DISCARDED

STUDIES IN EIGHTEENTH-CENTURY CULTURE

Proceedings

THE AMERICAN SOCIETY FOR EIGHTEENTH-CENTURY STUDIES

VOLUME 2

STUDIES IN EIGHTEENTH-CENTURY CULTURE

VOLUME 1: The Modernity of the Eighteenth Century
VOLUME 2: Irrationalism in the Eighteenth Century

STUDIES IN EIGHTEENTH-CENTURY CULTURE

IRRATIONALISM IN THE EIGHTEENTH CENTURY

edited by HAROLD E. PAGLIARO
Swarthmore College

THE PRESS OF
CASE WESTERN RESERVE UNIVERSITY
CLEVELAND & LONDON
1972

> Library of Congress Cataloging in Publication Data
>
> American Society for Eighteenth-Century Studies.
>   Irrationalism in the eighteenth century.
>
>   (Studies in eighteenth-century culture, v. 2)
>   Papers presented at the second annual meeting of the
> American Society for Eighteenth-Century Studies.
>   Includes bibliographies.
>   1. Civilization, Modern—18th century—Addresses, essays, lectures. 2. Eighteenth century—Addresses, essays, lectures. 3. Enlightenment—Addresses, essays, lectures. I. Pagliaro, Harold E., ed. II. Title. III. Series.
> CB411.A57   901.93'3   70-148731
> ISBN 0-8295-0239-4

Copyright © 1972 by The Press of Case Western Reserve University, Cleveland, Ohio 44106. All rights reserved.

Printed in the United States of America.

International Standard Book Number: 0-8295-0239-4.

Library of Congress Catalogue Card Number: 70-148731.

Contents

PREFACE
HAROLD E. PAGLIARO
Swarthmore College ix

THREE GENERATIONS:
A Plausible Interpretation of the French *Philosophes*?
LOUIS GOTTSCHALK
University of Chicago 3

AMERICA AND THE EIGHTEENTH-CENTURY
COMMUNITY OF LEARNING
HENRY STEELE COMMAGER
Amherst College 13

THE PROBLEM OF SCIENTIFIC ORDER VERSUS
ALPHABETICAL ORDER IN THE *ENCYCLOPÉDIE*
HUGH M. DAVIDSON
The Ohio State University 33

LEONARD EULER, SUPREME GEOMETER (1707–1783)
C. TRUESDELL
The Johns Hopkins University 51

FRENCH OPERA AND THE SPIRIT OF THE
REVOLUTION
PAUL HENRY LANG
Columbia University 97

LA PHILOSOPHIE DANS LE BOUDOIR;
or, A Young Lady's Entrance into the World
R. F. BRISSENDEN
The Australian National University 113

THE PROBLEM OF ARTISTIC STYLE AS IT RELATES
TO THE BEGINNINGS OF ROMANTICISM
FREDERICK J. CUMMINGS
The Detroit Institute of Arts 143

THE SICK ROSE AS AN AESTHETIC IDEA:
Kant, Blake, and the Symbol in Literature
JOHN NEUBAUER
Case Western Reserve University 167

LUDWIG TIECK:
English and French Sources of His *William Lovell* (1795/96)
FRANÇOIS JOST
University of Illinois, Urbana 181

CLARISSA AND THE TRAGIC TRADITIONS
SHELDON SACKS
University of Chicago 195

Symposium: Irrationalism in the Eighteenth Century

INTRODUCTION
RALPH COHEN
University of Virginia 223

THE RETREAT FROM REASON
BERTRAND H. BRONSON
University of California, Berkeley 225

IRRATIONALISM AND POLITICS IN THE EIGHTEENTH CENTURY
GEORGE ARMSTRONG KELLY
Brandeis University 239

FORMS OF IRRATIONALITY IN THE EIGHTEENTH CENTURY
GEORGE ROSEN
Yale University 255

UN ASPECT DE L'IRRATIONNEL AU XVIIIEMÈ SIÈCLE:
La Démonologie et son exploitation littéraire
P. VERNIÈRE
Université de Paris 289

THE IRRATIONAL AND THE PROBLEM OF HISTORICAL KNOWLEDGE IN THE ENLIGHTENMENT
HAYDEN WHITE
University of California, Los Angeles 303

PROGRAM OF THE 1971 MEETING	323
OFFICERS AND EXECUTIVE BOARD MEMBERS TO JUNE 30, 1972	327
LIST OF MEMBERS	329

Preface

THE AMERICAN SOCIETY for Eighteenth-Century Studies held its second annual meeting in College Park, Maryland, in April 1971. Its program chairman, Paul Kent Alkon, had arranged for the presentation of a wide variety of papers, from many disciplines. As a result, the essays that follow—all chosen from those read at the meeting—are diverse in their interests and methods. The title of the present volume was taken from the meeting's one symposium, which treated Irrationalism in the Eighteenth Century, even though no more than one third or so of the essays here presented fall under this heading. There are such obvious advantages to joining the actual meeting to the record of the meeting (these Proceedings) by means of a single title that the Publications Committee of the Society decided it might easily resign itself to the inaccuracy of a partial misnomer.

Surely no principle can make the eighteenth century coherent without reducing the age to a shadow of itself. Students of every age are probably right to suppose their period is complex, but there seems a particular justice in the claim when it is made by students of the eighteenth century—a conclusion borne out by the history of the histories that purport to explain it. Nevertheless one continues to believe that the period (at least aspects of the period) can be characterized in general terms, representing patterns of the age—patterns of idea and of action—in its art and its life. Though most of the essays in this collection confine themselves to limited subjects in one sense, almost without exception they offer generalizations that may be taken to be representative of the period. Whether they dwell, like Henry Commager's on the extra-national sense of man's obligation to man, or like François Jost's on Tieck's debt to Jonson, Restif, and others, they address themselves at least indirectly to ways in which the age may be defined, though ultimately in fairly broad terms. Professor Commager argues, for example, that the attitude towards learning in the age moved nations at war to cooperate in certain scientific matters, despite general hostilities. In a differently ordered realm, Professor Jost distinguishes epistolary novels whose characters write letters that *report* the action, from epistolary novels whose characters write letters that *stimulate* the action. In the process, he makes the point that English and German novels belong to the first, and French novels to the second group; and he notes a crucial exception to this general truth.

It should be obvious that each of these two essays goes about its individual business. On the other hand, each is able to offer a generalization that contributes to one's sense for the period, and not only in the obvious regard that it adds to one's knowledge of the more or less confined subject it nominally treats. Both essays as well add to or modify that structure in the mind of every reader which for him *is* the eighteenth century. Such structures are probably indispensable to the imagination. The doubts raised by some recent historiographers as to the possibility of writing history imply as much about the way in which men conceive and understand the past as they do about the "truth" of the past. It may be just a limitation of the mind that its control of past events is in flux. On the one hand, men seem to require simple, even primitive, formulations in order to grasp the relationship of events to each other—the myth or whole cloth. On the other, they remain critically unsatisfied with elements of the myth, which they restlessly modify or correct. Such "truth" about the past as the mind can accommodate apparently exists in the continuity of this tense process, which includes both the myth and its perpetual correction.

Treating irrationalism in the eighteenth century offers no peculiarly valuable opportunity for characterizing the age. Nevertheless it invites one to speculate once more—briefly and inconclusively, I hasten to assure the reader—about a psychological context that might include more than a few of the varied tendencies of the period—its scientific optimism and Tory gloom, lucid classicism and dark graveyard poetry, skepticism and enthusiasm, Mandevil-

Preface

lianism and benevolism, love of symmetry and of irregularity, its city ways and its primitivism, its analytical and its psychological art criticism. Needless to say such a context should not be thought of as "explaining" very much—only as providing a setting in which certain ideas and actions of the period are made to seem reasonable in each other's company. If the reader accepts my formulation, he will doubtless accept it advisedly, modifying and correcting it even as he entertains it.

It has often been observed that the eighteenth century was uniquely secular in its attitudes; and yet, such a view may appear to be contrary to certain obvious facts. Outstanding figures like Newton, Dryden, Defoe, Swift, Bolingbroke, Fielding, and Johnson were in various ways religious men, after all. One might also object that sectarian fervor and private enthusiasm—not to mention reverent commitment to Anglicanism or to Roman Catholicism—mark every decade of the century. Moreover, the literature of the pulpit—though much satirized—has seldom enjoyed such popularity. But it is nevertheless true that in certain important ways the seventeenth-century mind had precipitated a fundamental shift in responsibility from God to itself, so that men began to believe that they themselves, and not some power beyond them, were immediately accountable for their predicament on earth. They might not be responsible in the sense that they were culpable—they had not "caused" their plight—but they were responsible in the sense that they knew they could perform no ritual that would relieve their concerns as men. God might be remotely available, but he was no longer on the scene to help them. One may give point to this difficulty by suggesting that the problems of life required a new order of man's attention—while the fact of death required a new order of his emotional energy, such that the idea of death might be accepted in the new secular context, or attenuated by compensatory social action, or converted into psychological shapes that disguised its power to destroy.

In observing that tragedy makes the audience feel pity and terror, Aristotle involves himself in a shift in critical method. Until he makes that point in the *Poetics*, he argues as if he believed the evidence on which criticism must rely existed in the work under examination. For example, he amplifies the view that tragedy has six component parts, and in the process he is analytical or descriptive. But in making the new point, he inverts his method by locating the relevant evidence in the spectator of the work. Even if Aristotle is understood merely to have commented on a consequence of tragedy in referring to its effects of pity and terror, without intending to suggest that these effects in the spectator's mind constitute data for criticism, one would have to conclude that he sometimes thought about art (tragedy, at least) in the terms of the responses it engenders, and that he probably thought those responses more or less uniform among men. In so doing he implies the principle that subjects and objects are somehow meaningfully related to each other, at least potentially. Indeed the bulk of Aristotle's writings apart from the *Poetics* supports the view that reality is "here" (as well as "above") and that man is organically related to that reality (he is indeed a part of it), first through sense and then through reason. Accordingly, the transfer of his attention, in the *Poetics*, from object to subject—from the work of art to its spectator—amounts only to a variation in critical method and not to a philosophical inconsistency. Aristotle was an organicist who (taking appropriate precautions) might seriously regard evidence located anywhere on the subject-object axis.

The late seventeenth and the eighteenth centuries were divided over this and closely related issues. One effect of the new science was man's self-conscious belief that he is a spectator of the objects and events in the world outside himself. As a result of his enormously increased ability to look upon and measure the physical universe, he recorded a new sense of his own power. The record may take the form of optimism based on his ability to predict certain astronomical events (in a sense he thus guarantees the future), or the form of his presumed objectivity, which derives from his having confined his observation to quantifiable elements in the world outside him (in a sense he thus places himself beyond the reach of feeling). Simultaneous with this new sense of himself as impersonal observer and predictor, he developed an exaggerated idea of his private self as separated from things outside—an idea that culminated in his view that his mind was its own universe.

Preface

Almost immediately thereafter he invented modern analytical psychology. Inclined to be more concerned with its evaluative implications for the mind than Aristotle's collections of psychological essays (*De Anima* and *Parva Naturalia*), the psychology of the seventeenth and eighteenth centuries includes a drift of corrective argument—both optimistic and pessimistic—that reveals man to be remarkably independent as an appraiser of the world around him but remarkably limited as an initiator of action there. Assuming that man's religious expectations about his place in the scheme of things are not proved, the new psychology both elevates man as the best judge of his own case and eliminates him as one who may act significantly on his own behalf. Aristotle's psychology seems to add a rich dimension to human knowledge and experience, but the psychology of men according to Hobbes finds various ways of warning the reader that "*Whatsoever accidents* or qualities our senses make us think there be in the *world*, they be *not* there, but are *seemings* and *apparitions* only: the things that really *are* in the world without us, are those *motions* by which these seemings are caused" (*Of Human Nature*, Ch. II). It is remarkable that Hobbes is so intent on the mechanistic basis of "things . . . really in the world" that he never copes with an obvious question—how are these "things . . . in the world" converted into "seemings"? The reason for the omission may well have been his *preconception* of the world as a place in which men are without meaningful relationship to the things around them. In one sense, his willingness to declare all "seemings" to be matter in motion reduces man's legitimate expectation or his "natural" hope for something more in the way of kinship with the universe, with the result that he is brought to a kind of certainty, however barren. In *The Elements of Philosophy* (IV, xxv, 1), Hobbes expresses interest, in fact, in the causes of "phantoms which are perpetually generated within us"; his doubtful solution to the problem is to grant that certain organs of living creatures are fit for "retaining" the motions stimulated in them.

Hobbes' opponents, chiefly the Cambridge Platonists, who inspired Shaftesbury and a host of followers, at least obliquely, were in their own ways also committed to argue about things "outside" and "inside" man. Though generous in argument, the latitudinarians were warm contenders against Hobbes. Their mysticism, rationally argued to a point, offers the view that man somehow participates in the "truth" of the universe—the universe being informed by an *anima mundi*, of which he is a part. The mechanists, they held, allowed ". . . no other causes of things as philosophical, save the material and mechanical only; this being really to banish all mental, and consequently all divine causality quite out of the world; and to make the whole world to be nothing but a heap of dust, fortuitously agitated." Ralph Cudworth, who offered this representative view in *The True Intellectual System of the Universe* (1678), had much earlier expressed his own opinion as to the potential vitality of man's apprehension of "things" nominally outside him. In *A Sermon Preached before the Honourable House of Commons* (1647), he makes it clear that for him perception ideally—but only ideally—involves the perceiver's incorporation of qualities of things—". . . as if the *Soul of Musick*, should incorporate it self with the Instrument . . ."—and not the mere impingement of the motion of things on the mind. It is in a way strange that both Hobbes and Cudworth—whom I here, for want of space, assume to represent a broad spectrum of opinion in the age—are fascinated by the nature of the relationship of the observer to the thing observed. Indeed in one sense they seem to be confined by the problem it poses. Despite their quite different responses, both see the separation of subject from object as a threat —a threat to be accepted and defined, or to be reduced by its comparison with the religious alternative open to all men.

It seems fair to say that mechanists and Cambridge Platonists alike contributed to the sense that one's dwellingplace is the subject-mind and not the world outside. As Hobbes sought to define the mechanical relation of subject to object, he attributed to the mind a centrality it had never before enjoyed. That is, he explained the knowledge of experience in the terms of a spatial metaphor that placed man at the center of the epistemological action. Motions of things directed themselves towards man, where they "terminated," in one sense. Man was thus placed in the position of being their "natural" viewer and appraiser. Cudworth does much the same

Preface

thing, psychologically speaking, by declaring ontologically charged components to be incorporable in man, though in such a context as to require man to opt for the incorporation. Whether inevitably (with Hobbes) or willingly (with Cudworth), man is placed in an incredibly responsible position as the perceiver of events and their meaning. Among the chief results of his enormously increased status as subject was his preoccupation with his own processes. In one sense the new science (to which Cudworth no less than Hobbes is heir) sponsors man's location of emotional reality within himself, at the same time that it separates him from external reality— separates him by identifying it as the locus of quantities, not of qualities. Following Cudworth's advice, one might find meaning (qualities) in objects, of course, but one would have to labor to do so. Besides one would incorporate those qualities into oneself, and in the internalization, add to one's sense of interior being. Cudworth thought the kingdom of God was within. Still, there is no denying that for him God was abroad as well. Though not to the exclusion of important countertendencies, both the mechanist and the latitudinarian in different ways confirmed man's isolation from the world outside at the same time that they gave him enormous power over it, though in narrowly defined ways. Simultaneously they burdened him with responsibility for his own fate—he could turn to no one else—and stimulated him to enlarge the world of his own psyche, and to dwell in it.

Signs of the scientific author-observer and the indwelling man of feeling are apparent in the literature of the later age. One may discover in both art and criticism the tendency to apply the methods of science, though needless to say there were from the earliest times alternatives to this obvious bent, or modifications of it. Accordingly, the neoclassical ideal of the artist's control of his materials, of his use of traditional ideas and subjects, and of his clarity of statement go hand in hand with the scientific view that what is true is somehow measurable and explainable, and that what is measurable and explainable is somehow under the measurer's intellectual control. On the other hand, the wide acceptance of the *je ne sais quoi* of art and the idea of a grace beyond the reach of art seem to qualify art's faith in a scientific method. Nevertheless, the neoclassical author's belief in his cerebral control of his material is marked in a variety of ways—most characteristically, perhaps, by the speakers of poems, who are regularly distanced in time from the experiences they present, so that they are usually the informed observers of phenomena, not participants in an action that engages them passionately at the time they speak. Or if they are so engaged, they are often satirists who view the world with displeasure enough or comic detachment enough to be distanced from it. They are not caught up by the action they characterize, but rather angered or amused by it. To these practices sustaining the sense of the author's perpetual control over his subject may be added his use of discrete metaphors, which do not often reinforce each other at an emotional level—they make little use of the mood that assists meaning—and as a result one is at frequent intervals reminded of the author's cerebration. Quite another sort of eighteenth-century speaker is typified by his habit of expressing more feeling than his author has accounted for. Sometimes he is sentimental, and sometimes he indulges in something like uncensored self-revelation or self-examination. Though the sentimental voice may be sounded in verse, it is much more likely to speak in drama or prose narrative. The self-revealing or self-examining voice speaks parts of the graveyard poems and some of the poetry of Collins, Akenside, the Wartons, Gray, Cowper, and Blake.

On the face of it, these two speakers—the controlling and the controlled—seem strangely complementary. The one works to suggest his power over experience and the propriety of that power. The other reveals the tendency, perhaps the need, to allow experience to dominate him; or at least he reveals his willingness to allow the process of his involvement in the experience to become his subject matter. It may be useful to consider the fact of this division in relation to what I have said about the separation of subject and object, inside and outside, brought about by the new science. But first it seems worth observing that the very fact of the division may be significant. How can an age so have divided itself that on the one hand it may be characterized as exuberant and idiosyncratic and on the other as restrained and conforming?

Preface

With equal accuracy it may be thought of as aggressively inventive and cautiously traditional, equally predisposed to symmetry and to disorder, both intensely secular and intensely enthusiastic in its religious attitudes. Frankly, I doubt the view that these were in any obvious sense compensatory tendencies. If that were so, one might expect a greater balance than one finds in individual examples of literature and in the lives of individual men and women. To be sure *A Tale of a Tub* may be thought of as exemplifying the extremes of order and disorder, ancient and modern views, spare and prolix prose, and so on. And both Pope's life and his art may be regarded as running the full range of complementary extremes. But one labors to establish such a view of individual men and works of the age. It seems to me to make better sense to discover in these extremities—certainly not universal in the period—the signs of a uniquely divided imagination, such that to control intellectually and to be controlled emotionally were autonomous, and therefore excessive and compelling, operations of the mind. Eighteenth-century man was not first rational and then non-rational because he must express his non-intellectual side in order to compensate for his already expressed intellectual side. He was both the one and the other (when he was both) because he was often divided—unconsciously committed, alternately and discretely, to "reason" and then to "feeling," or to either one of these, more or less exclusive of the other.

Hobbes had characterized man as essentially isolated from his environment, or only mechanistically related to it, so that other than physical meanings about the interplay between inside and outside did not exist, except insofar as men supplied them. If outside and inside were joined only by one's idiosyncratic will, then whatever man might be (a minded body), he was alone. And if apart from unquestioning religious faith, he sought to discover a basis for new relationship with the world outside, then he must discover it in his analytical appraisal of the physical world and of himself. It is probably impossible to sort out antecedent and secondary factors so as to establish cause and effect, but whatever the precise relationship, many tendencies were more or less coterminous in the age: man's new barren relationship to his environment, his intense effort to define the world in analytical terms, his increased efforts to establish a science of psychology, his excessive interest in his own feelings and processes, and his (usually obliquely expressed) dread of aloneness—a secular terror without even the comfort of God's eternally punishing hand.

Small wonder that the Cambridge Platonists tried to demonstrate the existence of an *anima mundi* in which we all participate. If man's reason, as they claimed, could recognize God's presence in the natural world, then man was not alone after all. Their effort was not a dramatic failure. Many of their views were taken up, ethically and aesthetically, by Shaftesbury, Addison, and others, who modified them and spread them abroad, where they flourished in their new shapes. But in its original forms, their effort was a failure nevertheless, because it ran counter to the much more compelling force of the new science, which it seems was bent on defining man to himself in new and dangerous ways. Incidentally, as a result of what I take to be this compelling force, I find it hard to believe that the new definition of man was a simple function of "scientific discoveries." Man cannot just have "discovered" and then changed psychologically. It seems to me that in a way he must have been ready to accept the imaginative consequences of his investigative energies at the same time that he directed them to the farthest heavens to destroy an old truth and invent a new one. At least he was prepared with new rationalizations and emotional valves to cope with what he had found and wrought. Or else he would have interpreted what he saw differently from what he did. Indeed there were at the outset many varied and contending interpretations, which gradually gave way to the essentially secular interpretation that left man alone and responsible for his own life and death.

Man's differentiation of himself from God's creation, and so from God, was probably unconscious. In individual minds, like Newton's, for example, it may have resulted unintentionally from the desire to know God better by knowing His world better. Nevertheless, at some level of his being, having thus declared for himself the right to know about God's ways (not only lovingly to feel

Preface

them, but analytically to understand them), man adopted a position only slightly removed from the view that he was entirely separate from God, with autonomous rights and powers of appraisal. As he continued "scientifically" to define the world around him with success, he felt triumph in his independence. If he felt dislocation from his former comforting dependence, he might maintain his old religion; or like the Cambridge Platonists, he might re-explain the old religion using the new terminology; or, like Edward Young or Locke, become preoccupied with interior processes (his own psychology or mankind's); or, like Hobbes, experience fear at the prospect of war and death; or he might expend the newly available energy in public works, or in religious enthusiasm, or in generalized benevolence, or in sentimentality. No doubt many men and women of the period experienced few or none of these compelling shapes of energy. Others, like Colley Cibber, simply found ways of exploiting them commercially. But Samuel Johnson, for example, had breadth of character enough to experience most of them in a remarkable degree—and at the same time, at great cost to himself, he could maintain his hard-headed analytical ways.

As I see them, most of these processes, from old religion to new sentimentality, are both a result of the separation of man from his environment and an attempt to overcome the separation. There are exceptions. Let us assume the condition of religiousness to be the condition of nonseparation. Obviously to maintain one's old religion in the face of the new science would be an attempt to overcome the separation only if one had felt it. I believe that most of those who felt the implications of the new discoveries, and who held on to their religion—say Johnson—either paid the emotional price of compartmentalized minds, so that they experienced a special form of the separation, or—like Dryden—found that the religion they maintained had changed, having become somehow secularized, despite their conserving efforts. The Cambridge men—I do not question their sincerity—were clearly inspired by the threat of separation, and all their endeavor was to overcome it.

Non-religious expressions of feeling and idea are another matter. It may be true that the age's intense psychological preoccupation, its religious enthusiasm, its public works on behalf of the underprivileged, its benevolism, its sentimentality, and its rarely documented dread of death (Johnson, like Hobbes, reveals his fright) are also results of the separation brought about by the new science; but it is not obvious, surely, that they are also attempts to *overcome* that separation. My belief, simply expressed, is that the most straightforward effect of the new view of things was man's sense that to die is to "cease to be," as Keats was to put it later. The inanimate, cold world of Hobbes required an indomitable intellect for its perception (or was it an "invention"?), and it just as surely engendered a profound dread. All the other expressions of feeling in the list I have presented seem to me to be displacements of this primary sense, which operates unalloyed in consciousness only rarely. Accordingly, the unusual expressions of feeling in the eighteenth century are not, strictly speaking, compensations for an excess of intellection, but expiatory displacements of the unconsciously understood yet uniquely potent sense of death, which the mind of man had effectively accepted as man's, not God's, problem when he invented the new science. And intellection itself came to a new position of prominence. It had proved strong enough to effect the separation that thrust God's work on man. Moreover, it was required, in part to assure man that he could do God's work and in part to do it.

The new knowledge of seventeenth-century man, along with its motivations and its consequences, is in some ways a repetition of the Fall. Man, gratified and yet confined by the God-made paths and ways of the Ptolemaic universe, appropriates an aspect of knowledge whose dark assimilation brings death into the world and all our woe. The larger world through which man moves after he has destroyed his familiar home gives him more scope, but it also brings the threat of dissolution, which he must somehow cope with or dispose of. For some men Christ was reborn for the occasion. For many others, the fact of the new universe thrust the responsibility too squarely on man for Christ to help. For still others, the nature of the problem was unrecognized, though it nevertheless worked clandestinely in the mind. Intellectual optimism,

Preface

spiritual pessimism, the reaffirmation of faith, religious enthusiasm, benevolism, sentimentality, the eruption of death-preoccupied graveyard poetry, the new interest in society's unfortunates, the fascination with one's own psyche—all may be located at one place or another on the axis of the problem of death. Men at one end of the axis humbly returned the problem to God by denying that their science could penetrate the ultimate mystery. Men at the other, as they felt their essential helplessness, and as they located the extent of life in the here and now of earthly existence, either accepted Mandeville's view of society or assumed a new responsibility for helping their fellows in worldly ways. Both were reasonable courses to follow in a secularized universe, and both attested to man's ability to cope with the problem. Probably less rational and more unconscious was the radiation of warmth from benevolence and sentimentality, which sought to repudiate but in fact announced death's presence in a God-empty world. Equally irrational and unconscious were the enthusiasts, whose "god within" displaced death, and the graveyarders, whose death within broke out from confinement with incredible force. As I have implied already, no age is without these expressions of feeling, but no modern age is so persistently marked by them as the eighteenth century and the decades before it.

It seemed in keeping with the interdisciplinary nature of the Society to preserve the diversity of method as well as the diversity of substance of the papers presented at the annual meeting. Accordingly no effort has been made to normalize the language of the essays offered here, with the result that readers whose competence is in the realm of words may once or twice stumble over a mathematical equation. Though readers from many fields may be struck by the varied languages of discourse represented in these Proceedings, it seems fair to say they will find no essay in the volume so specialized as to be inaccessible. Notes too have been left in the form acceptable to the discipline that produced them.

I wish to express my thanks to Louis T. Milic, editor of the first volume of the ASECS Proceedings. Though other duties called him away from his work as editor of this second volume, his continued interest in the project has been enormously helpful to me. I wish also to thank my colleague in French literature, Professor Jean Ashmead Perkins, for seeing M. Vernière's article through the press.

HAROLD E. PAGLIARO

Swarthmore, Pa.
January 15, 1972

IRRATIONALISM
IN THE EIGHTEENTH CENTURY

Three Generations:
A Plausible Interpretation of the French Philosophes?

Louis Gottschalk

SEVERAL TERMS in the title of this address stand in need of precise definition. I borrow from Lester Crocker's *An Age of Crisis*[1] his definition of *philosophes*:

> By *philosophes* . . . we designate that group of eighteenth-century French writers who, refusing to abide by Christian doctrines and dogma and by the authority of the Church, searched for the truth in the light of reason and experience. They were not (excepting Condillac) systematic philosophers in the usual sense, but were primarily combative social and moral thinkers, usually with a strong tinge of scientific dilettantism.

By that definition my term *French philosophes* is a pleonasm, but I have expressly included the word *French* because I seek to avoid those English, Scottish, German, American, and other nationals who in the eighteenth century "searched for the truth in the light of reason and experience." I have found the French *philosophes* themselves hard enough to shoe-horn into three generations. The reader does not need to be reminded that the *philosophes* were not the whole of the Enlightenment but only an intellectual elite—more important perhaps to scholars of a later age than they were to their own contemporaries.

The three generations I have in mind comprise that dominated by Montesquieu (roughly 1721–50); that dominated by the *Encylopédie* (ending roughly around 1780, when the *Table analytique* was published); and that dominated by Condorcet (interrupted by but continuing beyond the outbreak of the French Revolution and Condorcet's death). I shall explain the choice of these chronological limits later.

The term *plausible interpretation* and the question mark (?) in my title are attributable to a *parti pris*. I have already committed myself in several publications to the contention that whereas the evaluation of evidence in the historiographical process is as scientific as any other process that examines a recognizable object for data that may be credited, debated, or discredited for a larger context, the choice of a historical context is an imaginative, creative decision that can rarely if ever be characterized by words like *factual* or *truthful* or *objective*, but must be, rather, by words like *plausible* or *tenable*. A context may thus be, as you all know, a theory or a hypothesis that must be discarded if it is found to be contrary to the facts derived from a scientific evaluation of the evidence or to the rules of logic, but it depends for general acceptance upon whatever conviction it carries as an interpretive concatenation or *Gestalt* of the relevant facts. It need not be the unique, exclusive truth, but it must have a factual, logical structure, though perhaps only one among several such.

From these definitions, it must now be abundantly clear, I mean to argue that the *philosophes* can convincingly be studied by a chronological ordering into three periods which, for want of a better name, I have called *generations*. A number of other students of the Enlightenment have already suggested that it may well be divided into two generations splitting somewhere about 1750. Let me cite some recent American examples. Henry Guerlac, in his study of the reputation of Isaac Newton,[2] indicated (as did several earlier writers)[3] that, about mid-century, French scientific circles were predominantly Cartesian and afterward became predominantly Newtonian.[4] Peter Gay cites with approval Arthur Wilson's quotation of the historian Ruhlière's address in 1787 to the French Academy: "It had been precisely in 1749, not a year earlier, or later—that philosophy had liberated itself from the [royal] Court," and Gay then goes on to show, now citing Ernst Cassirer, that Voltaire, d'Alembert, and other *philosophes* felt that at mid-century "public opinion was beginning to rule France" and that "the philosophes were beginning to rule public opinion," reflecting and producing "irreversible, if often subterranean, changes in Western politics, economy, and society."[5] Gay, furthermore, not only agrees that the triumph of Newtonianism over Cartesianism came in France by mid-century[6] but also points out that utilitarian doctrines began to compete with natural law in the late 1750's and dominated the second half of the Enlightenment.[7] Charles B. Paul attributes "a new turn in the *Weltanschauung* of the eighteenth century" to four significant works that appeared "around 1749"— Diderot's *Lettre sur les aveugles*, Condillac's *Traité des systèmes*, Buffon's preface to his *Histoire naturelle*, and d'Alembert's "Discours préliminaire" to the *Encyclopédie*—"writings of a new generation of intellectuals" who "called for an end to Cartesianism just as Descartes himself, more than a century earlier, had called for an end to scholasticism . . . an end to all untested generalizations, deductive systems, inquiries into final causes, and especially the *esprit de système* and the *esprit de calcul* in favor of 'facts, induction, observation, and experimentation.' "[8]

As already indicated, these American scholars are only a few of the more recent students of the subject to suggest that the Enlightenment might profitably be studied in two separate chronological parts, but they have said so only in *obiter dicta*, and they have not in fact done so themselves (although they have done very well what they did do). The usual ways of presenting the thought of the *philosophes* are those that Henri Sée used in two separate books with almost the same title. One was *Les Idées politiques en France au XVIIIe siècle* (Paris, 1920), and the other *L'Evolution de la pensée politique en France au XVIIIe siècle* (Paris, 1925). The first was organized partly genetically (at the beginning and in the conclusion) but chiefly biographically, each *philosophe* under consideration being given a separate chapter or subheading under two incidental headings, almost afterthoughts: "La Première Moitié du dix-huitieme siècle" and "La Deuxième Moitié du dix-huitième siècle." Admittedly unhappy with that organization, Sée put out the second work (1925), organized this time more thoroughly along topical and genetic lines, beginning with the "origines" and then grouping selected *philosophes* into schools labeled "La Doctrine libérale," "La Doctrine démocratique," "Les Réformateurs," and

"La Formation de la doctrine révolutionnaire." This nomenclature closely resembles that which Jacques Godechot subsequently used in the "Livre premier" of his book on the institutions of France during the Revolution and the Empire.[9]

Most writers who have dealt with the Enlightenment as a whole have mixed Sée's two methods, presenting the biographical material along with the topical, sometimes emphasizing the one and sometimes the other, but usually emphasizing the topical. That, for example, is the structure of the works of Kingsley Martin,[10] Mornet,[11] Hazard,[12] and Cassirer as well as of Gay. Monographic studies, of course, are by their nature more likely to be either predominantly biographical or predominantly topical. Except for a feeble attempt I made in treating the Enlightenment in a college textbook[13] and in breaking off at 1775 in Volume IV of the UNESCO *History of Mankind*,[14] and except for the brief but masterly pages of Crocker's "Introduction" to his anthology of Enlightenment literature,[15] I know of no attempt to make explicit the development of the whole *philosophe* movement as a succession of three generations, although (as I shall soon indicate) several authors of studies of discrete aspects of the Enlightenment found that they developed in three discernible chronological phases.

The suggestion that a tripartite chronological division of the *philosophes'* story might be justifiable first came to me in the 1920's with Albert Mathiez's certainly trenchant and perhaps deserved review[16] of E. Carcassonne's *Montesquieu et le problème de la constitution française au XVIIIe siècle* (Paris, [1927]) and his subsequent article entitled "La place de Montesquieu dans l'histoire des doctrines politiques au XVIIIe siècle."[17] Mathiez's thesis was that Montesquieu appeared a liberal only if looked back upon from the vantage of the French Revolution—in which case he might be regarded as an opponent of absolutism—but that, seen in his own setting, he was actually the outstanding reflector and propagandist of the dominant theme among political theorists of his day who, appealing to history or tradition for confirmation of their social preferences, found from their study of France's past that legally the aristocracy were entitled to share political and economic power with the king and that absolute monarchy was hence a usurpation. This conclusion, Mathiez pointed out, was also that of Saint Simon, Fénelon, and Boulainvilliers (among others), all of them nobles, and though it was opposed by other contemporary writers, particularly Dubos, the Marquis d'Argenson, and the Abbé de Mably, the influence of Montesquieu's *Esprit des lois* and of the *parlements*' remonstrances made it the dominant theme of French political thought until Montesquieu's death (1755) and a vigorous rival of other themes thereafter. I agree with Gay and others who state the obvious fact that "Montesquieu was far more than an ideologist for the nobles,"[18] and I hesitate to agree with Mathiez that Carcassonne was led astray primarily because he was a student of literature and not a historian or that Montesquieu's influence can be explained in terms of class-consciousness (Mably and D'Argenson were also nobles). Still, the thesis that Montesquieu and other leading lights of his generation looked, for rhetorical window dressing for their political preferences, primarily to history or tradition (no matter how much they might differ on what it taught) and that subsequent generations looked elsewhere reinforces the other reasons for dividing the *philosophe* movement into at least two parts at approximately mid-century.

What made me think in terms of a *three*-generation development of political thought among the *philosophes* was a series of dissertations prepared under my supervision. One of them was by Dr. Frances Acomb, entitled *Anglophobia in France, 1763–1789* (Duke University Press, 1950). Another was by Dr. L. C. Tihany, entitled "French Utopian Thought," presented in 1943, never published but summarized in an article in a *Festschrift* dedicated by some of my former students to their old professor.[19] Miss Acomb's thesis was that with the end of the Seven Years' War the vogue of Anglomania in France gradually gave way to Anglophobia, which became in its turn a conspicuous vogue with the growth in France of sympathy with the American insurgents of the 1770's and 1780's.[20] Tihany's thesis was that utopian thought in the eighteenth century passed through three successive stages: in the first, Utopia was located in vaguely remote lands, and its institutions, while constitutional-monarchical, were largely fantastic; in the second, Utopia was inhabited by real men in easily recognizable places, and its institutions were not equally fantastic and were sometimes republican; and in the third, Utopia was a frank blueprint for the political and social reform of France.[21]

Meanwhile the researches of Robert R. Palmer, in part begun under my supervision,[22] and my own studies[23] convinced me (in agreement with Bernard Fay,[24] Michael Kraus,[25] Jacques Godechot,[26] and Gilbert Chinard[27]) that a sufficient degree of intercommunication and cultural diffusion had occurred between Europe and America to justify speaking of "an eighteenth-century Atlantic community." Despite the convictions of some other scholars to the contrary,[28] I am still persuaded that the *philosophes*, somewhere around 1778, the year in which the Franco-American Treaty of Amity and Commerce and the Franco-American Treaty of Alliance were signed, and in which Voltaire and Rousseau died, and two years before the index volumes of the *Encyclopédie* were published, began to think of the United States of America as a model (*mutatis mutandis*, for they were monarchists) for a reformation of French institutions.

Perhaps some of you have already begun to wonder whether the studies under my supervision were not deliberate efforts of their authors to please their professor by regurgitating what he had fed them. I sometimes wondered about that myself, but several works by scholars personally unknown to me have come to conclusions similar to mine. Charles Vereker's *Eighteenth-Century Optimism: A Study of the Interrelations of Moral and Social Theory in English and French Thought between 1689 and 1789* (Liverpool, 1967) divides that subject into three successive phases—the first (to 1750) characterized by a metaphysical rationalism, the second by empiricism and scientific observation, and the third by "redemptive optimism"—i.e., the effort to improve men and abolish social evils. These three phases seem to coincide chronologically with the three phases of the *philosophes*' political thought —the *thèse nobiliaire* of Montesquieu and his *frondeur* disciples, the *thèse royale* of the Encyclopedists, and the *thèse nationale* or *républicaine* or *démocratique* of the pre-Revolutionary liberals. From the history of censorship Robert Darnton in his article "Reading, Writing, and Publishing in Eighteenth-Century France: A Case Study in the Sociology of Literature" (*Daedalus*, Winter 1971, pp. 214–56), adds another reason for dividing the *philosophe* movement into three parts. He holds that "before 1750 the [French] state had not often shown an enlightened attitude in its attempt to police the printed word"; in 1750 Malesherbes, as *directeur de la Librairie*, initiated a more lenient policy; and in 1771 a new censorship code tried to break the monopoly of the bookdealers' guild and "relaxed the rules governing privileges in order to 'augmenter l'activité de commerce' in favor of authors at the expense of bookdealers."[29] Chinard long ago mentioned that Benjamin Franklin was permitted to employ the "imprimeur ordinaire du roi" to propagate American constitutional ideas all over France,[30] and although Darnton demonstrates that book production actually slumped between 1774 and 1786, he attributes that slump to a campaign more against pornography than against constitutional ideas;[31] the books that continued to be published were "enlightened," advocating "individualism, liberty, and equality before the law as opposed to corporation, privilege, and 'mercantilist restrictions.'"[32]

It makes small difference for our present purpose whether one agrees with the writers who contend that the America the *philosophes* had in mind up to 1790 was a mirage that existed chiefly in their glamorizing imagination but had little substantive effect upon French institutions except perhaps the *Déclaration des droits de l'homme et du citoyen* of 1789.[33] I persist in believing, however, that, mirage or no, the American model had some influence, though sometimes (because influence is generally hard to demonstrate) indirect, tenuous, and rarely exclusive, upon such institutions as Franco-American commercial practices, the Société des Cincinnati (and hence the debate about hereditary titles and privilege), the toleration of Protestants, the "American" party on the eve of the French Revolution, a citizen militia, and the eventual written and amendable Constitution of 1791.

In the molding of the political ideas of the third generation of *philosophes* I find little reason to suspect that class-consciousness was a decisive factor, for although the outstanding men of the generation of the Encyclopedists, the generation of *philosophes* dominated by the *thèse royale*, were largely of "bourgeois" origin —Voltaire, Rousseau, and Diderot—those of the 1770's and 1780's, the generation of *philosophes* dominated by the *thèse nationale*, included noblemen like Condorcet, Turgot, Malesherbes, Chastellux, the Comte de Mirabeau, Mably, and Lafayette, as well as "bourgeois" or recently ennobled gentlemen like Raynal, the Abbé Sieyès, Brissot, Marat, Sylvain Bailly, and Dupont de Nemours.

Lest anyone object that some of the men just named are doubtfully classified as *philosophes*, let me point out that they were all "eighteenth-century French writers who, refusing to abide by Christian doctrines and dogma and by the authority of the Church, searched for the truth in the light of reason and experience." It was their luck (for better or worse) that the French Revolution caught them in mid-stream and made most of them more famous as men of revolutionary action than as "primarily combative social and moral thinkers." And lest anyone object particularly that Lafayette (rarely but not altogether unjustifiably considered a man of letters) seems a strange bedfellow for *philosophes*, let me quote Camille Desmoulins, sometime in 1790 after Lafayette removed his armorial bearings from his carriage and Bailly as mayor of Paris had put his servants in livery: "I blush for the honor of letters. The *philosophe* has become a marquis of dandies, and the marquis a *philosophe*."[34]

Of course the three generations of *philosophes* overlapped. The *parlements* in all three periods regularly called upon Montesquieu in defense of the *lois fondamentales* of France. Voltaire lived in both the first and second generation, Mably in all three, Turgot and Condorcet in the second and third. Mathiez makes a point of the change in political views that Mably underwent between his youth and his older years,[35] and Gay makes a point of the difference between the attitude continually revealed in Voltaire's earlier works, advocating (before it became the dominant theme of the *philosophes*) the *thèse royale*, and the wishful tenor betrayed in his *Idées républicaines* of the 1760's (likewise before the *thèse républicaine* became the *philosophes*' dominant theme).[36] Not being small men, Mably and Voltaire did not pursue the hobgoblin of consistency. It will come as no surprise to any of you that deservedly famous authors as well as lesser ones changed their minds and anticipated or followed the changes in the vogue of contemporary ideas, even when they helped to create and to propagandize them. In fact, whatever other claims they may have to fame, having anticipated or followed a vogue that became triumphant may well be counted among the reasons that made *philosophes* famous —posthumously at least, if not in their own day. For the struggle for predominance among the three *thèses—nobiliaire, royale,* and *nationale*—continued into the French Revolution and beyond, and the reputations of their champions among the *philosophes* (some of them now Revolutionary celebrities) rose and fell with the highs and lows of their respective causes.

NOTES

1. (Baltimore, 1959), p. xv.
2. "Newton's Changing Reputation in the Eighteenth Century," in Raymond O. Rockwood (ed.), *Carl Becker's Heavenly City Revisited* (Ithaca, N.Y., 1958), pp. 3–26.
3. Cf. Carl Becker, *The Declaration of Independence* (New York, 1922), pp. 40–47, and Preserved Smith, *A History of Modern Culture*, 2 vols. (New York, 1930–34), II, *The Enlightenment, 1687–1776*, pp. 37–39.
4. Guerlac also indicates a third generation in "the closing years of the century" of "overt anti-Newtonianism": *loc. cit.*, p. 24.
5. *The Enlightenment: An Interpretation*, 2 vols. (New York, 1970), II, 83. See also Arthur M. Wilson, *Diderot: The Testing Years, 1713–1759* (New York, 1957), pp. 194–95, and Ernst Cassirer, *The Philosophy of the Enlightenment* (New York, 1951), pp. 3–4.
6. *The Enlightenment*, pp. 129, 136–37, 142.
7. *Ibid.*, p. 459.
8. "Jean-Philippe Rameau," *The Proceedings of the American Philosophical Society*, CXIV, No. 2 (1970), 153.
9. "Les fondements," in *Les institutions de la France sous la Révolution et l'Empire* (Paris, 1951), pp. 3–25.
10. Kingsley Martin, *French Liberal Ideas in the Eighteenth Century: A Study of Political Ideas from Bayle to Condorcet* (Boston, 1929).
11. Daniel Mornet, *French Thought in the Eighteenth Century*, transl. Lawrence M. Levin (New York, 1929).
12. Paul Hazard, *European Thought in the Eighteenth Century, from Montesquieu to Lessing*, transl. J. Lewis May (Cleveland, 1965).
13. Louis Gottschalk and Donald Lach, *Europe and the Modern World*, 2 vols. (Chicago, 1951–54), I, 502–6, 513–19, 603–9, 621–22.

14. *The Foundations of the Modern World (1300–1755)*, Louis Gottschalk, Loren C. Mackinney, and Earl H. Pritchard (eds.) (Vol. IV of *History of Mankind: Cultural and Scientific Development*) (London, New York, and Evanston, 1969), pp. 453–55, 516–17, 544–46, 1012–18, 1047–48.
15. *The Age of the Enlightenment* (New York, 1969), pp. 11–23.
16. *Annales historiques de la Révolution française*, IV (1927), 509–13.
17. *Ibid.*, VII (1930), 97–112.
18. *The Enlightenment*, II, 680.
19. L. C. Tihany, "Utopia in Modern Western Thought: The Metamorphosis of an Idea," in Richard Herr and Harold T. Parker (eds.), *Ideas in History: Essays Presented to Louis Gottschalk by His Former Students* (Durham, N.C., 1965), pp. 20–38.
20. See esp. pp. 12–13, 29, 43, 66–67, 69–88, 98–103, 114–15, 121–23.
21. See esp. pp. 25–27, 30–31.
22. Palmer gives an account of his work and the criticisms of it in "The Age of the Democratic Revolution," in L. P. Curtis, Jr. (ed.), *The Historian's Workshop: Original Essays by Sixteen Historians* (New York, 1970), pp. 169–86.
23. See especially *The Place of the American Revolution in the Causal Pattern of the French Revolution* (Easton, Pa., 1948) and *Lafayette between the American and French Revolution* (Chicago, 1950).
34. *Révolutions de France et de Brabant*, No. 3, pp. 100–101.
    tury, transl. Ramon Guthrie (New York, 1927).
25. *The Atlantic Civilization: Eighteenth-Century Origins* (Ithaca, N.Y., 1949).
26. See especially *Les Révolutions, 1770–1799* (Paris, 1963), pp. 258–69.
27. Among Chinard's numerous works on Franco-American political and intellectual interchange see especially *Thomas Jefferson, the Apostle of Americanism* (Boston, 1929), and *La Déclaration des Droits de l'Homme et du Citoyen et ses antécédents américains* (Institut Français de Washington, 1945).
28. See Palmer, pp. 173–74, 181–82.
29. Pp. 229–31.
30. *La Déclaration des Droits*, pp. 10–11.
31. Pp. 235–36.
32. P. 238.
33. See Durand Echevarria, "Amérique devant l'opinion française, 1743–1870, questions de méthode et de l'interprétation," *Revue d'histoire moderne et contemporaine*, IX (1962), 57 (which seems to me to be contradicted *ibid.*, p. 60, and in the same author's *Mirage in the West: A History of the French Image of American Society to 1815* [Princeton, 1957], pp. 56–57, 70–72, 93, 100, 133, 162–63, 168).
34. *Révolutions de France et de Brabant*, No. 3, pp. 100–101.
35. "La place de Montesquieu," *loc. cit.*, p. 104.
36. *Voltaire's Politics: The Poet as Realist* (Princeton, 1959), esp. pp. 91–143, 217–38.

America and the Eighteenth-Century Community of Learning*

Henry Steele Commager

WE THINK OF our own time as an Age of Enlightenment, but it flouts and even repudiates two essential principles of the Enlightenment: first the priority of the claims of science and culture over those of politics, and second the cosmopolitan and even universal nature of science and culture.

The *philosophes* of the eighteenth century—the word embraces not only philosophers but scientists and statesmen, men of letters and critics—did not worship at the altar of nationalism; they were a fellowship bound together by common devotion to Reason in all of its manifestations, and they were sure that its primary and its most pervasive manifestation was in the realm of science, art, and learning. They believed in the universality of morals and of art. When they wrote history it was world history, as with Voltaire; when they studied religion it tended to be comparative religion, as with Christian Wolff; when they celebrated law it was the Spirit of the Laws, as with Montesquieu; when they contemplated art they sought the Universal in art, as with Winckelmann or Sir Joshua Reynolds; and their most characteristic poem was called quite simply an *Essay on Man*. Their scientists and men of learning were cosmopolitan, at home in every country, moving easily from country to country and from university to university—or more often than not, from academy to academy, for the univer-

---

* Portions of this essay have appeared as "Science, Learning, and the Claims of Nationalism," *The American Heritage*, April 1972. In its present form it first appeared in *Thoughts from the Lake of Time* (Josiah Macy, Jr., Foundation). Copyright © by Henry Steele Commager. All rights reserved.

sities of that day were, many of them, in the doldrums. They knew that the commonwealth of learning was older than the commonwealth of political nations; for the learned academy and the university had flourished some centuries before the rise of the modern state. With most of them the claims of science took precedence over the claims of the nation-state, for they equated science with truth; and as truth was universal and could never conflict with other truth, they held that the sciences were never at war—the phrase is from Edward Jenner. Condorcet, himself a victim of the new nationalism, spoke for all of his generation when he said that

> The philosophers of different nations who considered the interests of the whole of humanity without distinction of country, race or creed, formed a solid phalanx banded together against all forms of error, all manifestations of tyranny. Animated by feelings of universal philanthropy they fought injustice when it occurred in countries other than their own.

We have come a long way from this philosophy of the Enlightenment—the philosophy of Franklin and Jefferson and Tom Paine in America, of Joseph Banks and Edward Jenner and Joseph Priestley in England, of Rumford in Bavaria, of Linnaeus in Sweden, of Haller in Switzerland, and of Buffon and Lavoisier and Diderot in France—and it is by now increasingly clear that our shift in position represents a retreat rather than an advance.

Consider some of the characteristics of that world where the sciences were never at war, not even in time of war. It was an age when the United States, speaking through Benjamin Franklin, and the French government, speaking through Jacques Necker, could proclaim immunity in time of war for Captain Cook because he was "engaged in work beneficial to humanity"; when a Hessian officer, about to put to flame the house of Francis Hopkinson—one of the signers of the Declaration of Independence—was so impressed by the library and scientific apparatus that he ordered the flames extinguished, writing in the flyleaf of a book: "This man is clearly a traitor but he is a man of learning and science and must be protected"; when Frederick the Great could retain French as the language of his court while fighting France; when Napoleon's mother could safely put her money into British consols; when Goethe could receive the retreating general of the Allied armies, after Leipzig, with his Legion of Honor insignia across his chest; when in time of war the Royal Society could confer its gold medal on Franklin, and the Institute in Paris could give its gold medal to Sir Humphrey Davy—likewise in time of war. The same Napoleon who arranged that, arranged to spare the university city of Göttingen out of respect for the great classical scholar Heyne; it was fitting that Sir Charles Blagden should recommend in 1808 that the Emperor be made a member of the Royal Society in London.

The world of art, like the world of science, was cosmopolitan, and how fortunate that was for the rising Republic of the United States. There is no more charming chapter in the history of American art than that which recounts how George III, even in time of war, patronized painters from America. A group of benefactors had sent young Benjamin West over to Rome to study painting; he served his apprenticeship there and went on to London, where one of his paintings, typically a scene from the classical past, caught the fancy of the youthful George III. In 1772 West was appointed painter to the Court, a position he held, with George's friendship, throughout the Revolution and long after. It was during the years when the American colonies were fighting for independence that West received in his studio a succession of American apprentices —among them Charles Peale, John Trumbull, and Gilbert Stuart —all of whom were allowed to return to America. Meantime, other American artists were studying in France, all through the turbulent years of the Revolution and the Napoleonic wars, and soon the current of artists flowed, ever swifter and broader, to Rome and Florence where, at one time in the early nineteenth century, over fifty Americans were wielding brush and chisel.

The new United States in turn drew upon European artists and architects for her needs. Consider the creation of our national capitol, and indeed of the capital city itself. Was there ever a more cosmopolitan enterprise? The particular name of the city was Washington, but the generic name was Latin and, as it turned out, the architecture was Roman and the art almost entirely Italian.

The work of laying out the capital was originally entrusted to the Frenchman Major L'Enfant, who had come over to America with Lafayette and made himself part of the New World even while remaining French. Soon L'Enfant was joined by James Hoban, who had been born and trained in Ireland. He was chiefly responsible for the White House, for he rebuilt it after the disastrous fire in 1814. Next Stephen Hallet took over. He had been born and raised in France and had come to America in 1789 to set up a school of art in Richmond; alas, it never materialized but some of his other plans did. More valuable was William Thornton—responsible for the original design of the Capitol building, with all of its drawbacks. Born in the Virgin Islands—his father had been Governor of Tortola—he studied medicine at Edinburgh and architecture in Paris; then, ever restless, he travelled on the Continent with the naturalist Count Audriani. Only after this varied career did he come to America where he joined forces with poor John Fitch in making the first steamboats to float on American rivers; one of Fitch's steamboats was named *The Thornton*. It was while he was on his honeymoon in the West Indies that he submitted the winning design for the national Capitol; not content with that (and after the original decision, few were), he also designed the Octagon House, which still stands, and probably Homewood in Baltimore. One of his co-workers on the Capitol was George Hadfield from England. He had actually been born in Italy, had studied painting with the American Benjamin West, and was brother-in-law to that Maria Cosway who so charmed Thomas Jefferson.

Most colorful of all was Benjamin Latrobe, a product of Huguenot France and Moravian Germany, though born in England. Trained to the ministry in Germany, he had happily turned to art, practiced briefly in England, and then migrated to Virginia where he was an instant success. He designed a penitentiary, surprised that the New World should need one; he helped with the construction of the state capital in Richmond, which won him Jefferson's esteem; he helped improve the navigation of the James; he designed a new city water system for Philadelphia—what did he not do? Jefferson brought him to Washington and soon he was in charge of almost everything, for he was a man of cascading energy and endless resourcefulness. With the aid of Thornton—and of Jefferson's old friend Philip Mazzei—he imported a small army of sculptors and decorators from Italy. There were Guiseppi Franzoni and his brother Carlo, who did the statute of Liberty in the House of Representatives, and who designed the wonderful clock with the chariot of History flying over it, recording the deeds and the eloquence of members of the House with every passing hour. There was Luigi Persica, who did the statues of Peace and War and the Discovery of America in the Rotunda, her left hand pointing to Justice and her right showing the Constitution; and there was Enrico Causici of Verona who carved the panels of Daniel Boone and the Landing of the Pilgrims—how delightful that a Veronese artist should give us Daniel Boone; there was Francisco Lardella, who carved the tobacco capitals in the Senate lobby; and poor Guiseppe Valaperti, whose eagle in the frieze of the House was so absurd that he went off and drowned himself in chagrin, or so it was alleged. Nor does this exhaust the list of French and Italian artists—there was Antonia Capello, for example, a pupil of the great Canova whom Jefferson had hoped to lure to America, and the Frenchman Nicholas Gevelot who carved the panel of William Penn and others; but why go on? What an international undertaking it was, and how it went on, all through the Napoleonic wars and the early years of the Republic as long as the original Argonauts were in command.

Or consider those two remarkable presidents of the Royal Society, itself dedicated to the pursuit of science and learning for the benefit of all mankind: Sir Hans Sloane and Sir Joseph Banks. What an international figure was the first great President, Hans Sloane. Born in Ireland, he studied medicine under the German Nicolaus Staphorst; then off to France for his formal training at Paris and Montpellier and, just to even things up, at the (now long defunct) Protestant University of Orange. He sailed for the West Indies and botanized there, and the whole scientific world rejoiced when he brought back a cargo of botanical specimens from Jamaica. At his handsome mansion in London Sloane kept open house, just as did his successor Sir Joseph Banks; the famous Albrecht von Haller came to see him—not yet famous to be sure but destined to be "the most learned man in Europe." Linnaeus came to see him, with a letter from that greatest of medical professors, Boerhaave of Leyden, and after him Linnaeus's pupil Peter Kalm, who was to write the best botanical description of America; even Voltaire paid his respects, and that did not happen very often. Like Linnaeus at Uppsala, Sloane corresponded with botanists everywhere in the Western world, not least with Americans, who sent over thousands of specimens to the royal gardens; with William Byrd of *Dividing Line*; with Mark Catesby, who wrote *A Natural History of Carolina*; and with the elder Bartram, who presided over the most famous botanical garden in English America.

It was during the presidency of Hans Sloane that the stirring drama of the baby elephant was played out. "Un elephant en mignature" had been sent to the great Réaumur of Paris—his six-volume *History of Insects* was one of the capital works of its day—but was captured by a British man-of-war and brought to Portsmouth as a prize. Réaumur pleaded for his elephant, in vain it seemed, until Abraham Trembley of the Royal Society intervened. Trembley appealed to Fox, and eventually got permission to ship the baby elephant on. Meantime the creature had died. No matter. Trembley had him stuffed, the passports arrived, and in due time the baby elephant was delivered to Réaumur, and in good condition, too. What a triumph for science and for the baby elephant who achieved immortality in the pages of Buffon's great *Histoire Naturelle*.

Sir Joseph Banks continued the Sloane traditions and enlarged upon them: for forty years as head of the Royal Society he never permitted war or revolution to interfere with the beneficent role of science. As a youth he had sailed with Captain Cook, and it was he who had introduced the famous Tahitian Omai to England. He had botanized in Iceland, too, and, later on, when the British were at war with Denmark and Iceland was cut off from food and on the verge of starvation, he enlisted the sympathy of William Pitt and saved the island. It was Banks who arranged that gold medal for Franklin; it was he who intervened, again and again, during the war with France to enable the work of science to go for-

America and the Community of Learning

ward. Appealing to Grenville for permission for the French to ship a collection of specimens from Trinidad to Paris, he wrote that "the very application offers, during the horrors of a war, unprecedented in mutual implacability . . . an unconditional armistice to Science." Banks intervened, too, to save for France the great collection which La Billiardière had assembled in the East and which had been captured by a British naval vessel; he even persuaded George III and the exiled Queen of France to forego it, and finally shipped it through the blockade to the Jardin des Plantes. "That the Science of two Nations may be at peace, while their Politics are at war," he wrote, "is an axiom we have learned from your protection to Captain Cook, and surely nothing is so likely to abate the Rancour that Politicians frequently entertain against each other as to see Harmony and good will prevail among Brethren who cultivate science." He enlisted the aid of Lord Nelson and Lady Hamilton, and finally even of Napoleon himself, to obtain the release of Déodat de Dolomieu—the Dolomites bear his name—from the dungeon in Messina into which the Neapolitans had consigned him. At a time when Napoleon was threatening to invade England, Banks saw to it that the nautical almanacs, upon which safety at sea depended, were shipped over to France as usual.

Edward Jenner, he who had discovered inoculation against smallpox, was no less cosmopolitan than his colleague Banks. So great was his fame that he was almost a sovereign: a letter from him was more valuable than a passport; monarchs everywhere respected it. And it was Jenner who, in appealing for the release of the young Lord Yarmouth from captivity, penned the memorable phrase "The sciences are never at war. Peace must always preside in those bosoms whose object is the augmentation of human happiness."

We have no more illuminating example of the operation of the community of learning than that which records the acquisition by Harvard University of the Ebeling collection of Americana. How neatly all the parts, so miscellaneous and disparate, fit together once we apply this principle of the sovereignty of learning. Let us begin with Christopher Ebeling himself, one of those prodigious scholars who seem to have been the specialty of eighteenth-century Germany. He had been educated at the new university at Göttingen and had planned to go into the ministry but was diverted to the classics and to history—two of the Göttingen specialties. When we first meet him he is director of the commercial school at Hamburg, professor of Greek and Latin at the gymnasium and, for good measure, librarian of the city library. Somehow he found time to edit, translate, and write as well. Ebeling was fascinated by geography and by freedom: these interests pointed inescapably to America, and he set himself to write a multivolume *History and Geography of America*. He wrote other things, too, to be sure, thirty-four volumes altogether, on history, geography, even on music, for though he was deaf, music was his passion; he had translated the texts of Handel's *Messiah* and of Charles Burney's survey of European music: what had he not translated, from the Danish, the Dutch, the French, and the English—*Burnaby's Travels*, for example, which told so much about the distant colonies in America? For these remained the center of his interest, and it was to the history of America that he devoted the last quarter-century of his life.

For Ebeling had already projected an ambitious history—thirteen volumes, no less, one for each of the American states. But how write thirteen volumes on these states without books or documents? He called upon the community of learning and these difficulties vanished. He appealed to members of American learned societies—the American Philosophical Society (of which he was a member); to the newly organized Massachusetts Historical Society (which made him an honorary member); to Dr. Benjamin Smith Barton, who claimed (but did not have) a Göttingen degree; and Matthew Carey in Philadelphia; to Noah Webster and Dr. Mitchill in New York; to Dr. Ramsay the historian of South Carolina; to Jedediah Morse the geographer (not a very good one, Ebeling thought); to the Reverend Dr. Belknap, who combined history and fiction with science and theology; to President Willard of Harvard College; and, above all, to the learned Reverend William Bentley of Salem—Salem, the Weimar of America. All of them responded, and through the years of the Revolution and the Napoleonic wars a stream of books, journals, newspapers, and maps flowed across the turbulent Atlantic into the library of Professor Ebeling of Hamburg.

Now there were ample materials for the great history upon which he confidently embarked—*Erdschreibung und Geschichte von Amerika*. It was to be truly comprehensive; to embrace not only geography and history, but constitutions and laws, education and religion, commerce and trade, science and culture—a veritable encyclopedia. Although there were to have been thirteen volumes in all, Ebeling lived to describe only seven states, filling eight stout volumes. But it was nevertheless the best and most comprehensive history of the new nation that had yet appeared, and the most accurate, too. Nor was it all history and geography and statistics; Ebeling was an ardent liberal and a humanitarian. In American nationalism, liberty, and democracy he saw a model for Europe and especially for his own Germany, fragmented, shattered, and without a culture she dared call her own. As he had taken sides in the struggle for American independence (and this despite Göttingen which, being a Hanoverian university, was mostly on the other side) he continued to take sides in American politics, and his volumes voted for Jefferson whom he admired above all other Americans.

Turn now to Ebeling's Georgia Augusta University of Göttingen. It had been founded by George II of Hanover and England and flourished under his financial patronage and his intellectual neglect. But the days of an independent Hanover were numbered; after Jena (1806), Napoleon was master of Germany, and the following year he merged Hanover into a newly created Kingdom of Westphalia and assigned it to his brother Jerome. Would the great "Westphalian" universities go unscathed—Halle, Marburg, and Göttingen? The historian Chriostoph Meiners, who had written learnedly on the history of universities, hurried to publish a celebrated *eulogium* of Göttingen, but in German, which Jerome certainly could not or would not read. Something more was needed. The new Minister of Education in Westphalia, formerly a professor at the famous university, turned to Charles de Villers for help.

Villers, who had studied at Göttingen in that golden age when it was dominated by historians such as Schloezer and Heeren, Biblical scholars such as Eichhorn and Michaelis, classicists such as Gesner and Heyne; Villers, who commanded a world language and had a French, or at any rate non-German, talent for popularization. Villers responded with enthusiasm and within a few months a *Bird's Eye View of the Universities of Westphalia* appeared. This little book made clear that English universities were "opulent, Gothic and ridiculous," those of Italy like deserted palaces, those of France the servants of the Church, and those of Spain well below all the others. German universities, however, began where all others left off and, what is more, the universities of Westphalia were the most flourishing in Germany, and Göttingen the glory of them all—Göttingen with its world-famous scholars, its library of two hundred thousand volumes, its independence and secularism, its dedication to research.

Madame de Staël's interest in Germany was of long standing, but it was Villers who was chiefly responsible for turning her attention to the German universities. He was, she wrote, "an author who is always found at the head of all noble and generous opinions and who seems called, by the elegance of his mind and the depth of his studies, to be the representative of France in Germany and of Germany in France." He it was who provided an introduction to the German edition of her *De l'Allemagne*. Now Madame de Staël too was to play her part, albeit a minor one, in the drama of the transfer of the Ebeling library to America. That was as it should be, for she nourished a special affection for America: had she not modeled the hero of *Corinne*, Lord Nelvil, on the young Charlestonian John Izard Middleton, who lived in Rome and wrote on Grecian antiquities? Indeed at one time she had planned to move to America and to that end invested heavily in American lands; the imagination boggles at the impact of that dazzling mind and imperious morality on the pastoral American scene!

Madame de Staël had been banished from Paris by Napoleon for her radicalism, or perhaps merely for her contumaciousness, and had taken refuge in the family villa at Coppet, outside Geneva, where she looked across the lovely Lac Leman towards Mont

Blanc and bewailed her desolate position. There she settled down to write what was to be her most famous book, *De l'Allemagne*, a description of Germany and a paean of praise, too, for now that the Enlightenment had been betrayed by Napoleon, it was to Germany that the successors of the *philosophes* looked, the Germany of Goethe and Kant and the Humboldts, and of the universities. The three volumes were ready in 1810, and Madame de Staël was allowed to return to Paris to supervise their publication. Ten thousand copies had been printed when the Superintendent of Police descended on her, and on the printer, destroyed all the books (four miraculously escaped), and banished her once again from France. "You are not to seek the reason," wrote the Chief of Police, "in your omission of all references to the Emperor in your last work. That would be a mistake, for no place could be found for him in it that would be worthy of him. Your banishment is the natural consequence of the course you have pursued for some years past. It appears to me that the air of this country does not suit you. . . . Your last work is not French."

Madame de Staël fled from country to country, finding refuge finally in St. Petersburg where, as Georg Brandes remarks sardonically, she was able at last to breathe the air of freedom! Meantime she had managed to smuggle out one copy of her book, and it was published in London in 1813; next year—the United States was at war with Britain, as Britain with France, but that made no difference—saw it published in Boston.

Now came one of those conjunctions in intellectual history that happens so frequently that they cannot be chance. America had more than its share of philosophy and of science, but it did not yet have a learned class—the *érudites* of France, or the *Gelehrte* of Germany. Now, with peace, accumulated wealth, a broadening out of commerce and trade, and the growth of professions—the law and medicine chiefly—came a zeal for scholarship. Where were the books, where were the scholars, where were the universities to minister to these needs?

Here are four young men, soon to be joined by scores of others, who are recent graduates of Harvard and Dartmouth colleges and eager for more and better education than these provincial colleges could provide: George Ticknor, Edward Everett, George Bancroft, and Joseph Cogswell. Their friend the Reverend Joseph Buckminister of Boston's fashionable Brattle Street Church had already introduced them to German scholarship: to the prodigious erudition of that Old Testament scholar Johann Eichhorn; the matchless learning of the great classicist Christian Heyne and his successor Ludolf Georg Dissen; the originality of the pioneer philologist Georg Benecke; the intellectual vigor of the historian Arnold Heeren—all of Göttingen. Soon they could read in that most Bostonian of all magazines, the *Monthly Anthology*, three essays by Charles de Villers on German universities; soon, too, Ticknor had imported Villers' *Bird's Eye View* and read it with enthusiasm. Later he was to write on its title page, "this is the book which determined me to go to Göttingen and study," and he added his own italics on the margin of Villers' statement that "freedom of teaching and of learning were the palladium of the German universities." A few years later came confirmation from within the family, as it were. Early in 1813, Everett's brother, Alexander, who had acted as John Quincy Adams' secretary in St. Petersburg, published a long and fascinating essay on the study of German in Andrews Norton's new *General Depository and Review*. Germany was distinguished in every field of philosophy, he wrote, in the study of literature and of history, in the classics, and, indisputably, in theological and Biblical studies.

And now, in 1814, the young Bostonians fell on Madame de Staël's *De l'Allemagne* with enthusiasm. What they read confirmed what Buckminister had told them, what Villers had described, what Alexander Everett had observed—that the torch of learning had passed to Germany, that there, and there alone, were great universities, great libraries, and great scholars. And somehow the climax of the argument was always Göttingen, for though Berlin had already been founded, its fame was still to reach the New World. As soon as the long war with England was over, the Bostonians were off to Göttingen: Ticknor and Everett in 1815, Cogswell the next year, and then Bancroft, the youngest of them all.

What remarkable young men they were, these Argonauts of the search for a fleece more golden than any that Jason had imagined. All of them were scholars, or meant to be, frustrated by the limitations of the academy, the libraries, and the society of the neat little world of Boston and Cambridge; all were fired with a sense of obligation to country and to posterity and with the hope that they might create in Boston a new Athens, in Washington a new Rome.

There was George Ticknor, heir to a respectable fortune that exempted him from all claims but those of public service. He became the first Abiel Smith Professor at Harvard University; wrote a still unsurpassed *History of Spanish Literature*; founded the Boston Public Library; and presided over Boston's most distinguished literary salon. There was Edward Everett, whom Francis Jeffery of the *Edinburgh Review* pronounced "the most remarkable young man I have yet seen in America" when he was only nineteen. Two years later the authorities at Harvard were wise enough to appoint him Eliot Professor of Greek, and he in turn was wise enough to realize that he should prepare himself for the new chair by studying at the fountainhead of classical scholarship. He was the first American to receive a doctorate at Göttingen, where all the professors thought that he would be another Heyne, another Dissen. But he was not to be a scholar, after all, but governor of his commonwealth, president of his university, minister to the court of St. James's, and the orator who also spoke at Gettysburg.

There was George Bancroft, the youngest of the Argonauts and the least sophisticated, who went to Göttingen to study theology. He was revolted by the sterility of Biblical scholarship and soon found himself pursuing more secular studies, himself becoming more secular in the process, and more German, too. He learned "to see folly without regarding it as unnatural, and vice without being struck by it as anything out of the way," and he took on German mannerisms as he took on German erudition. When he returned he no longer fitted Harvard, and no longer yearned for a pulpit. He opened the Round Hill School in Northampton, he wrote the greatest of histories, he presided over the American naval establishment, he became a distinguished diplomat, and he returned to the Germany he had never ceased to love.

And finally there was Joseph Cogswell, rather old for this new career as a student, but ebullient and passionate. After graduating from Harvard College he had shipped to India as a supercargo.

He returned to Massachusetts and read law with the saturnine Fisher Ames and then with Judge William Prescott, whose son was to celebrate Spanish history as Ticknor celebrated its literature. But the law was not for him, nor the classics which he taught briefly at Harvard, and two voyages to the Mediterranean in the service of the great Salem merchant William Gray, though they nourished his wanderlust, did not win him to a mercantile career.

In 1816 Cogswell had a chance to go abroad as tutor-companion to young Israel Thorndike, son of another of the Salem merchants, Colonial Israel Thorndike, whose ships were on every sea. Where would he go but to Göttingen, to join his friends and to explore new worlds of science and learning? He planned to immerse himself in Greek, but when Professor Dissen told him that, after studying that language fifteen hours a day for eighteen years, he dared not read a single page without a dictionary at hand, Cogswell abandoned that notion and turned, somewhat illogically, to mineralogy. He walked the Harz Mountains, he climbed the Alps, he visited the museums of Dresden and Munich, he haunted the university libraries. He visited Goethe at Weimar and admired his great mineral collections at nearby Jena—after all, Goethe had written two impressive volumes on mineralogy—and when he left, the Master kissed him on both cheeks and "the tear in his eye convinced me that he felt what he expressed." What a triumph, to wring a tear from the eyes of Goethe! He returned to Harvard to become Professor of Geology and Librarian, and promptly introduced the Göttingen scheme of classification, by far the most scientific.

Ever restless, Cogswell abandoned these posts to set up what was to be the most famous school for boys in the country, at Round Hill in the Connecticut Valley, a school modeled on what he had seen in Switzerland and Germany, for he was convinced that "Germany is the only country where the science of education is thoroughly understood." When that failed, as inevitably it did, Cogswell edited the *New York Review*, became John Jacob Astor's advisor on book collecting, and eventually presided over the famous Astor Library which was to be the nucleus of New York's great public library.

America and the Community of Learning

Goethe was not the only magnet for the Argonauts. Far more important, as it turned out, was the learned Ebeling in Hamburg. Dr. Bentley of Salem had provided his young American protégés —it was of course Cogswell whom he knew best—with letters of introduction to this "affectionate, invaluable, and provident friend," who over the years had been one of his most faithful correspondents, and who had sent to him perhaps a thousand volumes of German literature and history—ample repayment for what Bentley and his friends shipped over to Hamburg. It was not until the spring of 1817 that Everett, Cogswell, and young Thorndike arrived in Hamburg to pay their respects to the great savant, and it was just in the nick of time. For Ebeling was now seventy-six and worn out by a lifetime of herculean labors; he died the next month. Everett and Cogswell moved swiftly to save the great library from dispersion at the auction block. Cogswell turned to his protégé's father, Israel Thorndike, who boasted one of the great fortunes of Salem, and he, always adventurous, put up the money that enabled Cogswell to snatch the library away from none other than Frederick III of Prussia. The next year it arrived in Cambridge—some three thousand volumes of books, three hundred and fifty volumes of newspapers, eight thousand maps—all in all the greatest library of Americana in existence, and perhaps the best selected, too, for it was a working library as well as a library of rarities, and contained many volumes not be found elsewhere in the United States. "It is to be hoped," wrote a rapt contributor to the *North American Review*, "that this most liberal foundation for a Bibliotheca Americana will stimulate the present age and posterity to supply whatever enlargement the superstructure will admit." That hope has been amply fulfilled.

Already by this time the community of learning was under pressure: a good many of the book shipments between Bentley and Ebeling seem to have been the victims of war. The change was dramatized by a minor incident of the nineties. In 1792 the prized Copley Medal of the Royal Society went to an American, Count Rumford, who was then Prime Minister of Bavaria; in 1794 it went to Alessandro Volta of Italy; 1793 is a blank. That year the medal was destined for the great Lavoisier, but the members of the society knew that Lavoisier was in deadly peril and they feared that an award from England would exacerbate that peril; so they held back. Alas, even that self-restraint did not save the great chemist. The story is familiar and prophetic: he was arrested, tried and condemned. He asked for time to complete some chemical experiments; "the Republic has no need for savants," said Coffinhal, and Lavoisier's head rolled beneath the guillotine. The authenticity of the story has been challenged, but not of the decapitation.

Nationalism, and national ideologies, now threatened the integrity of the community of learning. For nationalism, like romanticism, emphasized everything that was provincial and particular in culture rather than what was catholic and universal. It celebrated national origins, the national language, and even the provincial idiom, national literature and art and culture. It repudiated the world of the Enlightenment where scholars and scientists—and aristocrats, too, of course—had been able to ignore national barriers and move freely from country to country, even in time of war; where all men of learning shared a common language, French, a common education in the literature of the ancient world, and a common loyalty to science. It emphasized separation rather than unity, fostered dissension rather than harmony, and encouraged parochialism rather than cosmopolitanism. It not only set nation against nation, but introduced what we have come to call total war—not as total as ours, to be sure, for we have made some progress over the years, but involving a whole people and an entire nation. And, in between wars, nationalism erected barriers to the free movement of men, of goods, and of ideas. Finally, it largely invented the notion of National Character—the Enlightenment had sought what was universal rather than what was local about a people—and had discovered that in some Providential way one's own country boasted the best of all characters, the most advanced culture, and the most civilized society. From this it followed that even if you might raise awkward questions about the validity of the military or political hegemony, you could not question the validity of the cultural, for that surely was beneficent!

Would the new United States escape the ravages of the new nationalism? The auspices were favorable. It had been created in the age of Enlightenment and by men who were themselves enlightened philosophers. It lacked many of the institutions and traditions that accentuated, or exacerbated, nationalism: a national church, for example, a professional army, a national enemy—always excepting the Indians—a tradition of statism. The nation was still weak, and the War of 1812 had scarcely made it strong; the population was heterogeneous, and without strong common traditions; best, or worst, of all, the new nation did not develop cultural chauvinism for the elementary reason that there was as yet no culture to be chauvinistic about. Her language, literature, law, art, architecture, even her religion, were all inherited; it would have been ridiculous, as perhaps it still is, for Americans to insist either on the unique character of American culture, or on its superiority to all others.

But there were, from the beginning, countervailing forces—some of them the other side of the shield of the cosmopolitan forces. The very fact that Americans had to create their nation and their culture placed an unprecedented emphasis upon these; it is familiar enough, now that Germany and Italy and so many other new nations have had to cultivate a sense of nationalism and exalt a national culture. But it was new in the 1780s, and in America. The circumstances of American life, too, stressed the superiority of the New World over the Old, morally, socially, economically, and politically.

In the third quarter of the present century the United States has emerged as one of the most nationalistic and most chauvinistic of nations. It is chauvinistic not alone in the political realm—that is understandable enough in a world power—but officially (though not unofficially) in the scientific and cultural. The United States is, for the most part unconsciously, repudiating the principles of a Franklin, a Jefferson, a Banks, a Lavoisier, a Jenner. It is enlisting sciences in war, even at the risk of deflecting them from their traditional and proper purposes, which are those of peace and the advancement of humanity. What is true of the sciences is only less true of the humanities—less not because there is some special dispensation for the humanities, but because they are not considered very important.

IRRATIONALISM IN THE EIGHTEENTH CENTURY

All the great problems that confront us—the Cold War, nuclear war, pollution and the destruction of natural resources, racial animosities, population control—are global. None can be solved in the separate compartments of individual states. To the creation of all but the last, population, the United States has made a major contribution, and in all of them is a major offender. We are the leading offender in the assault upon nature; a leading offender, not merely in the past but in the present, in race relations; a leading offender in the reckless indulgence of warmaking. We have in all of these areas an inescapable responsibility to mitigate the ravages of national sovereignty and to enlarge and strengthen the scope of international action.

It is improbable that we shall at this time concede any limitation on national sovereignty. But if we are not about to act formally in the re-creation of an international community, we should strive all the more zealously to act informally. Government and the universities should join hands to emancipate science and learning from primary responsibility to nationalism, and encourage primary responsibility to the world community and to future generations.

Almost two centuries ago Jefferson, who had himself given up the whole of his energies in the struggle for American Independence and the creation of American commonwealths, wrote his young friend David Rittenhouse, then serving as President of the Council of Safety of Pennsylvania:

> Your time, for two years past has, I believe, been principally employed in the civil government of your country. Tho' I have been aware of the authority our cause would acquire with the world from its being known that yourself and Doctor Franklin were zealous friends to it, and am myself impressed with a sense of the arduousness of government and the obligation those are under who are able to conduct it, yet I am also satisfied there is an order of geniuses above that obligation, and therefore exempted from it. Nobody can conceive that nature ever intended to throw away a Newton upon the occupations of a crown. It would have been a prodigality for which even the conduct of providence might have been arraigned, had he been by birth annexed to what was so far below him. Cooperating with nature

in her ordinary economy, we should dispose of and employ the geniuses of men according to their several orders and degrees. I doubt not there are in your country many persons equal to the task of conducting government: but you should consider that the world has but one Ryttenhouse, and that it never had one before.

Here is the authentic note of the Enlightenment, and of the community of culture.

The Problem of Scientific Order Versus Alphabetical Order in *the* Encyclopédie

Hugh M. Davidson

*"L'empire des sciences et des arts
est un monde éloigné du vulgaire. . . ."*

THIS SENTENCE from the "Discours préliminaire" states the problem in the shortest possible way. As they look about them, d'Alembert and Diderot, the editors of the Encyclopedia-to-be, see on the one hand many bodies of technical knowledge, as yet unsystematized in a satisfactory way and out of contact with common understanding, and on the other hand a public—or as they say, with a satirical touch, the reading, not the talking, public. The general aim and the first rule of the encyclopedic enterprise must be to close this gap, to bring knowledge and people together; all other and consequent rules have to do with devising a suitable means to this end. The means they choose, of course, is a *dictionary*, i.e., a work composed according to the purely conventional order of the alphabet but called upon to reveal the purely logical order of thought in science and in art. This paradox and the effort to surmount it form the subject of most of my remarks, but, as I hope to show, the solution to the problem involves a second paradox, something like the near-death and renewal of an ancient verbal discipline.

I should add that my interest here lies in the design and spirit of the project: in what d'Alembert and Diderot sought to do rather than in what actually happened as the volumes of the *Encyclopédie* were constituted and published. I have decided to concentrate on what the two editors said in a small number of documents where intentions and rationale appear in a more or less pure state: the *Prospectus* (Diderot, 1750), the article "Art" (Diderot, 1751), the "Discours préliminaire" (d'Alembert, 1751), and the article "Encyclopédie" (Diderot, 1755).[1]

In order to see exactly what Diderot and d'Alembert wanted to do, we must remind ourselves of some things they take to be common to every discipline. Each one of them arises out of a contact between man and nature, a contact that turns, under the stimulus of human needs, into an activity designed to accomplish some end. To be more specific: (1) each one bears on a single object; (2) it involves the collection of data—either facts or rules—concerning that object; and (3) it seeks the order in which the data may be most properly disposed. For example, grammar concerns (1) speech which has (2) been reduced to rules that (3) form a system. Diderot asserts that what is true of grammar is true of the other arts and sciences. No matter how diverse the objects in question may be, no matter how widely his attention may range, he returns finally to this single notion or model of technical discipline. Even the most important distinction of all, that between science and art, does not obliterate the common features; in fact, it accentuates them.

> Si l'objet s'exécute, la collection et la disposition technique des règles selon lesquelles il s'exécute s'appellent *art*. Si l'objet est contemplé seulement sous différentes faces, la collection et la disposition technique des observations relatives à cet objet s'appellent *science*: ainsi métaphysique est une science, et la morale est un art. Il en est de même de la théologie et de la pyrotechnie.[2]

Collection, disposition: we must understand these words in an active sense which allows for the evolving state of any art or science at any particular time. In some instances, what the Encyclopedists are talking about is not an existing science but a problem area, a distinct field in which someone is collecting and disposing data, or should be doing so. One of the factors, the data, varies, obviously, as to number, whereas the second, the order or arrangement, remains always essentially the same.

> La seule ressource qui nous reste donc dans une recherche si pénible, quoique si nécessaire, et même si agréable, c'est d'amasser le plus de faits qu'il nous est possible, de les disposer dans l'ordre le plus naturel, de les rappeler à un certain nombre de faits principaux dont les autres ne soient que des conséquences.[3]

The artist or scientist always tries to arrange his data so that they fall into principles and consequences. When that happens in a problem area, we know that art or science is present there, and we can judge the discipline to be in a relatively complete state when a small number of principles can account for a large number of facts.

Of course it is possible to work in the opposite direction and to reduce the fullness of the account without sacrificing the ideal of order. That is, in fact, one of the Encyclopedists' most characteristic functions: to reduce sciences and arts to their *éléments*. (Voltaire had furnished one striking example of such a work, based on Newton's *Principia*). Diderot describes the task in his *Prospectus*:

> ... il a fallu donner à chaque matière une étendue convenable, insister sur l'essentiel, négliger les minuties, et éviter un défaut assez commun, celui de s'appesantir sur ce qui ne demande qu'un mot, de prouver ce qu'on ne conteste point, et de commenter ce qui est clair. Nous n'avons ni épargné, ni prodigué les éclaircissements.[4]

The elements turn out to be mainly matters of principle. One arrives at them by cutting out unessential facts, rules, and operations, by retaining the schematic framework of the discipline, by keeping before one the priority of certain principles, and by making clear what some of their consequences, both near and far, may be.

Since any single object of attention and the activities related to it form the starting point of an art or science, we would expect that this assignment—unifying and abridging bodies of knowledge—would correspond to a technical discipline. It does: it implies the art of logic.

> Il enseigne à ranger les idées dans l'ordre le plus naturel, à en former la chaîne la plus immédiate, à décomposer celles qui en

> renferment un trop grand nombre de simples, à les envisager par toutes leurs faces, enfin à les présenter aux autres sous une forme qui les leur rende faciles à saisir. C'est en cela que consiste cette science du raisonnement qu'on regarde avec raison comme la clef de toutes nos connaissances.[5]

I should like to call attention to two points here. First, this logic is both analytic and synthetic; it identifies elements and then combines them according to natural or other criteria. Secondly, it is a technique of presenting what is known. It not only looks backward to data and inward to ideas, but also outward and forward to those who do not yet know. Thus defined, as an art of communication as well as an art linked with scientific thinking (not necessarily with *discovery*: d'Alembert says that it does not have the first place in the order of *invention*), logic takes over concerns often thought to belong to other arts.

In fact, the paragraphs just following the lines quoted give us an interesting view of the re-alignment undergone by three traditional disciplines at the hands of d'Alembert and Diderot. It is the old trio, logic, grammar, and rhetoric, treated in that order, and not in the more usual order of grammar, rhetoric, and logic. Grammar has a place alongside logic, since words may and should mirror thought. Both logic and grammar have ideas as their object or subject matter, and both address themselves to the mind. What does that leave for rhetoric? The answer is: something powerful in effect but questionable in value, namely, *sentiment*.

> Les hommes en se communiquant leurs idées, cherchent aussi à se communiquer leurs passions. C'est par l'Eloquence qu'ils y parviennent. Faite pour parler au sentiment, comme la Logique et la Grammaire parlent à l'esprit, elle impose silence à la raison même; et les prodiges qu'elle opère souvent entre les mains d'un seul sur toute une nation, sont peut-être le témoignage le plus éclatant de la supériorité d'un homme sur un autre.[6]

D'Alembert goes on to limit severely the value of rhetoric; he criticizes the very idea of rules in such a field, where talent reigns. Orators are *not* made; only nature can do that (once more, as often in the philosophic movement of the eighteenth century, rhetoric

The Problem of Order in the Encyclopédie

is being put in the compromising company of poetry). A very meager art, if indeed it can be called an art, emerges. Concerned with "pedantic puerilities" that have been "honored with the name of rhetoric" (p. 36), it is to oratory what scholasticism is to true philosophy. This seems to recognize a place for a *genuine* discipline, but the emphasis is on the bad kind, which, it is hoped, will disappear some day. With the pedantic and childish aspects still in mind, d'Alembert concludes:

> Cependant quoiqu'on commence assez universellement à en reconnaître l'abus, la possession où elles [les puérilités pédantesques] sont depuis longtemps de former une branche distinguée de la connaissance humaine, ne permet pas encore de les en bannir: pour l'honneur de notre discernement, le temps en viendra peut-être un jour.[7]

But I must leave this digression on three of the liberal arts, though it has been necessary for what I want to say later about rhetoric, which goes out by the door but comes back in through the window.

For the moment the thing to note, it seems to me, is that the notions of science, art, and logic, as here used, are symptoms of something really basic—a habit of mind, a pair of intellectual reflexes. Almost everywhere we look in the "Discours préliminaire" and in the article "Encyclopédie," we see d'Alembert and Diderot *dividing* and *composing* in various ways. As I have not the time to treat this subject fully, I shall simply mention a few examples drawn from a long list. D'Alembert, in what he calls a genealogy of the sciences, follows the *va-et-vient*, the trials and errors, of the enquiring mind as it makes discoveries, gathers them together, forms them into sciences that become, in turn, elements capable of forming a general system. Or, he studies the results of the mind's meanderings as from a high point of vantage; he sees, as on a terrain below him, simultaneously rather than in sequence, objects known, operations applied to them, and connections binding them together: in such a perspective these factors again become parts of an organic whole, in which logical priorities are respected. Still, whether the account is cast in the form of a genealogy (more mythical than factual) or in the form of something like a map that forecasts the synoptic table of arts and sciences, the intellectual tendency is exactly the same.

Diderot presents a partial contrast with this way of proceeding. Whereas d'Alembert, in the Preliminary Discourse of 1751, tends to move synthetically from origins and elements to wholes, Diderot, in the article "Encyclopédie" of 1755, with four volumes behind him, seems to reverse the direction and to follow an analytical line of thought—which is natural, no doubt, in the case of an editor on the job. He describes the various kinds of "*ordre encyclopédique*" in a descending movement that begins with a panoramic view of knowledge and ends with reflections on what should go into the sections of a particular article in the Encyclopedia. Seen in this way, the task is staggering, indeed, paralyzing. I think it very significant that a mechanical analogy presents itself to him as he says to himself and to us what must be done.

> En général la description d'une machine peut être entamée par quelque partie que ce soit. Plus la machine sera grande et compliquée, plus il y aura de liaisons entre ses parties, moins on connaîtra ces liaisons; plus on aura de différents plans de description. Que sera-ce donc si la machine est infinie en tout sens; s'il est question de l'univers réel et de l'univers intelligible, ou d'un ouvrage qui soit comme l'empreinte de tous les deux?[8]

A machine has parts that fit together; so has the universe, since it is an infinitely large machine (composed itself of two unlimited universes, the real and the intelligible); and an encyclopedia, as an image or impression of the two universes must, by the force of the analogy, be a machine as well.

There are, in fact, five different and successive *ordres* for consideration, each less general than the preceding one; and in every case Diderot evokes a whole that is being analyzed. In the first place, the whole is the entire body of knowledge, and the parts are the divisions of that body according to the faculty—reason, memory, or imagination—most concerned in groups of sciences and arts. In the second order, the whole is again all of knowledge, but it now presents itself, as Diderot discusses it, with reference to *matières*: *Morale, Mathématiques, Théologie, Jurisprudence, Histoire naturelle*, etc., and the problem is to fix the right proportions among these parts. In the third order, Diderot narrows the field of view, turning from outer proportions to inner structure in the treatment of particular matters. Here the division is into axioms or principles versus consequences. Diderot makes his point in two magnificent periodic sentences, one based on the image of a tree, with its roots, trunk, and branches, and the other based on the image of a world map, with great regions, kingdoms, provinces, and areas. The fourth order brings us to the very point of setting up text in the *Encyclopédie*. This order is less general, Diderot says, than any of the preceding. What is the complex with which we begin here? It is a *dénomination* or head-word, with its various meanings, which forms or can form—the editor must try for this —something systematic:

> Il y a des termes solitaires qui sont propres à une seule science, et qui ne doivent donner aucune sollicitude. Quant à ceux dont l'acception varie et qui appartiennent à plusieurs sciences et à plusieurs arts, il faut en former un petit système dont l'objet principal soit d'adoucir et de pallier autant qu'on pourra la bizarrerie des disparates.[9]

In the fifth kind of "*ordre encyclopédique*" Diderot continues the treatment of a complex article, such as that considered under the preceding heading. Take a mineral, for example. The "dénomination" remains one and the same, but a number of people take turns in treating it: the grammarian, the naturalist, the physicist, the pharmacist, the doctor, the cook, the painter, the dyer. Each collaborator takes the substance as an undifferentiated whole and breaks it down into aspects of special interest to him. And so, in Diderot's five kinds of encyclopedic order, as well as in d'Alembert's historical and synoptical accounts of the sciences, we may discern the working of a single methodological impulse. It is so pervasive in their thinking that it may be judged, I think, an absolutely indispensable ingredient both in the conception and in the execution of their project. Let me emphasize for a moment the practical advantages.

(1) There is a sense in which the very possibility of distributing logically ordered knowledge into an alphabetically ordered work requires this analytical habit of mind. Since science and art have two distinct aspects, facts (or rules) and arrangement, and since facts or rules have a certain discreteness, different arrangements of essentially the same data become possible. The rearrangement into an alphabetical sequence, under such conditions, does not alter the data; it merely changes the order in which the elements follow each other. If you will allow me a bit of jargon from the land of computer science, we are talking about two *sorts* of the same *cards*. (I realize that the comparison is deficient, but it may help.) In any case, it is clear that knowledge can be and has been conceived in other ways, not dependent on such devices of analysis and synthesis, just as it is clear that encyclopedias can be and have been presented in formats other than alphabetical. The fact is that the particular view of art, science, and logic assumed by the Encyclopedists, and their frame of mind in general, lend themselves nicely to the solution of the problem created when an encyclopedia is to be also a dictionary.

I have something definite in mind here, and not merely a vaguely conceived tradition. The leading figures of the French Enlightenment simply do not agree on the nature of knowledge. Montesquieu finds it in the identification of causes, Divine, natural and rational, and in the study of ensuing relationships and effects; Rousseau finds it in the movement from contradictions of many different kinds toward unities, harmonies, and organisms; Voltaire looks for it, after tributes to the special validity of mathematics and mathematical physics, in the sifting of opinions, in acts of judging and doubting that are guided by common sense or clear results in practice. The views of Montesquieu and Rousseau hardly suggest moveable parts of knowledge that one may rearrange for purposes of exposition. The views of Voltaire, although they find expression in a dictionary giving *la raison par alphabet*, have nothing encyclopedic about them.

(2) This brings me to my second point of advantage, which concerns the reader. By nature, science is a closed, coherent organism. It leads normally to treatises where everything is *in order*: in order as to logical priority (principles come before consequences) and in order as to specification (broad distinctions subdivide so as to give an ever more thorough grasp of subject matter). The purity and unity of science are bound to be repellent to the unspecialized reader. As d'Alembert recognizes, the *Encyclopédie* might have been a collection of separate treatises. It would have met, then, one of its fundamental conditions, to keep the integrity and interrelationship of the sciences and arts, but, by making knowledge less available, it would have failed in its other major aspiration. The *Encyclopédie*, again, might have taken the form of a collection of separate dictionaries. That approach would have satisfied the condition of accessibility, but it would have failed to meet the need for encyclopedic order, since many words or entries would be repeated in separate dictionaries, with no effective linking of related subject matters and treatments.

The test of accessibility must be met first, or the Encyclopedists will have toiled in vain. It dictates the choice of an alphabetical presentation. At this point we see that rhetoric, the art for which d'Alembert expressed strong reservations and even contempt, is beginning to reassert itself, for we are now dealing unmistakably with three of the basic factors in any rhetorical situation: (1) something to be communicated; (2) the disposition or arrangement of subject matter; and (3) the character of the audience. Neither of the first two factors can be determined without reference to the third, which is decisive. Regarding arrangement, therefore, the task of the Encyclopedists becomes singularly complex. The members of this "society of men of letters and artists" must disengage, from (a) an original arrangement, such as might be found in a source work by Newton or Locke, something we might call (b) a technical arrangement, proper to disciplined thinking about the elements of an art or science; however, they cannot use this second order without change, because, though streamlined, it is still too elaborate, and so they translate it into (c) an alphabetical arrangement, in order that it may be immediately accessible to anyone who can read. Scientific order is logical, natural, and *forbidding*; while alphabetical order is illogical, conventional, and *inviting*: it supplies a place, a point of departure, where the curiosity of a reader may come to a first focus.

But this is a temporary expedient, as we know, for d'Alembert writes:

> Il nous reste à montrer comment nous avons tâché de concilier dans notre Dictionnaire l'ordre encyclopédique avec l'ordre alphabétique. Nous avons employé pour cela trois moyens, le système figuré qui est à la tête de l'ouvrage, la science à laquelle chaque article se rapporte, et la manière dont l'article est traité.[10]

He and Diderot will provide devices in each article that permit breaking out of the alphabetical order and returning to a logical and comprehensive sequence. There are three things to do: (1) identify the relevant science that stands behind the article; (2) situate that science in the ensemble of disciplines; and (3) reconstitute that science, within the limits possible in a work of this kind. To solve the first difficulty, the editors ordinarily include, just after the head-word or phrase, the name of the science or art to which the article may be referred. In cases where this key is omitted, they believe that reading the article will suffice: discussion given under the word "Bombe" obviously belongs to a military art, and the name of a city or a country to geography. In other instances, an article will suggest a second article, relating to a different science, and the process of identification may thus involve two or more sciences. To solve the second difficulty is easy, for all the reader has to do is to inspect the tree of knowledge, the *système figuré*, which shows him immediately the relative position of the science or sciences concerned in the article before him. The solution to the third difficulty is more complicated: the editors supply cross-references so that related subjects and articles may be properly linked. If these *renvois* do not appear explicitly in the body of the article, they may be present in another form as technical terms, and the reader may look them up in their alphabetical place, that is, in articles where their senses are defined and developed. It is important to note that d'Alembert understands these acts of cross-referral not merely as ways of explaining one article by another but as the means whereby the reader may re-assemble the members of a body, the parts of a whole: he intends not only *explication* but also *liaison*.

In brief, we may say that the alphabetical arrangement represents a temporary but quite indispensable concession to the reader; it puts him in contact with the line of scientific thinking on a subject; it allows him to start from where he is in puzzlement about a word and to move, by a series of combinations, toward a kind of understanding which is technical and ultimately encyclopedic; it takes him up, leads him on, and, if he stumbles because of unusual nomenclature, puts him, after a detour, back on the right path.

There is, however, an important epilogue to this story. As we have seen, in the article "Art," published in 1751, Diderot defined art and science as gathering and arranging rules and facts. In the "Discours préliminaire," also published in 1751, d'Alembert asserted that, at the crucial moment of presentation, rational order and alphabetical order may be reconciled so that the intellectual capital of the race may become, within limits, the property of all. Four years later, in 1755, when Volume V appeared, it contained the article "Encyclopédie." There Diderot clearly speaks from experience on many aspects, both theoretical and practical, of encyclopedia-making. He includes a long discussion of language, written from a retrospective point of view. The mood is that of one who now realizes too late what should have been done. His attitude can be best understood, perhaps, in the following way. D'Alembert had thought of language with an idea of synthesis in the back of his mind: words or phrases in the alphabetic sequence were essentially *terms*. Starting from those terms, the reader could move from article to article, retrace the steps that connect principles to consequences, identify sciences or arts, and see the places of these disciplines in the whole picture. D'Alembert's views reflect the mind of a mathematician. Diderot's views, as expressed in the article "Encyclopédie," sound more like those of a convinced empiricist. He conceives of the word less as a *term* than as a *sign*. An air of optimism pervades the "Discours préliminaire" on this point, as though words could be trusted, or, if not that, defined without great trouble. Diderot is now more cautious: he has an acute intuition—traceable to analysis rather than to synthesis—of the need to insure univocal meanings for words. The correct use of words as terms or elements presupposes attending to the problems of words as signs. All the hopes of the enterprise are at stake:

> ... la connaissance de la langue est le fondement de toutes ces grandes espérances; elles resteront incertaines, si la langue n'est fixée et transmise à la postérité dans toute sa perfection; et cet objet est le premier de ceux dont il convenait à des Encyclopédistes de s'occuper profondément. Nous nous en sommes aperçus trop tard; et cette inadvertance a jeté de l'imperfection sur tout notre ouvrage.[11]

Diderot can think of only one way to achieve fixity of meaning and freedom from ambiguities, and that is to refer living language to dead language. Since dead language exists only in authors, i.e., in writing, it is no longer subject to change. Greek and Latin could be used, the former where the latter does not supply what is needed. What would the result look like? As Diderot imagines it, we should have first the French radical, then the Greek or Latin radical, with a citation of the ancient author where the agreed-upon sense is present. Whatever we may think of the practicability of this plan, we can grasp without difficulty the ambition behind it. Each radical, after being defined and fixed, corresponds to a mental event. By its nature it signifies either simple and particular sensation or an abstract and general idea: each linguistic element is matched up with a psychological reality. In other words, Diderot forces us to approach at one and the same time the origins of both science and discourse. From these evident beginnings, where indivisible bits of thought and indivisible bits of language correspond exactly, scientific knowing grows into larger and larger ensembles of principles and consequences, and similarly, discourse follows it like a shadow, mimicking its every move. Such purified language would, indeed, remove the gap between technical thought and that done by the reader of the Encyclopedia. As we have seen from the "Discours préliminaire," Everyman, or at least Everyreader, can begin with the alphabet and then travel into the realm of science if one provides the necessary linking devices. Now, on a more fundamental level, we can see that every reader, starting from his own sensations and ideas, might, thanks to corrected linguistic usage, lock in at some point—wherever he chose, in the alphabetical sequence—with the thought of the scientist or of the artist, and go without ambiguity through a process of enlightenment to the level of the *éléments* of a science and to a grasp of where it lies on the total map of knowledge.

What we have here is a particularly fine example of the methodological principle to which I drew attention earlier: the impulse to move back and forth along a line, analyzing in one direction, synthesizing in the other. There was something metaphorical in my references to the principle when I spoke of discoveries gathered into treatises (synthesis), which were reduced to their elements (analysis), then distributed into articles and divisions of articles (further analysis) with means provided for recovering a view of a particular science and of the whole system (synthesis). The ultimate and literal acts of analysis and synthesis occur in the psychological and linguistic activity hinted at in the article "Encyclopédie."

The *Encyclopédie* did not succeed entirely; it did not realize the kind of blueprint that was present in the minds of d'Alembert and Diderot. It was necessarily more an aspiration and an inspiration than an accomplished project. For one thing, too many people were involved as collaborators over too long a time for the results to be uniform. For another, the *Encyclopédie* could often do little more than indicate problem areas. It could encourage exploration, but it could not give an account in formally satisfactory terms of all the territories it defined. It often had to content itself with partial coverage, with compilations, with recitals of different points of view, instead of the consensus and logical unity presupposed in the project. Moreover, because of the inevitable polemics, the Encyclopedists found themselves drawn into ways of thinking quite far from the calm progressions in thought that they associated with science and *philosophie*. The articles often have a curious antithetical structure, in which what ought to be is played off against what is; and this sort of dialectic is further complicated by the doubling and allegorizing that occur because of the need for indirection. Such antilogism and allegory strike any reader immediately as he turns from the programmatic statements to the articles of the *Encyclopédie*.

Nevertheless, where the arts and sciences strictly speaking were concerned, there was a purity of idea and aim in the minds of the two main editors. They saw themselves as being on the way to knowledge as a system of systems; and they invented an enormously appealing way to convey that view. One of the most commonly noticed features of eighteenth-century French literature is the way in which writers introduce theses and critical attitudes into poems, plays, and novels. No one can contest the value of such means of enlightenment. But they are subject to two serious objections. They make it difficult for an author to say in a truly technical or quasi-technical way what his message is; and they cannot give a complete and panoramic view of knowledge and human progress. The solution to both difficulties is the *dictionary*, an intellectual form or genre that Moréri, Bayle, Chambers, and others had already used. The Encyclopedists saw that it had possibilities as yet not exploited. An easily opened door to knowledge, it makes contact with the reader at a propitious moment, at a moment of "felt" need. But the special effectiveness or energy of an encyclopedic dictionary arises from the fact that, in spite of necessary abridgments, it is still both technical and systematic.

Artisans make discoveries, but think it more important to use them than to record them; geniuses make discoveries, but set them down in books that only a few can read. Whence the need for a "society," for a task force that will recover and assemble all that has been learned and then treat it, with a large audience in mind, as subject matter to be expressed, i.e., as *res* and *verba* (to

The Problem of Order in the Encyclopédie

use the old terms), subject to the rules of rhetoric. In other words, the *Encyclopédie* is a large-scale exercise in an art for which the principal Encyclopedists had little respect. Let us try to be precise, however. In the *Encyclopédie*, rhetorical thinking has been caused to coincide in essential aspects with scientific thinking. Ultimately and literally speaking, the scientist or artist starts with things, sensations of things, and ideas based on sensations. Now that is exactly where, as Diderot shows, the reader of the *Encyclopédie* is supposed to begin—with things, sensations, and ideas. Over the centuries, rhetoric has always interested itself in the opinions and even the prejudices of the audience; it has tended to become a *méthode d'agréer*, to take a phrase from Pascal. Not so here, however. Though it may start with opinion, this rhetoric leads us back to a prior point in the mind of the audience, where it may work with pristine and universal elements. We have thus a new version of an old discipline, new and different in the sense that it cannot be primary; nor can it have the last word; nor can it be the comprehensive art of arts (as it was for Cicero, for example). However, after waiting upon the labors of artists and scientists, it has a definite and, indeed, indispensable role to play.

It would be unwise, it seems to me, to reduce most of rhetoric to the art of arousing or communicating emotion, as d'Alembert would have us do. In fact, it appears quite improbable that any age of enlightenment can do without careful attention to rhetoric. (I mean the thing, not necessarily the term.) The reason is not far to seek. "Enlightenment" makes no sense unless it can distinguish between knowledge and opinion, and unless it undertakes to change opinion in the light of knowledge. But, in its various forms, rhetoric has always been a technique for influencing opinion. The interesting question for "enlightenment" literature is not, then, whether it involves rhetoric, but how it adjusts rhetoric to changing ways of conceiving the knowledge to be spread and the opinions to be modified.

The problem of scientific versus alphabetical order makes it possible for us to see, in outline, the approach of the Encyclopedists, who use a form of rhetoric as a technique for making, to some degree, scientists and artists of us all.[12] However, I am certain that this conception of rhetoric does not hold for Montesquieu or Voltaire or Rousseau. How could it, since each of these thinkers has attitudes and positions too pure and too distinctive for him to agree with the others in approaching this problem? If we wish to pursue this line of thought, we must not, I believe, take the works of Cicero and Quintilian as having more or less finally fixed the nature of this Protean discipline. Their eclectic contributions, though massive, brought about on the level of principles a serious reduction of certain Greek achievements, in which very different kinds of rhetoric were recognized or implied. Nor shall we want to fall into any of the more common reductions that have marked its history: to technique, narrowly defined; to speaking in public; to concern for ornate language; to emotional appeals; to this or that excess. Instead, broad attention to its premises, species, and applications may give us new means for understanding that aspect of the Enlightenment by which it appears as a vast movement of *mediation*, carried out by those who know, or at least know more, for the benefit of those whose thinking takes place for the most part in a climate of opinion.

NOTES

1. For the sake of my general argument I review briefly in passing some ground that has been covered by Professor Dieckmann in his essay "The Concept of Knowledge in the *Encyclopédie*" (pp. 73-107 in *Essays in Comparative Literature*, ed. Herbert Dieckmann, Harry Levin, and Helmut Moketat (St. Louis: Washington University, 1961). However, his problem and mine, though related at certain points, are not exactly the same.
2. From *Oeuvres complètes de Diderot*, ed. J. Assézat (Paris: Garnier, 1876), XIII, 360, "Art." I have used this edition for all citations from Diderot.
3. From the *Oeuvres complètes de d'Alembert* (Paris: Bélin, 1821), I, 28. I have used this edition for all citations from the "Discours préliminaire."
4. *Ibid.*, p. 91.
5. *Ibid.*, p. 33.
6. *Ibid.*, pp. 35-36.
7. *Ibid.*, p. 36. One of the Encyclopedists' mentors, Francis Bacon, is more sympathetic toward rhetoric. He defends it from some of the criticisms offered by Plato in his *Gorgias*, accepts essentially the work of Aristotle,

and finds it possible to establish four intellectual arts (inquiry, examination, elocution, and custody) by using four of the five traditional parts of rhetoric (invention, arrangement, expression, memory, and delivery).
8. Diderot, *Oeuvres complètes*, XIV, 451, "Encyclopédie."
9. *Ibid.*, p. 457.
10. D'Alembert, "Discours préliminaire," p. 51.
11. Diderot, "Encyclopédie," p. 429.
12. It should be noted that, with reference to the documents studied here, I have not attempted to deal with aspects clearly falling in the territory of a rhetoric designed to arouse enthusiasm for the idea of progress, for a long view of history, for reforms of abuses, or to provide an imaginative (even poetical) view of the Encyclopedic enterprise. In this connection, I wish to convey my thanks to Professor John N. Pappas of Fordham University for his close reading of my paper and his comments on it.

Leonard Euler, Supreme Geometer (1707-1783)*

C. Truesdell

ON AUGUST 23, 1774, within a month of his appointment as Ministre de la Marine and the day before he was made Comptrolleur Général of France, Turgot wrote as follows to Louis XVI:

> The famous Leonard Euler, one of the greatest mathematicians of Europe, has written two works which could be very useful to the schools of the Navy and the Artillery. One is a *Treatise on the Construction and Manoeuvering of Vessels*; the other is a commentary on the principles of artillery of Robins ... I propose that Your Majesty order these to be printed; ...
>
> It is to be noted that an edition made thus without the consent of the author injures somewhat the kind of ownership he has of his work. But it is easy to recompense him in a manner very flattering for him and glorious to Your Majesty. The means would be that Your Majesty would vouchsafe to authorize me to write on Your Majesty's part to the lord Euler and to cause him to receive a gratification equivalent to what he could gain from the edition of his book, which would be about 5,000 francs. This sum will be paid from the secret accounts of the Navy.

"The famous Leonard Euler," then sixty-nine years old and blind, was the principal light of Catherine II's Academy of Sciences in Petersburg. His name had figured before in the correspondence between Turgot, the economist and politician, and Condorcet, the

---

* Acknowledgment. I am grateful to Dr. Marta Rezler for correction of some details regarding Voltaire. The research reported here was supported in part by a grant of the U.S. National Science Foundation to The Johns Hopkins University.

prolific if rather superficial mathematician and littérateur soon to become Perpetual Secretary of the Paris Academy of Sciences, and later first an architect and then a victim of the Revolution. Just twenty years afterward Condorcet was to die because his hands had been found to be uncalloused and his pocket to contain a volume of Horace, but in 1774 equality, while already advocated and projected by Turgot, had not progressed so far. In a France threatened by bankruptcy a minister of state could still find time to write in letters to a friend his opinions and doubts and conjectures about everything from literature to manufacture, and by the way the solution of algebraic equations. It was such a minister who asked whether "this Euler, who lets nothing slip by unnoticed, might have treated in his mechanics or elsewhere" the most advantageous height for wagon wheels.[1]

In a time when intelligence was the highest virtue, when even men and women then thought to be lazy and stupid (and today proved by their words and deeds to have been lazy and stupid) were portrayed with little wrinkles of alertness around their sparkling, understanding eyes, the name of Leonard Euler, the greatest mathematician of the century in which mathematics was almost unexceptionally regarded as the summit of knowledge, was better known than those of the literary and musical geniuses, for example Swift and Bach. In the firmament of letters only Voltaire outshone Euler. True, in all the world there were but seven or eight men who could enter into discourse with him, Voltaire certainly not being one of them, and most of what he wrote could be understood in detail by only two or three hundred, Voltaire not being one of these either, but pinnacles could then still be admired from below. In the volume for 1754 of *The Gentleman's Magazine*, a British periodical of general interest the contents of which ranged from heraldry to midwifery, we find an article entitled "Of the general and fundamental principles of all mechanics, wherein all other principles relative to the motion of solids or fluids should be established, by M. Euler, extracted from the last Berlin Memoirs." The anonymous extractor concludes that Euler's principle "comprises in itself all the principles which can contribute to the knowledge of the motion of all bodies, of what nature soever they be." This principle we call today the *principle of linear momentum*. There are in fact two further general principles of motion, the *principle of rotational momentum* and the *principle of energy*. The former of these Euler himself evolved and enounced twenty-five years later; it was the culmination of his researches on special cases of rotation that had extended over half of the eighteenth century. The latter principle was left for the physicists of the next century to discover.

Euler was so prolific that an entire volume is required to contain the list of his publications. Approximately one third of the entire corpus of research on mathematics and mathematical physics and engineering mechanics published in the last three quarters of the eighteenth century is by Euler. From 1729 onward he filled about half of the pages of the publications of the Petersburg Academy, not only until his death in 1783 but on and on over fifty years afterward. (Surely a record for slow publication was won by the memoir presented by him to that academy in 1777 and published by it in 1830.) From 1746 to 1771 Euler filled approximately half of the scientific pages of the proceedings of the Berlin Academy also. He wrote for other periodicals as well, but in addition he gave some of his papers to booksellers for issue in volumes consisting wholly of his work. By 1910 the number of his publications had reached 866, and five volumes of his manuscript remains, a mere beginning, have been printed in the last ten years. There is almost no duplication of material from one paper to another in any one decade, and even most of his expository books, some twenty-five volumes ranging from algebra and analysis and geometry through mechanics and optics to philosophy and music, include results he had not published elsewhere. The modern edition of Euler's collected works was begun in 1911 and is not yet quite complete; although mainly limited to republication of works which had been published at least once before 1910, it will require about seventy-five large quarto volumes, each containing 300 to 600 pages. Euler left behind him also 3000 pages of clearly and consecutively written mathematical notebooks and early draughts of several books.[2] A whole volume is filled by the catalogue of the manuscripts preserved in Russia. Euler corresponded with savants and administrators all over Europe; the topics of his letters range more widely than his papers, going into geography, chemistry, machines and processes, exploration, physiology, and economics.) About 3000 letters from or to Euler are presently known; the catalogue of these, too, occupies a volume. About one third of the letters have been printed, many of them in volumes consisting of particular correspondences. The first such volume, published in 1843, was of great importance for its impetus to developments in the theory of numbers in the nineteenth century, more than fifty years after all the principals in the correspondence had died. This kind of permanence, difficult for literary men and historians and physicists to comprehend, is typical of sound mathematics.

It was Euler who first in the western world wrote mathematics openly, so as to make it easy to read. He taught his entire century that the infinitesimal calculus was something any intelligent person could learn, with application, and use. He was justly famous for his clear style and for his honesty to the reader about such difficulties as there were. While most of his writings are dense with calculations, four of his books are entirely elementary. One of these is a textbook for the Russian schools; one is the naval manual which Turgot caused to be reprinted in France; one is a treatise on algebra which begins with counting and ends with subtle problems in the theory of numbers; and the fourth, called *Letters to a Princess of Germany on Different Subjects in Natural Philosophy*, is a survey of general physics and metaphysics. This last is the most widely circulated book on physics written before the recent explosion of science and schooling. It was translated into eight languages; the English text was published ten times, each time revised so as to bring the contents somewhat up to date; six of the editions were American, the last one in 1872, a date four years closer to today than to 1768, when the original first appeared.

To study the work of Euler is to survey all the scientific life, and much of the intellectual life generally, of the whole eighteenth century. In this lecture, I cannot even list all the fields of science to which Euler made major additions. The most I can do is give some idea what manner of man he was.

Leonard Euler, Supreme Geometer

Leonard Euler was born in Basel in 1707, the eldest son of a poor pastor who soon moved to a nearby village. The parsonage there had two rooms: the pastor's study and another room, in which the parents and their six children lived. Euler was first instructed by his father, who had been an eager student of James Bernoulli, a mathematician of the days of Newton and Leibniz and an equally profound creator, but who had not continued into higher mathematics. The boy's talent was obvious, and he was soon sent to the Basel Gymnasium, which documents of the day show to have been in lamentable state, with fist-fights in the classroom and occasional attacks of parents upon teachers. Mathematics was not taught, so Euler was given private lessons by a young university student of theology who was also a tolerable candidate in mathematics.

At the age of thirteen, Euler matriculated in the faculty of arts of the University of Basel. There were approximately one hundred students and nineteen professors. Instruction was miserable, and the faculty, underpaid, was mediocre with one exception. The Professor of Mathematics was John Bernoulli, the younger brother of the great, and by that time deceased, James; John Bernoulli, (a mighty mathematician and ferocious warrior of the pen, was universally feared and admired as a geometer second only to the aged and long silent Newton. Bernoulli had returned, reluctantly, to the backwater of Basel despite brilliant offers of chairs in the great universities of Holland; he had had to return because of pressure from his patrician father-in-law. Single-handed, he had made Basel a mathematical center. Three of the four principal French mathematicians of the first half of the century had sought and received instruction from him; his sons and nephews became mathematicians, some of them outstanding ones. He hated the "scurvy English," as he called them, and like Horatius at the bridge he had defeated every British champion who dared challenge him.

Bernoulli discharged his routine lecturing on elementary mathematics at the University with increasing distaste and decreasing attention. Those few, very few, students whom he regarded as promising he instructed privately and sometimes gratis. By the time Euler was sixteen, Bernoulli had told him to study the major works of science of the day and was allowing him one hour every Saturday to express doubts and ask questions. As an old man, Euler remembered that he had studied hard so as to need ask little. He had already appeared as public opponent of claimants for chairs of logic and of the history of law; he had already given his own first public lecture, on the philosophies of Descartes and Newton; he was already bachelor and master of liberal arts. At nineteen he published his first mathematical paper, an outgrowth of one of Bernoulli's contests with the English; Euler had found that his teacher's solution of a certain geometrical problem, while indeed better than the English one, could itself be greatly improved, generalized, and shortened. In the case of his own sons, such turns aroused Bernoulli's jealousy and competition, but Euler at once became and remained the favorite among all his disciples.

The next year, at the age of twenty, Euler competed for the Paris prize. These prizes were the principal scientific honors of the century; golden honors they were, too, 2500 livres or even twice or thrice that much, not the empty titles of our time. John Bernoulli himself won the prize twice; his son Daniel, ten times; Euler was to win it twelve times, or about every fourth year of his working life. The assigned topics were usually dull or vague or intricate matters of celestial mechanics, nautics, or physics, never mathematics as such. Often they were directed toward the interests of a specific Frenchman who had something ready and was expected therefore to win, but the competitions were administered fairly, and when an outsider sent in a fine essay, in most cases he was given the prize. The Basler mathematicians had a knack of twisting an unpromising subject into something more fundamental, where mathematics could be brought to bear. The prize essays themselves only rarely solved the problem announced and usually were works of second class in the authors' total outputs, but the competitions caused the great savants to take up and deepen inquiries they might otherwise never have begun, so that the competitions tended indirectly to broaden the range of mathematical theories of physics. Thus they played, though at a more individual and aristocratic height, a role like that of military support for science in our time. The subject of 1727 was the masting of ships. Euler had never seen a ship, but his entry received honorable mention and was published forthwith. The winner was Bouguer, for whom the prize had been designed, and who had submitted an entire treatise he had been writing for some years; this treatise immediately became the standard work on the subject. The other two classics of the eighteenth century on naval science, one being much more general and mathematical and profound, and the other being the little handbook to which Turgot referred, were both to be written later by Euler.

In the same year, his twenty-first, Euler, at Bernoulli's recommendation, competed for the chair of physics. While he was quickly eliminated as a candidate, he published his specimen essay, *A Physical Dissertation on Sound.* With the clarity and directness that were to become his instantly recognizable signature, in sixteen pages he laid out in order and in simple words, without calculations, all that was then known about the production and propagation of sound, added some details of his own, and listed a number of open problems. This work became a classic at once; it was read and cited for over a hundred years, during which it served as the program for research on acoustics. Euler himself later wrote at least one hundred papers directly or indirectly related to the problems set here, and many of these he solved once and for all. The last page lists six annexes. The first denies the principle of preestablished harmony; the second asserts that Newton's law of gravitation is indeed universal; the fourth affirms that kinetic energy is the true measure of the force of bodies; while the remaining three announce solutions of problems concerning oscillation through a hole in the earth, the rolling of a sphere, and the masting of ships. The professorship was given to a man never heard of again, who in fact was interested primarily in anatomy and botany. Euler at twenty had entered the field of mechanical physics and philosophy as a challenger with definite positions, openly avowed, on every main question then under debate. At the same time, and in equal measure, he was able to announce definite and final solutions to several specific problems. When he died, fifty-five years later, his mastery of all physics as it was then understood, and his ability to solve special problems, were just the same. Indeed, most

Irrationalism in the Eighteenth Century

of the main general advances of the entire century had been made by him, and in addition he had solved many key problems and hundreds of examples. On the day of his death he had discussed with his disciples the orbit of the planet Uranus, which Herschel had discovered two years before. On his slate was a calculation of the height to which a hot-air balloon could rise. The news of the Montgolfiers' first ascent had just reached St. Petersburg, where Euler had been residing for most of his life.

Having had the good luck not to win the chair of physics at Basel, Euler went to Petersburg in 1727. John Bernoulli had been invited but felt himself too old; instead he offered one of his two sons, Daniel and Nicholas, and then adroitly required that neither should go unless the other went too for company and comfort. One was a professor of law and the other was studying medicine in Italy; and both were pleased to accept chairs of mathematics or physics. They promised the young Euler the first vacant place, but Russia's thirst for the mathematical sciences was slaked at the moment, so they suggested he take a position as "Student of Physiology." To this end they advised him to read certain books and learn some anatomy, which he did forthwith. He arrived in Petersburg on the day the empress died: an event that plunged the Academy into confusion.) During his trip the restriction to physiology had been forgotten, and Euler was made adjunct in the mathematical class.

The Academicians were all foreigners—Germans, Swiss, and a Frenchman, not only the professors but also the students. Thus language was not a problem, but the senior colleagues were. To a man the chiefs, like university officials today, were tumors, the only question being whether benign or malignant. The most promising mathematician, Nicholas Bernoulli, had died of a fever before Euler arrived. Euler's friends were Daniel Bernoulli, seven years older and already a world-famous mathematician and physicist, and Goldbach, an energetic and intelligent Prussian for whom mathematics was a hobby, the entire realm of letters an occupation, and espionage a livelihood. The Academy fell on evil days; its effective director was an Alsatian named Schumacher, whose main interest lay in the suppression of talent wherever it might rear its inconvenient head.

Soon most of the old tumors had been excised by departure or death. So had most of the capable men. Daniel Bernoulli, after having competed for every vacancy in Basel, in 1733 finally obtained the chair of anatomy. Once back, he felt himself a new man in the good Swiss air, but in the rest of his long life he never again reached the level and the productivity of his eight years in Petersburg, six of which were enlivened by friendly competition with Euler.

Euler stayed on. For him, these were years of growth as well as production. While he never lost his love for mechanics and the "higher analysis," he steadily enlarged his knowledge and power of thought to include all parts of mathematics ever before cultivated by anyone. He was able to create new synthetic theorems in the Greek style, such as his magnificent discovery and proof that every rotation has an axis. He sought and read old books such as Fermat's commentary on Diophantos. On the basis of such antiquarian studies he recreated the arithmetic theory of numbers, which had been scarcely noticed by the Bernoullis and Leibniz, in whose school of thought he had been trained. He gave this subject new life and discovered more major theorems in it than had all mathematicians before him put together. He was equally at home in the algebra of the seventeenth century. He also probed new subjects which were to flower only much later. One of these is combinatorial topology, in which he conjectured but was not able to prove what later became a key theorem, now called the Euler polyhedron formula.[3] Unifying and systematizing the work of many predecessors, he created analytic geometry as we know that discipline today;[4] from his textbook, and from others based upon it, and still others based on them, and so on, students of mathematics learned the subject from 1748 until the 1930's, when it was largely superseded by the rise of modern linear algebra. Students of natural science even today learn it in essentially Euler's way. Euler was the first man to publish a paper on partial differential equations, and the world has learnt most of the elementary calculus of partial derivatives from his books, although many of the results had been known to Newton and Leibniz but not published by them. It was mainly in his first Petersburg years that Euler developed his taste for pure mathematics, which has re-

IRRATIONALISM IN THE EIGHTEENTH CENTURY

mained forever after, in a tradition deriving straight from him and unbroken by the most violent political changes, a Russian specialty. About one third of his total output was regarded as "pure" mathematics in his own day; in the classification of our time, this term would apply to only about one fifth of his work; but that small fraction includes many of his deepest and most permanent contributions. One of these is the concept of real function: namely, a rule assigning to certain real numbers other ones. In his earlier years Euler, like his predecessors, had used a far more restricted, and vague, concept of function, but his own discoveries in the theory of partial differential equations and wave propagation had shown him the clear way,[5] which every mathematician since his day has followed. Other great discoveries were the law of quadratic reciprocity[6] in number theory and the addition theorem for elliptic functions,[7] but these came much later than the time of which I am now speaking.

There is no evidence that Euler preferred any one part of mathematics to the rest. The only sure conclusion we can draw from his prodigious output is that he sought to enlarge the domain of mathematics and its applications with an eager dedication like that which led Don Giovanni to seduce even ugly girls *pel piacer di porle in lista*, but Euler's outposts, even those ridiculed by some of his contemporaries, have been bridgeheads to future and permanent total conquests.

The first Petersburg years brought Euler success, instruction in the facts of life, and misfortune. He became Professor of Physics in 1730, but, as often happened in the Enlightenment, he could not collect all of his salary. In 1731 there was a matter of promotion: four little men, who up to that time had been receiving less than he, were set equal to him. In a formal protest Euler wrote,

> That we shall each be treated on the same footing is something I can't get through my head at all.... It is true that I have never applied myself so much to physics as to mathematics, but nevertheless I doubt much that you can get from the outside such a person as I for any 400 rubles. In the matter of mathematics, I think the number of those who have carried it as far as I is pretty small in the whole of Europe, and none of those will come for 1000 rubles.

Leonard Euler, Supreme Geometer

(We should take note of Euler's estimated difference of salaries: 400 for a physicist, 1000 for a mathematician. In those days physics was a speculative or experimental science, not a mathematical one.)[8] When Euler wrote these words, he was twenty-four and had published seven papers. If he thought this kind of talk would get him anywhere, he was mistaken. Schumacher advised the President of the Academy not to grant him the least concession, since otherwise he would straightaway grow impudent. Euler had to be content with 400 rubles, like the four little men who were raised to his rank and pay. Euler learned a lifelong lesson from this experience: It is futile to argue with administrators but easy to outwork them.

Two years later Euler was made Professor of Mathematics at a salary of 660 rubles, and then he married. Of course he chose a Swiss wife, the daughter of a court artist; in this way he continued the tradition of the Bernoullis, all of whom were either professors or painters, and his younger brother also became a painter. The first of Euler's many children was born the next year. A few weeks later a violent fever destroyed the sight of one of Euler's eyes. Two years afterward he became supervisor of the department of geography. His remaining eyesight was severely strained by the work, but he was really interested in constructing a good general map of Russia, and he succeeded in doing so. He wrote to order a school arithmetic text and a great treatise on naval science, receiving for this latter 1200 rubles, in this way nearly doubling his salary for two years. His Swiss talent for making money was beginning to show itself.

In 1740 Euler was asked to cast the horoscope of the new Czar, who was only a few weeks old. While such a task would have been normal a century earlier, for the Enlightenment it was *retardataire*. Euler smoothly passed the honor on to the Professor of Astronomy. The contents of the horoscope is not known, but in less than a year the child Czar was deposed and hidden; twenty-four years later, still in prison, he died.

In 1740 Frederick II ascended the throne of Prussia. This eccentric and semi-educated general, flute player, and homosexual lay under the spell of France and French men. He wished to create in Berlin a combined French Académie des Sciences and Académie

Française. Voltaire was his Apollo, and Voltaire recommended as director a trifling but extremely eminent French scientist named Maupertuis, whom he dubbed "Le Grand Aplatisseur" because he had led an expedition to Lapland so as to measure the length of one degree of meridian and had concluded thereby that the earth was flatter at the poles than at the equator. For Voltaire, who endorsed mathematical philosophy but did not understand it, this proved Descartes wrong and Newton right about everything. The later *philosophes* followed his judgment; the British gleefully followed them; and somehow this minor and highly precarious side issue has assumed in the folklore of science an importance it never for a moment deserved or enjoyed among those who knew what was what in rational mechanics. In addition to being an argonaut, Maupertuis was an *héros de salon* and a *causeur*, a fit table companion for the king; notwithstanding that, he had been a disciple of John Bernoulli, and though no geometer himself, he knew mathematics when he saw it. He proposed to bring all the Bernoullis and Euler to Berlin.

Only Euler came, and no sooner had he arrived than the king's wars overturned everything and nearly killed Maupertuis, who withdrew from Prussia until he was sure Frederick's seat was firm. Euler, meanwhile, was writing mathematical papers. Every associate member of the Academy was required to compose for publication at least one memoir per year; every pensioner, at least two; Euler never presented fewer than ten.

The keys to the treasurehouse of learning in the eighteenth century—I should be tempted to say also today, were it not that any such statement would be empty because "learning" has been taken off the gold standard—were the Latin language and the infinitesimal calculus. Frederick II understood neither; he detested both. He ordered his Academy to speak and publish only in French, and he encouraged it to cultivate the sciences useful in promotion of trades and manufactures, in the restraint of savage passions, and in the development of a subject's duties. Euler, despite his thoroughly Classical training and his consummate mastery of the new "analysis of curves," easily accepted these conditions. He continued his connection with the Academy of Petersburg, not only sending it a stream of papers, mainly on pure mathematics, but also serving as virtual editor of its publications; in addition, he conveyed to Schumacher information of all sorts regarding the scientific life of the West. In return, of course, he received a salary. These relations continued even during the Seven Years War, when Russia joined the alliance against Prussia and at one time overran Berlin. When a farm belonging to Euler[9] was pillaged by the Russians, their commander, General Tottleben, saying he did not make war upon the sciences, indemnified Euler for more than the damage sustained, and Empress Elizabeth added a further gift, so that the loss was turned into a handsome profit. Euler also lodged and boarded in his house Russian students sent by the Petersburg Academy, one of these being Rasumovski, hetman of the Cossacks, who later became president of the Academy. Euler gave these students instruction in mathematics, this being as close as he ever came to what is called "teaching" in universities now. Euler taught mathematics and physics to the whole world, and down to the present time his influence on instruction in the exact sciences has been second only to Euclid's. Like Euclid, he taught by written words, not by the now-exalted personal contact.

By no means all of Euler's books were popular ones. Until about fifteen years ago unopened copies of his more advanced works turned up at low prices on the book market. At least five of these were the first treatises ever published on their subjects, and while easy for a dedicated reader to study, they seemed abstruse to the laity. Few as were the copies sold in Euler's own day,[10] they fell into the right hands. His treatises on rigid-body dynamics, infinite series, differential and integral calculus, and the calculus of variations were mother's milk to three or four generations of mathematicians and theoretical physicists, including the great Frenchmen of the Napoleonic revival, as well as the less eminent but equally influential German and Italian professors of the same period; from the teaching of these three schools the basic core of Euler's work has passed into the common tradition of the mathematical sciences.[11] While it is a rare young Doctor of Philosophy in America today who can decipher a page of Johnson's *London* without a dictionary if not a crib or coach, and while in another academic generation we can confidently expect that *Robinson Crusoe* will have to be translated into "modern English," even the mediocre juniors in engineering the world over have learned and are able to use a dozen of Euler's discoveries. With the music of the same period, the contrast is even more striking. For example, in the eighteenth century no one outside Hamburg can have heard Telemann's *Der Tag des Gerichtes*; few can have been those who heard even some part of Bach's *Messe in H-moll*, and no one, certainly, had heard the whole of it or any part at all of *Die Kunst der Fuge*. While these works seem to us now to stand at the summit of the Enlightenment, even their authors had in their own day merely national or local reputations. Not so with Euler, who was famous far, far beyond the tiny though international circle of those who could understand what he wrote. He was one of those favored few who achieved even from their own contemporaries the respect of which posterity has judged them worthy. Euler won his later fame by the usual method: the merciless trials by the fire and water of time. In his own day, from his twenty-fifth year onward, he was a senior academician, and he made full use of the advantages his position gave him.

The academies of the eighteenth century, although few in number, dominated its science, which had become professional. While in the earlier Baroque period there had been many savants, mostly amateur, who had contributed in some degree to the spring tide of the new natural philosophy, by the time of the Enlightenment science had become a serious business, valued and rewarded though little understood. The high positions were paid well. Euler's initial salary in Berlin was 1600 talers; Maupertuis received nearly twice as much; the junior members, about 300. The number of positions was small, and competition for them was intense. As senior professor in Basel and "the Archimedes of his age," as he justly regarded himself, old John Bernoulli at the end of his life received only about as much as a "student" or "adjunct" in one of the great academies. It is difficult to estimate equivalents in modern currency, but in terms of goods and services I think the value of Euler's 1600 talers was around $40,000, tax-free. For example, in 1742 he bought a fine house with a large garden for 2000 taler, one and one quarter year's salary, while the wages of a professor

Leonard Euler, Supreme Geometer

today for the same length of time, after income taxes, would barely equal the price of a run-down row house. However, we must not be misled by today's social-democratic guilt syndrome, which dictates that the greatest genius of the age must not be paid more than twice the wages of idleness for a congenital fool. The Enlightenment, as its name might suggest, was a period of economic variety, in which Euler found himself further from the top than from the bottom. It would have cost a whole Paris prize to buy a Savonnerie carpet fourteen feet square, had the royal monopoly let any be sold. This is one point where comparisons might be thought simple, since the factory still exists. A carpet of the same size, presumably one of the garish sprays of splotches now regarded as art, costs $36,000; as in the Enlightenment, today the total product of the factory is reserved, though no longer for the splendid galleries of kings and their pretty mistresses' bedrooms but rather for the upper beaches washed by the flux and reflux of interchangeable functionaries of the Nth Republic.

Euler practised the thrift for which the Swiss are justly famous. In 1753 he bought a farm for 6000 talers, and with its produce of hay, grain, vegetables, and fruit he cut his household expenses in half. He lodged there his widowed mother, his younger children, and their private tutors. A portrait of the time, a fine pastel by Handmann, shows him in an elegant nightcap and a dressing gown of light and dark blue strips of satin, presumably his working clothes. In this portrait, his blind right eye is turned aside from the beholder. The mouth has a somewhat confused expression that is due only to damage to the pastel and does not reflect the ease and decision visible in other portraits of Euler.

To learn what an Academy of the eighteenth century was, we may begin with Gulliver's third voyage, published the year before Euler first went to Petersburg. Swift had the Royal Society of London in mind, but the glove fits the more formal academies of the Continent almost as well. First there was the mathematical class:

> ... a race of mortals ... singular in their shapes, habits, and countenances. Their heads were all reclined either to the right or the left; one of their eyes turned inward, and the other

directly up to the zenith. Their outward garments were adorned with the figures of suns, moons, and stars, interwoven with those of fiddles, flutes, harps, trumpets, guitars, harpsichords, and many other instruments of music, . . . I observed here and there many in the habit of servants, with a blown bladder fastened like a flail to the end of a short stick, which they carried in their hands. In each bladder was a small quantity of dried pease, or little pebbles. . . . With these bladders they now and then flapped the mouths and ears of those who stood near them . . . ; it seems the minds of these people are so taken up with intense speculations, that they neither can speak, nor attend to the discourses of others, without being roused by some external taction upon the organs of speech and hearing; for which reason those persons who are able to afford it always keep a flapper. . . . And the business of this officer is, when two or more persons are in company, gently to strike with his bladder the mouth of him who is to speak, and the right ear of him or them to whom the speaker addresseth himself. This flapper is likewise employed diligently to attend his master in his walks, and upon occasion to give him a soft flap on his eyes, because he is always so wrapped up in cogitation, that he is in manifest danger of falling down every precipice, and bouncing his head against every post, and in the streets, of justling others, or being justled himself into the kennel. . . .

At last we entered the palace, and proceeded into the chamber of presence, where I saw the King seated on his throne, attended on each side by persons of prime quality. Before the throne was a large table filled with globes and spheres, and mathematical instruments of all kinds. His Majesty took not the least notice of us, although our entrance was not without sufficient noise, by the concourse of all persons belonging to the court. But he was then deep in a problem, and we attended at least an hour, before he could solve it. . . . My dinner was brought. . . . In the first course there was a shoulder of mutton, cut into an equilateral triangle, a piece of beef into a rhomboides, and a pudding into a cycloid. The second course was two ducks, trussed up into the form of fiddles; sausages and puddings resembling flutes and hautboys, and a breast of veal in the shape of a harp. The servants cut our bread into cones, cylinders, parallelograms, and several other mathematical figures. . . .

The knowledge I had in mathematics gave me great assistance in acquiring their phraseology, which depended much upon

> that science and music; and in the latter I was not unskilled. Their ideas are perpetually conversant in lines and figures. If they would, for example, praise the beauty of a woman, or any other animal, they describe it by rhombs, circles, parallelograms, ellipses, and other geometrical terms, or by words of art drawn from music, needless here to repeat. . . .

(We remark that the mathematicians of the Enlightenment shared the common passion for music. Euler himself wrote a major treatise on harmony, which as far as it goes has never been superseded; he projected a treatise on composition; and he published some short papers concerning the function of dissonances. D'Alembert likewise wrote a treatise on music. Some musicians returned the compliment: Rameau wrote,

> Music is a science which should have secure rules; these rules should be drawn from an evident principle, and this principle can scarcely be known to us without the aid of mathematics. Thus I must admit that despite all the experience I could get from music in practising it for so long a time, nevertheless it is only by the help of mathematics that my ideas have grown clear. . . .

Whatever Rameau's study of mathematics may have been, no sign of it may be detected in his book, in which even the experimental facts of acoustics as they were then known are partly misrepresented.)

In Laputa,

> . . . their houses are very ill built, the walls bevil, without one right angle in any apartment, and this defect ariseth from the contempt they bear to practical geometry, which they despise as vulgar and mechanic, those instructions they give being too refined for the intellectuals of their workmen, which occasions perpetual mistakes. And although they are dexterous enough upon a piece of paper in the management of the rule, the pencil, and the divider, yet in the common actions and behaviour of life, I have not seen a more clumsy, awkward, and unhandy people, nor so slow and perplexed in their conceptions upon all other subjects, except those of mathematics and music. They are very bad reasoners, and vehemently given to opposi-

tion, unless when they happen to be of the right opinion, which is seldom their case. Imagination, fancy, and invention, they are wholly strangers to, nor have any words in their language by which those ideas can be expressed; the whole compass of their thoughts and mind being shut up within the two forementioned sciences.

Most of them, and especially those who deal in the astronomical part, have great faith in judicial astrology, although they are ashamed to own it publicly. But what I chiefly admired, and thought altogether unaccountable, was the strong disposition I observed in them towards news and politics, perpetually enquiring into public affairs, giving their judgments in matters of state, and passionately disputing every inch of a party opinion. I have indeed observed the same disposition among most of the mathematicians I have known in Europe, although I could never discover the least analogy between the two sciences; unless those people suppose, that because the smallest circle hath as many degrees as the largest, therefore the regulation and management of the world require no more abilities than the handling and turning of a globe. But I rather take this quality to spring from a very common infirmity of human nature, inclining us to be more curious and conceited in matters where we have least concern, and for which we are least adapted either by study or nature.

These people are under continual disquietudes, never enjoying a minute's peace of mind; and their disturbances proceed from causes which very little affect the rest of mortals. Their apprehensions arise from several changes they dread in the celestial bodies. For instance, that the earth, by the continual approaches of the sun towards it, must in course of time be absorbed or swallowed up. That the face of the sun will by degrees be encrusted with its own effluvia, and give no more light to the world. That the earth very narrowly escaped a brush from the tail of the last comet, which would have infallibly reduced it to ashes; and that the next, which they have calculated for one and thirty years hence, will probably destroy us. For if in its perihelion it should approach within a certain degree of the sun (as by their calculations they have reason to dread) it will conceive a degree of heat ten thousand times more intense than that of red-hot glowing iron; and in its absence from the sun, carry a blazing tail ten hundred thousand and fourteen miles long; through which if the earth should pass at the distance of one hundred thousand miles from the nucleus or main body of the comet, it must in its passage be set on fire, and reduced to ashes. That the sun daily spending its rays without any nutriment to supply them, will at last be wholly consumed and annihilated; which must be attended with the destruction of this earth, and of all the planets that receive their light from it.

They are so perpetually alarmed with the apprehensions of these and the like impending dangers, that they can neither sleep quietly in their beds, nor have any relish for the common pleasures or amusements of life. . . .

The mathematicians Swift described lived upon an island magnetically suspended in the air. They were able to control its motions perfectly and so dominate the low earth beneath them. At this baser level lay the practitioners of applied and natural science, who inhabited the Grand Academy of Lagado:

This Academy is not an entire single building, but a continuation of several houses on both sides of a street, which growing waste was purchased and applied to that use.

I was received very kindly by the Warden, and went for many days to the Academy. Every room hath in it one or more projectors, and I believe I could not be in fewer than five hundred rooms.

The first man I saw was of a meagre aspect, with sooty hands and face, his hair and beard long, ragged and singed in several places. His clothes, shirt, and skin were all of the same colour. He had been eight years upon a project for extracting sun-beams out of cucumbers, which were to be put into vials hermetically sealed, and let out to warm the air in raw inclement summers. He told me he did not doubt in eight years more he should be able to supply the Governor's gardens with sunshine at a reasonable rate; but he complained that his stock was low, and entreated me to give him something as an encouragement to ingenuity, especially since this had been a very dear season for cucumbers. I made him a small present, for my lord had furnished me with money on purpose, because he knew their practice of begging from all who go to see them.

I went into another chamber, but was ready to hasten back, being almost overcome with a horrible stink. My conductor pressed me forward, conjuring me in a whisper to give no offence, which would be highly resented, and therefore I durst not so much as stop my nose. The projector of this cell was the most ancient student of the Academy; his face and beard were of a pale yellow; his hands and clothes daubed over with filth. When I was presented to him, he gave me a close embrace (a compliment I could well have excused). His employment from his first coming into the Academy, was an operation to reduce human excrement to its original food, by separating the several parts, removing the tincture which it receives from the gall, making the odour exhale, and scumming off the saliva. He had a weekly allowance from the society, of a vessel filled with human ordure, about the bigness of a Bristol barrel.

I saw another at work to calcine ice into gunpowder, who likewise showed me a treatise he had written concerning the malleability of fire, which he intended to publish.

There was a most ingenious architect who had contrived a new method for building houses, by beginning at the roof, and working downwards to the foundation, which he justified to me by the like practice of those two prudent insects, the bee and the spider.

There was a man born blind, who had several apprentices in his own condition: their employment was to mix colours for painters, which their master taught them to distinguish by feeling and smelling. It was indeed my misfortune to find them at that time not very perfect in their lessons, and the professor himself happened to be generally mistaken: this artist is much encouraged and esteemed by the whole fraternity.

In another apartment I was highly pleased with a projector, who had found a device of ploughing the ground with hogs, to save the charges of ploughs, cattle, and labour. The method is this: in an acre of ground you bury, at six inches distance and eight deep, a quantity of acorns, dates, chestnuts, and other mast or vegetables whereof these animals are fondest; then you drive six hundred or more of them into the field, where in a few days they will root up the whole ground in search of their food, and make it fit for sowing, at the same time manuring it with their dung. It is true, upon experiment they found the charge and trouble very great, and they had little or no crop. However, it is not doubted that this invention may be capable of great improvement.

I went into another room, where the walls and ceiling were all hung round with cobwebs, except a narrow passage for the artist to go in and out. At my entrance he called aloud to me not to disturb his webs. He lamented the fatal mistake the world had been so long in of using silk-worms, while we had such plenty of domestic insects, who infinitely excelled the former, because they understood how to weave as well as spin. And he proposed farther that by employing spiders the charge of dyeing silks should be wholly saved, whereof I was fully convinced when he showed me a vast number of flies most beautifully coloured, wherewith he fed his spiders, assuring us that the webs would take a tincture from them; and as he had them of all hues, he hoped to fit everybody's fancy, as soon as he could find proper food for the flies, of certain gums, oils, and other glutinous matter to give a strength and consistence to the threads. . . .

I was complaining of a small fit of the colic, upon which my conductor led me into a room, where a great physician resided, who was famous for curing that disease by contrary operations from the same instrument. He had a large pair of bellows with a long slender muzzle of ivory. This he conveyed eight inches up the anus, and drawing in the wind, he affirmed he could make the guts as lank as a dried bladder. But when the disease was more stubborn and violent, he let in the muzzle while the bellows were full of wind, which he discharged into the body of the patient, then withdrew the instrument to replenish it, clapping his thumb strongly against the orifice of the fundament; and this being repeated three or four times, the adventitious wind would rush out, bringing the noxious along with it (like water put into a pump), and the patient recover. I saw him try both experiments upon a dog, but could not discern any effect from the former. After the latter, the animal was ready to burst, and made so violent a discharge, as was very offensive to me and my companions. The dog died on the spot, and we left the doctor endeavouring to recover him by the same operation. . . .

I had hitherto seen only one side of the Academy, the other being appropriated to the advancers of speculative learning, of whom I shall say something when I have mentioned one illustrious person more, who is called among them *the universal artist*. He told us he had been thirty years employing his thoughts for the improvement of human life. He had two large rooms full of wonderful curiosities, and fifty men at work. Some were condensing air into a dry tangible substance, by extracting the nitre, and letting the aqueous or fluid particles percolate; others softening marble for pillows and pin-cushions; others petrifying the hoofs of a living horse to preserve them from foundering. The artist himself was at that time busy upon two great designs; the first, to sow land with chaff, wherein he affirmed the true seminal virtue to be contained, as he demonstrated by several experiments which I was not skillful enough to comprehend. The other was, by a certain composition of gums, minerals, and vegetables outwardly applied, to prevent the growth of wool upon two young lambs; and he hoped in a reasonable time to propagate the breed of naked sheep all over the kingdom.

So much for the Department of Doing Material Good to Humanity. You may think that these long quotations from *Gulliver's Travels* are no more than a fantastic parody and so digress from my subject; on the contrary, for each episode in the Third Voyage a specific source, either in the *Philosophical Transactions* or in other scientific literature available to Swift, has been traced.[12] The truth was so bizarre as to need only recounting to serve as satire of itself. Today we sometimes forget that the abuse which accompanied the rise of the experimental method amounted to a second childhood of the human mind.

Crossing the walk, Gulliver arrived at the part where resided "the projectors in speculative learning," that is, to the Department of Moral and Humanitarian Studies.

The first professor I saw was in a very large room, with forty pupils about him. After salutation, observing me to look earnestly upon a frame, which took up the greatest part of both the length and breadth of the room, he said perhaps I might wonder to see him employed in a project for improving speculative knowledge by practical and mechanical operations. But the world would soon be sensible of its usefulness, and he flattered himself that a more noble exalted thought never sprang in any other man's head. Every one knew how laborious the usual method is of attaining to arts and sciences; whereas by his contrivance the most ignorant person at a reasonable charge, and with a little bodily labour, may write books in philosophy, poetry, politics, law, mathematics, and theology, without the least assistance from genius or study. He then led me to the frame, about the sides whereof all his pupils stood in ranks. It was twenty foot square, placed in the middle of the room. The superficies was composed of several bits of wood, about the bigness of a die, but some larger than others. They were all linked together by slender wires. These bits of wood were covered on every square with paper pasted on them, and on these papers were written all the words of their language, in their several moods, tenses, and declensions, but without any order. The professor then desired me to observe, for he was going to set his engine at work. The pupils at his command took each of them hold of an iron handle, whereof there were forty fixed round edges of the frame, and giving them a sudden turn, the whole disposition of the words was entirely changed. He then commanded six and thirty of the lads to read the several lines softly as they appeared upon the frame; and where they found three or four words together that might make part of a sentence, they dictated to the four remaining boys who were scribes. This work was repeated three or four times, and at every turn the engine was so contrived that the words shifted into new places, as the square bits of wood moved upside down.

Six hours a day the young students were employed in this labour, and the professor showed me several volumes in large folio already collected, of broken sentences, which he intended to piece together, and out of those rich materials to give the world a complete body of all arts and sciences; which however might be still improved, and much expedited, if the public would raise a fund for making and employing five hundred such frames in Lagado, and oblige the managers to contribute in common their several collections.

He assured me, that this invention had employed all his thoughts from his youth, that he had emptied the whole vocabulary into his frame, and made the strictest computation of the general proportion there is in books between the numbers of particles, nouns, and verbs, and other parts of speech. . . .

We next went to the school of languages, where three professors sat in consultation upon improving that of their own country.

The first project was to shorten discourse by cutting polysyllables into one, and leaving out verbs and participles, because in reality all things imaginable are but nouns.

The other project was a scheme for entirely abolishing all words whatsoever; and this was urged as a great advantage in point of health as well as brevity. For it is plain that every word we speak is in some degree a diminution of our lungs by corrosion, and consequently contributes to the shortening of our lives. An expedient was therefore offered, that since words are only names for *things,* it would be more convenient for all men to carry about them such things as were necessary to express the particular business they are to discourse on. And this invention would certainly have taken place, to the great ease as well as health of the subject, if the women, in conjunction with the vulgar and illiterate, had not threatened to raise a rebellion, unless they might be allowed the liberty to speak with their tongues, after the manner of their ancestors; such constant irreconcilable enemies to science are the common people. However, many of the most learned and wise adhere to the new scheme of expressing themselves by things, which hath only this inconvenience attending it, that if a man's business be very great, and of various kinds, he must be obliged in proportion to carry a greater bundle of things upon his back, unless he can afford one or two strong servants to attend him....

Another great advantage proposed by this invention was that it would serve as an universal language to be understood in all civilised nations, whose goods and utensils are generally of the same kind, or nearly resembling, so that their uses might easily be comprehended. And thus ambassadors would be qualified to treat with foreign princes or ministers of state, to whose tongues they were utter strangers.

I was at the mathematical school, where the master taught his pupils after a method scarce imaginable to us in Europe. The proposition and demonstration were fairly written on a thin wafer, with ink composed of a cephalic tincture. This the student was to swallow upon a fasting stomach, and for three days following eat nothing but bread and water. As the wafer digested, the tincture mounted to his brain, bearing the proposition along with it. But the success hath not hitherto been answerable, partly by some error in the *quantum* or composition, and partly by the perverseness of lads, to whom this bolus is so nauseous, that they generally steal aside, and discharge it upwards before it can operate; neither have they been yet persuaded to use so long an abstinence as the prescription requires.

Thus we see that "relevant" studies were subsidized by the governments of the Enlightenment, that they employed large staffs and needed costly apparatus, and that of modern educational tools only television and computerized dating were yet to be discovered. None of the products of these gossamer schemes for human betterment led to anything we now value. On the other hand, the military projects rarely if ever brought any improvement in the arts of warfare, but they did yield as by-products much basic science which every man curious to understand the world around him must learn today, science upon which rests much of our ordinary technology, that ubiquitous and supremely ugly technology whose products the most humanitarian of humanists insist upon having, and at low cost, however much they may despise the kind of learning that has produced them. For example, Euler's treatise on naval science was based largely on assumptions about the inertial and frictional resistances of water and air which were later shown to be false, so his tediously scrupulous calculations of the efficiency of sails, oars, and paddle wheels, the design of hulls, and the courses of sailing ships, while correct as calculations, can have been nothing but useless to the Russian navy, yet his book contains also the first analysis of the stability of floating bodies in general and of the motion of rigid bodies about a variable axis. One device based upon Euler's basic theory but not invented until over 150 years after his death is the gyrocompass, which has saved at least a thousand times the number of lives it has helped to destroy.

Swift did not mention the disputes of the academicians and the precarious finances of the academies. Although by disposition somewhat irascible, Euler was not quarrelsome; he was exceptionally generous, never once making a claim of priority and in some cases actually giving away discoveries that were his own. He was the first to cite the works of others in what is now regarded as the just way, that is, so as to acknowledge their worth. Up to his time citation had been little more than a weapon of attack, to show where predecessors went wrong. Euler's intellectual generosity can hardly be set as an example, any more than a rich man's scale of giving can be imitated by a poor one: Euler was so wealthy in theorems that loss of a dozen more or less would not be noticed.

It was a different matter with religious issues. Euler maintained for his entire life the simple Protestant faith his father had preached. It had no pretensions in science, and science for Euler had no just pretensions in morality and religion. Thus for Euler the atheism or deism or agnosticism of the French *philosophes* was devilish. King Frederick, on the other hand, while regarding organized religion as desirable for the ignorant, upheld the supremacy of the human intellect so long as it impinged only upon God's rights, not those of earthly kings. A Swiss Protestant was ready to bow to his king, but not to the Devil. Euler published anonymously a booklet called *The Rescue of Divine Revelation from the Objections of the Freethinkers*.

In addition, Euler was a philosopher in his own right. Whereas the *philosophes* ridiculed him as naive, Kant later was to derive his own metaphysics from his study of Euler's writings, but he was not able enough in mathematics to understand Euler's major metaphysical paper, *Reflections on Space and Time*. The ridiculously narrow doctrine of the physical universe we are accustomed to associate with Kant and his successors in German philosophy was evolved after Euler's death, and Euler's point of view did not come into its own until the rise of non-Euclidean geometries and relativity, one and two centuries later.[13]

Maupertuis, President of the Berlin Academy, was not precisely a *philosophe*. Euler was loyal to him, and he stood between Euler and the dislike, even contempt, of the king. Maupertuis had sputtered an overriding law of nature, the Law of Least Action, according to which all natural operations rendered something the smallest it could possibly be. Maupertuis' attempt to phrase this law in its application to mechanics was wrong, and ridiculously so. A year earlier Euler had found a correct statement for the case of a single particle, greatly more special than Maupertuis' pronouncement, but, as far as it went, right. When he heard of Maupertuis' principle, far from claiming any credit, Euler published his own result as being a confirmation of Maupertuis' grand idea, which he praised beyond measure.

Not so the rest of the world. A distinguished non-resident member of the Academy named König, a good mathematician and a friend and former protégé of Maupertuis, had some objections, which he confided to Maupertuis in a private conversation. A break followed, for Maupertuis tolerated no criticism. The next year König published his objections, along with counterexamples, and he mentioned that in any case the idea had been sketched in a letter of the long-dead Leibniz, an extract from which he included. A dreadful rumpus ensued in Berlin. König could not produce the letter, which he said he had seen in the possession of his unfortunate friend Henzi, whom the fathers of the Canton of Bern had beheaded because he had made some suggestions regarding the government. Euler came to the defense of Least Action and Maupertuis. Having handed over to Maupertuis as a gift his own discovery of the one case in which the principle could then be proved right, he was sure Maupertuis could not have stolen it from Leibniz, and he had shown that something could be done with the principle if properly corrected. Unfortunately he chose to launch a counterattack against König, claiming that the letter was forged.[14]

Meanwhile Voltaire, who after the death of his mistress the Marquise du Châtelet had no agreeable lodging, came to visit King Frederick at Potsdam. Formerly Voltaire had been a great admirer of Maupertuis and had written:

> *Héros de la physique, Argo-*
> *nautes nouveaux*
> *Qui franchissez les monts, qui*
> *traversez les eaux,*
> *Dont le travail immense et*
> *l'exact mesure*
> *De la terre étonnée ont fixé*
> *la figure.*

> Heroes of physics, new
> Argonauts,
> Who cross the mountains and
> the seas,
> Whose immense labor and
> exact measurement
> Have fixed the figure of the
> astonished earth.

After having sat for a while as the rival of Maupertuis at the king's table, Voltaire changed his mind and republished the quatrain with "hero" replaced by "courier" and with the couplet about immense work and exact measurement replaced by:

> *Ramenez des climats, soumis aux*
> *   trois couronnes*
> *Vos perches, vos secteurs, et*
> *   surtout deux Lapones!*

> You bring back from climes
>   subject to the three crowns
> Your poles, your sectors, and
>   above all two Lapp girls.

Indeed Maupertuis had a strange household, which his Lapp mistress had to share with tropical birds, exotic dogs, and a black man, but this was only the beginning. Just at that time Maupertuis published a medley called *Letter on the Progress of the Sciences*, in which he proposed numerous things worthy of the Academy of Lagado: investigations of the Patagonian giants, methods of prolonging life, a college composed of perfectly educated representatives of all nations, vivisection of criminals, a town where only Latin would be spoken, boring a study hole into the earth, use of drugs to allow experiments on the brain, and other metaphysical matters. Voltaire was thus well prepared to regard the treatment of König by Maupertuis as unjust, and Maupertuis' eccentricities and silly pretensions furnished an admirable subject for a satire: *Dr. Akakia, Physician of the Pope*. The doctor's mission was to cure Maupertuis of his dreadful case of insufferable arrogance.

The king, while presumably amused by the wit displayed, was insulted by the attack on his own President. It must be remembered that the king himself regularly participated in the doings of his Academy by composing essays on moral philosophy for its memoirs. He forbade Voltaire's satire to be printed. Voltaire printed it anyway, using a permit issued for another work. The king, doubly insulted, had the edition burnt by the hangman. The satire was reprinted in Holland, and Berlin was flooded with copies. Voltaire, in increasing disgrace, left town as quickly as he could gain permission to do so. On his slow progress to Switzerland he was in fact arrested and detained for a while by the king's officers. Maupertuis, already sick to death with tuberculosis, also left Berlin to take refuge in the home of one of the Bernoullis in Basel, where in a few years he died. Voltaire published a sequel, in which Akakia induced Maupertuis and König to sign a treaty of peace. Article 19 concerns Euler:

> ... our lieutenant general L. Euler hereby through us openly declares
> I. that he has never learnt philosophy and honestly repents that by us he has been misled into the opinion that one could understand it without learning it, and that in future he will rest content with the fame of being the mathematician who in a given time has filled more sheets of paper with calculations than any other...."

Unfortunately the further sections of this article of the treaty, while equally witty, repeat some of the specific objections of the Englishman Robins about mathematical points, objections which reflect only the inability of Robins to understand the advanced mathematics of his day. In a typical effusion of literary philosophy, Voltaire had done no more than blindly copy passages of bad science.

After Maupertuis' departure all the duties of the presidency fell on Euler, but the king would not have a German (for as such he regarded Euler) assume the title, be given the powers, or receive the pay of the office. The Academy had to finance itself from the sale of almanacs, and Euler had to direct their production and marketing. The depression caused by the Seven Years War was severe. Serious disputes with the king ensued. Meanwhile, the Academy grew smaller from attrition, until besides Euler there was only one other man of any capacity, namely, the lately arrived, self-taught Genevan genius Lambert, whom Frederick regarded as a bear and could only with great difficulty and after long delay be persuaded to accept.

While throughout his long life Frederick again and again expressed his contempt for the infinitesimal calculus, the elements of which, it seems, he had tried to learn several times but in vain, he insisted upon having a mathematician for President of his Academy. At the same time this mathematician had to be a man of the world, a lion of society. Few indeed in all history have been the mathematicians of this kind, but Frederick found one.

In 1759, when Maupertuis died, there were besides Euler and Lambert only two other major mathematicians in the whole world: Daniel Bernoulli and d'Alembert. The former did not fit any of Frederick's qualifications. The latter, a Frenchman ten years younger than Euler, was at the height of his fame; he was Frederick's ideal, being a man of wit, a *philosophe*, a major collaborator on Diderot's *Encyclopédie*, and a light of literature. Even seven years earlier the king had offered him a salary of 12,000 francs, which was seven times what he was receiving in Paris, and also free lodging in the royal château and meals at the royal table, but d'Alembert had preferred freedom in poverty to the dangerous vicinity of a king. Moreover, d'Alembert had quarreled with the Berlin Academy over one of its prizes, and for a time he seemed to be a rival of Euler in mechanics and in some parts of analysis. The major scientific dispute of the mid-century, that over the tones and motions of the monochord, was at its hottest; the disputants were d'Alembert, Euler, and Daniel Bernoulli, three powerful parties each consisting of just one man, since there was no one else who could understand the mathematics enough to form a founded opinion, let alone take part. In this dispute,[15] as in several others, the eighteenth century is unique: never before had mathematics been so highly regarded by the community of learning, but never before or after were there so few persons able to enter the arena of mathematical research.

D'Alembert came to visit Frederick at Potsdam in 1763. The Academicians, most of whom were Swiss, feared the worst. D'Alembert spoke graciously to them and recommended them to the king. In particular, he declined the presidency and recommended Euler for it; the king positively refused, and indeed all along he had spoken contemptuously of Euler, written to him with harsh disrespect, and declined to grant him the least of the requests he had submitted from time to time on behalf of his family and friends. After d'Alembert had returned to Paris, Frederick wrote for his advice on all matters concerning the Academy of Berlin, to the extent that when the Academicians wished to suggest something to the king, they found it best to convey the message first to d'Alembert in Paris, who thereupon, if he agreed, offered it to the king as his own idea.

Euler then found the position intolerable. For a long time he had been negotiating intermittently regarding a return to the Petersburg Academy. With the accession of a German princess as Catherine II of Russia in 1762, the auspices for the arts and sciences there improved greatly, and Euler succeeded in obtaining an excellent appointment. He tendered his resignation to King Frederick, who brusquely told him to stop petitioning. Euler desisted from taking part in any activity of the Academy. D'Alembert, meanwhile, had found a replacement for him, the young Lagrange, a Piedmontese who had begun in 1760, at the age of twenty-four, to pour forth brilliant research on analysis and mechanics at Euler's own level and speed. Euler had tried to induce him to come to Berlin, but Lagrange, seeing that he had to choose between Euler and d'Alembert, took d'Alembert as his foster father in the politics of science, though in research he always followed tacitly in Euler's footsteps. The choice reflected Lagrange's sagacity. D'Alembert, though not old, had ceased to produce anything worthwhile and had become merely a conniver; he had quarreled with all mathematicians of his own age or older, and he was detested by his fellow academicians in Paris; vain, he badly needed an admirer at the highest echelon of mathematics. Euler was at the summit and plateau of his creative powers, was on excellent terms with everyone except d'Alembert, König, and King Frederick, and needed nothing but money and rank. D'Alembert arranged that Lagrange go to Berlin as Euler's successor.[16] In order to do so, d'Alembert had to tell Frederick a white lie, namely, that Lagrange was a *philosophe* and man of the world. In fact he was neither; he had no interests outside mathematics and a narrow outlook within it, but in society he knew how to keep his mouth shut when not expressing deference to the views of his seniors. In addition, he could pass more or less for a Frenchman, and he later became one.[17]

In all of Euler's vast correspondence there is no mention of politics and little reference to social conditions. Evidently one country, government, or party was the same as another for him, provided it allowed free worship in the Protestant faith his father had taught him and the chance to do a mountain of mathematics for a good salary. Like many other men of the Enlightenment, Euler expressed a general interest in human wellbeing and in good works such as widows' pensions, charity for orphans and cripples, and common measures for prevention of disease and promotion of trades and manufactures, but his own contribution to these estimable objectives seems to have been confined, beyond a few special mathematical studies, to a morally exemplary personal life and a miraculously creative and ageless exercise in mathematical science. Again and again he stated that truth of all kinds, knowledge in general, and mathematics in particular led to the betterment of man's condition, and he never showed evidence of seeing any conflict between service to his prince and service to humanity. While obviously neither a Prussian nationalist nor a Russian one, Euler served both countries with the total loyalty which in those days was regarded as the ordinary moral duty of a servant to his master. The personal failings of Frederick II as a candidate for God's lieutenant on earth must have been more than obvious to Euler, but it was not these that drove him from Berlin. Rather, he sought a social and financial position worthy of himself and, above all, advancement for his children.

Finally Frederick granted Euler leave to depart with most of his family and some of his servants, eighteen persons all told. Euler, then in his sixtieth year, was entertained en route by the King of Poland and the eminent nobility, and upon arrival in Russia was received by the empress. In addition to his salary of 3000 rubles he was given 8800 rubles to buy a good house and 2000 rubles for furniture. He was not burdened with duties, but his counsels were requested regularly and generally followed. His greatest reward was that good places in the Academy or the imperial service were found for his sons, and marriages into the nobility were arranged for his daughters.

In his last years in Petersburg Euler had more free time for mathematics than ever before. He very soon lost the sight of his

Leonard Euler, Supreme Geometer

one remaining eye. Like Bach, he underwent the torment of an operation for cataract, which was unsuccessful and rendered him almost totally blind. If anything, this enforced end to most of the ordinary duties of life left him still freer to work. About half of his 800 publications were written in these, the last seventeen years of his life. In 1766, the year he moved, Euler composed the first general treatise on hydrodynamics; it was to be about one hundred years before anyone wrote another. The next year Euler wrote his famous *Complete Introduction to Algebra*. After Euclid's *Elements*, this is the most widely read of all books on mathematics, having been printed at least thirty times in three editions and in six languages; selections were being used as textbooks in the Boston schools seventy years afterward. The next year, 1768, Euler wrote his three-volume treatise on geometrical optics and his tract on the motion of the moon; both of these are filled with colossal calculations, and the latter contains a single table 144 pages long. In 1770 he wrote a monograph on the difficult orbit of a comet which had appeared the year before.

Euler's total blindness put an end to composition of such long treatises, and the great increase in the annual number of his publications reflects the change in his method of work. In the middle of his study he had a large table with a slate top. Being barely able to distinguish white from black, he could write a few large equations. Every morning a young Swiss assistant read him the post, the newspaper, and some mathematical literature. Euler then explained some problem he had been sleeping on and proposed a method of attacking it. The assistant was usually able to produce the outline for a draught of a short memoir, or part of one, by the next morning. In 1775, for example, Euler composed more than one complete paper per week; these run from ten to fifty pages in length and concern widely different special problems.

Euler's memory, always remarkable, had by now become phenomenal. He could still recite the *Aeneid* in Latin from beginning to end, remembering also which lines were first and last on each page of the edition from which he had learned it some sixty years earlier. Enormous equations and vast tables of numbers were ready on demand for the eye of his mind. He became one of the sights of the town for distinguished visitors, with whom he usually spoke on non-mathematical topics. Amazed by the breadth and immediacy of his knowledge concerning every subject of discourse, they spread unbelievable fairy tales about what he could do in his last years.

Only recently have we been able, by study of the manuscripts he left behind, to determine the course of Euler's thought. We now know, for example, that many of the manuscript memoirs published in the two volumes of posthumous works in 1862 he wrote while still a student in Basel and himself withheld from publication for a reason—which usually was some hidden error or an unacceptable or unconvincing result. The first page of one of these memoirs is reproduced here as a figure. The memoir it opens is the one that served to introduce Euler to Daniel Bernoulli and was important in securing him his first post in Petersburg. There can be only one reason Euler did not publish it: Daniel Bernoulli had obtained the same result at about the same time by somewhat different means, and Euler did not wish to detract from his friend's glory. The result itself, the solution of the problem of efflux of water from a vessel, became known through Daniel Bernoulli's book, published twelve years later.

The manuscript is a typical one. The spots are ink from the other side showing through. There are few corrections in the smooth, easy writing. The manuscripts of the books Euler wrote in later life are much the same, but in many cases there remains one or even two complete earlier manuscripts of the whole, showing many differences from the final one. When Euler wished to revise something, he wrote it all out afresh, neat and clean. Like Mozart, he revised in his head and did not begin to use paper until the revision was complete.

The most interesting of all Euler's remains is his first notebook, written when he was eighteen or nineteen and still a student of John Bernoulli. It could almost be described as being all his 800 books and papers in little. Much of what he did in his long life is an outgrowth of the projects he outlined in these years of adolescence. Later, he customarily worked in about four domains of mathematics and physics at once, but he kept changing these from year to year. Typically he would develop something as far

De Effluxu Aquæ ex Tubis Cylindricis utcunque inclinatis ex inflexis

§. I.

Quæ hucusq contemplati sumus vasa, e quibus aqua effluat, ejusmodi omnia fuere, ut circa axem verticalem quaquaversus æqualiter fuerit diffusa. Jam quâ lege aqua erumpat ex tubis vel inclinatis ad horizontem vel inflexis vel incurvatis. Quod quidem attinet ad inclinatos tubos, facile posse colligi videtur ex motu de descensu super plano inclinato principiis aquam inde effluxuram, eâ prorsus velocitate quâ ex tubo verticali ejusdem altitudinis, cujusque foramen ad basin eandem habet. Ne autem temere aliquid admittere videar, tubos inclinatos et inflexos Theoriæ subjiciam.

§. II.

Sit itaq tubus inclinatus cylindricus $ABCD$ sit ejus sectio recta AB. Sectio autem horizontalis fundum DC, quod similmente EF quoq ellipticô et perpertusam sit vena effluens esse, cujus sectio recta, eg. Sit verticalis BG, et horizontalis CG, ut habeatur angulus inclinationis BCG, et ratio sinus totius BCG sinum anguli inclinationis BCG, quam dic a ad b. Sit ratio sectionis cylindri rectæ AB ad sectionem venæ rectam eg seu quod eodem

First page of Euler's first paper on fluid mechanics.

as he could, write eight or ten memoirs on various aspects of it, publish most of them, and drop the subject. Coming back to it ten or fifteen years later, he would repeat the pattern but from a deeper point of view, incorporating everything he had done before but presenting it more simply and in a broader conceptual framework. Another ten or fifteen years would see the pattern repeated again. To learn the subject, we need consult only his last works upon it, but to learn his course of thought, we must study the earliest ones, especially those he did not himself publish.

In an age when genius, intellectual ambition, and drive were common, no man surpassed Euler in any one, and none came near him in combination of all three. Nevertheless, histories of the eighteenth century and social or intellectual histories in general rarely mention him. The explanation was written by Fontenelle, before Euler was born:

> On traite volontiers d'inutile ce qu'on ne sait point, c'est une espèce de vengeance; & comme les Mathématiques & la Physique sont assez généralement inconnues, elles passent assez généralement pour inutiles. La source de leur malheur est manifeste; elles sont épineuses, sauvages & d'un accès difficile....
>
> Telle est la destinée des Sciences maniées par un petit nombre de personnes; l'utilité de leur progrès est invisible à la plupart du monde, sur-tout si elles se renferment dans des professions peu éclatantes.

ANNOTATED BIBLIOGRAPHY

BIOGRAPHY:

Nicolaus Fuss, *Lobrede auf Herrn Leonhard Euler . . . 23 Octob. 1783 vorgelesen . . .* , Basel, 1786 = L. Euleri *Opera Omnia* (I)**I**, XLIII–XCV, Leipzig and Berlin, 1911.

M.-J.-A.-N. C de Condorcet, "Eloge de M. Euler," *Hist. Acad. Roy. Sci. Paris* 1783, 37–68 (1786) = L. *Euleri Opera Omnia* (III) **12**, 287–310, Zürich, 1960.

O. Spiess, *Leonhard Euler, Ein Beitrag zur Geistesgeschichte des XVIII. Jahrhunderts*, Frauenfeld/Leipzig, 1929.

Note: Fuss did not meet Euler until 1773, Euler's sixty-seventh year; Condorcet never met him at all. Neither was competent in more than a small part of the range of science enriched by Euler; both were younger than he by more than thirty years, and neither seems to have studied Euler's early work in detail. Their necrologies of Euler are heavily weighted by hearsay and treat his early years as already legendary. Nevertheless the accounts of Euler's life and work in the general histories of mathematics or collected biographies of mathematicians are mainly if not entirely their authors' personal embroideries upon odds and ends pecked out of the two necrologies. The biography by Spiess, on the other hand, is based upon extensive study of unpublished letters and documents as well as all published sources concerning Euler's life. However, it is a biography in the literary sense; while Spiess made some attempt to write what is now called intellectual history, his understanding of the contents of Euler's researches was limited not only to what in Spiess' day was called pure mathematics but even to elementary matters such as quadratures, properties of particular curves, explicit sums of series, etc. Thus, inevitably, Euler appears in Spiess' pages as the most dazzling of mathematical jugglers but not as the great creator of concepts and organizer of doctrines he really was. In general, the critical reader who would understand Euler's conceptual frame and intellectual achievement can find today no intermediary between himself and Euler's own writings.

LISTS OF PUBLICATIONS AND MANUSCRIPTS:

G. Eneström, "Verzeichnis der Schriften Leonhard Eulers," *Jahresbericht der Deutsch. Math.-Ver.* **4**. *Ergänzungsband* (2 Lieferungen), 388 pp. (1910) and **22**, 191–205 (1910).

Manuscripta Euleriana Archivi Academiae Scientarum URSS, Tom. 1, Moscow-Leningrad, 1962. (This volume describes the scientific manuscripts preserved in Russia. According to Eneström, the manuscripts left in the Archives of the Academy in Berlin were once described by Jacobi. I have not seen his

description and do not know if it was ever published or if the manuscripts still exist.)
Leonhard Eulers Briefwechsel (Beschreibung und Resümees), Leningrad, 1967.

WORKS:

Memoirs, books, and manuscripts published at least once before 1911:
L. *Euleri Opera Omnia,* Leipzig or Zurich, 1911–:
  Series I. *Opera Mathematica* (complete in 30 parts).
  Series II. *Opera Mechanica et Astronomica* (23 of 31 parts published by the end of 1972).
  Series III. *Opera Physica et Miscellanea* (10 of 12 parts published by the end of 1972).
  Note: Some of the volumes have prefaces containing analyses or at least summaries of the contents. At the present time these prefaces constitute the best approximation available to a scientific biography of Euler.

Manuscripts not published before 1911:
Manuscripta Euleriana Archivi Academiae Scientiarum URSS, Tom. 2, Moscow-Leningrad, 1965.

Letters:
  J. Stepling, *Litterarum commercium eruditi inprimum argumenti,* Breslau, 1782. (Letters from Euler to J. Stepling are printed on pp. 273–75 and 420–26.)
  P. Prevost, *Notice de la vie et des écrits de Georges Louis Le Sage de Genève,* Geneva, 1805. (Letters from Euler are printed on pp. 381–90.)
  P. H. [and N.] Fuss, *Correspondence Mathématique et Physique de Quelques Célèbres Géomètres du XVIIIème Siècle,* St. Petersburg, 2 vols., 1843, reprinted in N.Y. and London, 1968.
  Note: These volumes, which contain the correspondence of Euler with Goldbach and letters to Euler from John I Bernoulli, Daniel Bernoulli, and Nicholas II Bernoulli, have

been largely superseded by the better editions listed below.

R. Wolf, "Zwei Briefe aus Christoph Jezlers Correspondenz," *Mittheil. Naturf. Ges. Bern* **1851**, pp. 53–58.

Oeuvres de Frederick le Grand **20**, 1852. (Letters from Euler are printed on pp. 199–203.)

G. Karsten, "Briefe von Leonhard Euler und von Joh. Alb. Euler an Wenzeslaus Joh. Gust. Karsten," *Allg. Monatsh. f. Wissensch. u. Lit.* **1854**, 325–49. (This is one of the most interesting of Euler's correspondences. The publication gives only extracts from the letters of L. and J. A. Euler to Karsten. Karsten's half of the correspondence, unpublished, is in the Archives of the Academy of Sciences of the USSR.)

Briefe von Christian Wolff aus den Jahren 1719–1753, St. Petersburg, 1860. (See especially pp. 233–35.)

L. Euleri Opera Postuma . . . **1**, St. Petersburg, 1862. (Pp. 519–54 contain letters to Nicholas II Bernoulli and Frederick II of Prussia.)

Ch. Henry, "Lettres inédites d'Euler à d'Alembert," *Bull. Bibliogr. Storia Sci. Mat. Fis.* **19**, 136–48 (1886).

Oeuvres de Lagrange **14**, Paris, 1892. (The correspondence between Euler and Lagrange occupies pp. 135–245.)

A. Le Sueur, *Maupertuis et ses Correspondants*, Paris, 1897. (The correspondence between Euler and Maupertuis occupies pp. 144–79.)

G. Eneström, "Der Briefwechsel zwischen Leonhard Euler und Johann I. Bernoulli," *Bibliotheca Math.* (3)**4**, 344–88 (1903); **5**, 248–91 (1904); **6**, 16–87 (1905).

G. Eneström, "Der Briefwechsel zwischen Leonhard Euler und Daniel Bernoulli," *Bibliotheca Math.* (3)**7**, 126–56 (1906/7). (Most of Euler's letters in this correspondence are missing. Draughts of some of them, not included in this publication, are preserved in Leningrad.)

P. Stäckel, "Ein Brief Eulers an d'Alembert," *Bibliotheca Math.* (3)**11**, 223–26 (1910/11).

K. Bopp, "Eulers und Johann Heinrich Lamberts Briefwechsel," *Abh. Preuss. Akad. Wiss.* 1924.

M. G. Bigourdan, "Lettres inédites d'Euler à Clairaut," *Comptes Rendus Congrès Soc. Savantes Paris et Dép.*, Lille (1928), 26–40 (1930).

Ученая Корреспонденция Академии Наук XVIII Века, Акад. Наук СССР Труды Архива Выпуск 2, 1937.
> (This collection includes five letters from or to Euler and several from or to his son J. A. Euler.)

Die Berliner und die Petersburger Akademie der Wissenschaften im Briefwechsel Leonhard Eulers **1** (Correspondence of Euler with G. F. Müller), ed. Juškevič and Winter, Berlin, 1959.

Ibid., **2** (Correspondence of Euler with Nartov, Razumovski, Schumacher, Teplov, and the Petersburg Academy), ed. Juškevič and Winter, Berlin, 1961.

Леонард Эйлер, *Письма к Ученым*.
> (Correspondence of Euler with nineteen savants), Moscow and Leningrad, 1963.

Leonhard Euler and Christian Goldbach, Briefwechsel 1729–1764, ed. Juškevič and Winter, Berlin, 1965.

R. Lamontagne, "Lettres de Bouguer à Euler," *Rev. Hist. Sci.* **19**, 225–46 (1966).

Relations Scientifiques Russo-Françaises, ed. A. T. Grigorian & A. P. Youschkevitch, Leningrad, ed. Nauka, 1968. (Pp. 127–279 contain the correspondence of Euler with Delisle.)

Euler's Place in the History of Science:

Note: Although it would be hard to find any history of mathematics or physics that does not say something about one or more aspects of Euler's work, and although his name is used as a label for a dozen or more of the commonest and most useful theorems in the mathematical sciences, the bulk and level of his works seem to have discouraged critical study of them.

Even volumes of essays devoted to celebrations of Eulerian anniversaries often contain no more than musings by senior scientists who have merely glanced at a few pages before composing variants of the sweeping generalities imparted to them by their teachers in elementary courses half a century earlier. In regard to eighteenth-century mathematics and physics the general histories of science or mathematics or physics are grossly unreliable, since they are based largely on tale-bearing or caprice or both. Some of the prefaces to individual volumes of *L. Euleri Opera Omnia* explain some part of Euler's work in the broader setting of the time, especially those in Volumes (I)24 (by Carathéodory), (II)11_2 (by Truesdell), (II)12 (by Truesdell), (II)13 (by Truesdell), and (II)15 (by Ackeret). For mechanics one may consult also C. Truesdell's *Essays in the History of Mechanics*, New York, 1968, though this work treats Euler merely incidentally. Except for the paper by O. B. Sheynin, "On the mathematical treatment of observations by L. Euler," in *Archive for History of Exact Sciences*, Volume 8 (in press), only in the Russian language are there any further substantial and founded analyses of Euler's work.

However, a distinguished mathematician of our day, Georg Polya, has composed a treatise on methods of discovery in mathematics which refers to Euler so often, even including analyses and schemas of some of his papers, that Euler might be said to be the hero of the work. This treatise is *Mathematics and Plausible Reasoning*, 2 vols., (Princeton, 1954). Polya's estimate of Euler, on p. 90 of Volume 1, is as follows:

> Of all mathematicians with whose work I am somewhat acquainted, Euler seems to be by far the most important for our inquiry. A master of inductive research in mathematics, he made important discoveries (on infinite series, in the Theory of Numbers, and in other branches of mathematics) by induction, that is, by observation, daring guess, and shrewd verification. In this respect, however, Euler is not unique; other mathematicians, great and small, used induction extensively in their work.

Yet Euler seems to me almost unique in one respect: he takes pains to present the relevant inductive evidence carefully, in detail, in good order. He presents it convincingly but honestly, as a genuine scientist should do. His presentation is "the candid exposition of the ideas that led him to those discoveries" and has a distinctive charm. Naturally enough, as any other author, he tries to impress his readers, but, as a really good author, he tries to impress his readers only by such things as have genuinely impressed himself.

NOTES

1. This remark is enlightening. The book to which Turgot refers is Euler's famous *Mechanica*, published in 1738. One of the most abstract works of the century, it never comes near anything concerning a wheel, let alone a wagon. Respect unsupported by even vague familiarity with the contents of this book is not limited to statesmen but is shown even by modern general histories of science or mathematics, which regularly and in positive terms provide it with a purely imaginary description as being the "analytical translation" of Newton's *Principia*. In fact it is a treatise on the motion of a single point whose acceleration is induced by several kinds of rules. Were it not for the headings, only an initiate would be able to recognize the contents' relevance to mechanics.
2. There are also four classes of manuscripts of memoirs and books:
   1. Manuscripts from which, perhaps with some correction, the works were set in type in Euler's lifetime.
   2. Manuscripts intended for publication and published in the regular volumes of the Petersburg Academy after Euler's death.
   3. Manuscripts which Euler withheld from publication but which were published in the posthumous volumes entitled *Commentationes Arithmeticae Collectae* (St. Petersburg, 1849) and *Opera Postuma*, 2 vols. (St. Petersburg, 1862).
   4. Manuscripts of works not published until 1965 or still not published.
3. Namely, in any simple polyhedron the number of vertices plus the number of faces is greater by two than the number of edges. Euler could not have known that the same assertion lay in an unpublished manuscript of Descartes. Euler did publish a proof, but it is false.
4. Analytic geometry is ordinarily attributed to Descartes. Of course, like any other mathematical innovation, it was neither without antecedents nor incapable of improvement. The reader who doubts my statement should draw his own conclusion by comparing Descartes' *La Géométrie*, Volume 2 of Euler's *Introductio in Analysin Infinitorum*, and a textbook of the 1930s.
5. The "clear way" is commonly attributed to Dirichlet or other mathematicians of the nineteenth century.
6. That is, in the notation of Gauss, of the two congruences $x^2 \equiv q \pmod{p}$ and $x^2 \equiv p \pmod{q}$, p and q being prime numbers, either both or

neither are soluble, unless $p \equiv q \equiv 3 \pmod 4$, in which case one is soluble and the other is not.

7. That is, in the notation of Jacobi,
$$\mathrm{sn}(u+v) = \frac{(\mathrm{sn}\,u)(\mathrm{cn}\,v)(\mathrm{dn}\,v) + (\mathrm{cn}\,u)(\mathrm{sn}\,v)(\mathrm{dn}\,u)}{1 - k^2 (\mathrm{sn}^2 u)(\mathrm{sn}^2 v)}$$
and related formulae.

8. This difference in their predecessors is recognized by both mathematicians and physicists today, since the latter are wont to say that the greatest discoveries in mathematics were made by (theoretical) physicists, while the former often remark that most of the major discoveries in theoretical physics were made by mathematicians (until very recently). Usually they are speaking of the same persons, e.g., Huygens and Newton and Euler and Lagrange and Cauchy and Fourier.

9. The episode has come down to us only through Condorcet's *Eloge*; we do not know whether Euler had more than one farm.

10. Euler's correspondence with Karsten shows that the printing of his book on the motion of rigid bodies, an acknowledged masterpiece of mechanics, was delayed four years for lack of interest. The publisher demanded subscriptions for 100 copies, but after waiting eighteen months he had received only thirty. Euler finally waived royalties; instead, he requested twenty free copies but said he would be satisfied with twelve. It seems this latter number was what he did in the end receive. Twenty-five years later, and after Euler's death, the same publisher found it worthwhile to issue the work in a second edition, adding some of Euler's major papers on the subject as an appendix.

11. It is well known that the British school of the mid-nineteenth century, the greatest representatives of which were Green, Stokes, Kelvin, and Maxwell, learned mathematics and mathematical physics primarily from French books.

12. A colleague in literature has kindly brought to my attention the fascinating, learned article in which these sources are discovered and quoted: Marjorie Nicolson and Nora M. Mohler, "The scientific background of Swift's *Voyage to Laputa*," *Annals of Science* 2, 299–334 (1937). The reader of the article of Nicolson and Mohler cannot fail to notice also their opening comments on the third voyage: "There is general agreement that in interest and literary merit it falls short of the first two voyages. It is marked by multiplicity of themes; it is episodic in character. In its reflections upon life and humanity, it lacks . . . philosophic intuition. . . . Any reader sensitive to literary values must so far agree with the critics who disparage the tale." On the contrary, I think that such critics have approached it without first learning the language in which it is written. They have forgotten that in the eighteenth century the cultivators of literature, unlike most of their successors today, did not despise science and vaunt their ignorance of it, but rather did their best to understand it, or at least pretended they did, as may be noted for instance in Uncle Toby's reference to the *Acta Eruditorum* and in Samuel Johnson's disturbingly precise recol-

lection of the contents of volume upon volume of popularized science (cf. also R. B. Schwartz, *Samuel Johnson and the New Science* [Madison: Univ. Wisconsin, (1971)]. Even pragmatically, how can the literary critics have for a moment fancied that so accomplished, artful a writer as Swift would have published a "pointless" book, a satire of "slight importance," which would not strike home to the general reader of his own day?

The critics, few of whom have written great satires themselves, here remind me of the man born blind who engaged himself to mix colors for painters. For him who reads all four books, the satire bites deeper from each voyage to the next. The practitioners of music, mathematics, applied natural philosophy, and projective humanitarianism were the intellectual elite of the Enlightenment. To smite such men, who would have felt themselves little touched by the pettiness and brutality encountered in the first two voyages, Swift rose in the third. In the fourth the moral philosophers, superior both to the arrogant dessication of the Laputan judicial astrologers and to the sordid scheming of the Lagadian quacks, found themselves revealed as being no more than Yahoos.

To strike the mathematicians and projectors where they were weakest, Swift paraphrased their own writings. The truth was more bizarre than any imagination. Nevertheless, Swift's deadly penetration selected such representative examples to picture not only the Royal Society but also any other academy of the day and, with weird vision, even a great range of professional science, pseudoscience, and progressive learning 250 years later. When the third voyage is read out loud to an audience of scientists today, though their professionally glazed eyes have never seen nor ever will see a Lilliputian, Brobdingnagian, or Houyhnhm, they instantly recognize in it a harsh picture of their enemies, their friends, and themselves.

13. Euler did not anticipate these much later specific theories, but they are in no way contradictory or repugnant to the general conceptions of space and time he formulated.

14. In Euler's entire life this episode is the only one that has given rise to any *suspicion* of wrongdoing. With the gleeful desire now in fashion to show that *everyone* is as evil as everyone else—or conversely, that nobody is better than anybody—so that no moral or intellectual values can have any but transitory and subjective, and hence meaningless, meaning, every biographical notice on Euler, no matter how short, manages to mention his unfairness toward König.

15. While it had antecedents going back for over a century, the dispute began with a paper by d'Alembert published in 1749 and continued through d'Alembert's remaining life. According to T. L. Hankins, *Jean d'Alembert: Science and the Enlightenment* (1970) (see p. 48), in a final volume of his *Opuscules*, which exists in manuscript but was never published, d'Alembert conceded defeat. On the whole, the controversy was not resolved during the lifetimes of any of the main disputants but rather just died out. Euler solved all the relevant prob-

lems correctly and in generality. Daniel Bernoulli's point of view has been used more often subsequently and is susceptible of greater generalization, but he himself was unable to do much on the basis of it, since the mathematical theory essential for exploiting it was not developed until the middle of the next century. Lagrange also took part from 1760 onward, but his work is largely incomplete or incorrect. While it made a great stir in its day and drew high praise from both Euler and d'Alembert, it stands up but ill under critical scrutiny. For a review of the whole matter, see pp. 237–300 of my *Rational Mechanics of Flexible or Elastic Bodies, 1638–1788*, L. *Euleri Opera Omnia* (II)II_2 (1960).

16. The relations between Euler and d'Alembert in 1763–66 are too complicated to trace here. Like most other savants of the period, Euler despised d'Alembert's character, and he did not wish to remain in the Academy if d'Alembert were to become its president. By the time d'Alembert came to decline the presidency, Euler wished only to leave Berlin and feared that d'Alembert's recommendation of him might result in his being retained against his will; and by the time it came to persuading Frederick to accept Lagrange as Euler's successor, d'Alembert's actions were in Euler's best interest, since without a replacement Euler would not have succeeded in getting permission to go.

17. Lagrange's native language was Italian, and his first publication was in Latin. The errors of language in his earliest papers in French have been silently corrected in the reprints in his *Oeuvres Complètes*, the editors of which, unfortunately, have not taken similar pains with the numerous errors in mathematics.

French Opera and the Spirit of the Revolution

Paul Henry Lang

THIS PAPER, which is the scenario for a larger essay, owes its existence to certain unexplained discrepancies I became interested in while working on a book on operatic esthetics. As is well known, Meyerbeer and his French grand opera of the early nineteenth century changed operatic history not only in France but everywhere else. In France also, sixty-odd years earlier, Gluck's celebrated reform of the lyric stage, which is supposed to have determined the future course of opera all the way to Wagner, occurred. But in fact there is no connection between Gluck and Meyerbeer, as there is none between Gluck and Wagner, for the earnest reformer's ideas gained acceptance only in a small circle of disciples in Paris. Mozart, the principal master of opera in the latter part of the century, ignored Gluck and followed the Italians. That Wagner designated Gluck as his official forerunner proves nothing, because history does not ratify the appointment.

Now between these operatic strains there is, almost unnoticed, the French *opéra comique*, which somehow leads directly to romantic grand opera. But no one has yet told us how this lowly genre, made of innocent little songs called *vaudevilles* connected by spoken dialogues, developed into the pathetic and wildly romantic grand opera, completely devoid of comic scenes. Looking at the title page of the first printed edition of *Carmen* (1875), I was startled to see that this red-hot drama of sex and murder was still called "an opéra comique in three acts." This is assuredly curious, and so I began to investigate by proceeding backward until I reached the origin of the species. This transformation of down-to-earth merriment into bloody romantic tragedy is the subject of this paper, and since in France everything has literary origins, we must search for the point of departure in French literary and theatrical history.

Political, social, economic, and cultural life in France flowed uninterruptedly toward 1789, from the death of Louis XIV to the storming of the Bastille, from the improvised pieces of the *théâtre de la foire* to Méhul's operas, from the *Lettres persanes* to *Le Marriage de Figaro* and *Paul et Virginie*. The atmosphere of Mme. de Lambert's salon around 1720 did not differ materially from that of Mme. de Geoffrin's in 1770. Nevertheless, literary and artistic taste did change toward the middle of the century, and Voltaire on the one hand, and Rousseau and Diderot on the other, are on different sides of the watershed. Voltaire still upholds classical taste, attempting to breathe new life into the traditional genres, but with Rousseau and Diderot *sensibilité* gains the upper hand. The French comic theater, from which we must make our departure, has changed. Full-throated laughter is replaced by irony, biting satire, and sentimentality. The themes are predominantly social and the tone philosophical; the figures of the play are no longer ridiculous, only their altercations are so; and everything is illuminated by the brilliant artistry of the language. Side by side with this development in the comedy, there arose the utterly sentimental type of play, the *comédie larmoyante*. The situation was ripe for a superior intellect to reconcile the extremes in a compromise genre designed to elevate what was sanctioned by practice to esthetic doctrine. This superior intellect was Diderot, who in the *comédie sérieuse* elected to dwell on man's virtues and obligations. Diderot's theory of drama was based on the validity of natural feelings and on the humanity and dignity of these feelings. The difficulty he faced was that human virtue was often confused with sentimentality, and while the period was passionately interested in virtuous men, it watched them with moist eyes. What had been a frivolous, sophisticated, and malicious society became sentimental. In Louis XV's last years it tired of sparkling wit; the piquant was relieved by the moving; the beauty spots disappeared because only expressive faces were now admired; and we see at this period the first appearance of the frail romantic hero who carries on him the mark of death. In 1768 Baron Grimm introduces Grétry, the head of the new school of opera, with these words: "He is young, his face is pale, expressing suffering, behold the sign of genius."

There is, then, a definite turn toward bourgeois sentimentality just at the time when the famous "quarrel of the buffoons" started. Indeed, Diderot stated that the drama should be essentially a domestic bourgeois tragedy. He was convinced that a play is made cheerful, serious, or tragic, not so much by its subject as by its tone, its passions, its characters, and above all by the extent of audience involvement. Such a view presents the historian with an entirely new situation and with a new dramatic species in which passion is combined with social interest. This drama, the *comédie sérieuse*, presents middle-class occupations and family situations which are within the audience's own experiences and concern. Historians of music have attributed the emergence of the *opéra comique* solely to the impact of the Italian *opera buffa* and the quarrel it created. My contention is that the influence of the *opera buffa*, while considerable, was restricted to some of its musico-technical features, and that while it did emerge from the quarrel of the buffoons, this French *opéra comique* owes its existence to the *comédie sérieuse*, and is in fact a genre that has very little in common with Italian opera. Before I attempt to connect these literary developments with the lyric stage, we must take a look at French musical esthetics.

To the French of the seventeenth and eighteenth centuries the point of gravity in an opera rested on the declamation of the text; they considered music as accessory to the words. Let me quote a few typical opinions. Le Cerf de la Viéville, *Comparaison de la musique italienne et de la musique française*, 1704: "The aim of music is to color the poem." Yves-Marie André, *Traité sur le Beau*, 1741: "The principal aim of a good composer is always the delectation of the intellect." Abbé Pluche, *Spectacle de la nature*, 1746: "If it sounds only on an instrument, the most beautiful melody is only like a handsome garment which is not worn but is kept on a clothes rack." D'Alembert: "We must admit that music exerts its full ability to affect when it is tied to words or to the dance. Music is like a language without vowels; it is the task of the action to fill this void." And finally, Charles Batteux, the leading esthetician, in his *Les Beaux Arts réduits à un même principe*, 1746, flatly declares that "in a symphony, music is only half alive."

Obviously, there was much more behind the quarrel of the buffoons than the relative singability of French and Italian, or even the relative value of the music of the two nations. The statements I have just read would have been anathema to any Italian composer of the eighteenth century, while, in contrast, the essence of French musical esthetics was that music is a sort of sonorous rhetoric, distinctly inferior to literature. Even Diderot, when discoursing on music, always deals with vocal music, and he even saw the origins of music in the verbal inflections of language.

In the meantime one musician, Rameau, stood up against this universally held doctrine and challenged single-handed the entire body of *philosophes*. His art represents substantial gains for *sensibilité* at the expense of the prevailing esthetics, for the minute that part-writing, harmony, and orchestration adhere inseparably to the melody constructed on the words, the musical setting acquires values independent of the text. Rousseau, too, soon came to the conclusion that the composer must convey the feelings which the appearance of things elicits in him. The term he uses to designate this procedure is still "imitation," but what is really understood by it is "expression." Henceforth we are justified in considering *sensibilité* an early romantic phenomenon, even as manifested in Diderot's requirements concerning *mis en scène*, decor, and acting. The new theater demands a realistic milieu and the creation of what we call "atmosphere." Diderot goes into considerable detail, prescribing the costumes, the actors' attitudes, even single gestures. He expects maximal empathy from the actor, counting on his sighs and tears and bodily movements. He often sprinkles his discussion of the theory of drama with musical examples and similes which can be very unfortunate, but we must not be misled by them; Diderot's musical importance lies in his dramaturgy, not in his musical obiter dicta. Characteristically, it is precisely when he speaks of the renewal of the musical stage that he proves to be surprisingly conservative. After much speculation he advances a theory about the new opera: "We must introduce into the lyric stage realistic tragedy." But this view does not accord with the new compromise, or middle-ground, everyday bourgeois play he advocates for the spoken theater. "In a work intended for the lyric stage," he says, "there should be measured verse, but in my opinion bourgeois tragedy cannot be versified." In other words, in music Diderot still clings to the old *tragédie lyrique* of Quinault and Lully, which the *philosophes* tried to supersede. Yet we shall see that opera, contrary to Diderot's beliefs, will be renewed under the sign of the very *genre sérieux*, the sentimental bourgeois drama, which he championed for the theater but denied to opera.

As we watch the events in France, it seems that all this theorizing was in vain; the buffoon war threatened to extinguish French opera altogether. I shall not retell the story, it is well enough known, but certain of its aspects need to be examined. The most important single fact is that the cause of opera drew the elite of French intellectual life onto the firing line. Rousseau, the commander-in-chief of the Italian party, states in his *Confessions* that the quarrel was more intense than any political or religious controversy. The grand seigneurs, the rich, and the great ladies supported French music, and they were in the majority; the other party, more lively, more enthusiastic and proud, consisted, he says, of the real connoiseurs, the talented, and the geniuses. But what did the *philosophes* know about music? They knew a great deal about physical acoustics, knew the theoretical writings from the Greeks to Rameau, and of course they were thoroughly versed in the literature on musical esthetics. But they were not musicians, not even Rousseau, who actually composed music (with a little outside help). The embittered old Rameau just listened to what he called the *philosophes'* dilettante musical prattle, but when they started to teach him harmony and composition he bristled and threw himself into the war on the side of French opera. Rameau's judgment concerning the *philosophes'* lack of knowledge of music was justified, but their importance in the history of music does not rest on their silly musical opinions, even though these opinions were, and in some quarters still are, taken seriously. Since the *philosophes* wanted to establish an ideal French operatic dramaturgy and taste, and the Italian *buffa* seemed to exemplify many of their ideas, they chose to regard all other kinds of music invalid or at least of a lower order. The principal point in their doctrine was that the *buffa* incarnates the truth and simplicity of nature and avoids the artificial and the *recherché*. There was a good deal of merit in this "return to nature," and they fought for their ideal with passion. It was this aim, good theater with plausible plots and protagonists, that excuses the *philosophes*' many mistakes, sins, and distortions. The literary historians are not aware of these mistakes, many of them downright hilarious, while the music historians have not bothered to investigate the ideas that prompted them. I should like to quote some specimens of the *philosophes*' musical animadversions.

Grimm vaguely understood the primacy of melody in vocal music, but to underscore this he goes on record as saying that "the orchestral parts only hide the composer's lack of talent." Rousseau, who as a composer had much trouble with harmony, was angered by what he called Rameau's aristocratic thesis about the origin of melody from harmony, declaring that "music with elaborate harmony expresses neither feeling nor character." It would follow, then, that polyphony also must be condemned, and sure enough, Rousseau proclaims that "two independent parts sounded together cancel each other and thus the intended effect is destroyed." In *La Nouvelle Héloïse* he goes even further: "So far as I am concerned, I am convinced that no harmony can be as pleasant as singing in unison, and if we feel the necessity of harmony, it is because our taste has deteriorated." Then this sometime composer assures his readers that "it is a proven fact, rooted in nature, that every accompaniment in which all the chords are full, creates much noise and contains little expression, and it is precisely that which characterizes French music." And here is a choice paragraph from the *Lettre sur la musique française*:

> As to fugues, double fugues, mirror fugues, strettos, and all the other complicated idiocies which the ear cannot suffer and the mind cannot accept, these are obviously the remnants of barbarism and bad taste, which, like the portals of Gothic cathedrals, still exist solely to demonstrate the disgrace of their erstwhile creators.

French Opera and the Spirit of the Revolution

Now all this is pretty ridiculous, and musical historians love to quote such statements—of which there are many—to demonstrate the utter incompetence of their authors. The historian does not see that the dramaturgical theory hidden by the critical inanities is sound and that without it the reform of opera could not have been carried out. Incidentally, I must tell you how much I was surprised by the continued influence of Addison's much earlier writings. He almost seems like an English—a very English—edition of the French opera critic. He too could say appalling things about music, yet he too was on the right track. In French writings I have repeatedly come across camouflaged sentences, even whole paragraphs, taken from Addison; on the other hand, I have also seen unmistakable borrowings in Addison from St. Evremond. This intertwined Anglo-French musical criticism by laymen goes all the way to Leigh Hunt and Théophile Gautier.

As we turn to the musical stage to see the outcome of the war of the buffoons, we find a new conception of the theater in the fifties, that is, years before Gluck and his reform. That this reform, purely French and carried out by Frenchmen, has been neglected by historians creates a grievous hiatus in operatic history. It is once more the old no-man's-land lying between literary and musical scholarship which we must enter, for this new opera is the creation of literary minds, the musicians simply following suit. The first bona fide librettists appeared at this time. They respected Diderot's dramaturgical theories, and in little more than a decade this new comic opera prepared for, and in a large measure created, romantic opera. A contributing factor to this neglect on the part of historians has been the rather exclusive cult of Gluck and his reform. The nineteenth century made Gluck into the arch-classical founder of the true music drama; but his influence on operatic history was in fact strictly local and valid only for the *opera seria*; the real action was elsewhere. The Gluckian reform of opera is another area that badly needs restudy and reevaluation.

We shall have to start the story by recounting a pleasant fraud. Monnet, the director of the theater at Saint-Laurent, was a shrewd observer of French tastes and fashions, and decided to take advantage of both the slogans of the opera war and the lack of musical experience of public and critics alike. He commissioned a pair of Frenchmen to produce an opera. D'Auvergne, the composer, put it together using chansons and ariettes, virtually creating the first French comic opera in 1753. *Les Troqueurs* was highly successful, but the canny Monnet declared it to be the work of an Italian composer residing in Vienna. By the time the true state of affairs was disclosed, Monnet had won the battle; he had proved that the French language could be set to music and that French composers could compete with the Italians. At this point there enters the playwright Charles Simon Favart (1710–92), an old hand at devising vaudevilles and parodies for the Foire St. Germain, who now advanced to real comedies with *Bastien et Bastienne* (1753), *Ninette à la cour*, (1755), and other successful works. Everyone was eager to set Favart's librettos to music; even Gluck, then in Vienna, picked up his ears.

The next important librettist was Michel Jean Sédaine (1719–97), the literary ancestor of Scribe and Dumas, who established an organic connection between the drolleries of the *théâtre de la foire* and music. Librettos were now constructed with an eye to their suitability for musical treatment, and thus the true comic opera was born. There were ensembles, dance scenes, and all sorts of other opportunities for the composer to show his wares. At this point Sédaine caught up with Diderot's dramas. Favart was an amiable marketplace Molière, but Sédaine was intelligent and cultivated, and his handling of the musical numbers, especially the ensembles, shows talent bordering on virtuosity. Rather surprisingly, Sédaine took his subjects from Lafontaine; eight of his librettos were based on Lafontaine's fables, which he worked over into contemporary stories with considerable skill. It is well to remind you once again that all this took place around 1760, that is, well before Gluck's arrival in Paris.

Now there is a surprising turn, entirely due to the literary and social currents as guided by the *philosophes*. A new libretto was set to music by Philidor in 1765, and its very choice was to have lasting effects on the future of opera. The librettist, Poincinet, took Fielding's *Tom Jones* and reworked it into an opera libretto. To take as a subject a contemporary work—*Tom Jones* had been written only sixteen years before—was unheard of in the annals of opera. It was the first time that an opera libretto was based on a fresh, modern, literary work, but henceforth this sort of thing, novels, plays, short stories, even newspaper items, would be the source for *opéra comique* librettos. Poincinet and Philidor were acting wholly in Diderot's spirit when they took as their hero not Orpheus, or Nero, but a foundling. It is most interesting to observe how with this work the *opéra comique* begins to depart altogether from the Italian *opera buffa*, the cause of the whole musical war, and steadily develops toward romantic opera. Poincinet restricted the plot to Tom's and Sophie's relationship and, omitting all the novel's other concerns, gave a prominent place to the disclosure of Tom's origin. The social conflict was boldly exposed; the opera takes up arms against social prejudice, demanding sympathy for the rejected. With this libretto the path leads to a wide social highway, and for half a century librettists followed it faithfully. Presently, the *opéra comique* began to absorb elements coming from the serious opera. There is a duet in *Tom Jones* in C minor, marked *allegro avec colère*. We hear diminished seventh chords employed dramatically, deceptive cadences creating suspense, and Philidor ends the act with a septet, which, too, was a thing unheard of in those days.

This was in 1765. Four years later there appeared another opera, *Le Déserteur*, in which the new dramatic and social thought produced a pattern that was copied by composers for decades. A poor soldier is arrested and condemned to death; the prisoner is visited in jail, writes a farewell letter, and in the end is pardoned. Every one of these scenes represented a mood-type used by countless later composers. Just think of the letter aria in Tchaikovsky's *Eugene Onegin*, or the prison scene in Beethoven's *Fidelio*; as a matter of fact, there was scarcely an opera without a prison scene for some time to come. But there is more to this opera than what I have just related—it is also a harbinger of romantic opera of the nineteenth century. Could there be a more touching spectacle than little Louise, the soldier's sweetheart, standing in her bare feet before the king (the stage directions are quite explicit), her apron filled with gold pieces donated by the sympathetic officers? But she casts away this fortune in order to be able to run faster to her lover with the good tidings of the king's pardon. The contemporary newspapers tell us that the audience shed torrents of tears. Surely, this is a very curious "comic" opera. Though the reprieve comes from the king, who appears as the just and benevolent monarch of the fairy tale, this is a genuine "rescue opera." If so, what about the long-accepted theory that it was the Revolution that created this distinct type? The date, as I must again remind you, is 1769; we are still a long way from the Revolution, but the fact remains that the French lyric theater had already become the mouthpiece of bourgeois ideals and sentiments. Curiously enough, such plays in the form of spoken dramas could not reach their intended public in the 1760's. Diderot's plays remained somewhat didactic, and were received with cool intellectual detachment. But Sédaine's librettos, which followed Diderot's dramaturgical theories, when equipped with music evoked a tremendous response from the public. It was this role that Diderot intended for the drama, but until the appearance of Beaumarchais the role was played by the musical drama, still perversely called *opéra comique*. And it was this so-called comic opera, with its serious subjects, that actually prepared the climate for the Revolution decades before its advent. For the theater was immensely popular and reached a large public; and during the Revolution, as Mme. Cherubini put it, "in the morning the guillotine was kept busy, and in the evening one could not get a seat in the theater."

Let us jump a few years, into the nineties. The revolutionary leaders envisioned a model vaguely taken from classical antiquity: music should serve the common weal; it should solidify morals, fortify patriotism, impart courage and perseverance; it should extol the greatness of the nation and the majesty of the people's ideals. Of course this was anything but the old Platonic ideal; it was filled with the illusions of the Revolution that *liberté, égalité,* and *fraternité* represent not only a democracy of the whole people but the dawn of a new humanity. Perhaps I should quote a few excerpts from the Constitutional Assembly's minutes. December 21, 1793: ". . . every occasion should be celebrated with the singing of hymns praising the fatherland, liberty, equality, and fraternity, because hymns have the power to endow the citizens with all manner of virtues." Another excerpt, this one from the Education Bill: "The pupils should be particularly trained in song and dance so that they can participate in national festivals." In the curriculum of the elementary schools, decreed in 1794, it is recommended that there should be a collection of songs for the use of the pupils, praising heroic deeds.

Music became a public matter not only through legislation and curriculum, but also because of the increasingly frequent festive gatherings. Robespierre stated the purpose of these gatherings clearly: "There is an institution that must be regarded as a most important part of public education: the national festivals." Such festivals were celebrated, at least in theory, almost every week. Their list began with the first anniversary of the destruction of the Bastille; the others followed in an unending stream. The nature of these festivals determined not only the role but also the form of music: it had to be suitable for mass participation. As a rule these compositions—hymns, marches, and cantatas—were primitive; their titles show that their sole purpose was to contribute to revolutionary zeal. There were hymns to liberty, to humanity, to the majesty of the people, hymns to celebrate Robespierre's oath, and so forth. Then there were songs of the Republic, songs for every victory of the army, and one unique hymn that I find particularly attractive: it was entitled "Hymn of Jubilation for the Occasion of the Victorious Entry of the Art Treasures Brought from Italy." So the piratical enrichment of the Louvre by the young Napoleon was made the occasion of national pride and rejoicing. But texts aside, the music had plenty of martial and revolutionary momentum—the "Marseillaise" dates from 1792. The accompaniments to these compositions were of course furnished by instruments, but the orchestra of the Revolution had to share the spirit established by the songs. What was new was its tone and acoustics, those of the out-of-doors. The *Journal de Paris* expressed this preference for the outdoor performance quite succinctly in 1793:

> The national festivals cannot have any other boundary but the firmament, for the ruler, that is the people, can never be shut in,

and since on such occasions we demand the greatest pomp, we have no use for stringed instruments. The wind instruments are preferred because the open air does not influence their sound, which is eight times as strong as that of the strings.

Where they got the precise ratio of strength I cannot imagine, but it does not matter; the important fact is that this concentration on wind instruments had considerable bearing on the development of the orchestra. Following the Revolution an entirely new ideal of orchestral sound was cultivated because of the great ensembles that played on the open squares and in large halls. The character of the sound rests on the traditions of military music, the strings having a minor role, and everything being concentrated in the winds, especially the brasses. It seems that Apollo put down his lyre, donned a red cap, and picked up a trumpet. Here is the origin of Berlioz's monster orchestra, and it is here that music begins to adopt the tone used by the people's tribunes. This tone invaded every corner of music, not excluding church music, as an organic part of the change that was taking place between 1789 and 1800.

Now let us turn to the principal artistic arena of that time, the theater—for our purposes, the musical theater. Like the titles of the chansons, most of the operas reflected the calendar and were directly inspired by the recent momentous events. Beginning with 1790, there is an abundance of pieces with political tendencies, with immediate propagandistic aims, often written in haste, and of a poster-like design, ignoring all tradition. Let me quote the titles of a few of these propaganda operas, all of them still carrying the designation *opéra comique*. *Sacrifice on the Altar of Liberty*; *The Siege of Lille*; *Republican Discipline, a Historical Picture in One Act*; *The Real Sansculotte or the Boatman*; *The Crimes of the Ancien Régime*; *Hymn to the Supreme Being—with Ballets*; *The Republican Nurse*; and so forth. The anti-religious attitude becomes noticeable, and with typical French ruthlessness the mob invades the church itself. A musical play entitled *The Taking of the Bastille* was performed, with appropriate noise, in Notre Dame.

French Opera and the Spirit of the Revolution

These Republican operas, patriotic and historical tableaux, and dramatized hymns helped to increase the sensational quality of the *opéra comique* by increasing the demand for exciting plots that would reflect the tensions of the revolutionary times and would represent the principal experience of the period: rescue from tyranny, from servitude, from prison; that is, what we have come to call the rescue opera. The public was passionate and sentimental, but also rude. It was not interested in the beauty of music, but in savoring and controlling the ideas coming from the stage; it demanded instantaneous and active experience of certain aspects of a play or opera, and the pleasure of exercising radical judgment on the spot. This public had no feeling for the wholeness of life, it recognized only good or bad. The actor or singer whose lot was to represent a tyrant was lucky if the public's antipathy was not extended to him personally. In their naive enthusiasm people would vault the orchestra pit, clamber up on the stage, and beat up the unsympathetic characters and destroy the decor. The sympathetic heroes received ten or twenty curtain calls, and they usually rewarded the public by singing with them a Republican song. Performances were often interrupted by spontaneous singing, and in well-known operas the already popular tunes were always sung by the public along with the singers. The intensely patriotic and Republican citizens started the singing even before the beginning of the performance and continued between the acts, often teaming up with the equally patriotic orchestra in popular songs. At first only "La Marseillaise" was regarded as officially sanctioned, but soon the right of the public to choose the songs to be sung during the performances was acknowledged, as this sort of singing was considered a profession of faith in the political actualities of the day. After a while the situation worsened as ardent Republicans became more and more suspicious of laggards and saboteurs in their midst. On one occasion the public, finding that the orchestra of the Théâtre Feydeau did not play "Ça ira" with sufficient enthusiasm, stormed the pit and bloodied the musicians. It was in this climate that the rescue opera was fully developed, and it openly acknowledged its political aims in an opera of 1790 based on a recent newspaper account. Entitled *The Rigors of the*

Convent, the most interesting thing about this work is its political character and its frankness, but the theme itself and the locale are also significant and quite unusual. Otherwise, the musico-dramatic disposition of the opera is traditional in almost every respect and Berton's music poor and conventional. He starts in E-flat and never manages to get beyond B-flat, but the opera made a tremendous impression on his contemporaries.

In the first act, laid in the convent garden, Lucile, a nun, and the Count, disguised as a gardener, sing a duet from which we learn that the two are in love but that Lucile cannot violate her vows and so tells the Count to leave forever. There follows a big ensemble, an *ensemble de scandale*, as the nuns come from all corners of the convent to discuss the big news: the Mother Superior has discovered a love letter in Lucile's cell, and she makes the poor girl read it aloud in front of the assembled crowd. Lucile is so exhausted by the ordeal that she collapses. In the second act the scene represents a vaulted crypt lighted by a single lamp; from both sides dull sunlight filters in, on the right there are benches, further back there is a tomb with an urn on top of it, next to the tomb an iron grille covers a dungeon, and on the other side there is a large cross. (I am quoting this description from the score, the manuscript of which is in the Bibliothèque Nationale.) This theatrical picture and the mood that goes with it is characteristic of the heavy Romanticism that invaded the French operatic stage in the 1790's. This, as well as the political nature of the experience of the rescue, is what makes Berton's opera significant in musical history; its music can be safely forgotten.

Now the nuns, led by the Mother Superior, gather to pronounce sentence. Lucile is led to the grille, behind which, in the small dark cave, she is to pass the rest of her life. But noise is heard offstage; soldiers, led by the Count, break in and rescue Lucile from the dungeon. Though called a comic opera, this is plainly romantic horror opera, but with a political twist; the commanding officer of the National Guard makes sure of that by making a speech. Humanity, he says, no longer permits crimes to be committed under the pretext of religious sanction. The laws, he continues, addressing his words to the Mother Superior, "which we swore to uphold, and which no one is entitled to ignore, and which you, Madame, are also obliged to respect, have broken the barriers of your religious prison and will return to nature those unfortunates who were unjustly torn from society." Now all join in singing the final number, "O liberty, goddess of France, we would rather die than live without you."

After 1794 and Bonaparte's rise, the exaggerated revolutionary mood paled, and there ensued a period of hesitation as the French nation began to follow with interest the general's victories. The revolutionary pride was transferred to the French armies, which were seen as liberators of the oppressed countries, and France basked in this progressive, humanitarian role. Beginning with 1798 the rescue opera took notice of the change. Now its theme became the liberation of foreign peoples or individuals suffering under absolutism. The opera that inaugurated this trend with great success was *Léonore, ou l'amour conjugale* by Bouilly and Gaveaux. Bouilly was a prolific man of letters of the lachrymose kind, though in private life he was a police chief and prosecutor. I mention his official position not because the combination seems odd and a bit amusing, but because as police chief during the revolutionary years he acquired insight into human character and the ways of fate. Two of his librettos became world famous: *Léonore* of 1798 was translated into German and set by Beethoven as *Fidelio*, and the other, *Les deux journées*, of 1800, composed by Cherubini, was still a repertory piece (called *The Water Carrier*) in my youth. Cherubini's opera is now forgotten, very unjustly, because it is a masterpiece; but *Fidelio*, an exact copy of the original French opera, both textually and musically, is ever present, and I shall conclude by saying a few words about the model for this great work that crowns the history of the rescue opera.

The title is significant. Under *Leonora, or Wedded Love*, we read "A Spanish historical play in two acts," and we observe that this new rescue opera of the Bonapartean age omits the earlier wildly romantic elements and relies on history. The ideas apotheosized gain in clarity and nobility, and become ideals, in this case the courage and faithfulness of a loving wife and the triumph of liberalism over tyranny. *Léonore* has nothing in common with the crudely propagandistic operas of the immediate past; the motif of the rescue itself is elevated from romantic adventure to universal human significance. With this work the mystery is solved. The designation *opéra comique* has lost its erstwhile meaning and became a rather misleading technical term. Any French opera that contains spoken dialogue is called by that name, no matter how serious and elaborate. The nineteenth century, accustomed to the sonorous splendor of grand opera, would not admit to its sacred precincts the *opéra comique* unless the spoken dialogues were equipped with music; both *Carmen* and *Fidelio* were converted for the carriage trade, and we must endure the pitiful recitatives added to these masterpieces by nonentities, though of late, and thanks to Bruno Walter, the Metropolitan Opera has divested *Fidelio* of Arthur Bodanzky's feeble additions.

We have seen that under the pressure of social and political forces a new direction had opened for the opera composer, and its guiding theme was a new and concrete social view, expressed in the motif of rescue, of liberation. It is a long and tortuous way from the simple *opéra comique* of the 1760's to the tremendous dramatic power of Beethoven, but without traversing those animated, confused, passionate, ridiculous, and bloody years, we shall never understand the development of this particular corner of musical history.

La Philosophie dans le boudoir;
or, *A Young Lady's Entrance into the World**

R. F. Brissenden

For ANYONE concerned with sentimentalism, in all the senses of that complex term, the last ten years of the eighteenth century, the decade dominated by the French Revolution, are of particular interest. To talk of one revolution is misleading: there were many revolutions.[1] One of these, perhaps the most important, consisted of a conscious attempt to realize in political actuality an ideal theory of man, "[to put] into laws," as Robespierre said, "the moral truths culled from the works of the philosophers."[2] These moral truths can, in a strictly technical sense, be described as *sentimental*: that is, they were grounded in the belief that man's ability to act morally is related to the degree of psychological and physiological sensitivity with which he can spontaneously respond to the world about him, related, to use the language of the day, to his *sensibility*. With this belief went the hope that if people were allowed to exercise their sensibilities freely they would act in a "humane" way. As Henri Peyre succinctly puts it, "The eighteenth-century writers [who] prepared the way for the Revolution without wishing for it . . . taught a secular code of ethics . . . [in which] they gave first importance . . . to the love of humanity, altruism and service due society or our fellow man."[3] "Humanity" functioned as a concept at once empirical and idealistic; and it is significant that it was not until the eighteenth century that the English word "humane" as distinct from "human" (an

---

* I wish to thank the William Andrews Clark Memorial Library, University of California at Los Angeles, whose grant of a Senior Research Fellowship enabled me to complete this paper.

orthographic distinction which cannot be made in French) took on exclusively the meaning it has today. According to the *OED*, the word, which had long existed as a variant form of "human," only then "became restricted to a particular group of senses," viz., those "marked by sympathy with and consideration for the needs and distresses of others; feeling or showing compassion and tenderness . . . ; kind, benevolent." It was in a democratic mood of sympathy with and tenderness for the needs and distresses of others that the National Assembly, in 1790, accepted Dr. Guillotin's proposal that "in cases of capital punishment the privilege of execution by decapitation should no longer be confined to the nobles, and that it was desirable to render the process of execution as swift and painless as possible."[4] Three years later Robespierre, invoking another moral principle, the sanctity of the general will, was to condone and direct the employment of the guillotine for the purpose of creating forcibly the conditions under which people could be genuinely free. No doubt it is true, as Lester G. Crocker has observed, that "the cruelty and bloodthirstiness of the Terror were due to revolutionary dynamics, not to any ideas of the *philosophes*."[5] Nonetheless the uses to which Dr. Guillotin's mercifully efficient machine were put demonstrated convincingly that man, in his attempt to be humane, could be only too appallingly human.

I am, of course, stating the obvious. My excuse for doing so is that the irony of the situation presented itself in just such brutally obvious ways to the people at the time. One did not have to be on the scaffold oneself to appreciate the force of Madame Roland's remark: "O Liberty, what crimes are committed in thy name!" In England, in 1798, the same charge was laid at the door of Sensibility:

> Sweet child of sickly Fancy! — her of yore
> From her loved France Rousseau to exile bore . . .
> Taught her o'er each lone vale and Alpine steep
> To lisp the story of his wrongs and weep . . .
>
> Mark her fair votaries, prodigal of grief,
> With cureless pangs, and woes that mock relief,

> Droop in soft sorrow o'er a faded flower;
> O'er a dead jack-ass pour the pearly shower; —*
> But hear, unmoved, of *Loire's* ensanguined flood,
> Choked up with slain; — of *Lyons* drench'd in blood;
> Of crimes that blot the age, the world with shame,
> Foul crimes, but sicklied o'er with freedom's name . . .
> Parent from child, with ruthless fury torn, —
> Of talents, honour, virtue, wit forlorn,
> In friendless exile, — of the wise and good
> Staining the daily scaffold with their blood . . .
> Of hearts torn reeking from the human breast, —
> They hear — and hope, that ALL IS FOR THE BEST.[6]

These lines, written by a young politician and statesman, George Canning, occur in the long poem later called *The New Morality*, which took up most of the final issue of *The Anti-Jacobin*, a short-lived but brilliant Tory satirical review. The poem, to which the Prime Minister, Pitt, himself contributed a brief passage, was accompanied by a large Gillray cartoon in which a motley radical crowd are depicted worshipping the French idols, Justice, Philanthropy, and Sensibility. On the altar Sensibility occupies a dominant position and is shown "holding Rousseau's works in one hand, and weeping over a dead bird, while her foot rests on the decapitated head of the martyred Louis."[7]

From the role assigned here to Sensibility it is obvious that the ideas it represented were felt to be of special importance. "Sensibility," in both its French and its English form, is indeed an important and an unusually complex word, and I should like to say something very briefly about it—although to attempt to cover properly the variety of meanings with which it was invested during the eighteenth century would require a separate undertaking. It is, of course, like "sense" and "sentiment," a key term in the vocabulary of sentimentalism, a group of words which exhibit a remarkable range and complexity of meaning combined with great and often vague connotative power. In this period they operated across the broadest spectrum of thought and discourse. At the

---

* See Sterne's "Sentimental Journey."

highest level they played an essential part in the languages of physiology, psychology, and philosophy. If I may borrow a term from Thomas S. Kuhn's *Structure of Scientific Revolutions*,[8] a concept such as "sensibility" can be seen as functioning "paradigmatically" both for philosopher-psychologists like David Hume, Adam Smith, and Helvétius, and for physiologists like Albrecht von Haller—it provided them, that is, with hypotheses about the nature of man, which they could take both as established and as capable of future development. The philosophical or scientific meaning of the concept is probably extended to its limits by Diderot in *Le Rêve de d'Alembert*, where *sensibilité* comes finally to denote the basic primal force by which the material universe, both organic and inorganic, is animated or energized. At the lowest level, however, sentimental concepts formed part of what Steven Marcus, in his study of sexual literature in the Victorian age, has characterized as the "fantasies" of a period, that "mass of unargued, unexamined and largely unconscious assumptions"[9] which forms the basis of that view of the world which everybody at a particular time and in a particular society seems to share without perhaps being fully aware of the fact.

"Sensibility" at this level was intimately involved with one of the deepest fantasies of the age, the assumption that man is innately benevolent. But the way in which the term was used also often reflected the fear that man's capacity for benevolent action was very limited, and that to be endowed with a delicate sensibility was to be cast inevitably in the role of a victim. Sensibility in many contexts carried with it connotations of weakness, passivity, femininity, and of impotence, often of a specifically sexual kind. At the same time a heightened sensibility could be taken as an index of sexual responsiveness. Some of the most symbolically significant figures of the day combined these characteristics in a peculiarly fascinating manner: Parson Yorick, for instance, on his sentimental journey, continually shows us how his better feelings, his moral sensibilities, are aroused by his allowing himself to become involved in sexual liaisons, which he is either unable or unwilling to consummate. Jean-Jacques Rousseau, as he presents himself in his *Confessions*, glories in his possession of a feeling heart and at the same time complains that it is the source of all his troubles. His sexual idiosyncracies follow the same pattern: he tells us that he has an almost feverishly acute response to sexual stimulation, or to the prospect of it, but is almost incapable of fully enjoying a woman in any normal way. Born free, he finds complete sexual satisfaction only in his chains.

Rousseau's masochism is clearly a subject to tempt the wildest speculations. Without indulging in anything too extravagant, however, I feel that one is justified in pointing to the closeness with which Rousseau's autobiographical persona in the *Confessions* accords with some of the most pervasive fantasies of the age, in particular with the assumption that a delicate sensibility could be taken as a sign at once of moral superiority or excellence, of a high potentiality for erotic excitability and responsiveness, and of personal weakness and ineffectuality. When such notions are allied to the highest political, ethical, and social aspirations it is not surprising that the resulting concept should exercise a powerful fascination, or that, in the wake of the Terror, it should arouse the contempt and disgust which are expressed in the poem I have quoted.

Simple and sentimentally optimistic notions of human nature had of course been challenged during the eighteenth century long before the Revolution—*Gulliver's Travels*, *The Fable of the Bees*, *The Dunciad*, *Candide*, and *Rasselas*, to mention but a few of the more obvious examples, are sufficient testimony of that. Sentimentality, both literary and moral, had been laughed at on the stage; and within the novel, as the work of Sterne and Smollett in particular demonstrates, there had long existed a relationship, ambiguous but dynamic, between sentimentalism and satire.[10] The dangers both of over-indulging one's own feelings and of placing too great a trust in someone who appears, deceptively, to be endowed with a genuine sensibility became a favorite theme. A great many novelists would have been happy to claim, as Mrs. Jane West does in her dedication to *A Gossip's Story*, that their aims were "to illustrate the Advantages of CONSISTENCY, FORTITUDE, and the DOMESTICK VIRTUES; and to expose to ridicule CAPRICE [and] AFFECTED SENSIBILITY."[11]

Towards the end of the century—ironically enough during the period of warmest revolutionary enthusiasm—criticism of sentimentalism began to assume a more direct and specific form. The clichés of the novel of sensibility and its cousin-german the gothic novel were burlesqued, inverted, and parodied within "underground" variants of the novel form itself, in some cases by people who were themselves producing or who went on to produce the very material they were satirizing. Matthew Gregory Lewis, for instance, author of the most notorious of all gothic novels, *The Monk*, which appeared in 1796, wrote when he was sixteen a brief and unfinished skit called *The Effusions of Sensibility*. Courtney Melmoth, a most prolific sentimentalist, and William Beckford, author of *Vathek*, both wrote parodies of the genre. And Jane Austen began her career as a writer with a series of little burlesque novels which she produced in her early 'teens for the private amusement of her family. The most substantial of these, *Love and Friendship*, written when she was about fourteen, is a surprisingly accomplished work, and despite its brevity the best and most thoroughgoing of all the burlesques of sentimental fiction.

One of the most interesting things about these parodies is the spontaneity with which they appeared. Young "Monk" Lewis, and the younger and even more precocious Jane Austen, were not following any set satiric tradition when they produced their skits; they were merely amusing themselves by playing with the worn-out formulæ of popular fiction. Nor did they write for publication: Lewis' piece was not printed until 1839, some time after his death;[12] *Love and Friendship*, with the rest of Jane Austen's juvenilia, remained in manuscript until this century, and even *Northanger Abbey* which, although it contains elements of parody, is a novel in its own right, did not appear during the author's lifetime. The book, which had been written in 1797–98, was not published until 1817, the year in which Jane Austen died. It is, if nothing else, an interesting coincidence that, almost simultaneously and quite independently, these two young writers should have decided to send up the novel of sensibility. The coincidence becomes even more interesting if we take into account another, and in many

La Philosophie dans le boudoir

ways very different, work which was published at the same time: *Justine, ou les Malheurs de la Vertu*, the first edition of the Marquis de Sade's first novel. The manuscript of *Love and Friendship* is dated June 13, 1790; *The Effusions of Sensibility* was written in 1791; and it was in this latter year that *Justine* first appeared, although the first draft of the book had been completed in 1787. *Justine*, of course, is more than a mere skit; but like all of Sade's fiction it can be regarded as at once an extension and development of the novel of sensibility and of the gothic novel and a parody of these forms—a parody whose purpose is to invert and attack the values which they embody and express. The same can to some extent be said of Jane Austen's novels, especially the early ones, *Northanger Abbey* and *Sense and Sensibility*, which are most closely related to the parodies she wrote as a girl.

The ways in which Sade, both as a writer and as a human being, differs from Jane Austen are so glaringly obvious that it may seem rather embarrassingly pointless to look for any similarities at all. Nonetheless some points of resemblance do exist, and they are, I believe, of some interest and significance. To discover one of the simplest one needs look no further than the opening pages of *Justine*, Sade's first novel, and the corresponding section of *Sense and Sensibility*, which Jane Austen commenced in 1797, and which, when it appeared in 1811, became the first of her novels to be published.

Each novel has for its central characters two sisters (there is also a third in *Sense and Sensibility*, but she is not very important), and the situations in which they are revealed to us at the beginning of their stories are basically the same. Justine and her sister Juliette, at the tender ages of twelve and fifteen, are suddenly bereft of their parents and their fortune: their father dies a bankrupt, his wife soon follows him to the grave, and after "two distant and heartless relatives [have] deliberated what should be done with the young orphans"[13] they are given a small legacy and thrust out into the world to fend for themselves. Jane Austen's two sisters, Elinor and Marianne Dashwood, are not in such desperate straits as Juliette and Justine, but like them they have lost their father, have been deprived of the money they could reasonably have expected to inherit, and are treated with high-minded selfishness by their brother and his wife.

The parallels do not end here. Each author makes a point of contrasting the characters of his heroines in rather similar terms. Elinor Dashwood, Jane Austen tells us, "possessed... strength of understanding, and coolness of judgment... her disposition was affectionate, and her feelings were strong; but she knew how to govern them."[14] Her young sister, Marianne, however, was "sensible and clever; but eager in everything... she was generous, amiable, interesting: she was everything but prudent... Elinor saw, with concern, the excess of her sister's sensibility."[15]

No one could say that Juliette's "disposition was affectionate," but in her own utterly libertine way she certainly exhibits "strength of understanding and coolness of judgment"; she has, Sade tells us, "a philosophic acuity far beyond her years."[16] Justine's resemblance to Marianne is much more direct: "Full of tenderness, endowed with a surprising sensibility..., she was ruled by an ingenuousness, a candor, that were to cause her to tumble into not a few pitfalls."[17] Like Elinor, though for somewhat different reasons, Juliette also "saw with concern, the excess of her sister's sensibility," and

> she rebuked her for her sensitiveness [*elle lui reprocha sa sensibilité*]; she told her... that in this world one must not be afflicted save by what affects one personally; that... true wisdom consists infinitely more in doubling the sum of one's pleasures than in increasing the sum of one's pains; that, in a word, there was nothing one ought not do in order to deaden in oneself that perfidious sensibility from which none but others profit while to us it brings naught but troubles.[18]

Elinor's "sense," though very different from the amoral or antimoral "reason" represented by Juliette, is not altogether unrelated to it; and if we allow for the obvious dissimilarities there still remains a real parallelism between the situations in *Justine* and in *Sense and Sensibility*: both Sade and Jane Austen are concerned (though for somewhat different ends) with exposing the weakness of sensibility, and the folly and danger of trusting completely to it. There is nothing very original in their attempting to do this: in the novels written in the last thirty years of the century the heroine who has to learn how to keep her sensibility under prudent control and how to distinguish between true and false sensibility becomes something of a stock figure. It is during this period, some time in the 'eighties, that "*sensiblerie,*" the French word for affected, hypocritical sensibility—"*sensibilité feinte et stérile*" is a definition given in a work published in 1799[19]—appeared in the language. Even the device of two sisters with contrasting characters, one of whom is distinguished by her sensibility, appears to have been to some extent conventional. A novel called *The Twin Sister; or the Effects of Education* was published in 1788; *Melissa and Marcia, or the Sisters,* appeared in the same year; and Jane West's *A Gossip's Story,* which is also concerned with two sisters, and which has been called "an embryo *Sense and Sensibility,*"[20] was published in 1796. Even more profoundly conventional—so well-established indeed as to warrant our calling it (in Marcus' sense) a fantasy—is the dichotomy reflected in Jane Austen's title: the conflict between sensibility and sense, heart and head, the passions and reason, men of feeling and men of the world, innocence and experience, nature and art, is one of the most pervasive and persistent of all themes in the literature and thought of the eighteenth century.[21]

The situation in which Sade and Jane Austen initially involve their heroines is also conventional: the situation in which a young and innocent heroine is suddenly thrown on her own resources, "at this period crucial to [her] virtue," as Sade puts it.[22] It is a situation, of course, which has fascinated man's imagination ever since he has had the leisure and opportunity to think about young and innocent heroines. But in the eighteenth century it assumed a special significance; and it did so partly because the status of women was undergoing a revolutionary change—it is in the eighteenth century, significantly, that women's liberation as well as the liberation of slaves may be said to have begun—and partly because of the particular complex of values which were attached, as I have suggested, to the concept of sensibility. There were no doubt other reasons as well, among them the special relation, both as writers and readers, in which women stood to the novel, but those I have mentioned are the most obviously important. But for whatever reason, the entrance of a young lady into the world—which is the sub-title to Fanny Burney's *Evelina* as well as to this paper—became an established and enduring theme in eighteenth-century fiction, and one which was to exercise the imagination of the novelist until at least the beginning of this century. We see the final and fullest development and exploration of the theme probably in some of the novels of Henry James, *Portrait of a Lady* and *The Wings of the Dove* particularly.

It was, of course, a social ritual of considerable importance. When a young lady made her debut, either through presentation at court or through her first formal appearance at a country ball or a ladies' tea-party, it indicated that she was on the marriage market. It also indicated that she was fair game for every scoundrel who might wish to seduce her before she was safely wedded. It is an old story, but in the eighteenth century this familiar *rite du passage* assumed an unusally wide significance. A stock description of a stock situation may suggest just how great this significance was. It comes from the first chapter of *The Monk*. When *The Monk* appeared in 1796 it seemed remarkably novel and daring, but what is really striking about the book is the way in which it brings together into one work so many long-established fictive patterns and devices. Nothing could be more conventional than the warning Lorenzo, a young gallant, issues to one of the heroines, Antonia, who has just felt an equally conventional and sentimental thrill of sympathy for Ambrosio, the Monk. "Surely," she cries, "the warmth of sympathy cannot have deceived me?" Indeed it has, for Ambrosio eventually rapes and murders her. She would have done well to heed Lorenzo's warning:

> You are young, and just entering into life. . . . your heart, new to the world, and full of warmth and sensibility, receives its first impressions with eagerness. Artless yourself, you suspect not others of deceit; and viewing the world through the medium of your own truth and innocence, you fancy all who surround you deserve your confidence and esteem. What pity, that these

La Philosophie dans le boudoir

gay visions must soon be dissipated! What pity, that you must soon discover the baseness of mankind....[23]

The universal significance with which the situation is invested is perhaps the most notable feature of this statement. Lorenzo is not merely warning her, as so many girls in so many songs and stories have been and still are warned, that in affairs of the heart men are deceivers ever. What he is saying is that once Antonia enters the world or life—the terminology could not be more sweeping—she will not only lose her innocence but also because she is innocent, she "*must* soon discover the baseness of *mankind*"—the baseness, that is, of humanity as a whole. In making her entrance into the world this young lady, like a great many of the young ladies in eighteenth-century fiction, symbolically represents not merely sexual innocence or the supposedly mystical power of virginity but something more. Pamela and Clarissa, the archetypal heroines from whom Antonia is descended, are not just young women attempting to defend their honor in difficult situations; they are representatives of a whole constellation of social and moral values which include but transcend the merely sexual. The debates between Clarissa and Lovelace, like the debates and lectures which precede and follow practically every rape and orgy in Sade's fiction, are debates about fundamental moral and metaphysical issues. The status of individual human beings—are they free, are they fallen, are they innately good or innately evil, have they inalienable rights?—and the question of whether there is or is not a God are discussed at the theoretical level by lovers, or by rapist and victim, and the conclusions they reach are often given a practical demonstration through the way in which the sexual relations between these people are brought to a conclusion. Ambrosio, the Monk of Lewis's novel, is deliberately presented as a Faust figure. But he is not tempted by the chance of exercising absolute power, as Faustus is; he is tempted by love and by the desire to lead a life of sexual freedom and fulfillment. Since this too is what most of the other characters in the novel want, Ambrosio is also something of a revolutionary and Promethean hero: his destruction placates the terrible authoritarianism of the Church, which has been presented as the most repressive instrument of organized society. And his temptations, and the theological and philosophical analyses to which he subjects them, take place, not surprisingly, for the most part in the bed-chamber, although for Ambrosio and his unfortunate mistresses the bed-chamber tends more often than not to be cold, damp, stony, and occupied by corpses and the things that feed upon them.

One could say that the association of philosophical speculation and debate with sexual activity goes back to the Garden of Eden; or, if one wishes to be classical rather than Christian, to Plato's Symposium. But *La Philosophie dans le boudoir*, the title chosen by Sade for one of his briefer and perhaps for this reason more effective pieces, assumes a special significance in the seventeenth and eighteenth centuries. To be a libertine meant practically from the beginning to be both a free-liver sexually and a free-thinker philosophically,[24] and the salon was both symbolically and often actually the ante-chamber to the boudoir. It is no accident that Diderot should have located his thoroughly philosophical exploration of the concept of *sensibilité* in d'Alembert's bed-chamber, even though, ironically enough, it was probably no boudoir in the erotic sense. Practically all Sade's philosophizing takes place in the boudoir, or at least amid scenes of sexual intercourse, and while this association of activities reflects Sade's own obsessive preoccupation with sex, like so many other things in Sade's work it also represents the logical culmination of much that is implicit in the philosophy and the fiction of the preceding century. "Il y a un peu de testicule au fond de nos sentiments les plus sublimes et de notre tendresse la plus epurée,"[25] Diderot once remarked. It was Sade's purpose, pursued with manic energy, to demonstrate that this, though true, was only half the truth. In Sade's view, the sentimental image of man denied not only the sexual elements in his nature, but also his inherent violence, aggressiveness, selfishness, and cruelty. Long before the Terror Sade was suggesting that the sentimental ideals by which the Revolution was inspired were based on a grossly inadequate account of human nature; and the force of his criticism was not lessened by the deficiencies and distortions in his own view of man.

La Philosophie dans le boudoir

The point of the satire in Jane Austen's *Love and Friendship* can be seen, in this context, to be remarkably sadistic; and the work even has a connection, unhappy and fortuitous, with the Revolution. Jane Austen dedicated the little novel to "Madame la Comtesse De Feuillide." The countess was her cousin Eliza, and Eliza's husband, Jean Capotte, Comte de Feuillide, was to be guillotined four years later during the Terror. This unfortunate occurrence is not out of keeping with the argument of *Love and Friendship*, which is basically that sensibility as such has nothing necessarily to do with moral worth, and that human beings are fundamentally selfish—or, rather, that to believe that men in general are basically *un*-selfish is to be dangerously deluded. The heroes and heroines in *Love and Friendship* are all creatures of the most exquisite sensibility and the most ruthless and unscrupulous selfishness. "A sensibility too tremblingly alive to every affliction of my Freinds [sic], my Acquaintance and particularly to every affliction of my own," confesses Laura, the main character, "was my only fault."[26] Her husband Edward and her friends Augustus and Sophia are "Exalted Creatures [who] scorned to reflect a moment on their pecuniary Distresses & would have blushed at the idea of paying their Debts."[27] They do not blush to rob their parents and relatives, however, and purely out of principle they marry in defiance of their parents' wishes. Having "constantly refused to submit themselves to such despotic Power," they disentangle themselves "from the Shackles of Parental Authority" and then contrive to live with the help of "a considerable sum of Money which Augustus had gracefully purloined from his Unworthy father's Escritoire."[28] Sophia, of course, like Laura, is "all Sensibility and Feeling,"[29] so much so that when Augustus is finally removed to Newgate she cannot bear to visit him: "my feelings are sufficiently shocked by the *recital* of his Distress, but to behold it will overpower my Sensibility."[30] Deserting their husbands, Laura and Sophia flee to Scotland where they are given shelter by Sophia's "relation" MacDonald. In return for his hospitality they rob him and corrupt his daughter. She had been happily going to marry a young man of whom he approved, but, says Laura, "[Janetta's] errors in the Affair had only arisen . . . from a want of proper confidence in her own opinion, & a suitable contempt of her father's. We . . . had no difficulty to convince her that it was impossible she could love Graham, or that it was her duty to disobey her Father. . . ."[31] They soon pack her off to Gretna Green with a lover who is suitably sentimental—that is, a man who is in her father's opinion, which is doubtless justified, "an unprincipled Fortune-hunter."

The four main characters in this story all marry in defiance of the wishes of at least some of their parents; they behave in thoroughly anarchic and self-centered ways; and, with one exception, they come to a variety of sticky ends (Laura survives with a reasonably handsome annuity). They do enjoy a period of complete happiness, however, and this is when they are able to live together as a group quite cut off from the world of normal social responsibilities. "In the Society of my Edward & this Amiable Pair," writes Laura, "I passed the happiest moments of my Life: Our time was most delightfully spent, in mutual Protestations of Freindship, and in vows of unalterable Love, in which we were secure from being interrupted, by intruding & disagreeable Visitors. . . ."[32] It would be too much to describe this as a commune of sexually liberated swingers, but it does bear some interesting resemblances to the isolated groups of criminals and libertines which are a dominant feature of Sade's fantasies.

The same pattern appears in the reunion of Laura with her cousins Philander and Augustus towards the end of the story. Although they have robbed and deserted her, she finds her unscrupulous cousins much more congenial than her other companions: "whilst the rest of the party were devouring Green tea & buttered toast, we feasted ourselves in a more refined & Sentimental Manner by a confidential Conversation."[33] In the course of the conversation she learns that this small *Societé des Amis du Crime* has had a typically Sadean inception: the commission of a criminal act which leads to the death of parents. Their mothers, they tell Laura, were sisters and always lived together.

> They were neither of them very rich; their united fortunes had originally amounted to nine thousand Pounds, but as they

had always lived upon the principal of it, when we were fifteen it was diminished to nine Hundred. This nine Hundred, they always kept in a Drawer ... for the Convenience of having it always at Hand. Whether it was from this circumstance, of its being easily taken, or from a wish of being independant [sic], or from an excess of Sensibility (for which we were always remarkable) I cannot now determine, but certain it is that when we had reached our 15th year, we took the Nine Hundred Pounds & ran away ... to London & had the good luck to spend it in 7 weeks & a Day ... [We then] began to think of returning to our Mothers, but accidentally hearing that they were both starved to death, we gave over the design & determined to engage ourselves to some strolling company of Players, as we had always a turn for the Stage.[34]

The most obviously sadistic passage in Jane Austen's work does not, however, occur in *Love and Friendship*, although it is included in the collection of juvenilia, *Volume the Second*, in which *Love and Friendship* appears. It is a short piece which bears the title, "A Letter from a Young Lady, whose feelings being too strong for her Judgement led her into the commission of Errors which her Heart disapproved." It begins as follows:

Many have been the cares & vicissitudes of my past life, my beloved Ellinor, & the only consolation I feel for their bitterness is that on a close examination of my conduct, I am convinced that I have strictly deserved them. I murdered my father at a very early period of my Life, I have since murdered my Mother, and I am now going to murder my Sister. I have changed my religion so often that at present I have not an idea of any left. I have been a perjured witness in every public tryal for these past twelve Years; and I have forged my own will. In short there is scarcely a crime that I have not committed. — But I am now going to reform.

She is going to reform because she has just helped Colonel Martin of the Horse Guards defraud his brother of eight million pounds. "The Colonel in gratitude waited on me the next day with an offer of his hand—. I am now going to murder my Sister. / Yours Ever. / Anna Parker."[35] With its family murders, irreligion, and a crime involving an enormous sum of money this reads like a synopsis of one of the episodes in *La Nouvelle Justine*.

From the novels Jane Austen went on to write it is abundantly clear that she did not believe that everyone was like Anna Parker, or even that everyone was so thoroughly selfish as the characters are in *Love and Friendship*. But she knew that all of us, even the most amiable, have a streak of Miss Parker in our make-up and that to pretend otherwise is a sentimental delusion. One of the few really chilling moments in her fiction comes in *Northanger Abbey* when we are made simultaneously to realize both that General Tilney is not a murderer out of a gothic novel and that he is a ruthless, self-centered man who, given the right provocation and the right circumstances, could possibly be tempted to kill someone. It is her ability to include the potential cruelty and nastiness of ordinary people together with their more admirable and pleasant qualities in one balanced image of humanity that in part makes Jane Austen a great novelist.

The Marquis de Sade, although he is a literary figure of major importance, is not a great novelist, and the image of humanity presented in his writings can hardly be called balanced. As a philosopher he is both highly intelligent and, I think, fundamentally confused, although the confusion is a fruitful one so far as his imaginative work is concerned. His novels, which are all in a sense one novel, are the result of a continuous and unrelenting attempt to resolve the radical inconsistencies in his position, inconsistencies which stem directly from his sexual peculiarities. Simone de Beauvoir has observed very perceptively that "it is neither as author nor as sexual pervert that Sade compels our attention; it is by virtue of the relationship which he created between these two aspects of himself. Sade's aberrations begin to acquire value when, instead of enduring them as his fixed nature, he elaborates an immense system in order to justify them."[36] And because of the particular character of his aberrations, Sade's attempt to justify them led him into direct conflict with that complex of ideals, fantasies, and theories about the nature of man and society which can be called sentimental. Against the image of man as a social, sympathetic, generous, benevolent, and good-natured being Sade sets his diametrically opposed image of man as an isolated, anarchic, selfish, cruel, violent, and aggressive being. Yet he shared with

La Philosophie dans le boudoir

sentimentalism the belief that all knowledge and all systems of value stem basically from the individual experience; and that the ideal society is one in which individual men and women can determine as freely as possible their own destinies.

It is not surprising then that Sade should have been pre-occupied with the theme of a young lady's entrance into the world, just as so many "sentimental" novelists were—particularly Richardson, for whom, like Jane Austen, Sade had an unqualified admiration. The entrance of a young lady into the world is an occasion in which the individual comes directly into conflict with society, and on the outcome of this conflict depends the degree of independence and freedom with which the mature individual, the adult woman with the values she represents, can lead her life. In its basic form it is an act of sexual initiation; and when the conflict between the desire for freedom and the pressure to conform is violent, as it is in *Clarissa*, the act of initiation can itself be violent and painful. The rape of Clarissa by Lovelace is one of the most significant actions in the whole of eighteenth-century fiction. The threat and possibility of rape lurk in the background of most sentimental novels; and Sade, of course, was obsessed with the subject. Justine, the heroine of his first novel, is raped continuously. Every sexual act to which she submits is a violation; she remains, metaphorically at least, a perpetual virgin who is forced again and again to enter the world—a symbol, like Clarissa, of the impossibility of ever completely reconciling the values of the world with the sentimental and Christian ideal of virtue. For Juliette, her sister, however, the act of sexual initiation is liberating: she becomes free, powerful, and criminal; instead of being crushed by the world she dominates it.

The most successful of Sade's works of fiction is *La Philosophie dans le boudoir*, and since its subject is the sexual initiation of a young woman this is understandable. Also it is relatively short; it has a single coherent dramatic action—it is presented as a dramatic scenario rather than a novel—and it is much more tightly controlled than any of Sade's other explicitly sexual pieces. The philosophical debates are brief, lucid, and pointed; no one is actually killed; and that feature of his perversity which, as Gilbert Lely observes, "belongs . . . to the sphere of real lunacy,"[37] his coprolagnia, is for the most part kept out of sight. It is even at times, in Sade's own black way, grotesquely funny; and one has the reassuring feeling that Sade on this occasion was sufficiently distanced from his subject to be aware of the fact. At the height of one of his incredibly complicated group acts of coition, when everyone is uttering the usual Sadean screams of joy, pain, ecstasy, and execration, he remarks with unusual tact that "the fear of appearing monotonous prevents us from recording expressions which, upon such occasions, are all very apt to resemble one another."[38]

La Philosphie dans le boudoir is powerful and disturbing, and despite the simplicity of its structure, unusually complex. It is also in some ways, like *The Monk*, remarkably conventional; and it is to these conventional aspects of the work that I should like briefly to draw attention. The central character is a young girl, fifteen years old, of great sensibility, Eugénie de Mistival, and in the course of the action she is introduced by a group of libertines to practically every form of sexual activity. She is an apt and eager pupil, and her sexual education is accompanied by a series of philosophical discussions in which the generally accepted notions of religion and morality are systematically destroyed. The situation in which, as Barry Ivker observes, "the heroine's philosophic inquiries . . . parallel her discoveries in the sexual sphere,"[39] had already become well established as a convention in libertine fiction; and Sade himself, in a footnote to the third version of *Justine*, draws attention to some earlier examples of the genre: Argens's *Thérèse philosophe*, Chorier's *L'Académie des dames*, Latouche's *Le Portier de Chartreux* and Mirabeau's *L'Education de Laure*. But Sade goes much further than his predecessors in his emphasis on the natural savagery, selfishness, and cruelty of human beings. And in *La Philosophie dans le boudoir* he takes particular pains to demolish the notion that sensibility, especially sensibility in women, can be taken as evidence of a generous, benevolent, kind, humane disposition. On the contrary argues Dolmancé, one of the most eloquent of Sade's libertine philosophers, it is a sign of a capacity for exercising the most exquisite cruelty.

La Philosophie dans le boudoir

> [This] species of cruelty, fruit of extreme organic sensibility, is known only to them who are extremely delicate in their person, and the extremes to which it drives them are those determined by intelligence and niceness of feelings; this delicacy, so finely wrought, so sensitive to impressions, responds above all, best, and immediately to cruelty; it awakens in cruelty; cruelty liberates it.[40]

This is too much for Eugénie, who is driven into a frenzy of sexual excitement by Dolmancé's remarks. Taking her in her arms, Madame de Saint-Ange, her female instructress, cries out: "Adorable creature, never have I beheld a sensibility like yours, never so delightful a mind!"[41] And indeed it is in the mind, in her imagination, that Eugénie experiences her greatest ecstasy. Inflamed once more by Dolmancé's calm dismissal of "the useless virtues of generosity, humanity, charity, all those enumerated in the absurd codes of a few idiotic religious doctrines" and his argument that the individual has the right to assert himself against society by criminal acts, Eugénie exclaims, "wild-eyed," "I want a victim."[42] The victim she wants is her mother, and the mere thought of what she may now be at liberty to do to her is enough to bring this delicate creature with her exquisite sensibility to a sexual climax. Later the mother appears, and in the concluding scene she is raped, beaten, infected with venereal disease, and kicked out the door.

Remarkably unpleasant and grotesquely fantastic as all this may be, it has an inner psychological and dramatic coherence, and an intellectually ordered development which make it in its own terms convincing, and for that reason rather more disturbing than the gory extravaganzas which crowd the interminable pages of Sade's longer works. It is, of course, quite patently Oedipal or Electral in its structure; and it is in this pattern (of which the education of the heroine in philosophical libertinism may be seen as a variant) that what I have called its conventionality may be seen basically to lie. But what is involved is more than the simple destruction of a parent; it is the implications with which this act is charged that are really troubling. The point is that Eugénie is already free when she tortures and humiliates her mother; but in order to validate and authenticate her liberty she needs this ritual confirmation of the fact, just as Dolmancé, like Sade's other atheist libertines, feels the need to blaspheme at the moment of sexual triumph, even though he is convinced that God is a "disgusting fiction."[43]

Precisely the same pattern may be seen to operate throughout *Love and Friendship*. Jane Austen's loving couples are absurd because they defy and disobey their parents *when there is no need to*. "My Father . . . insisted on my giving my hand to Lady Dorothea," says Edward. "No never exclaimed I. Lady Dorothea is lovely and Engaging; I prefer no woman to her; but know Sir, that I scorn to marry her in compliance with your wishes. No! Never shall it be said that I obliged my Father."[44] The deaths of the mothers of Philander and Augustus and the way in which their unscrupulous sons accidentally learn of the fact and light-heartedly dismiss it has a similar tone. "The DISTRESSES that may attend the Misconduct Both of PARENTS and CHILDREN, In Relation to MARRIAGE," as Richardson describes it on the title page of *Clarissa*, was of course a theme of enduring interest to novelists and their readers in the eighteenth century. There are some fairly obvious reasons why this should have been so, especially in view of the fact that the majority of novel-readers were women. But the determination of the proper relationship between child and parent had a significance that extended beyond the question of whether a daughter or a son had the right to choose her or his own marriage partner. It comprehended—to quote again from the title page of *Clarissa*— "*the most* important Concerns *of* Private LIFE"; it comprehended, as Sade felt his work comprehended, the whole issue of the liberty and the rights of the individual.

And it is in *Clarissa* that we find the closest parallel to the situation in *La Philosophie dans le boudoir*. Clarissa is initiated into the world by Lovelace when he rapes her. The rape, like the sexual initiation of Eugénie, is carried out before a group; Lovelace is assisted by Mrs. Sinclair, the keeper of a high-class brothel, and her girls. Clarissa, of course, cannot accommodate herself to Lovelace's world; she preserves her freedom, and dies—going, as she says to Lovelace ambiguously, to wait for him at her father's house. But her freedom, like the liberation of Eugénie, is also accompa-

La Philosophie dans le boudoir

nied by the ritual destruction of figures of parental authority. Her own parents survive—Richardson contriving, as always, to have his cake and eat it—but their surrogates, Mrs. Sinclair the bawd and Captain Tomlinson, Lovelace's assistant, both die. Clarissa's experience in the brothel can be read very convincingly as a nightmare analogue of her experience at Harlowe Place: Mrs. Sinclair and her helpers force, cajole, and trick her into submitting to Lovelace just as her own mercenary and selfish parents had tried to force, cajole, and trick her into marrying the repulsive Mr. Solmes. The agonizing and physically horrible death of Mrs. Sinclair cannot be exactly equated with the destruction of Madame de Mistival, but it certainly performs an analogous function in the symbolic structure of the story.

The implications of *Clarissa*, like the implications of everything Sade wrote, are saddening and disturbing; and when they are set in this context, so too are the implications of Jane Austen's otherwise delightful burlesques. An excessive indulgence in sensibility, or a blind faith in man's capacity to follow the dictates of his heart, to act in accordance with his better feelings, is foolish and deserves to be ridiculed. But to cast doubt on or, as Sade does, to attempt to destroy entirely, the ideals embodied in the concept of sensibility is to attack something which must be regarded as fundamental to any view of man that is at all rational or hopeful. "It suffices that man is what he is," wrote d'Holbach,

> or that he is a sensible being [i.e., a being endowed with sensibility] in order to distinguish what gives him pleasure or displeasure. It suffices that one man knows that another man is a sensible being like himself, to perceive what is useful or hurtful to him. . . . Thus the feeling and thinking being has only to feel and think, in order to discover what he must do for himself and others. I feel, and another feels like me; this is the foundation of all morals. . . .[45]

This is stating in its most optimistic form the enlightened, the *sentimental* assumption; and if this is not in some sense true, no matter how limited that sense may be, then there is not much hope for mankind. Sade, with his eerily prophetic visions of genocide and universal annihilation, obviously wants us to believe that there is not; and if we were to read *Love and Friendship* as tragedy rather than comedy we could perhaps come to a similarly bleak conclusion. Seen in a balanced rather than an unduly pessimistic light, and read in the context of the revolution, these works do of course suggest that the sentimental ideal, though a noble and indeed an essential one, is frail and delicate; and that for man to realize it, to achieve his potentially humane destiny, he needs to be protected from the more ferocious and self-centered elements in his humanity.

These parodies of sentimentalism go further than this, however, in their implication that there is a connection between the experience of, and the desire for, freedom and the urge to cruelty and destruction. This makes them particularly disturbing to people who read them, as we do today, in an atmosphere thick with the rhetoric of dissent and revolution, charged with the threat of violence. The simple explanation of and excuse for the bloodshed which can accompany social revolution is that it is a political or military necessity; people have to be killed so that objectives felt by the revolutionaries to be legitimate may be achieved, objectives which have been rendered otherwise completely unattainable by repressive and inflexible authority. Revolutionary violence can thus be seen both as an expression of frustration and disillusionment, and as something which is intended to serve a functional purpose. Sadean cruelty can partly be explained in this way: his great criminals like Juliette and St. Fond commit atrocities in order to gain power and wealth. But these "necessary" acts of cruelty are far less important in Sade's world than the murders, tortures, blasphemies, and desecrations which accompany the sexual activities of people who are already in a state of complete liberty, who no longer need to attain their freedom.

Ritual cruelty and violence are of course essential elements in the fantasy life of psychopathological sadists. They can also be essential elements in the fantasy life—and the real life—of societies. The Terror, like many political purges, was in part symbolic: as Hazlitt very beautifully observes in his *Life of Napoleon Buonaparte*, "it was the phantom of kingly power that was struck

La Philosophie dans le boudoir

at, that tottered and fell headless with Louis XVI"[46] (and decapitation itself is, quite fortuitously, a highly symbolic mode of execution). Sade reminds us continually of the social and political significance of anarchy, violence, and cruelty; and this reminder is all the more ominous when we bear in mind that he had established his intellectual position and written much of his work during the period of greatest revolutionary hope and enthusiasm, the period which culminates in the Declaration of the Rights of Man. Sade was himself, in his own way, a political revolutionary, and in *La Philosophie dans le boudoir* he includes a substantial political manifesto, "Yet another Effort, Frenchmen, if you would become Republicans." It has been suggested that this destroys the unity of the work,[47] and it certainly has a distinct identity since it was apparently extracted and distributed widely as a pamphlet during the revolution of 1848. But Sade, who was highly conscious of the relationship between sexual and political activity, clearly intended I think to place it where he did; and the reading aloud of the document by Dolmancé forms an ironically fitting climax to the philosophizing which has gone on in Madame de Saint-Ange's boudoir.

The causes of and motivations for social and political violence are extraordinarily complex; but Sade suggests more vividly than most writers one of the areas in which an explanation of these things can be sought. Moreover the line of approach which Sade opens up has a quite special relevance to what is happening today. I am touching here, of course, on the fringes of an enormously complex subject; but it is worth observing that the new radicalism, not only in the United States but possibly in all urban, highly industrialized societies, is openly and at times aggressively sexual, extremely sentimental—both in the good sense, in its commitment to humane values, and in the bad sense, in its self-pity and self-deception—and increasingly violent. A thoroughly anarchic and libertine document like Jerry Rubin's *Do it!*, for instance, which is sub-titled *Scenarios of the Revolution* and which chronicles the transformation of the relatively sentimental Berkeley Hippie into the activist Chicago Yippie, presents a very familiar pattern to anyone who has read Sade. (In other ways—in its good humour, in the use of the physical appearance of the book to reflect its apparent anarchy and incoherence, and in its zany charm—*Do it!* is also very reminiscent of *Tristram Shandy*).⁴⁸ Let me cite one more example: *Defiance*, the first issue of "A Radical Review," published in October 1970. It is interesting, in the context of this present discussion, for a number of things. First, it is concerned to a surprising degree with what, in eighteenth-century terminology, would have been called the difference between true and false sensibility. Richard Poirier, for instance, in an extremely thoughtful essay, which contrives, nonetheless, to give somehow the impression that the eighteenth century never occurred, begins by asserting that "the future induces even more sentimentality than does the past," and arrives at the conclusion that while "there has probably never been a time before . . . when there were such irresistible demands on feeling . . . what is probably being discovered are the possible restrictions of human compassion, sympathy and feeling."⁴⁹ Second, it is remarkable in how many of the semi-documentary reports from the revolutionary front contained in *Defiance*, political conversion or illumination is presented as being associated with an act of sexual initiation. And today, as Dodson Rader, the editor, suggests in his somber article "On Revolutionary Violence," the world is once more proving too much for the young lady: "Violence on the left . . . [arises out of] sexual disorder compounded by a sentimentalist, neo-Romantic sensibility available in the literature of revolt."⁵⁰ The idealistic enthusiasm of the civil rights struggle of the 'fifties has soured. Now, says Rader, the "English majors handling dynamite . . . are beyond despair, and death has claimed their vision. For they have understood that to destroy all limits is, in a perverse sense, to be truly free. To destroy is to *feel* free."⁵¹

Sade himself could have written that final sentence. "Il faut toujours en revenir à de Sade, c'est-à-dire à *l'homme naturel*, pour expliquer le mal,"⁵² Baudelaire confided to the pages of his journal. Sade may not explain evil, but he certainly shocks us into a fresh awareness of its existence. Natural man undoubtedly has elements of sadism in him—as does civilized man—and to return to Sade is to be made painfully conscious of our potentiality for cruelty, ferocity, and selfishness. If the heavenly city of the philosophers is one possible and imaginable condition of man's existence,

La Philosophie dans le boudoir

the hellish dungeons beneath the snow-bound castle of the Duc de Blangis, running with blood and excrement, provide us with another: and any balanced view of mankind must somehow take them both into account. The Marquis de Sade, limited and horribly distorted though his own image of man may be, forces us as few other writers do to acknowledge this. But if we must return to Sade we should also return to Jane Austen, for even in the slightest and most inconsequential of her works she offers us the reassurance that with wit, intelligence, and a sense of humour it is possible, at least for most of the time, to contemplate and even bear the condition of being human.

NOTES

1. "There were many revolutions within one Revolution, each with its own 'causes,' and there were also 'causes' which explain why all these interlocked. Each of these processes of change has its own 'for' and 'against,' if one chooses to argue them, and each is a causal change which runs athwart the others." J. McManners, "The Historiography of the French Revolution," in *The New Cambridge Modern History* (Cambridge, 1965), VIII, 651.
2. "What does this mysterious science of government and legislation amount to? To putting into laws the moral truths culled from the works of the philosophers." Robespierre, in a speech to the Convention. Quoted in the article "The French Revolution," in *Encyclopaedia Britannica*, 14th ed. (1929).
3. "The Influence of Eighteenth Century Ideas on the French Revolution," *The Influence of the Enlightenment on the French Revolution*, ed. William F. Church (Boston, 1966), p. 94; reprinted from *Journal of the History of Ideas*, X (1949), 63–87.
4. Article "Guillotine," in *Encyclopaedia Britannica*, 14th ed. (1929). Guillotin did not invent the machine: he perfected a device which in various forms had been used in Scotland, England, and various parts of the Continent since the Middle Ages.
5. *An Age of Crisis: Man and World in Eighteenth Century French Thought* (Baltimore, 1959), p. 470.
6. *The Poetry of the Anti-Jacobin*, ed., with Introduction and Notes, by L. Rice-Oxley, M.A. (Oxford, 1924), pp. 176–77. *The New Morality* runs to 465 lines and is the most substantial of all the poems published in the review. All those associated with producing the *Anti-Jacobin*, William Gifford, John Hookham Frere, George Ellis, Canning, and possibly Pitt, contributed to the poem. The most sustained passage, 11. 71–157, is by Canning. It attacks the intellectual basis of the new morality—"French philanthropy," the "new philosophy"—and culminates

in the invocation of Sensibility. Frere, Ellis, Canning, and Pitt were all members of Parliament.
7. *The Works of James Gillray, the Caricaturist,* ed. Thomas Wright, (London, n.d.), p. 246. Gillray entitled the cartoon *The New Morality, or the Promis'd Instalment of the High-priest of the Theophilanthropes, with the homage of Leviathan and his Suite.* This gave the title to the poem when it was later printed in *The Poetry of the Anti-Jacobin.*
8. In *The Structure of Scientific Revolutions,* 2nd ed., enlarged (Chicago, 1970), Kuhn argues for the adoption of the word "paradigm" to describe a certain kind of achievement, one "that some particular scientific community acknowledges for a time as supplying the foundation for its future practice" (p. 10). Adam Smith's *Theory of Moral Sentiments* (1759) in the field of the social sciences, and Albrecht von Haller's *De Partibus Corporis Humani Sensibilibus et Irritabilibus* (1752) in the field of medicine are very clear examples of paradigms in Kuhn's sense. "Sensibility" is a concept of central and fundamental importance in each of these works.
9. *The Other Victorians: A Study of Sexuality and Pornography in Mid-Nineteenth Century England* (London, 1966), p. 1.
10. Ronald Paulson's *Satire and the Novel in Eighteenth-Century England* (New Haven & London, 1967) is particularly illuminating on this matter.
11. *A Gossip's Story, and a Legendary Tale* (London, 1796), Vol. I, Dedication.
12. *The Life and Correspondence of M. G. Lewis* [by Mrs. Margaret Baron-Wilson] (London, 1839), II, 241–70. For an excellent account of this and other parodies of the novel of sensibility see Archibald Bolling Shepperson, *The Novel in Motley: A History of the burlesque Novel in English* (Cambridge, Mass., 1936).
13. *Justine, or Good Conduct Well Chastised,* in *The Marquis de Sade: the complete* Justine, Philosophy in the Bedroom *and other Writings,* compiled and translated by Richard Seaver & Austyn Wainhouse (New York, 1966) (hereafter, *The Complete Justine*), p. 459.
14. *Sense and Sensibility* (London, 1811) I, 10.
15. *Ibid.,* p. 11.
16. *The Complete Justine,* p. 460.
17. *Ibid.,* p. 459.
18. *Ibid.,* p. 460.
19. Mercier, *Le Nouveau Paris* (1799), II, lxx. Quoted in Paul Robert, *Dictionnaire alphabétique et analogique de la langue française* (Paris, 1966). Mercier places the appearance of the word in the 'eighties when, "quelque temps avant la Révolution, les gens de bon ton avaient adopté une certain philosophie *sentimentale* qui était l'art de se dispenser d'être vertueux."
20. J. M. S. Tompkins, *The Popular Novel in England, 1770–1800* (London, 1932).

La Philosophie dans le boudoir

21. This is reflected in such titles as *Sense and Sensibility*; *The Man of Feeling* and *The Man of the World*, by Henry Mackenzie; *Songs of Innocence and of Experience, shewing the Two Contrary States of the Human Soul*, by William Blake; *Man as he is* and *Hermsprong, or Man as he is Not*, by Robert Bage; and *Nature and Art*, by Mrs. Elizabeth Inchbald.
22. *The Complete Justine*, p. 459.
23. *The Monk* (London, 1796), I, 28–29. *The Effusions of Sensibility* is also concerned with the theme of a young lady's entrance into the world. Honoria, the heroine, leaves the country and goes to London. At her first ball she too "[discovers] the baseness of mankind": tripped by a jealous rival, she falls and sprains her great toe. See also note 36, below.
24. The original meaning of "libertine," which goes back to Roman times is simply "a freedman; one manumitted from slavery" (*OED*). But in the sixteenth century *"libertin"* (French) and "libertine" were applied to religious freethinkers: "the name given to certain antinomian sects of the early sixteenth century, which arose in France and elsewhere on the Continent" (*OED*). By the 1590's the word could mean "a man who is not restrained by moral law, esp. in his relations with the female sex" (*OED*); and in the seventeenth century the word both in French and English became firmly identified with philosophical scepticism and sexual freedom. It is at this time that pornographic prose fiction first appears in Europe; see David Foxon's *Libertine Literature in England, 1660–1745* (London, 1964).
25. Letter to Falconet (July 1767), quoted by Charly Guyot in *Diderot par lui-même* (Paris, 1953), p. 37.
26. *Volume the Second*, ed. B. C. Southam (Oxford, 1963), pp. 5–6.
27. *Ibid.*, p. 24.
28. *Ibid.*, p. 23–24.
29. *Ibid.*, p. 20.
30. *Ibid.*, p. 27.
31. *Ibid.*, p. 35.
32. *Ibid.*, p. 22.
33. *Ibid.*, p. 60.
34. *Ibid.*, pp. 61–62.
35. *Ibid.*, pp. 202–4. *Volume the Second* also contains a brief piece, "Letter the first From A Mother to her friend" (153–57), which gives an account of the "first entrée into life" of two sisters; they go to drink tea with a neighbor and her daughter, but not before receiving the conventional warning: "You are this Evening to enter a World in which you will meet with many wonderfull Things: Yet let me warn you against suffering yourselves to be meanly swayed by the Follies and Vices of others. . . ."
36. "Must We Burn Sade?," in *The 120 Days of Sodome and other Writings by the Marquis de Sade*, compiled and translated by Austyn Wain-

house and Richard Seaver (New York, 1967) (originally published as "Faut-il brûler Sade?" *Les Temps Modernes*, December 1951 and January 1952), p. 6.
37. *The Marquis de Sade: A Biography*, transl. Alec Brown (London, 1961), p. 304. Originally published in Paris in 1952, Lely's biography gives a sympathetic account of Sade. Lely notes that while more than half the six hundred sexual incidents related by the female story tellers in *Les 120 Journées de Sodome* involve the eating of excrement, Krafft-Ebing lists only one example of coprophagy in his nine hundred case-histories.
38. *Philosophy in the Bedroom*, in *The Complete Justine*, p. 272.
39. "Towards a definition of libertinism in 18th-century French fiction," *Studies on Voltaire and the eighteenth century*, LXXXIII (1970), 231. Mr. Ivker's extremely informative article and David Foxon's *Libertine Literature in England, 1660–1745* provide an excellent account of libertine fiction (before Sade) in the seventeenth and eighteenth centuries. Donald Thomas's Introduction to *The School of Venus* (New York: Signet Edition, 1971) is also very helpful. The main works in the libertine tradition appear to be Pietro Aretino's *Sonnetti Lussuriosi* (1527) and *Ragionamenti* (1534–36); *La Rhetorica della Puttana* (1612); *La Puttana Errante* (c. 1650), probably by Niccolo Franco; *L'Escole des Filles* (1655) by Michel Millot and Jean L'Ange (translated as *The School of Venus* some time before 1688); *Le Meursius Français ou L'Académie des dames* (1680; Latin version, *Satyra sotodica*, 1660), by Chorier; *Vénus dans le cloître* (1683), by Jean Barrin; *Le Portier des Chartreux* (1743), by Latouche; and *Thérèse Philosophe* (1748), by the Marquis d'Argens. Many of these works and even exact bibliographical details concerning them are hard to come by, and I have not yet been able to read all of them.
40. *Philosophy in the Bedroom*, in *The Complete Justine*, p. 255.
41. *Ibid.*, p. 257.
42. *Ibid.*, pp. 287, 288.
43. *Ibid.*, p. 241. "[Be] not astonished at my language: one of my largest pleasures is to swear in God's name when I'm stiff. It seems then that my spirit . . . abhors, scorns this disgusting fiction; I would like to discover some better way to revile it . . . and when my accursed musings lead me to the conviction of the nullity of this repulsive object . . . I . . . would instantly like to re-edify the phantom, so that my rage might at least fall upon some target."
44. *Volume the Second*, p. 11.
45. From *Good Sense* (1772), an abridged version of *Le Système de la Nature* (1770), transl. J. P. Mendum, included in *The Enlightenment: The Proper Study of Mankind*, an anthology edited by Nicholas Capaldi (New York, 1967), p. 81.
46. *The Life of Napoleon Buonaparte* (London, 1830), I, 269. H. M. Stephens in his *History of the French Revolution* records that during the Terror "little guillotines were worn as brooches, as earrings, as

La Philosophie dans le boudoir

clasps, and the women of the time simply followed the fashion without realizing what it meant. Indeed, the worship of the guillotine was one of the most curious features of the epoch. Children had toy guillotines given them; models were made to cut off imitation heads, when wine or sweet syrup flowed in place of blood; and hymns were written to La Sainte Guillotine, and jokes made upon it as 'the national razor.' " *A History of the French Revolution* (New York, 1902), II, 359–60.

47. Introduction to *Philosophy in the Bedroom*, in *The Complete Justine*, 180.
48. Jerry Rubin, *Do It! Scenarios of the Revolution*; Introduction by Eldridge Cleaver (New York, 1970).
49. "Escape to the Future," *Defiance: A Radical Review*, #1 (New York, 1970), pp. 163 and 178–79.
50. *Defiance*, p. 202–3.
51. *Ibid.*, p. 201.
52. *Romans et Nouvelles*, in *Oeuvres Complètes* (Paris, 1952), XIII, 12.

The Problem of Artistic Style As It Relates to the Beginnings of Romanticism

Frederick J. Cummings

DESPITE THOSE WHO HAVE FOUND it primarily a mid-nineteenth-century confrontation, Honoré Daumier's caricature of the *Combat des Ecoles* (Fig. 1), published as a lithograph in 1855, summarizes one hundred years of a "battle of styles" reaching deep into the eighteenth century. The towering personality of Jacques-Louis David, here portrayed in the guise of an emaciated warrior (ultimately drawn from his *Rape of the Sabines* [Fig. 2] shown at the Salon of 1799) looms over this drama. In David's painting a virile Romulus is deterred by a noble and desirable Sabine who separates the opposing warriors with extraordinary grace.

Daumier's contender is no virile youth keen on capturing a Sabine woman from a somewhat older, less effective warrior. On the contrary, we sense that he has lost much of the battle. His teeth are gone, he wears spectacles, and his limbs are bony and thin. He retains only the nobility, dear to the Academy, of his somewhat questionable nudity. His weapon is the classical maulstick and his shield an oval palette. His antagonist is a suspiciously Courbet-like *sansculotte* in wooden shoes with a goat's hoof for a paintbrush and a makeshift palette.

If we were not already aware of the need, Daumier's reference to types from eighteenth-century art would suggest that we look there for a key to the meaning of his print. It was actually created at the end of a tradition; therefore, its historical implications extend far beyond the immediate battle of the official art of David with the naturalistic art of Courbet to which it refers.

Daumier's reference to David establishes in itself the link between the battle of the schools and a broader, more interesting and variable situation regarding visual choices in the late eighteenth century. Numerous attempts have been made to bring the many-faceted condition of art in the last half of the eighteenth century into focus, that is, to make it manipulable by means of unifying historical concepts. This paper, quite simply, is another attempt to do that.

Some art historians have attempted to deal with the problem of visual multiplicity by reducing the rapidly shifting attitudes of the late eighteenth century to one or two important ones.[1] Rudolf Zeitler, in his *Klassizismus und Utopia*,[2] has described the period as characterized by a thoroughgoing dualism. His treatment is in keeping with the traditional assignment of elements of the period's art to the poles of Neoclassicism or Romanticism.

The other tendency is to view the period in terms that insist on an essential pluralism. Rudolf Bisanz, writing in 1970 on the German artist Philipp Otto Runge, who worked at the turn of the eighteenth century, dispenses with all attempts to see any consistent features except a thoroughgoing multiplicity. His characterization is a perfect example of the uncertainty regarding this period. I quote:

> In view of these unmitigable circumstances it is logical to disavow the practice of assessing qualitatively the art of the nineteenth century on grounds other than each artist's singularity as an individual human being, the sincerity and comparative peculiarity of his *ideational* posture, the relative uniqueness of his personal style, the degree of his conditional expressive "functionalism," and the measure of elective affinity to the spirit of an ethnic, religious, philosophical, regional, or national group. If grounds exist for assuming in addition also supranational cross-influences and those issuing from a conditional "historicism" or conditional "electicism" [sic] to affect his collective makeup, then these should be explored separately and on the basis only of specific data peculiar to him as an individual artist rather than on grounds which force his integration into a preconceived, at times highly doubtful, at times wholly unfunctional, configurational *gesamt*-structure.[3]

Artistic Style and the Beginnings of Romanticism

Rarely have more exotic verbalisms been invoked to disguise a failure in dealing with a problem. Bisanz seems to have been anxious to avoid the Neoclassicism-Romanticism problem and has fallen into the deeper pitfall of total multiplicity. I submit this as an example of the historical chaos which is the everyday condition of the art historian specializing in the latter half of the eighteenth and the early nineteenth centuries.

The multiplicity referred to by the author of the Runge monograph and the dualism of Zeitler do not really help us in discerning the secret longings and motivations of late eighteenth-century artists. The textbook treatments which rely largely on the concept of historical revivals are also inadequate. Indeed, it is possible to conceive a Neoclassical style and a Neoclassical period, a Romantic style and a Romantic period, a Realistic style and a Realistic period only by an undue emphasis on three or four personalities, that is, by a distortion which rarely allows us to see the entire lay of the land. Thus, on most general issues we are lost. And when faced with the ultimate goals of the art historian, that is, periodization in terms of the visual qualities of a group of works of art related in time, we achieve our goals only by extraordinary omissions or unwarranted emphasis.

The battle of styles, or what I shall call the issue of visual alternatives, may provide a key with which to unlock the secrets of late eighteenth-century art. In fact, it is the condition of visual alternatives rather than the issue of historical revivals that finally must serve as the basis for understanding this period. The condition of visual alternatives is the more fundamental in that it gives us a clue to the artist's intentions, while the fact of historical revivals manifests his application of visual choices.

To understand the situation with regard to visual choices we will have to go well beyond the surface forms of late eighteenth-century painting to discern the attitudes and the new techniques used by artists. This will necessitate a keen awareness of the emotional tensions in the life of the typical artist of the period. These tensions, whose variety and pitch can scarcely be overemphasized, alone allowed the age to break through the restrictions set down by Renaissance attitudes, which were gradually dispensed with and sloughed off. The greatest source of information about its lively emotional life is its visual art. In fact, it is through the images of this art alone, where perception and imagination are interlocked, that we are able to gain insight into the stirrings and rumblings which reveal its true character.

The battle of the schools of 1855 actually began one hundred years earlier, with the essay of Winckelmann whose title in English is *Reflections on the Imitation of Greek Art in Painting and Sculpture*.[4] The new techniques introduced by his contemporaries were ultimately to develop an increasingly elaborate series of choices for the artist. As Daumier illustrated, these rich possibilities burgeoned in so many directions that ultimately the schools, out of necessity, took on the role of controlling them through academic theory, training, and the statement of official positions. Despite the schools, the intellectual energies unleashed in the eighteenth century could not be brought under one system. Daumier's emaciated warrior shows the official attempt to do so when that attempt was already crumbling. This intricate and bureaucratic aspect of the story is much less attractive than the original, initial sensations out of which it developed.

I do not wish to present an analysis of Wincklemann's *Reflections* here. It is among the most "modern" documents of the eighteenth century, in that it presents ideas which were to alter fundamentally the way of looking at and using works of art. Its wording does not sound as modern as that of Jean-Jacques Rousseau, whose feelings about the world are seemingly our own, nor does it sound as modern as lines from Diderot, which are so frank as to seem almost without academic trappings, an omission that adds to their apparent modernity. Winckelmann's *Reflections* are in the form of the traditional academic essay or lecture, not unlike Bellori's seventeenth-century *Idea della Bellezza*.[5]

But let us listen: the sensations, the intuitions are new and startlingly fresh. Speaking specifically of the importance of an artist's living model, Winckelmann writes of the necessity for an entire civilization and culture, unpolluted and perfect even in its life's blood, to prepare for the artist's sensation that will produce the specific line on the canvas. Does he not speak our language? He writes: "Only the inner sensation brings forth the essence of truth; the artist who wants truth in his figures will not even grasp a shadow of it unless he interpolates those elements that the soul of an indifferent model cannot possibly experience or express through passionate gestures."[6]

The importance of Winckelmann's *Reflections* is that it states not only a highly intellectual view of that beauty with which the Greeks lived from day to day but offers reasons why it owes its character to the climate, the physical configuration, and the way of life which was brought to climactic expression in Greek sculpture. In doing so it extends the conception of artistic style beyond the manner of the individual artist to include the artistic creations of an entire historical period, reflecting its philosophy, its climate, its way of life, and the general tenor of its entire civilization. This association of visual alternatives with one civilization, as opposed to one artist or antiquity in general, is the overwhelming contribution of Winckelmann.

In the *Reflections* Winckelmann summarizes well the academic tradition of his predecessor Bellori; but Bellori could not have been historically informed enough to assert that his ideal beauty was found only in Greek art, and it would never occur to him to do so. Winckelmann's informative essay is presented with a new sense of nervousness, a high state of emotion, and a keen sense of the pervasive necessity for Grecian beauty. There is in fact a voracious desire evident in his sentences for the beauty known only to the Greeks.

Without realizing it Winckelmann had opened Pandora's Box. By connecting ideal beauty with a specific historical context, he invented the eighteenth and nineteenth centuries. His achievement was to make the selection of style, and thus the representation of visual appearance, more than it had ever been in the past, a conscious and deliberate act on the part of the artist. By linking the goal of the artist with a historical locus he made the artist's series of choices abundant, even endless. The inclusiveness and intellectual force of Winckelmann's essay, linked with his almost trembling emotional impetus, offered a condition of visual alternatives that was essentially new. Even Picasso's reference to African or Iberian sculpture is ultimately a derivation from this new perspective.

It is at this point that many art historians have stopped, and it is on this basis that historicism, the matrix for one interpretation of this period, rests.[7] Was it not enough to invent the idea of a civilization attaining its embodiment in unified visual creations, whose qualities, when properly described, tell us the story of men's lives and even of their innermost sensations? Was it not enough to invent what the Germans like to call historicism? It is indicative of the omnivorous appetites of the eighteenth-century individual that this extraordinary insight must here take a minor position, for the moment, in order that I may isolate other contemporary interests and techniques that provided the artist with visual choices.

In the mid-eighteenth century three systems by means of which artists might represent experience visually existed together in a kind of constellation, often interacting, but quite definitely distinct from each other. This is a simple basic fact. It is one that has not been stated, and therefore it is one whose implications have not been grasped. The situation has been observed, but no one has felt it necessary to describe these systems with a view that each could be operative in relation to style. And indeed, one of these systems—the most important of all and the last to be discussed in this paper—has been relegated to a subordinate, sometimes inoperative, place in art-historical treatments of this period.

The first to be mentioned is that essentially medieval tradition of the style established and handed down by the artist's atelier or workshop. This tradition was strongest and firmest in Italy, where it dominated much official art of the time. The workshop tradition as we know it in the art of the Tiepolos is perhaps the best example. The father, Giambattista (1696–1770), early in the eighteenth century established a style taken up in the second generation by his son Giandomenico (1727–1804) and his students. The Tiepolos span almost the entire eighteenth century and extend into the nineteenth. Their art illustrates supreme intellectual and technical refinement. It is an art admirable and gratifying beyond words. But in the visual arts, at least, the modern world has given up this incredibly satisfying tradition, supplanting it with an emphasis on individual and, at times, on private sensation. The gain is that, though we no longer use the refined technical tradition that made the Tiepolos' creations possible, we still value their art, a state of affairs for which, once again, we can thank Winckelmann at least in part.

The possibilities for selection of style within the workshop tradition are minimal. The style of the atelier can be changed only if it deteriorates or alternatively if it is regenerated by the force of one great personality whose exceptional talents and skills bring new variations on established ideas and gestures. Usually, this kind of alteration is not a matter of conscious or immediate choice.

A second sponsor of visual choice was the Academy, where it was quite consciously cultivated through the lectures, seances, and tracts of its members. The numerous art academies organized in Europe in the late eighteenth century were a symbol of modern culture keeping in step with the times, and they play an increasingly important role in what we might call the administration of the arts. The overall thrust of the Academy, beginning in the fifteenth century, was to supplant the atelier tradition by providing a corpus of art theory. This theoretical basis was extended by a certain amount of technical apparatus of which the most important tools were the living model—that is, nature as it is—and antique sculpture or Old Master paintings, which were thought of as the embodiment of ideal form, or nature as it should be. The result of this emphasis on art theory was increasingly to make artists into intellectuals and to make works of art intellectual phenomena as opposed to creations of the hands and of the body.

Within this context, from the fifteenth century onwards the polarity of nature and of ideal form established the basis for discussions about works of art. This was essentially a Renaissance manifestation, which was early formulated in the writings of Leon Battista Alberti (1404–72). Despite its abundant prevalence in the late eighteenth century, this tradition was on the wane; nevertheless, like the atelier tradition, it was slow to disintegrate. Even though its effect on the bureaucracy of the academy, on the new institutions called museums, and on art critics and historians should not be underestimated, its value for eighteenth-century artists should be weighed continuously.

After the founding of the Royal Academy of Arts in London in December, 1768, its president, Sir Joshua Reynolds, delivered annual lectures, beginning in 1769.[8] His *Discourses*, as the lectures were called, summarize the long tradition of academic theory to that moment. It is literally impossible to find a new idea in Reynolds' writings. His colorless essays are as well milled and as carefully sifted as super-refined flour. It seems extraordinary today that Reynolds should have been echoed, in most essentials, by John Henry Fuseli,[9] James Barry,[10] and John Opie.[11] Each repeats essentially the same ideas. It is clear that these were official compendiums intended as summaries for the guidance of students. As such, they had a profound influence, and they were operative in providing certain visual choices.

These lectures and much other writing about art in the eighteenth century involved a system of aesthetic considerations which is surprisingly strict. This system presents three basic possibilities for determining the representation of visual experience. It is based on aesthetic categories or modes which are given specific visual qualities. This method of categorization will be familiar from the writings, for example, of Edmund Burke. The "sublime," the "beautiful," the "picturesque," "ideal nature," "common nature" —these are the terms inevitably encountered in these tracts, and each carries with it a grouping of stylistic qualities.

Within this system the most highly regarded aesthetic category is called the sublime by some and the ideal by others. A second or middle level of aesthetic category is called the beautiful, often with reference to the archetype of Raphael. The lowest aesthetic category is sometimes called common nature, and includes the imitation of everyday objects as we see them. No matter what the author's terms, or the number of his categories, they typically cover the range from the natural through the beautiful to the ideal.[12]

The tendency of scholars today is to attempt to differentiate the subtle nuances among these different usages.[13] In other words, it is asked, what is the sublime for Burke and how does it differ from the sublime for Fuseli, Coleridge, or Goethe?[14] This is an intellectual parlor game so fascinating that many have been led into its maze for a clue to the overall character of the period.[15] The introduction of archetypes for these categories complicates the parlor game; we find Raphael in the top category for some but in the middle for others, and of course, we have to know why. But to be drawn into this system in search of a historical concept, a clue to the trembling emotion of Winckelmann, is to be lost. These categories of aesthetic response and the objects of experience that may induce such responses are mere derivations of the idealized Renaissance presentation of man and his noblest moments. They were developed in sixteenth-century discussions of individual artistic styles such as that of Raphael as opposed to that of Titian. The hierarchy of artistic types, with the representation of man at the top and the imitation of nature in still-life paintings at the bottom, is an extension of these categories. The hierarchy of genres and the hierarchy of styles are basic for understanding seventeenth-century discussions in academic treatises. Erwin Panofsky in his book entitled *Idea*[16] and Rensselaer Lee in his *"Ut Pictura Poesis"*[17] have both discussed these concepts at length as they should be understood within the Renaissance tradition.

The prevalence of these three aesthetic categories in the least sophisticated eighteenth-century traveler's commentary should suggest to us that their common currency represents an ancient tradition. They became increasingly complicated and fragmentary as the century wore on. It is clear that they were less and less critical for artists and more and more important for the appreciation or evaluation of works of art. Their vitality diminishes totally in the nineteenth century. The very dryness, the grayness, of these tracts, which repeat outworn ideas, implies that they have become formulas. It is one of the leading facts about late eighteenth- and nineteenth-century art that the hierarchies of artistic types and of aesthetic modes were slowly and inevitably being eroded and dispensed with.

For this reason, the theory of modes should take a secondary or tertiary role in a consideration of late eighteenth-century art. By this I suggest no more, for example, than that Burke's theory of the sublime should not be invoked routinely to establish the effective features of this period of art. We should not take too seriously Sir Joshua Reynolds' repetition of the theory of the grand style and the hierarchy of genres as useful in putting together an art-historical characterization. Reynolds' ideas were so completely out of date by the time he repeated them to his students that it is almost impossible to find any freshness in them. This does not mean that his students didn't listen. Often, they listened too carefully. William Blake understood this point well, and that is why he put Reynolds down so emphatically in his notes on the *Discourses* and in the text accompanying his Laocoon print. Blake was caught up in a reevaluation of spiritual experience, which is one of the new concerns of certain late eighteenth-century artists, like those I shall take up at the end of this paper.

Neither the atelier system nor the modal system of the Academy can form the basis for a general discussion of the critical factors operative in visual choice in the late eighteenth century. Accordingly, we must turn to a third system. At its basis lies what I shall refer to as the critical evaluation of experience. This principle of evaluation was to lead to the greatest alteration in the appearance of works of art and was to become the most fruitful source for alternatives in the visual representation of experience.

I would like this phrase, "the critical evaluation of experience," to be understood in the broadest terms. My use of it will be confined to the visual representation of the world in which eighteenth-century man lived; the visual representation based on his exploration of experience in the past; his investigation of human emotions in every kind of dramatic situation; his examination of experience through literature, including Homer, Shakespeare, and Dante, for emotional situations of a different type from those in historical tracts; and his scientific analysis of the world around him for the sake of making the visual representation of experience more concrete.

The principle of the critical evaluation of experience as the basis for creating works of art involved two general urges. On the one hand, it relied on a wish to expand experience with new information; on the other, it involved a wish to make the experience

Artistic Style and the Beginnings of Romanticism

of the past or of distant places concrete, actual, and present. If we turn this idea around, we can make the following generalization. In their urge to make experience actual and present by visual means, no matter how far away in space and time a subject or little-explored an emotional situation, they gave art a new function by using it to expand the horizons of human experience. It will be realized at once that this is essentially different from the ecclesiastic, didactic, and decorative functions to which art was previously devoted.

In every area where the urge to evaluate human experience critically is apparent, an often new technique was devised to make its application possible. I wish to illustrate this by selecting four areas of subject matter where this principle is apparent, mentioning in each the new techniques for realizing the artist's goals.

The first area of subject matter may seem simple, but it illustrates my interpretation well. It is the introduction of a vast number of new topographical representations through works of art. The research technique used, if we can term it a technique, was travel to the site in order to record its actual configuration.

The dramatic increase in the number of artists working in the late eighteenth and early nineteenth centuries in itself is an expression of a new urge toward increased communication and an inceased appetite for visual information. In the French Salon of 1759, 37 painters exhibited, while in the salon of 1806 there were 302 artists, some 50 of whom were women. Anyone who knows the salon *livrets* from 1750 to 1850 will have noted that from thin pamphlets they came to be novelettes.

If there was an increase in the actual number of fine artists, there was an efflorescence in the number of print-makers, and many devoted themselves to preparing topographical views which were purchased rapidly. The vast increase in publications necessitated an increasing number of print-makers, especially to illustrate books of travel. At the same time there was a substantial increase in the number of artists painting landscapes, city-scapes, archaeological sites, Alpine scenes, and city views. Within these types there is a dramatic tendency for new landscape subjects to be introduced. The new subjects included not only delighted appreciations of the Greek Doric temples[18] at Paestum in southern Italy but also representations of the South Seas, then being explored by Cook, whose artist, William Hodges, painted landscapes like that in the National Maritime Museum, Greenwich, England, showing Easter Island. These artists traveled to little-known parts of the Alps and hitherto little-explored areas of England and Wales for new themes.[19] Richard Wilson's haunting view *Cader Idris* (National Gallery of Art, London) is one of the most famous examples. Canaletto's and Guardi's views of Venice, and Volaire's views of Vesuvius are manifestations of a genuine thirst for an emotionally moving record of a place, and often a place not easily accessible to the general public. If we simply pass over these by calling them picturesque we shall miss a central point about the need they filled. The use of works of art as a means of visualizing or as a record of research into the unknown, the exotic, or simply distinctive parts of the world in which they lived is an important aspect of the new function being performed by works of art.

The actualization of experience through a given research technique allowed new doorways to be opened on experience, and new insights to be gleaned along with new information. Thus, people not only found the South Seas or the Alps emotionally satisfying; they became familiar with them and were led to increase their knowledge. The need for information as an element in the function of these works will continue to make accuracy in rendition and research on the site for the sake of accuracy leading priorities of this art.

By viewing these works in this way, that is, on the basis of their subject and intention, we are able to link Canaletto or Guardi, Volaire, Hodges, and Marieschi without any uncomfortable hedging about Guardi still being Rococo as opposed to Neoclassical. That is, surface mannerisms of style must find their proper balance in relation to artistic intention. In a view of Venice by Canaletto, the figures may be Rococo in style, but the important thing is the photograph-like recording of the city-scape.

A second subject is that of research by the artist in the realm of psychological responses and emotional expression, that is, in the realm of psychic experience. An understanding of this urge is es-

Figure 1: Honore Daumier, *Battle of the Schools*. Lithograph (from K. Lankheit, *Revolution und Restauration*, 1965)

Figure 2: Jacques Louis David, *The Sabine Women Stopping the Battle Between the Romans and the Sabine Men*. Paris, Louvre

Figure 3: Jacques Louis David, *Socrates at the Moment of Taking Hemlock* (*Death of Socrates*). New York, The Metropolitan Museum of Art. Wolfe Fund, 1931

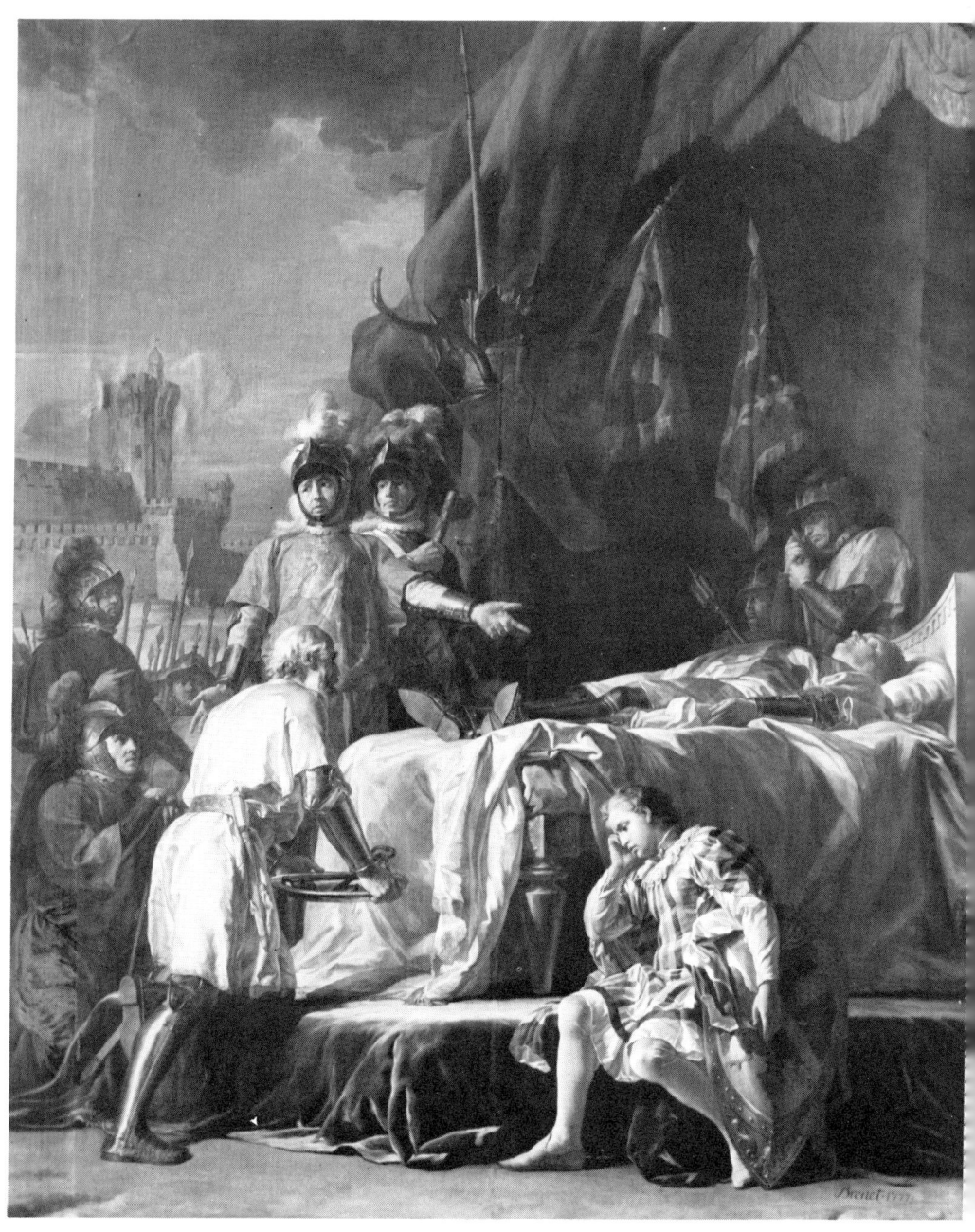

Figure 4: N. G. Brenet, *Honors Given to Commander-in-Chief DuGuesclin*, Versailles, Musée National

Figure 5: Francois Ménagéot, *Leonardo da Vinci Dying in the Arms of Francis the First*. Amboise, City Hall (Photo: Henry)

Figure 6: Henry Fuseli, *The Nightmare*. The Detroit Institute of Arts

Figure 7: Joseph Wright of Derby, *The Woodman and Death*. Hartford, Wadsworth Atheneum. The Ella Gallup Sumner and Mary Catlin Sumner Collection

Figure 8: Benjamin West, *Agrippina Landing at Brundisium with the Ashes of Germanicus*. Yale University Art Gallery. Gift of Louis M. Rabinowitz

sential for our understanding of this period, and it is much more complex than the appreciation of landscape. I have already mentioned the emotional tensions which stimulated these individuals to move rapidly in many directions almost simultaneously, and in so doing to break down established traditions. This is a fundamental feature of the change in the emotional climate of the cultivated European in the last half of the eighteenth century. All of the points under discussion may be seen to relate to, and to be an outgrowth of, this new emotional intensity. If the appetite for new information about experience is great, the appetite for intense emotional experiences, whether new or not, is overwhelming, and those who could satisfy this need reaped unusual rewards.

Contrary to some views of this period, the best eighteenth-century artists were not satisfied with the rhetoric of emotional expression; they wanted the real thing. They selected those subjects that took them to the extremes of emotional life, where they grappled with the most intense emotional responses. To take an established subject, I show David's *Death of Socrates* of 1787 (Fig. 3).[20] All of you will be familiar with the fact that the death scene is often used in late eighteenth-century painting. Few of you will be aware that every history painter did this subject at least once and many painters repeated it often. Every historical, literary, and contemporary source was scanned for emotionally impacted subjects of this type. The deaths of warriors like Duguesclin as portrayed by Brenet (Fig. 4),[21] of Marat as portrayed by David,[22] the deaths of great generals like Wolfe,[23] the deaths of artists like Leonardo da Vinci as seen by Ménageot (Fig. 5),[24] the deaths of heroines like Alcestis,[25] the deaths of the heroes of Livy and Homer were used. Inevitably, these are the deaths of the noble, the virtuous, the talented, the great, which allow the observer by association to participate in the pageant of the ultimate human drama. An enormous thirst for deeply felt emotions lies behind these obsequies and funereal pageants.

The deathbed scene is close to that of the Deposition or the Lamentation over the Body of Christ and therefore has a long history in west European painting. But the late eighteenth-century artist also represened emotional situations rarely employed before. It is in these, where the known boundaries of emotion are scanned, that we must look for clues to their lively emotional curiosity. Henry Fuseli's *The Escapee*[26] of ca. 1772 shows a deranged man attempting to flee from his deathbed while priests approach to perform the rites of extreme unction. In horror the man, pursued by priests and his own family, attempts to flee from the chamber of death. Fuseli's *Nightmare* (Fig. 6)[27] of 1782, in Detroit, is extraordinary because of the simple fact that it shows a woman having a nightmare. So anxious is Fuseli to give this scene palpability in order to strike the imagination of the observer that he includes the actual bog fiend seated on her body, and his night steed looks on through the curtains. It is clear that Fuseli's tentacles of sensation were exploring realms far beyond those academic boundaries which circumscribe his lectures to students. In such drawings and paintings one can discern the secret dramas, the ill-understood yearnings, for the examination of which works of art were now employed and to which they gave the most moving expression.

No matter what the subject there is a tendency for the late eighteenth-century artist to represent emotions in a way that will make the visual presentation more intense and convincing. Standard gestures and expressive types continued to appear, but they became less and less acceptable.[28] I wish to illustrate this with an example from the fables of Aesop, which will also show how the artist was searching avidly through a wide variety of literary sources for new and fresh emotional situations. This use of literary sources, made available through more exacting literary translation, is the third area of experience I wish to reexamine.

Joseph Wright's *The Woodman and Death* (Fig. 7) of ca. 1773, now in the Wadsworth Atheneum, Hartford, illustrates a fable of Aesop as embodied in the Latin poetry of Phaedrus. (Wright probably knew these fables through his acquaintance with their translator, Sir Brooke Boothby.[29]) On an immediate level, we see an old man terrified by an approaching skeleton. By association, we immediately recall the medieval theme of the Dance of Death, through which we are reminded that death is just around the corner, and we quickly grasp what is happening. That the man is actually a woodman we gather from the bundle of

Artistic Style and the Beginnings of Romanticism

sticks fallen by his side. It is evening, and he is returning home from his labors, carrying a bundle of fagots on his shoulder, when he stumbles and falls. Tired and chagrined, he implores death to come and to remove the burdens of his life. At once, death appears to grant his wish. But the terrified old man is now anxious only to replace his burden and to hurry homeward. The moral comes at the end of the fable and reads in Boothby's starkly tense translation:

> Man any miseries will endure
> Rather than seek from death a cure.[30]

These succinct lines are the distillation of Wright's poignant message. The skeleton holds out his hands with the arrow pointed away from the man to suggest that he may choose or reject death. The old man fallen onto the ground holds up his arm in terror and actually grabs a stick to beat off the invited, yet now unbearable, spectre. Each landscape element is selected to amplify the central meaning. The scene is reminiscent of the decayed garden mentioned in Goethe's *Werther* and includes Gothic architecture, ruins in the process of further disintegration under the ravages of time, a watery landscape, not picturesque but rather dying or dead trees, all of which contribute to the melancholic association with death.

The moment selected for arrested action is emotionally the most impacted with psychological implications. Every element in the picture has been chosen with the eye of a scientist to quicken the spectator's emotional responses. The human skeleton was studied by Wright from the most up-to-date edition of the *Anatomy of Albinus*. Death itself does not appear at night, in a mist, or in a blinding flash, but in the limpid clear light of the afternoon. Its figure moves; it gestures; it seems to look; it has its own shadow. The response of the woodman is as incisively observed as the ribs of the skeleton. In his face, which establishes for us the very pulse of their eagerness for intensely felt emotion, every eyelash trembles. The central concentration of the Romantic artist, the emotional response to actual experience, is here succinctly revealed. Such a work makes clear that the late eighteenth-century individual was not about to accept a kind of text-book presentation of human emotions. Wright here steps outside the standard emotional expressions published in the academic model books of Charles Le-Brun,[31] illustrating well his reliance on his own observations and his use of them to make his drama more palpable and convincing.

The fourth area for the critical examination of human experience to be discussed here is that of history; there the techniques used were archaeological investigation and coordination of its findings with existing literary sources. In the search for new and more varied emotional experiences the qualities of a given historical period were the most stimulating to the imagination and the most rewarding. Once unlocked as a source for subject matters and for artistic form, the possibilities of historical experience were seemingly endless. The emotionally avaricious late eighteenth-century man awakened to these possibilities with the enthusiasm of one finding a particularly rich and easily retrievable treasure. Hawthorne's opening paragraphs in *The Marble Faun* or Keats' intense state of longing in his *Ode on a Grecian Urn* best characterize this sense of urgency.

Although Greece and Rome were their most immediate inspiration, Egypt, Gothic art, Chinese art, and the art of Medicean Florence were close behind. These avid travelers to remote times and places give the bewildering impression of running away in all directions almost at once. Their compulsion to realize the experience of the past extended to dressing in costumes like those of the Greeks, drinking from antique kylikes, and sitting on Grecian furniture. Most important, they wished to partake of the dramas of ancient life.

The tragedy of the blind Oedipus as seen by the painter Harriett[32] was as emotionally serviceable as the medieval epic of the life of St. Louis as seen by Durameau, Vien, and Noel Hallé.[33] The Welsh bard as presented by William Blake[34] was as rewarding as the despair of the Biblical Nebuchadnezzar in the wilderness as treated by Volaire, Blake, and John Hamilton Mortimer. The errors of the modern man Newton, as treated by Blake, were as pertinent as those of the early English queen Philippa[35] as portrayed

Artistic Style and the Beginnings of Romanticism

by Benjamin West. The shocking story of the invention of the Scottish bard Ossian by Macpherson is a perfect illustration of an historical acquisitiveness that is irrepressible. To satisfy this unquenchable appetite for new sensations, no stone which might reveal a clue to the emotional life of the past was left unturned. The most sophisticated research and the best technological methods were used to satisfy this need, including archaeological investigation and the fresh examination of literary sources.

This industrious *recherche du temps perdu* is made more benignly complex for us because increasing knowledge led to increasing discrimination. The Tuscan order, which was appropriate for early Italic subjects, was used by David in his *Oath of the Horatii*. The palace of Diocletian, although anachronistic, was considered appropriate for Agrippina's landing on the east coast of Italy at Brundisium as visualized by Benjamin West, and the Roman reliefs on the Ara Pacis the appropriate source for her funereal procession with the ashes of her husband Germanicus (Fig. 8).[36]

West's Agrippina is a visual concretion of past experience. It could only have come into being after a new structure had been given to the past. Ancient art and literary texts were now related to each other in such a way that one could form from them a coherent image of the world in which Agrippina lived, as West presents it for us. The result was an emotionally new kind of experience based on the principle of grasping related, rather than isolated, phenomena from the past.

It is essential to make clear that these re-creations of the past in late eighteenth-century paintings exemplify a search for the "real thing." They are actualizations of the past. Through them the past is made present. The concern for archaeological accuracy in these works is the bridge to emotional palpability. The antique costume, heroic nudity, the palace of Diocletian—these are merely the techniques and the trappings of style. Historicism and archaeological correctness are the techniques of historical re-creation and the means for achieving historical presence. These works reveal to us the artist's emotional longing to have the great dramas of the past, in his own world and in his own time, as intellectual fare available for emotional satisfaction. The emotional longing for antiquity as it was, for the South Seas as it is, are very close to Courbet's absorption with his world as it was.

I cannot be emphatic enough in saying that the tendency on the part of late eighteenth-century man to describe the past or the exotic is not a wish to escape. On the contrary, it is a wish to partake, to acquire, to have the past or that which is distant, in his own time, within his grasp. It is the most emphatic expression of an insatiable desire to make the products of the historical imagination concrete.

An almost sentimental longing for past time is the most essential of the prerequisites for exploring human experience. Late eighteenth-century man possessed this longing in a remarkable degree. It includes an extraordinary self-consciousness, at once the source and expression of a general urge to shape the past imaginatively and to make it actual. A truly new dimension of human experience, the temporal dimension that makes available the experience of the past, had come into being. This is the most important discovery of the modern world. We overlook it only because it is so fundamental that we cannot imagine our emotional life without a historical context. Before this, men, with the exception of rare intellectuals, lived as individual entities. After it, men lived within and by the standard of continuities. This was achieved through the elaboration of the techniques of observation, recording, publication—that is, through research, or what I have called the critical evaluation of human experience.

Before leaving the subject, I should like to stress a point I have already made—that the method of historical reference to visual materials is essentially different from the modal system, and is an arch enemy of the system inherent in the hierarchy of genres and the ideal style of the Academy. These older systems involve entirely different ways of dealing with visual materials. The modal system is based on an archetype of sublimity or beauty. Sometimes this was thought to be embodied in a historical locus such as Greek art, and when this appeared to be the case, the modal and historical systems came together briefly. However, the system of modes values the ideal type most of all; that is, it values the world as it is not, and as it has never been. The historical system is based on the premise of re-creating human experience as it actually existed. As stated already, this method derived from the concurrent wish to use the visual arts for representing experience as it actually is. Hand in hand go the needs not only to extend the horizons of human experience but to make it concrete, measurable, identifiable, emotionally present, and therefore assimilable and satisfying.

To conclude, the battle of styles of the late eighteenth century is a very different matter from the battle of the schools of the nineteenth. The situation we find in late eighteenth-century art is the continuation of the atelier tradition of the medieval world, the Renaissance or Albertian tradition involving a view of ideal form and a system of aesthetic modes, alongside a distinguishable group of essentially new and modern premises for establishing the appearance of works of art. In every case the modern system realizes a new attitude linked with a new technique for giving it visual form.

With the introduction of the need to actualize that which was far away, deep in the past, little known, little understood, or to re-create the great events of his own day, the artist was forced into the position of creating his own visual form in accordance with the requirements of the subject. He did this through research and what I have called the critical evaluation of experience. I would contend that this may be the case even when contemporary subjects are presented, as for example in West's *Death of Wolfe* (National Gallery of Canada, Ottawa) or Géricault's *Raft of the Medusa* (Musée du Louvre, Paris), which required research in order to lend the events they depict that authenticity essential for emotional appreciation.

This historical method resulted in the creation of works of art that were substantially more intellectual than earlier paintings, in that the artist was increasingly responsible for their rationale and references. Once the artist was made responsible for rethinking, researching, and establishing his own visual form, the possibilities open to him multiplied. Even something approaching total abstraction was possible, as in Flaxman's outline drawings, which are mere hieroglyphs, recalling antique dramas. Indeed, these historically inspired works of art tend to be increasingly abstract, even when their goal is to "make actual." A photograph is totally abstract, even though the intention of this abstraction is to actualize, to preserve, to make, and to keep present a moment in past time. The photograph, indeed, is ultimately an outgrowth of the need to actualize that appears in late eighteenth-century works of art.

This responsibility for establishing visual form within a rich context offering multiple visual choices is the very crux of a fundamental change that takes place in mid-eighteenth-century art. It is intimately bound to the new function given to works of art of expanding the limits of man's experience. It is only when we grasp these central ideas and the age's deep need for and commitment to rapidly changing emotional alternatives that we grasp how modern these men are—how intensely their spirit reaches out to us. Their conception of visible form is at the root of the twentieth-century principle that the artist creates his own form to suit the needs of a given conception and the requirements of its actualization.

NOTES

1. Please see notes 1 and 2 of my review "Robert Rosenblum, *Transformations in Late 18th Century Art*, Princeton, 1967," *Journal of the Society of Architectual Historians*, XXVIII, no. 2 (May 1969), pp. 137–38. Please also see notes 1 and 2 of my essay "Romanticism in Britain, 1760–1860," in *Romantic Art in Britain, Paintings and Drawings 1760–1860* (Detroit/Philadelphia, 1968), p. 24.
2. Rudolf Zeitler, "Klassizismus und Utopia," in *Figura*, V (Stockholm, 1954), 10.
3. Rudolf M. Bisanz, *German Romanticism and Philipp Otto Runge, A Study in Nineteenth-Century Art Theory and Iconography* (DeKalb, Ill., 1970), p. 7.
4. Johann J. Winckelmann, *Gedanken über die Nachahmung der Griechischen Wercke in der Mahlerey und Bildhauer-Kunst* (Dresden, 1755). This treatise was translated by John Henry Fuseli as *Reflections on the Painting and Sculpture of the Greeks* (London, 1765). A second edition of Fuseli's translation was entitled *Reflections Concerning the Imitation of Grecian Artists in Painting and Sculpture* (Glasgow, 1766).
5. Giovanni P. Bellori, *Le Vite de' pittori, scultori ed architetti moderni* (Rome, 1672).
6. "Die innere Empfindung bildet den Character der Wahrheit, und der Zeichner, welcher seinen Academien denselben geben will, wird nicht

einen Schatten des Wahren erhalten, ohne eigene Ersetzung desjenigen, was eine ungerührte und gleichgültige Seele des Modells nicht empfindet, noch durch eine Action, die einer gewissen Empfindung oder Leidenschaft eigen ist, ausdrücken kan." J. J. Winckelmann, *Gedanken*, p. 8.

7. In fairness it should be said that Nikolaus Pevsner and Hans Gerhard Evers have not stopped with a simplistic view of historical revivals. Both have attempted to extend the term "historicism" in such a way as to incorporate the basic attitudes toward artistic form in the late eighteenth and nineteenth centuries. Pevsner distinguishes five facets within his concept of historicism, while Evers envisions two definite attitudes toward form in his..(See Nikolaus Pevsner, "Möglichkeiten und Aspekte des Historismus, Versuch einer Frühgeschichte und Typologie des Historismus," in *Historismus und bildende Kunst* [Munich, 1965], pp. 13–24; Hans Gerhard Evers, "Historismus," in *ibid.*, pp. 25–42.) Both scholars have suggested that historicism provides a comprehensive and unifying art-historical concept for the period. A critical examination of this premise must reveal that no matter how broadly viewed, it is too limited to provide a tool whereby we can penetrate to all of the essentials of the period.
8. *The Works of Sir Joshua Reynolds* (London, 1797), 2 vols.
9. John Knowles, *The Life and Writings of Henry Fuseli* (London, 1831), 3 vols. Fuseli's lectures were delivered between 1800 and 1825.
10. *The Works of James Barry . . . Historical Painter* (London, 1809), 2 vols.
11. John Opie, *Lectures on Painting* (London, 1809).
12. The system of aesthetic modes as it applies to a specific work of art was discussed in my essay "The Selection of 'Style' in Neo-Classical Art as Exemplified in Antonio Canova's *Hercules and Lichas*," in *Stil und Uberlieferung in der Kunst des Abendlandes, Akten des 21. Internationalen Kongresses für Kunstegeschichte in Bonn, 1964*, I (Berlin, 1967), 232–35. The best general treatment of the application of modes to the visual arts is the essay by Jan Bialostocki, "Das Modusproblem in den bildenden Künsten, zur Vorgeschichte und zum Nachleben des 'Modusbriefes' von Nicolas Poussin," *Zeitschrift für Kunstgeschichte*, XXIV, no. 2 (1961), 128–41. Bialostocki's notes include numerous references to eighteenth-century treatises which utilize the concept of modes extensively. For Poussin's famous letter on the modes, see Ch. Jouanny, *Correspondance de Nicolas Poussin* (Paris, 1911), no. 156.
13. Meyer H. Abrams, *The Mirror and the Lamp: Romantic Theory and the Critical Tradition* (New York, 1958).
14. For Goethe's essay on aesthetic modes see, "Einfache Nachahmung, Manier, Stil," first published in the *Teutscher Merkur*, February, 1789. Johann W. von Goethe, *Goethes Werke*, 127 volumes (Weimar, 1887–1912), part I, XLVII, pp. 77–83.
15. Christopher Hussey, *The Picturesque: Studies in a Point of View* (London, 1927).

16. Erwin Panofsky, *Idea*, 2d ed. revised (Berlin, 1960).
17. Rensselaer W. Lee, "*Ut Pictura Poesis*: The Humanistic Theory of Painting," *The Art Bulletin*, XXII (1940), 197–269.
18. S. Lang, "Early Publications of the Temples at Paestum," *Journal of the Warburg and Courtauld Institutes*, XIII (January 1950), 13–48.
19. Allen Staley, "British Landscape Painting, 1760–1860," in *Romantic Art in Britain*, pp. 25–30.
20. *Socrate au moment de prendre la cigue*, Paris Salon, 1787, no. 119. The painting is in the Metropolitan Museum of Art, New York.
21. *Honneurs rendu au Connétable du Guesclin*, Paris Salon, 1777, no. 18. The finest version of this painting is at Versailles, signed and dated 1777. The horizontal version at Dunkerque appears to be signed and dated 1778. I have not seen the Dunkerque painting, but the photograph suggests that it should be examined carefully before the attribution is accepted.
22. Royal Museum of Fine Arts, Brussels; painted in 1793.
23. The most famous example is *The Death of General Wolfe* by Benjamin West. The painting is in the National Gallery of Canada, in Ottawa. See also T. Crombie, "Death of Wolfe in Paintings: a tricentenary review," *The Connoisseur*, CXLIV (September 1959), 56–57.
24. François Ménagéot, *Léonard de Vincy, mourant dans les bras de François premier*, Paris Salon, 1781, no. 151. The painting is in the Mairie of Amboise.
25. When it was first shown at the Salon of 1785 (no. 178), the painting was entitled, *L'Héroisme de l'amour conjugal (Alceste s'étant dévouée volontairement à la mort, pour sauver les jours de son époux, fait ses adieux à son mari, que le désespoir accable)*. Today the painting is in the Musée du Louvre, Paris.
26. The drawing is in the British Museum, London. It was shown in the exhibition *Romantic Art in Britain*, Detroit/Philadelphia, 1968, no. 66.
27. In the same exhibition, no. 68.
28. See Frederick Cummings, "Charles Bell and the *Anatomy of Expression*," *The Art Bulletin*, XLVI (June 1964), 191–203.
29. See the various discussions of this painting as referred to in *Romantic Art in Britain* (no. 29), and in Benedict Nicolson, *Joseph Wright of Derby, Painter of Light* (London/New York, 1968), II, 243 (no. 220).
30. Brooke Boothby, *Fables and Satires, Translated from Phaedrus and others with a Preface on the Esopean Fable* (Edinburgh, 1809).
31. For Charles LeBrun, see Jennifer Montagu, "Charles LeBrun's 'Conférence sur l'expression général et particulière,'" Ph.D. dissertation, University of London, 1959.
32. Fulchran Jean Harriett, *Oedipe à Colone*, private collection, Paris. The drawing that presumably prepared for this painting was shown in the Salon of 1796 (no. 202).
33. These scenes from the life of St. Louis were commissioned for the chapel of the *Ecole Militaire*, Paris, in 1773. The paintings can be seen there today.

34. Blake's watercolor illustrations for Thomas Gray's *The Bard* were prepared about 1800–1801. There is a discussion of this series in *Romantic Art in Britain*, pp. 160–61 (no. 94).
35. *Queen Philippa Soliciting Her Husband, Edward the Third, to Save the Lives of the Brave Burghers of Calais*, Royal Academy Exhibition, London, 1788, no. 89.
36. See Allen Staley, "The Landing of Agrippina at Brundisium with the Ashes of Germanicus," *Bulletin, Philadelphia Museum of Art*, LXI (1965–66), 10–19 (nos. 287–88).

The Sick Rose as an Aesthetic Idea:

Kant, Blake, and the Symbol in Literature

John Neubauer

I

CHAPTER 59 OF KANT'S *CRITIQUE OF JUDGMENT* asserts that beauty is the symbol of morality, but the explanation is so sketchy that H. W. Cassirer, the most detailed commentator of the work in English, simply omitted this chapter, not being able to follow Kant's argument.[1] Without presuming to fill the gap, I would like to outline the symbolism that leads Kant to his final assertion.

Kant believes that, strictly speaking, neither language nor mathematics is symbolic, because their representative signs are arbitrary; that is, they have no unique relationship to the concepts involved. Thus the word "cat" can tell us nothing about the essence and behavior of that animal without referring us to experience. Kant calls such signs characterizations, and he distinguishes them from schematical and symbolical representations.[2]

In order to understand what schematical and symbolical representations are, it might be useful to recall that for Kant knowledge is a joint product of intuition, imagination, and understanding:

> What must first be given—with a view to the *a priori* knowledge of all objects—is the *manifold* of pure intuition; the second factor involved is the *synthesis* of this manifold by means of the imagination. But even this does not yet yield knowledge.

> The concepts which give *unity* to this pure synthesis, and which consist solely in the representation of this necessary synthetic unity, furnish the third requisite for the knowledge of an object; and they rest on the understanding.[3]

The fundamental assertion of Kant's first Critique is that both intuition and understanding (or perceptions and concepts) are necessary for genuine knowledge: "Thoughts without content are empty, intuitions without concepts are blind."[4]

Now schematic representations do indeed involve an interaction between understanding and intuition: for instance, we may start with the concept "animal," and, by applying the rules of understanding, construct the corresponding perception, say the neighbor's cat called "Frisbee" (Column I in the accompanying diagram). In schematical representations, then, we demonstrate a concept by supplying a corresponding sensible intuition.[5] In symbolic representations the procedure is similar, but here we start not with demonstrable concepts but with rational ideas, for instance God, Justice, or Love, to which no sensible intuition can be adequate. Kant gives the example of despotic states, which do not have perceptual equivalents. But we can represent despotic states symbolically, if not schematically, for instance by a machine. Once the association between machines and despotic states is established, we might extend the symbolism by regarding constitutional states as organic bodies (Column II in the accompanying diagram). Clearly, the relationship between despotism and a machine is neither as arbitrary as the connection between the word "cat" and the animal itself, nor as uniquely determined as the tie between the concept "animal" and a specific cat called "Frisbee." The machine is neither implied by the notion of a despotic state nor identical with it, for their relationship is based on mere analogy: reflections about the machine may yield thoughts and observations comparable to those that a contemplation of despotic states might yield.

Much of our language, especially poetic language, is indeed of such a metaphoric type, in that it employs analogical-symbolical representations. But if Kant's pattern holds for poetry, the poet starts with an *a priori* concept and seeks for it an adequate sensuous rep-

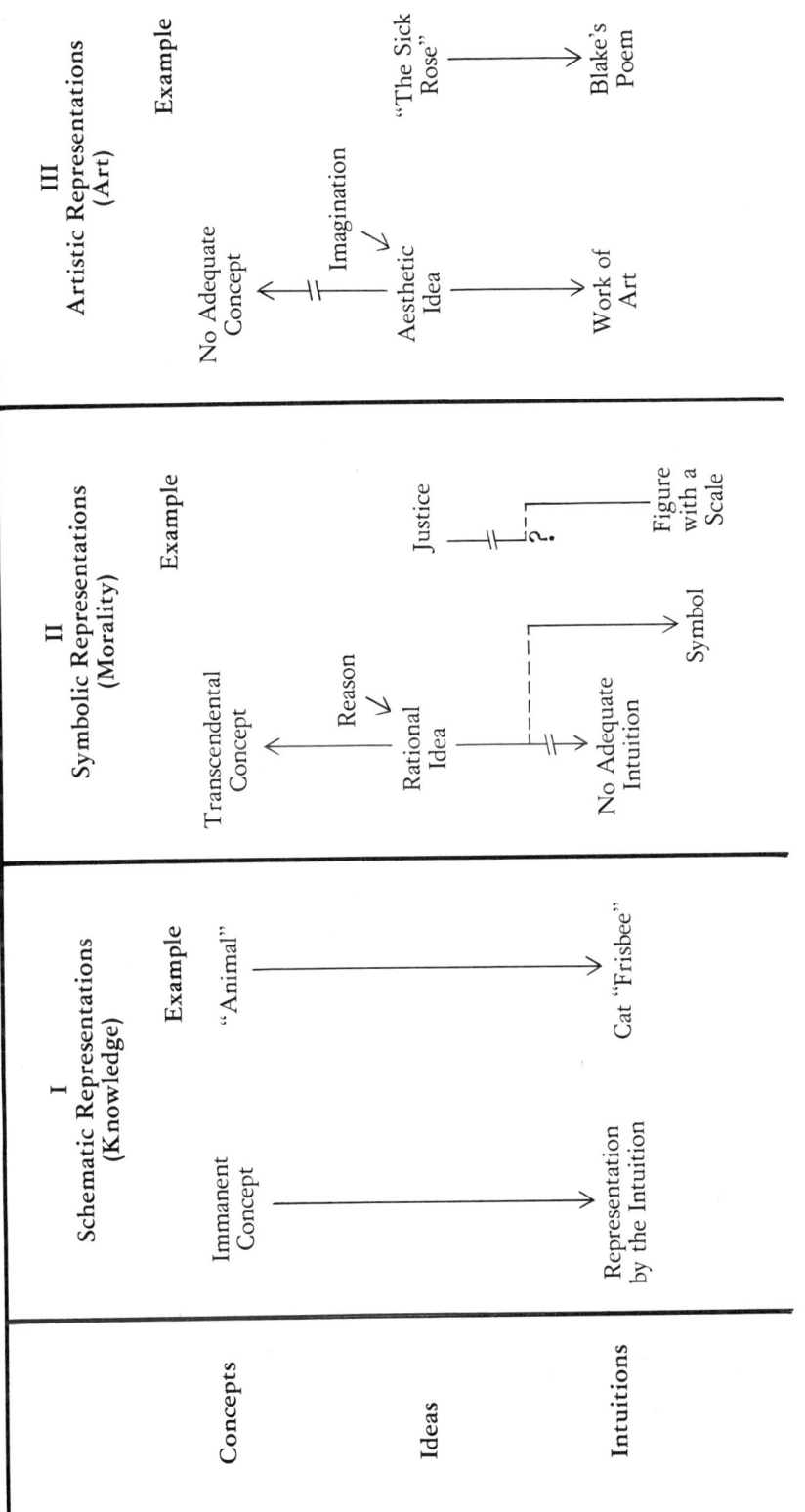

resentation—to paraphrase it with Eliot's term: an "objective correlative." The success of the symbolic representation depends on the reader's reaction, and its effectiveness is measured by the degree to which the reader's thoughts resemble the poet's *a priori* concept. The contemplation of the representation should lead the reader back to the original concept; in other words, the reader should invert the process of poetic creation by retranslating the representation into the concept. Such a procedure would, I believe, more appropriately be called allegorical. Let me hasten to add that, although Kant uses the term "symbolism" for such representations, his account of the poetic process, which I describe later, is different.

II

O Rose, thou art sick!
The invisible worm
That flies in the night,
In the howling storm,

Has found out thy bed
Of crimson joy:
And his dark secret love
Does thy life destroy.[6]

Blake's "The Sick Rose" possesses a baffling and deceptive simplicity: no syntactic irregularities, no precious refinement of language, no private and enigmatic myths of the kind one encounters in some of Blake's longer works. Yet a naturalistic reading of the poem immediately encounters difficulties: worms, however passionately in love, do not fly, and rose-beds are not crimson, though the roses themselves may be. The poem seems to contain objects of our experience, but instead of nature it refers us to some imaginary landscape which bears resemblance to the concrete world only inasmuch as certain elements of it are denoted with words of everyday experience: like much of romantic poetry, Blake's *Songs of Experience* appeals to our internal rather than external senses.

The Sick Rose as an Aesthetic Idea

The poem is then neither simple nor realistically descriptive: its mystery seems to ask for clarification and interpretation. But to interpret a poem of pure poetic idiom implies an attempt to transpose its poetry into conceptual language, the way the Kantian symbol asks to be converted into its original concept. Let us not ask for the moment whether such an interpretive undertaking is proper, merely whether it is feasible. The transposition of "The Sick Rose" into conceptual language is extremely difficult and uncertain because Blake provides us with no clues about the proper mode: the poem is a single image with no commentary, no generalization, no hint at allegorical intentions. In its hermeneutic circle it resembles the works of Kafka rather than the philosophically discursive poems of Wordsworth or Shelley. Yet precisely this enigmatic self-enclosure challenges us to search for a hidden meaning, a clue that would crack the code of verbal signs. And with the aid of some ingenuity it is indeed possible to construct patterns of explanations, some of which I would like to consider briefly.

On the elementary level one may attribute an allegorical structure to the poem. Since roses suggest femininity and fragility, one could conceive of the flower as a Richardsonian Pamela, endangered by some despicable seducer. One shudders to think with what profit a cruder Freudian analysis might exploit the "bed of crimson joy" and the undeniably erotic atmosphere of the poem. Yet, if we associate the rose and the worm with human figures, if we embark upon an anthropomorphic interpretation of the poem, we are obliged to complete the translation and decode all elements of it. Now a despicable man may readily be called a worm; but why should such a worm of a man fly in a "howling storm"? Is the storm his personal passion, a riot, a war, an apocalyptic disaster? The choice is all but arbitrary, and one can find other interpretive possibilities with equal ease: a virgin humanity raped by sinister and invisible capitalistic powers, early sexuality emerging in an infant, artistic purity endangered by a corrupt and materialistic society, the corruption of the glorious French Revolution, and so forth. The difficulty with all such interpretations is that the poem allows all but supports none: the conceptual patterns will have to stand on their own feet. One need not be a New Critic to hold that biographical, historical, and social references merely accentuate one or the other aspect of the poem without wholly encompassing it.

We may try a less concrete approach by reading the poem in terms of the general categories of "innocence and experience"— an approach to which we are invited by Blake himself. But there is little agreement among critics about the relationship between the two parts of the *Songs* and about Blake's attitude towards innocence and experience. E. D. Hirsch, one of the most astute commentators on the *Songs*, aligned the polar forces of the poem with the negative and positive values of *Songs of Experience*[7] and concluded that the poem satirizes love that is perverted by society, that the rose "is sick for the same reason London is sick, and the revolution that will make London healthy is a political manifestation of the psychological revolution that will cure the rose."[8] Hirsch quite rightly stresses elsewhere that the sickness of the rose is an internal decay as well as an external attack,[9] but he ultimately explains the inner perversion by the repressive and hypocritical customs of society. One may well ask whether it is legitimate to introduce into the interpretation a social context which is wholly absent from the poem itself, even though it is part of some of the other poems in *Songs of Experience*. One feels that the condition represented by the poem is more profound and more general, that it reflects a psychological rather than social situation, a human rather than social condition. The rose's sickness appears as a foreboding, an internal anticipation of the external corruption, and as such it suggests deep affinities between pursuer and pursued.

We might then be tempted to read the poem as an archetypal "Fall" from the garden of innocence, where the seductive worm, that is, snake, merely induces to action the self-destructive forces in the rose. This reading seems a great deal more convincing and coherent; yet it merely represents a more sophisticated technique in translating: we are now not converting figures into figures, but figures and events into archetypal situations that still require a complete translation of the poem. But the "howling storm" of the night seems singularly inappropriate to that primeval happiness and light which we attribute to Eden. The locale and mood of the poem

The Sick Rose as an Aesthetic Idea

are no closer to the spirit of paradise than Kafka's father figures are representations of an Old-Testament God or Abraham. In both cases it might be useful to compare the poetic and Biblical worlds, as long as we realize that analogies naturally stress what is common but, as Kafka scholarship demonstrates, usually fail to reveal the differences. Archetypal comparisons focus on the general pattern of a work at the price of neglecting its essential individuality.

Perhaps nobody has commented upon the poem more sensitively than Maurice Bowra:

> If we ask what the poem means, we can answer that it means what it says, and that this is perfectly clear. It conjures up the vision of a rose attacked in a stormy night by a destructive worm. . . . But, as in all symbolical poems, we can read other meanings into it and make its images carry a weight of secondary associations. We may say that it refers to the destruction of love by selfishness, of innocence by experience, of spiritual life by spiritual death. All these meanings it can bear, and it is legitimate to make it do so. But the actual poem presents something which is common and fundamental to all these themes, something which Blake has distilled so finely from many particular cases that it has their common, quintessential character. And this Blake sees with so piercing and so concentrated a vision that the poem has its own independent life and needs nothing to supplement it.[10]

III

The theoretical foundations for this view of poetic symbolism were actually laid down in Kant's *Critique of Judgment*. According to Kant, works of art are "purposive without purpose," which means that they have a design or structure that is not directed towards any particular end. If we say that a poem has a design, we do not imply that it was designed to fulfill a purpose, merely that there is a designer behind it. The cardinal point of Kant's theory of creativity is that there can be no rational rules for the construction of artistic designs; the genius that engenders the work is incapable of explaining the artistic process because genius is merely an innate mental disposition through which nature itself gives the rules to art. It follows that the design or purposiveness of a work of art cannot be put into conceptual language, that the meaning of a poem cannot be formulated in terms of a concept or a cluster of concepts, lest we do violence to its very nature.

For similar reasons, aesthetic judgments cannot be based on concepts, and hence cannot yield objective knowledge. Cognition and aesthetic judgments overlap, inasmuch as they both rely on our perception of things; but whereas in cognition this sensory material is then organized by the understanding, in aesthetic judgments the sensory impressions are immediately referred to our feeling of pleasure, and this feeling alone arbitrates our judgment.

Yet the understanding does have a function in aesthetic judgments, a function which is, however, different from the role it has in the construction of scientific and logical knowledge. The key to this special function is Kant's notion of an aesthetic idea. As discussed earlier, symbols, for Kant, are representations of rational ideas which are lacking in adequate sensuous representations (Column II in the diagram). Now, aesthetic ideas are the counterpart to rational ideas: if the latter belong to reason, the former are products of the imagination; if rational ideas cannot be expressed adequately by intuition, aesthetic ideas cannot be exhausted by concepts (Columns II and III in the diagram). As Kant puts it, an aesthetic idea is a representation of the imagination "which occasions much thought, without, however, any definite thought, i.e. concept, being capable of being adequate to it" (192 f.). I cannot think of a better example for the untranslatability of aesthetic ideas than Blake's "sick rose," which is wholly embodied in the image of the poem itself and cannot be put into conceptual language.

The conceptualization of an aesthetic idea is nevertheless useful, and we may generate patterns of explanation, provided we recognize that no particular systematization of poetic language is adequate. "Purposiveness without purpose" implies that works of art point towards the conceptual language of everyday life, without being identifiable with any particular segment of that life and without being capable of changing it. The curious isolation of the aesthetic idea, its separation from practical reason (action) and theoretical reason (science) is for Kant its *raison d'être*, its quasi-metaphysical justification. If no particular concept is adequate to it, nevertheless it can generate a spectrum of thoughts wherein each element is a variation of the idea itself. The aesthetic idea triggers the imagination and stimulates the reader to engage in the construction of imaginative associations. Such constructions do indeed utilize the understanding, as well as the imagination, without limiting it to a particularity. The pleasure of aesthetic contemplation consists of a free and harmonious cooperation between imagination and understanding: the image of the sick rose will not yield knowledge, but it may set us in a frame of mind where the essence of humanity, our practical freedom, is manifest.

IV

It was my purpose to show that the theoretical statement by Kant and the poetic practice of Blake's poem illuminate each other. In closing I would like to give a brief justification for identifying the aesthetic idea with the literary symbol and, lest I prove my point too well, point out some fundamental differences between Kant's position and Blake's.

With respect to the symbol I rely on the authority of Goethe, who gave the following definition: "Symbolism transforms the phenomenon into an idea, the idea into an image, in such a way that the idea always remains inexhaustibly effective and unattainable in the image, and even though expressed in all languages will remain inexpressible."[11] Actually, neither Goethe's definition nor what I have singled out in Kant and Blake agrees fully with what is generally recognized as symbol in the modern tradition—even though Goethe is usually credited with the first modern formulation of it. Kant, Blake, and Goethe insist on the self-contained finality of art; their symbolism is "hermetic," whereas symbolism in the more usual sense is rather "referential," that is, the representation points towards an abstract idea or an undefined feeling. Thus William York Tindall, after consulting Webster, describes the symbol as "a visible sign of something invisible" and as "an outward sign of an inward state."[12] The *Encyclopedia of Poetry and Poetics* says that "the literary symbol unites an image (the analogy) and an idea or conception (the subject) which that image suggests or evokes."[13] Such conceptions of the referential symbol are probably closer to Kant's definition of symbolism, as I characterized it at the beginning of my paper, than his notion of the aesthetic idea. Of course, most modern poetry falls into the wide spectrum between purely hermetic and purely referential symbolism.[14]

It has been suggested by several critics, among them by Erich Kahler, Northrop Frye, and Erich Heller, that the rise of referential symbolism is inextricably linked to the emergence of modern science and the concomitant disintegration of commonly held myths and beliefs.[15] The Greek gods were perceived as concrete manifestations of nature, and Greek natural science, as R. G. Collingwood puts it, was based "on the principle that the world of nature is saturated or permeated by mind."[16] Similarly, medieval realists held that universals possess concrete existence. Symbolic links between mind and matter, ideas and things, inwardness and outer world become necessary only when abstraction and experience have become separated.

The Cartesian dualism of mind and matter, the mechanical view of nature, and the de-mythologizing of natural events came with the rise of science. Kant did not merely register this division in modern consciousness; he helped to create it. His Critiques represented a surgical operation in which matters we may know scientifically became separated from articles of faith and principles of action: the sources of knowledge had to be as pure as the judgments of art and the principles of morality. And in his theory of knowledge Kant relied largely on the Newtonian method of constructing theories—the very method against which Blake's greatest rage was directed. While it seems fairly certain that Blake did not read Kant, he was comrade-in-arms of those German romantics who reacted against Kant's compartmentalization of human faculties, because he unknowingly fumed against it: whatever he says about Newton or Locke is applicable to Kant.

The hermeneutic natural imagery of "The Sick Rose" represents a highly successful attempt to reestablish an earlier unity between mind and nature, in that it fuses the idea with the objects of representation, and re-mythologizes nature. If this spiritualization of nature may be regarded as a form of naturalism then, and only then, one may agree with E. D. Hirsch that "The Sick Rose" and the *Songs of Experience* are naturalistic. Schiller's concept of the "naive," as described in *Naive und sentimentalische Dichtung*, would seem to be a better characterization of that poetic mode.

The symbolism of "The Sick Rose" is, however, not the only poetic mode in which Blake attempted to overcome the increasing abstraction of reason and the disappearance of myths. If his symbolism in the early nineties appears as an attempt to recreate the natural unity of a prescientific age, the equally self-enclosed symbolism of his later works, above all *Jerusalem*, seems to anticipate the poetry of such modern figures as Yeats and Rilke, where the universal language of religious myths is replaced by a new and personal mythology of private language and individual creativity.

One may detect in Kant a tie between art and religion which is both similar to and different from Blake's poetic practice. For Kant believed that the universal claim of aesthetic judgments was grounded in the *a priori* principle that the empirical laws of nature were consistent among themselves and with the structure of our mind, as if these laws were created by a mind that is similar to ours but not identical with it. To be sure, Kant never claimed that this principle, or the existence of such a mind, could ever be proven scientifically; but certain passages in his third Critique do suggest that he thought of art as the concrete manifestation of a metaphysical order. One faintly perceives here the anticipation of the Romantic view that art should absorb all the energies that were previously invested in faith, for art is the earthly presence of the divine. Is it justified to see in Kant the anticipation of an aesthetic religion? The answer is perhaps buried in the enigmatic language of that chapter on "beauty as the symbol of morality"—but unearthing it might prove as difficult as the conceptualization of an aesthetic idea.

NOTES

1. H. W. Cassirer, *A Commentary on Kant's Critique of Judgment* (London: Methuen, 1938).
2. I. Kant, *Critique of Judgment*, transl. J. H. Bernard, p. 255 f. The page reference is to the second edition of the work in German (Berlin: Lagarde, 1793). All further references made in the body of my text will be to this edition.
3. I. Kant, *Critique of Pure Reason*, transl. Norman Kemp Smith, p. 104. The page reference is to the second edition of the work in German (Riga: Hartknoch, 1787). The exact nature of the relationship between intuition, imagination, and understanding in Kant's philosophy is very controversial. For an exposition of the problems involved see A. H. Trebels, *Einbildungskraft und Spiel. Untersuchungen zur Kantischen Ästhetik*, Kantstudien, Ergänzungshefte, No. 93 (Bonn: Bouvier, 1967), esp. pp. 15–51.
4. *Critique of Pure Reason*, p. 75.
5. Such representations also involve the "transcendental schema," a concept that Kant describes in his *Critique of Pure Reason* (pp. 176–87).
6. *Blake: Complete Writings*, ed. Geoffrey Keynes (London: Oxford U. Press, 1966), p. 213.
7. E. D. Hirsch, *Innocence and Experience: An Introduction to Blake* (New Haven: Yale U. Press, 1964), p. 91.
8. Hirsch, p. 94 f.
9. Hirsch believes that the rose's ignorance is "her spiritual disease because in accepting 'dark secret love' she has unknowingly repressed and perverted her instinctive life, her 'bed of crimson joy' " (p. 234).
10. C. M. Bowra, *The Romantic Imagination* (1949; rpt. New York: Galaxy Books, 1961), p. 44.
11. J. W. v. Goethe, *Werke* (Hamburg: Wegner, 1948), XII, 470: *Maximen und Reflexionen*, no. 749. My own translation.
12. W. Y. Tindall, *The Literary Symbol* (New York: Columbia U. Press, 1955), p. 5.
13. *Encyclopedia of Poetry and Poetics*, ed. Alex Preminger (Princeton: Princeton U. Press, 1965).
14. The situation is actually considerably more complex, since we should really distinguish several different modes within referential symbolism itself. Thus Baudelaire's famous "Correspondances" suggests two types of referential symbolism: one that relates the senses in synaesthetic experience, and another that establishes a forest of symbols between nature and poetic language. We find another kind of referential symbolism again in that ironic "Glassbeadgame" with traditional religious symbols in which some twentieth-century authors, such as Thomas Mann, James, Joyce, T. S. Eliot, or Sartre, engage.
15. Erich Kahler, "The Nature of the Symbol," in *Symbolism in Religion and Literature*, ed. Rollo May (New York: Braziller, 1960); Northrop Frye, *A Study of English Romanticism* (New York: Random House, 1968), esp. pp. 3–49; Erich Heller, "The World of Franz Kafka," in

The Disinherited Mind (1952; rpt. New York: Meridian Books, 1959), esp. pp. 209–15.
16. R. G. Collingwood, *The Idea of Nature* (1945; rpt. New York: Galaxy Books, 1960), p. 3.

Ludwig Tieck:
English and French Sources of His William Lovell (1795/96)

François Jost

WE THINK OF LUDWIG TIECK mainly as one of the founders and exponents, with the brothers Schlegel, of German Romanticism, which he illustrated in many ways, especially in his long series of plays and stories. Today the cultured public often identifies him only as the author of *Der blonde Eckbert* and *Der gestiefelte Kater*. The literary scholar, however, remembers other aspects of his work. Although Tieck was born rather late in the eighteenth century and helped importantly during his lifetime to shape the spirit of the nineteenth—he died in 1853, at the age of eighty—quite a few of his publications present characteristics of the age of Enlightenment, often mingled, it is true, with elements of the new trends.

The Enlightenment milieu is dominant in one of his very first novels, *Die Geschichte des Herrn William Lovell*, which appeared in three volumes in 1795 and 1796. To a certain extent it is the "story of Mr. Ludwig Tieck," not so much in regard to the details of the plot as in regard to the ideas expressed and the *Weltanschauung* the author expounds. But other sources than the young novelist's personal experience may be discovered. In point of fact, *William Lovell* clearly shows essential links between Tieck's own philosophy and that of his masters or inspirers, and reveals striking analogies between his technical devices or patterns of structure and those of his models. When he first thought of writing the novel and started to work out its major parts, Tieck was a student of English literature, successively at Halle, Göttingen, and Erlangen, specializing in Elizabethan drama.[1] He also knew French, as did every educated man of the time, and as an authentic German —his birthplace was Berlin—he felt very strongly the spell of Italy: these are, in general terms, the foreign sources of *William Lovell*.

The initial spark for the work was provided, it seems, by Ben Jonson's *The New Inn or the Light Heart*;[2] on the other hand the narrative technique as well as many episodes and ideas echo parts of *Le Paysan perverti* by Restif de la Bretonne,[3] and most of the action takes place in Italy.[4] A similar combination of sources can be discovered in one of Tieck's latest works, his novel *Vittoria Accorombona*, dealing with Italian post-Renaissance mores, which he planned at the age of twenty and wrote at the age of sixty-seven. The fate of the "Famous Venetian Curtizan," as John Webster called her, a lady of the aristocracy who died in 1585, first became the theme of a literary work when, in 1608, *The White Devil* was performed.[5] Webster's drama is clearly Tieck's main source. And at the time Tieck was writing his novel, Stendhal had just published his *Chroniques italiennes* (1837), which also includes the story of Vittoria Accoromboni. But we are concerned here with Tieck's early work, *William Lovell*.

Herbert Lovel, one of the main characters of Jonson's play, seems to have transmitted not only his name to Tieck's hero, but also quite a few traits of his character. The "melancholy guest" of the English comedy becomes the melancholic Epicurean in the German novel. *The New Inn*, it is true, does not count among Jonson's masterpieces, and Tieck never commented on it at any length. The two volumes of his *Altenglisches Theater*, published in 1811, contained plays of Shakespeare exclusively. But internal and circumstantial evidence may shed some light on the nature of the relations between *The New Inn* and *William Lovell*. Indeed we may limit ourselves to one aspect of such evidence: why did Tieck choose for his hero the name Lovell? Obviously he could have taken it from anywhere. In the eighteenth century, Lovel, or Lovell, or Lowell were common names in literature and in everyday life as well. In Shakespeare's *Richard III* there is a Lord Lovel—with one "l"—and Tieck's copy of that play, now in the British Museum, is more plentifully sprinkled with annotations than are his copies of any other play. In *Henry VIII* there is a Lovell with two "l's," whose role is twice as important as that of the Lovel with one "l." In Richardson's *Clarissa*, one discovers a Lady Lovel, the godmother of Jacob, Clarissa's brother, among the *dramatis personae*. And, after all, Clarissa's seducer could be the godfather of Tieck's hero, whose name is formed with the first five letters of Lovelace. In Clara Reeve's novel *The Old English Baron, A Gothic Story* (1778), the action takes place in the "Castle of Lovel," the hero of the plot being Arthur Lord Lovel, son of Richard Lord Lovel. To put an end to these frivolous speculations, let us quote a line of Pope's which could have served as a motto for Tieck's novel, and anachronistically for Jonson's comedy:

Is it, in heav'n, a crime to love too well?

On the other hand, no Mr. Lovell appears in Pope's *Elegy to the Memory of an Unfortunate Lady*, from which this verse is taken. Again, only a vague analogy can be noticed here, while significant parts of *The New Inn* appear to be real sources of inspiration. Jonson's choice of the name and the word-play in which it figures suggest this conclusion. In the first act of the play the innkeeper asks his guest Herbert Lovel, "But is your name Love-ill, Sir, or Lovewell?" This line points the way to a striking connection between the two works, for the pun corresponds in part to a declaration by William Lovell, who in relating the details of some love affair, says: "Never was I so pleased to be Mr. Lovell."[6]

The play on words may remind one of the fourteenth-century poet William Langland, whose *Piers Plowman* includes the episodes of "Do-well," "Do-bet," and "Do-best." Such examples of onomastic symbolism are as old as literature. Proper names foreshadow or explain the acts and behaviour of many major Biblical figures. For the reader of *Tom Jones* unaware of this symbolism, the names of benevolent Mr. Allworthy and of the pedantic divine Square would be interchangeable. And without that symbolism Camus' "stranger," Meursault—meurt-sot—might be thought to have died for a good reason or even a good cause, whereas he actually died "sottement," absurdly. Herbert Lovel's name is symbolic, and so is William Lovell's. As their names suggest, both Jonson's and Tieck's heroes represent a specific conception of love. Jonson's does so in speeches, revealing notions very much like Plato's; Tieck's, in actions and discussions, reflecting the views of Epicurus and Catullus, of Helvétius and La Mettrie, of Choderlos de Laclos and Restif de la Bretonne.

William Lovell (1795/96) and *Le Paysan perverti ou les dangers de la ville* (1775) may be compared with each other on several levels: the general outline of the plot, the distinctive character of the protagonists, and the specific technique used in both works. Before Tieck started writing his novel, Restif's had appeared five times in German translation: first in 1784, with the title *Das Verderben des Landmanns, oder die Gefahren der Stadt*. The translator, Ludwig Wilhelm Meyer, was not a famous writer, but he certainly exercized some influence as librarian-in-chief at the University of Göttingen, where, nine years later, Tieck became fascinated by the story he imagined and decided to tell. Other early translations of *Le Paysan perverti* were entitled *Der verunglückte Bauer*, *Der verführte Landmann*, and after 1796, *Der ausgeartete Landmann*. There are more German translations than French editions of the novel.[7] This is to say that Tieck did not have to go to a rare book room in order to get acquainted with Restif's work, which was reviewed in all the important literary gazettes of the time. However, the author of *William Lovell* probably read *Le Paysan perverti* in French.

The general theme, the contrasts between country and town, or "rus in urbe," the peasant in the city, had often been treated in novels, especially in France. Earlier novelists like Marivaux and the Chevalier de Mouhy, however, did not really exploit the seamy side of city life. In town, Jacob's qualities grow more vigorous; Marivaux's hero, who is far from being a model for all virtues, becomes a *paysan parvenu*, thanks to his sound judgment and his strength of character. Jeannette, too, in Mouhy's *La Paysanne parvenue*, finally overcomes the dangers of Paris and sets an example for feminine behaviour in a society of vice. Tieck's and Restif's heroes, on the contrary, belong to another generation, that of the utopists of Evil, of the Marquis de Sade.

To compare in some detail *Le Paysan perverti* and *William Lovell* would require a good knowledge of both books. It is necessary to remember that Edmond, Restif's main character, is a young farmer's son sent to town in order to learn a handicraft. There, he soon declares his love for his master's wife, Mrs. Parangon. At almost the same time he enjoys the favors of some young ladies who help him to progress rapidly on the path of immorality and corruption. A certain Abbé Gaudet extirpates the principles given to Edmond by a traditional Christian education and replaces them with those of contemporary atheism. After a series of adventures and crimes Edmond gets caught in the net of human justice; and divine justice, too, contributes to convert and to punish the unfortunate sinner. On the very day he is supposed to marry Mrs. Parangon, by then a widow, the prospective husband, who has lost one arm and one eye in the course of his turbulent life, has his chest crushed by the wheel of a carriage and dies.

Tieck's William Lovell is sent from England to the continent as an apprenticeship in life. Before leaving his home, he falls in love with Amalie, whom he plans to marry upon his return. But he is torn away from her by a number of other women he meets during his long journey. Little by little the conception of life which had been taught him at his family estate is replaced by a new one: gratification of the senses soon appears to him to be the supreme and unique good; a certain Rosa, an uncle of his living in Rome, contributes to the acceptance of a philosophy of existence which leads him to a bitter end. He is killed in a duel by Amalie's avenger.

The parallels between the two stories are striking. Edmond and Lovell express in similar words an identical astonishment and criticism at their first arrival in Paris: it is the reaction that Saint-Preux, the lover of Julie in the *Nouvelle Héloïse* had already shown, and Restif is known as a fervent disciple of Rousseau. Not only are both heroes extraordinarily successful lovers, but both are incorrigible gamblers. Furthermore, Lovell follows exactly the same procedure in seducing Rosaline as Edmond does in seducing Laure: promising marriage and wearing down continued resistance by tender reproaches for her lack of confidence in refusing and ignoring true love. Of course in both novels the girls, as soon as seduced, are abandoned. In both novels, too, the corrupters, Gaudet and Rosa respectively, suggest this tactic to their disciples. Other general analogies: both Edmond and Lovell become libertines by the corrosive and corruptive action of big cities. In both cases the moral depravation takes place mainly under the influence of women—although both heroes aspire to an ideal love symbolized by Madame Parangon and Amalie—and the intellectual corruption takes place under the influence of specific characters, Gaudet and Rosa, masters of sophistry and wickedness. Virtue and vice, they both teach, are not only relative but identical in their effects. Gaudet writes:

> Le méchant et l'homme vertueux font tous deux ce qui leur plaît davantage; tout dépend de la position du point de vue, de la détermination qui les a mis en mouvement. Penses-tu que saint François d'Assise ne trouvât pas plus de plaisir dans la macération et dans la pauvreté qu'il n'en eût trouvé dans toutes les délices mondaines?[8]

This idea, found also in Laclos and Sade, is widely commented on in Tieck's novel. Virtue exists only in our imagination: "Die Tugend *ist* nur, weil ich sie *gedacht*,"[9] writes Rosa's pupil. This doctrine inspires the action in both novels. The heroes act according to this fundamental principle, which provides the chief resemblance between the two main characters.

Le Paysan perverti and *Die Geschichte des Herrn William Lovell* are both epistolary novels.[10] If one remembers that the letter form was one of the most popular in eighteenth-century prose fiction, one may be tempted to discard this similarity as too general to be significant. On closer examination, however, one discovers that Tieck's and Restif's works both belong to a particular class of epistolary novels, precisely that kind which, though common in France, was hardly known to any major German or English novelist of the time.

Epistolary novels may be divided into two basic groups, with three major variants in each group. In the first, letters are addressed to a confidant or to several confidants of either one or of several protagonists. Within this group, the three types are illustrated by Marivaux's *La Vie de Marianne*, which is an epistolary autobiography in retrospective; by Goethe's *Die Leiden des jungen Werther*, where a sole hero relates the events, as they occur, to his intimate Wilhelm; and by Richardson's *Clarissa*, consisting mainly of two sets of letters in which the principal characters, Clarissa and Lovelace, narrate to their friends all the phases of the action in which they are participating. In all the types of this group the reader learns about the plot by means of "confidential letters." These essentially "lyrical" or narrative letters, however, do not in the slightest influence the plot itself. The method, therefore, might be called static, or passive.

The method used in the second group of epistolary novels, on the other hand, may be called active, or dynamic. In these works, the addressees of the letters are the principal characters, who directly confront each other. Having done talking *about* their antagonists, the heroes of these novels speak *to* them. They are not seeking compassion: because they intend to be the masters of their destinies, they write directly to their beloved or their adversary. In such novels, instead of progressing *in* the sequence of letters, the plot progresses *by means of* the sequence. It is from the clash produced by them that the spark flies, enflaming heart and mind. Guilleragues' *Lettres portugaises* represents a one-way correspondence between the protagonists; Dostoevski's *Bednye lyudi* (Poor Folk) is an exchange of letters between the two principal characters; and Laclos' *Liaisons dangereuses* is a circular correspondence. It is in this last that the kinetic method reaches perfection. For Laclos' novel and those of its type, instead of assuming the form of a monologue, as does *Portuguese Letters*, or of a dialogue, as does *Poor Folk*, develops a "polylogue." That is, the characters involved in the story write to each other. (A glance at the accompanying diagrams will provide my reader with additional information about these relationships.)

Both the *Paysan perverti* and *William Lovell* exemplify the Laclos type, as the three tables reproduced here help to illustrate. This fact obviously does not in itself constitute the slightest proof that Tieck followed Restif's procedure. The resemblance in method, however, will seem to be something more than haphazard similarity to anyone who examines the sorts of epistolary novel that were published in Germany, England, and France at the time Tieck wrote his *William Lovell*. Among the most popular German works one finds Gellert's *Schwedische Gräfin* (only partly in letter form) and Hermes' *Sopiens Reise von Memel nach Sachsen*. Both authors use the passive method, and so do the authors of all the best-known German epistolary novels published during the last third of the eighteenth century: Goethe in *Werther*, Schiller in *Der Geisterseher* (only partly epistolary), Heinse in *Ardinghello*, and Hölderlin in *Hyperion*. The same holds for Great Britain. In the greatest English epistolary novels the letters are not exchanged among the main characters of the plot; these novels employ the static technique, just as do the German masterpieces which they partly inspired. All three epistolary works of Richardson, *Pamela*, *Clarissa*, and *Sir Charles Grandison,* are of this kind, and so are Smollett's *The Expedition of Humphry Clinker,* Fanny Burney's *Evelina,* and Goldsmith's collection of sketches *The Citizen of the World*. All the famous French epistolary novels, on the contrary, are of the dynamic type—Guilleragues' *Lettres portugaises*, Rousseau's *La Nouvelle Héloïse*, Restif's *Le Paysan perverti,* Laclos' *Liaisons dangereuses*, Madame de Staël's *Delphine*. In fact, *Die Geschichte des Herrn William Lovell* is the only celebrated and commonly known epistolary novel in Germany written according to French patterns. Furthermore Tieck mentions *Le Paysan perverti* in the foreword to his novel, though without alluding to any specific narrative device. These numerous items of circumstantial evidence all but require the inference that there exists not only an analogical, but also a cause and effect relation between Tieck's and Restif's works.

I

Ludwig Tieck: 'Die Geschichte des Herrn William Lovell' 1795/96 (a)

Senders \ Receivers	William Lovell	Rosa	Eduard Burton	Mortimer	Karl Wilmont	Andrea Cosimo	Rosaline	Amalie Wilmont	Others	Total: letters sent
William Lovell		59 (5)	18 (–)	– (–)	– (–)	1 (–)	4 (–)	4 (–)	9 (–)	95 (5)
Rosa	13 (4)		– (–)	– (–)	– (–)	2 (4)	– (–)	– (–)	2 (3)	17 (11)
Eduard Burton	5 (–)	– (–)		15 (3)	– (–)	– (–)	– (–)	– (–)	– (–)	20 (3)
Mortimer	– (–)	– (–)	11 (–)		9 (–)	– (–)	– (–)	– (–)	– (1)	20 (1)
Karl Wilmont	– (–)	– (–)	1 (1)	12 (–)		– (–)	– (–)	– (–)	1 (–)	14 (1)
Andrea Cosimo	3 (1)	3 (5)	– (–)	– (–)	– (–)		– (–)	– (–)	– (1)	6 (7)
Rosaline	11 (–)	– (–)	– (–)	– (–)	1 (–)	– (–)		– (–)	– (–)	11 (–)
Amalie Wilmont	2 (–)	– (–)	– (–)	– (–)	1 (–)	– (1)	– (–)		6 (2)	9 (2)
Others	21 (1)	5 (1)	2 (–)	4 (2)	– (–)	3 (5)	4 (–)	7 (3)	36 (5)	76 (13)
Total: letters received	55 (6)	67 (11)	32 (1)	31 (5)	11 (–)	3 (5)	4 (–)	11 (3)	54 (12)	268 (43)

Total of letters in 'Die Geschichte des Herrn William Lovell' a) ed. 1795/96: 311; b) ed. 1828: 268

Total of one-way correspondences: 55 (8)

a) The figures are those of Tieck's final edition of 1828. The first edition contained forty-three more letters and eight more correspondences. (see figures in parentheses).

**Restif de la Bretonne:
'Le Paysan perverti'
1776**

II

Senders \ Receivers	Edmond	Gaudet	Pierre	Mme. Paragon	Zéphire	Laure	Ursule	Manon	Others	Total: letters sent
Edmond	■	46	45	6	1	1	1	1	16	117
Gaudet	25	■	–	1	–	–	3	4	1	34
Pierre	20	–	■	9	–	–	–	1	7	37
Mme. Paragon	7	2	5	■	–	1	1	1	3	20
Zéphire	–	–	4	2	■	17	–	–	1	24
Laure	1	1	–	–	10	■	1	–	1	14
Ursule	–	5	–	2	–	–	■	–	–	7
Manon	–	5	–	–	–	–	–	■	–	5
Others	8	2	3	5	–	–	–	1	10	29
Total: letters received	61	61	57	25	11	19	6	8	39	287

Total of the letters in 'Le Paysan perverti': 287

Total of one-way correspondences: 66

III

Choderlos de Laclos: 'Liaisons dangereuses' 1782

Senders \ Receivers	Valmont	Mme. de Merteuil	Cécile	Mme. de Tourvelle	Danceny	Mme. de Volanges	Mme. de Rosemonde	Sophie Carnay	Others	Total: letters sent
Valmont		33	2	12	2	–	–	–	2	51
Mme. de Merteuil	21		2	–	2	2	–	–	1	28
Cécile	2	4		–	8	–	–	11	–	25
Mme. de Tourvelle	10	–	–		–	5	9	–	–	24
Danceny	4	3	9	–		1	2	–	1	20
Mme. de Volanges	–	1	–	2	1		9	–	1	14
Mme. de Rosemonde	–	–	–	6	1	1		–	2	10
Sophie Carnay	–	–	–	–	–	–	–		–	–
Others	2	–	–	–	1	–	1	–		4
Total: letters received	39	41	13	20	15	9	21	11	7	176

Total of the letters in 'Liaisons dangereuses': 176

Total of one-way correspondences: 36

The purpose of this study in sources was not to minimize Tieck's originality. In one of his *Pensées* Pascal says, "Qu'on ne dise pas que je n'ai rien dit de nouveau; la disposition des matières est nouvelle." Originality does not mean *creatio ex nihilo*, but transformation of diverse elements, whether taken from books or from life; it consists in the art of fusing raw materials and making out of them a homogeneous compound. This is Tieck's chief merit.

NOTES

1. Some of the most important sources of information about Tieck's acquaintance with English literature are: Rudolf Köpke, *Ludwig Tieck. Erinnerungen aus dem Leben des Dichters nach dessen mündlichen und schriftlichen Mittheilungen*, 2 vols. (Leipzig, 1855); H. Lüdeke, *Ludwig Tieck und das alte englische Theater* (Frankfurt am Main, 1922); Walther Fischer, "Zu Ludwig Tiecks elisabethanischen Studien: Tieck als Ben Jonson-Philologe," *Shakespeare-Jahrbuch*, LXII (1926), 98–131; and Edwin H. Zeydel, *Ludwig Tieck and England* (Princeton, 1931). In *Tiecks William Lovell* (Halle, 1912) Fritz Wüstling does not insist on the parallel between Tieck's novel and *The New Inn* (pp. 120–22). See also James Trainer, "William Lovell, Tieck's World of Chaos," *Etudes Germaniques*, XXIII (1968), 191–201; idem, *Ludwig Tieck, from Gothic to Romantic* (The Hague, 1964); A. Gillies, "Ludwig Tieck's English Studies at the University of Göttingen, 1792–1794," *The Journal of English and Germanic Philology*, XXXVI (1937), 206–23; Harvey W. Hewett-Thayer, "Tieck and the Elizabethan Drama: His Marginalia," *ibid.*, XXXIV (1935), 377–407; idem, "Tieck's Marginalia in the British Museum," *Germanic Review*, IX (1934), 9–17.
2. For *The New Inn* I am following the George Bremner Tennant edition, *Yale Studies in English*, XXXIV (New York, 1908). The comedy was first performed in 1629 and was printed two years later.
3. The relationship between Tieck's and Restif's novels has been the topic of a Greifswald dissertation: Karl Hassler, *Ludwig Tiecks Jugendroman "William Lovell" und der "Paysan perverti" des Restif de la Bretonne* (1902).
4. There is no book however, on Tieck's affinities with Italy, but one on *Tieck et le théâtre espagnol*, by J. J. A. Bertrand (Paris, 1914).
5. See Köpke, *op. cit.*, I, 151.
6. "Noch nie hab ich mich so darüber gefreut, dass ich Lovell bin." Book IV, letter 47. I quote according to *Ludwig Tieck in vier Bänden*, ed. Marianne Thalmann, I (Munich 1963).
7. See J. Rives Childs, *Restif de la Bretonne, Témoignages et jugements. Bibliographie* (Paris, 1949), esp. pp. 239–40.

8. Letter LXIX. I am referring to my edition of the *Paysan perverti* (Paris, 1972).
9. Book III, letter 23.
10. A bibliography of the epistolary novel can be found in F. Jost, *Essais de littérature comparée*, 2 vols. (Fribourg-Urbana, 1964–68), II, 92–93 and 380–402.

Clarissa *and the* Tragic Traditions

Sheldon Sacks

I

EXPLORATION OF general principles realized in unique literary works, always difficult, is at worst an innocuous pursuit. It is somewhat unjust, then, that any critic who interprets a favorite convention as if it were a permanent principle of literary construction may be threatened by ridicule in future generations and with undue frustration in his own day.

On the morning of May 17th, 1712, John Dennis went into "a strange and deplorable frenzy." According to Pope he entered Lintot's shop and "opening one of the Volumes of the *Spectator*, in the large Paper, did suddenly, without the least provocation, tear out that of No. 40 where the author [Addison] treats of Poetical Justice, and cast it into the street."[1] E. N. Hooker suggests that Dennis' public deviation from Neoclassic decorum on this occasion was the consequence of his belief that "Steele was conducting a campaign to undermine his reputation" and that personal resentment rather than philosophical rage impelled the advocate of Poetical Justice to reply in terms that sometimes seem closer to one of the dramatic rants moderately condemned in the offending *Spectator* than to reasoned criticism."[2] There are, writes Dennis:

> as many Bulls and Blunders, and Contradictions in it almost as there are Lines, and all delivered with that insolent and that blust'ring Air, which usually attends upon Error, and Delusion, while Truth, like the Deity that inspires it, comes calmly and without noise.... But what will this dogmatick Person say now,

when we shew him that this contemptible Doctrine of Poetical Justice is not only founded in Reason and Nature, but is it self the Foundation of all the Rules, and ev'n of Tragedy itself? For what Tragedy can there be without a Fable? or what Fable without a Moral? or what Moral without poetical Justice? What Moral, where the Good and the Bad are confounded by Destiny?[3]

That "dogmatick person" did have more to say about the problem, and indeed did so in Spectator 548, in a letter which, together with the offending No. 40, supplied Samuel Richardson, both in his Postscript to *Clarissa* and in his voluminous correspondence, with the bulk of his arguments for sending his heroine victoriously to heaven rather than delicately into the arms of a converted Lovelace. Yet, as R. F. Brissenden has suggested, Richardson's attitude towards poetical justice was far more ambivalent than might be implied by his defense of Clarissa's death.[4] In fact, precisely as recommended by Spectator 548, every villainous character in *Clarissa* is punished so severely, though psychologically and morally rather than physically, that Rymer himself—though surely he would have protested against the heroine's death—might well have rejoiced in the everlasting torments of her enemies; furthermore Richardson takes reiterated pains in his correspondence to show that his punishments are aesthetically as well as morally just. In 1748 he wrote to Edward Moore, for example:

> Methinks I would be above justifying a Fault merely because it is past & irretrievable. But have I not dealt in Death & Terrors? Was it not time I shd. hasten to an end of my tedious Work? Was not Story, Story, Story the continual demand upon me. I did not desire that the *Reader* sh'd pity Lovelace: but I w'd not punish more than was necessary in his *person*, a poor Wretch whom I had tortured in Conscience (the punishment I always chose for my punishable Characters.)[5]

Again in 1749, in a letter castigating Frances Grainger,

> I have made Clarissa shew a great regard to [parental authority.] Why? Because there is much more Likelihood that Children should think too lowly than too highly of it: And because

she had to reflect, that for 18 out of 19 Years of her Life, she had the Love, the Admiration, and almost the Adoration of her Parents and Uncles. And if for that one year they were despotic, arbitrary, tyrannical, were ever Parents more severely punished for their Tyranny than they?[6]

No matter how profoundly twentieth-century critics may wish to relegate the concept of "poetical justice" to some historical limbo where the spirit of Rymer's *Edgar* does ludicrous penance alongside Nahum Tate's perversion of *King Lear*, its ghostly presence reappears. It reappears first as a subtle influence on new forms that developed as the soul of tragedy transmigrated from drama to narrative, even when, as in the case of Richardson, the novelist consciously tried to exorcise it. And it may be seen to haunt the twentieth century as strongly as it did the eighteenth—no matter how different our views seem from those offered by Rymer and Dennis—whenever we attempt to answer questions about the most desirable relation between the ethical and the tragic—the relation that originally led to the formulation of "poetical justice" as a critical concept.

It indeed seems strange that the novelist whose initial fame rested on the contemporary popularity of a novel subtitled *Virtue Rewarded* was forced to defend his own punishment of innocence to his own greatest admirers, and that he even made a vain attempt at persuading Garrick to perform Shakespeare's rather than Tate's version of *King Lear*.[7] But it is more ironic still that, despite his stated plan and conscious intention to write a work of the "tragical" kind in *Clarissa*, the novelist, accused of being too harsh to his innocent heroine in his own day, failed to accomplish his intention—at least he failed according to the brand of twentieth-century criticism which insists that whereas "a tragic figure is always *defeated* in his efforts to impose his will on events," Clarissa "asserts her triumph; not only her own personal triumph but the triumph of all the values her creator wishes to emphasize."[8]

In this respect Richardson finds himself in interesting company. With rhetorical flourishes similar to those Rymer employed in condemning *Othello* as an absurd deviation from poetical justice, which he conceived of as a necessary principle of tragic construction, a distinguished modern critic deplores the ending of Conrad's *Victory* as a culpable deviation from the desirable starkness of a "tragic vision," which he conceives as being the most desirable modern relationship of the ethical to the tragic, although almost the opposite of poetical justice. We are told that the ending of Conrad's fine novel "is a retreat from the tragic to the sentimentally ethical that asks for blind faith in life and love and for the comforting cinematic outburst, 'together we can lick the world, Baby.' " . . . Conrad, we are assured, "has himself run a risk: unwilling to abide with the tragic vision and able only to withdraw before it since he cannot go beyond, he has still dared to try high tragedy."[9] Is Heyst's victorious sacrifice reducible to or even explicable by its vile paraphrase, "Together we can lick the world, Baby"? Or is it simply that, with the abolition of poetical justice, any victory, any sacrifice, however meaningful, must be regarded as a betrayal of true tragedy? In fact, the ease with which we can use the same formula to reduce even Lear's final affirmation of the value of his love for Cordelia to a similar facile paraphrase suggests that the desirable relationship between ethical affirmation and the sense of the tragic in drama or fiction is far more complex than that specified as immutable law, either by the twentieth century's "tragic vision" or by the seventeenth century's "poetical justice," though either relationship may indeed be present in a large number of good tragedies. More important for my purpose in this paper, *both* concepts imply serious questions about the very nature of tragic catastrophes and about the degree to which tragic actions are defined as such by their endings.

The most perceptive discussion of these matters is, I think, contained in the following passages:

> [Shakespeare's] is the only Lear to come to an unhappy end; the Lears of the other versions have their kingdoms restored, and die of old age. Why must we have *this* ending. Is it made necessary or probable by the antecedent action? It is not. As a matter of fact the catastrophe *seldom* is in the great tragedies of Shakespeare. What in the plot necessitates that Emelia should come too late to save Desdemona? Hamlet's death wound, poisoned though the sword is, is a mere possibility of combat. The

> defeat of Cordelia's forces is the mere fortune of war, and nothing prevents Edmund from speaking in time to save Cordelia. The catastrophe is no more probable than its contrary; and yet we must have the unhappy ending. Why? Because it is an emotional necessity.
>
> But again we may ask *why?* ... let me simply say that in every true tragedy the audience is compelled to transcend a *lower* set of moral values to a *higher*; it is compelled to fear and pity, for instance, only to acknowledge in the end that in a higher judgment there are worse evils than those it has been fearing and pitying; and by confronting great misery it has learned, momentarily at least, something of the great conditions on which human happiness truly depends, and something of the high dignity of which man is capable. ... Frequently in Tragedy—in Lear, for instance—the tragic hero himself experiences that transcendence of values, and his merest acknowledgment of that experience is in itself a human triumph. ... Lear must forget royal pride and the stings of ingratitude and all else, and realize the supreme value of love; he must put by his kingship and all the world, gladly, for the sake of his loved daughter; and then he must learn the value of love again as only loss can teach it; and so Cordelia must die. Her effort to save Lear, then, must be in vain. ...[10]

If these observations are even close to being accurate and the catastrophes in good tragedies may satisfy the demands of "emotional necessity" rather than those of literary or naturalistic probability of action, then at least one further inference would seem strongly warranted: we must read or see any such tragedy *as* a tragedy long before the catastrophe is actually represented, and, probably, before we even know the precise shape it is to take; otherwise there is no possible reason for the catastrophe to *become* an emotional necessity. It may even be the case that a given fate for any character or characters is revealed as a catastrophe by the identical pattern that made it an emotional necessity. (If the ending of *Tom Jones* were lost, Tom's plight in prison where, among other horrors, he seems doomed to hang, would still be interpreted as a temporary bar to promised fulfillment rather than as a tragic catastrophe, even though Tom is threatened by a fate which, considered apart from the comic pattern of the novel, would be perfectly appropriate for the catastrophe of a tragedy.)

These assertions are both complicated and abstract, but perhaps I can clarify them somewhat by posing a brief sequence of admittedly rhetorical questions: Does anyone read *The Eumenides* as a comedy because Orestes is finally freed of his madness, because justice is brought to Athens, and the curse of the house of Atreus is at last removed? For that matter—though it may indeed have vitiated somewhat the force of the last scene—did eighteenth-century audiences watching Garrick playing Tate's version of Lear react to the hero's torments as they did to those of Tom Jones comically imprisoned, threatened with loss of his beloved Sophia, with execution, and with eternal damnation for committing murder and incest? But, if the answers to these questions are negative—and obviously they are—why should a moral victory or even an absolute affirmation of the tragedian's positive values destroy the effect of tragedy?

To experience a work as tragic, serious, or comic is, after all, never the consequence of a mere increment of consistent local effects. Instead, the intuited pattern—the synthesizing principle—of any coherent action permits appropriate subordination even of ostensibly incompatible local effects, each of which contributes to the full realization of a single power. Writers both of dramatic and narrative comedies, for example, have long been aware that even scenes of intensely represented suffering, when properly represented, will be interpreted only as temporary barriers to comic fulfillment implied early in the work. George Bernard Shaw was critically shrewd as well as correct when he referred to his own *St. Joan* as a special kind of comedy rather than a tragedy: the epilogue is the emotionally satisfying conclusion precisely *because* the play's structure *is* comic. Similarly, though on another scale, Jane Austen was able fully to convey Anne Elliot's suffering in *Persuasion* and, at the same time, defeat pathos by assuring us by the pattern implicit in the first three chapters that the pain would soon dissipate and Anne would receive as her morally serious comic reward all the good things we wished for her.[11]

There is a crucial sense, in other words, in which a literary work is constructed and read or seen as tragic only when a character or characters who are represented as partly or completely sympathetic are portrayed in a plausible sequence of events moving towards a fate that we are *required* to interpret as a significant kind of "doom"—but the significance of that doom, far from being destroyed, may be emphasized by an ending that is a moral victory, as in *Clarissa* or as in *One Flew Over the Cuckoo's Nest*; it can be made especially poignant by the contrasting happiness of a set of related characters, as in *Anna Karenina* or *Light in August*, or even, as in *Adam Bede*, by the renewal of the sense of continuity as the tragic characters themselves live out lives subsequent to their doom in relative prosperity.

Indeed, Aristotle himself never insisted that tragedy end in catastrophe, though he argues cogently that "the critics . . . are wrong who blame Euripedes for . . . giving [many of his tragedies] an unhappy ending. It is, as we have said, the right line to take." That such a defense was necessary surely points to the existence of Macedonian counterparts of Rymer and Dennis. Indeed, even in the offending Spectator 40, Addison attacks the notion of poetical justice with considerable moderation and admires tragedies that do end happily; he writes:

> Terrour and Commiseration leave a pleasing Anguish in the Mind; and fix the Audience in such a serious Composure of Thought, as is much more lasting and delightful than any little transient Starts of Joy and Satisfaction. Accordingly we find, that more of our *English* Tragedies have succeeded, in which the Favourites of the Audience sink under their Calamities, than those in which they recover themselves out of them. The best Plays of this Kind are the *Orphan, Venice Preserv'd, Alexander the Great, Theodosius, All for Love, Oedipus, Oroonoko, Othello*, etc. *King Lear* is an admirable Tragedy of the same Kind as *Shakespear* wrote it; but as it is reformed according to the chymerical Notion of Poetical Justice, in my humble Opinion it has lost half its Beauty. At the same time I must allow, that there are very noble Tragedies which have been framed upon the other Plan, and have ended happily; as indeed most of the good Tragedies, which have been written since the starting of the above-mentioned Criticism, have taken this Turn: As the *Mourning Bride, Tamerlane, Ulysses, Phaedra* and *Hyppolitus*, with most of Mr. Dryden's. I must also allow, that many of *Shakespear's* and several of the cele-

brated Tragedies of Antiquity, are cast in the same Form. I do not therefore dispute against this Way of writing Tragedies, but against the Criticism that would establish this as the only Method; and by that Means would very much cramp the *English* Tragedy, and perhaps give a wrong Bent to the Genius of our Writers.[12]

Surely nothing said here should have been capable of infuriating Dennis; and surely Richardson, who relied so heavily on Addison for his defense, had he been concerned simply with the problem of the victorious destruction of Clarissa, might have rested content with so admirable and admired a champion. But, of course, the concept of poetical justice has much wider implications than those for tragic endings, and indeed Dennis scores some sharp points when he claims, on Christian grounds, that arguments about justice in a Christian afterlife are irrelevant to the tragedian since he is not God and is not creating the world but is a poet and must follow the rules of poetry to create good tragedy. He scores still more heavily, I think, when he points out that many of the best tragedies that Addison had named as ending unhappily did actually follow the laws of poetical justice, since, in fact, the tragic hero was punished for moral culpability, just as Aristotle, as interpreted by Horace, as interpreted by Rapin, as interpreted by Rymer, as interpreted by Dennis, had always insisted.[13]

The real problem for Richardson was that in writing the first tragic novel in English he had indeed shown his heroine making an irreversible blunder extremely early in the action. But, as Hardy, Conrad, and Dostoevsky were to do in later centuries, he had used every one of his considerable stocks of creative narrative devices, including the protagonist's own self-blame, to transmute what might have been seen as tragic choice into the illusion of tragic inevitability No sensitive reader could react to her running off with Lovelace, despite the supposed evil of such an act and despite the subsequent insights into her own sexual motives, as anything but external coercion. As a consequence, her "unjust" suffering was prolonged and especially emphasized as mental torment precisely to the degree Richardson had become adept at using his epistolary techniques to reveal internal states of consciousness. This practice not only defied the laws of "poetical justice" but in fact threatened to reduce the heroine to that crushed worm that Aristotle—without the help of the commentators quoted above—had warned us about. To make things worse, or better, Richardson had indeed portrayed Clarissa making a sequence of crucial choices but also represented her—again with consummate narrative skill—making not only the "right" ethical choice in each instance but the very one designed to raise her virtues in our estimation from mere domestic goodness to tragic nobility as it moved her towards tragic destruction.

It may be useful to see, as only a random example, how Richardson himself viewed one major choice. Clarissa can theoretically insist upon her inheritance and therefore become free of the pressure to marry Solmes, the pressure to deal with Lovelace at all, and certainly the pressure to marry him. The advocate of this decision—at a number of crucial points in the action—is Anna Howe, represented not as she frequently is, at her best, but as she is when, through her very liveliness, realistic attitudes, and vulgarity, she is made a foil to Clarissa's nobility; indeed, if we may judge from Richardson's letters, heaven help even his most ardent admirers who misunderstand Miss Howe's role or who find fault with Clarissa in anything but her correspondence and unwilling flight with Lovelace. In 1752, for example, he wrote to Sarah Chapone, "Well, Dear Madam, do you observe, that I 'designedly drew Clarissa with some Defects in Judgment, and that even in palpable Cases, in order to give an Air of Probability to the Character.' And I have made her ever ready to point out, and accuse herself of those Faults."[14] But Clarissa's fault is limited in the letter only to her undertaking a correspondence with Lovelace, and even here is completely mitigated by Richardson's reminder that the correspondence was continued

> (for prudential Reasons, as supposed, and for the Sake of preventing Mischief from so high a Spirit if provoked) with the Connivance of her too timid Mother; which she never, however, pleads in her own Behalf, when matters become arduous tho' her Mother was afraid she would. She was too noble a Creature to involve her Mother in Difficulties, tho' in her own Defence,

and tho' her Mother tamely deserted the just Cause of her Child. She charges herself with this Fault, I think very exemplarily in the Woodhouse—when surprized and terrified at finding from behind the Wood, a Man coming towards her, who proved to be Lovelace.—"O thought I, at that Moment, the Sin of a prohibited Correspondence."[15]

But, alas, for poor Mrs. Chapone, she had discovered other faults in the heroine, such as the virtuous refusal to demand her own estate and here, Richardson responds:

> ... it was a pretty Piece of Advice, was it not, Madam, in Miss Howe, for a Clarissa to follow, in the *early* time of the Misunderstanding, to lay Claim to Independence, though under Age; to take Possession of her Grandfather's Estate, ousting her Father's Agents; to shine away in her Chariot, and to shut her Gates against those of her own Family, who would not be willing to submit to the advised Independence. Upon the whole, we may say, That if Clarissa was not fit to be her own Judge in this Case, Miss Howe was much less fit, and Clarissa would have been much less excusable had she followed her Advice.[16]

And indeed, though Richardson could be kind and admiring in his portrait of Anna Howe, both in the novel itself and in his comments about her later, his charity and admiration disappeared when any of his correspondents failed to realize the extent to which her function as a good, lively girl, morally inferior to the heroine, was to ennoble Clarissa even more. In the same letter, he takes Mrs. Chapone to task:

> ... let me ask you, Madam—Don't you think too highly of Miss Howe's Character? Surely it has great Blemishes as well as Beauties. Clarissa loves her, yet blames her. She wanted Generosity to the Man she intended to have. She and Lovelace, tho' nobody else, treated him so ludicrously. ... Was she not as inferior in true Courage to Clarissa, as in Meekness? ... But Clarissa is a Heroine: And by her Meekness where neither her Virtue nor her Honour, nor her Friendships, nor her Piety were concerned; and her Courage where they were; she showed *that* Magnanimity, which ever will be the Distinction of a true Spirit.[17]

If one is writing the first tragic novel in English during an age that takes its poetical justice seriously, this is obviously not the attitude to take towards a heroine that must be hectored, forced into not-so-subtle captivity, drugged, raped, rejected by all she has most loved, and then, mercifully, buried. And, after all, it was Richardson who attempted to console Aaron Hill for his disappointment over the rejection of *Merope* by reminding him "that it is necessary for a genius to accommodate itself to the mode and taste of the world it is cast into, since works published in this age must take root in it, to flourish in the next. . . ."[18] What consolation might our century offer the printer who thought he had "created a new species of writing" that was "more than a novel or Romance," and was "of the tragic kind" were he to read the evaluation of his *Clarissa* by so sensitive a critic as Joseph Wood Krutch:

> . . . Clarissa became above all else the model for sentimental fiction, by which term we mean here to denominate that vulgar sort of demi-tragedy produced when goodness is substituted for greatness as the necessary qualification of the hero and when, as a result, the catastrophe reveals him, not going down in rebellious defeat, but tamely acquiescent to the forces which destroy him. . . . All the supremely great artists have instinctively avoided this pattern and the sort of satisfaction it gives to an audience, but the essentially vulgar soul of Richardson felt its way slowly but unerringly towards it.[19]

II

In our day, the literary historian has been most persuasive in Richardson's defense. The writings of Alan D. McKillop[20] and Ian Watt,[21] even without support from more recent studies, are sufficient to replace the image of *Clarissa*'s origin as that of "a vulgar soul [feeling] its way slowly but unerringly towards" a debased form of sentimental fiction with a picture of a conscious artist employing profound aesthetic intuition to create major innovations in novels which, nevertheless, reflect literary conventions and social needs of his own time. The sense of Richardson's literary consciousness and his innovative use of literary convention is reinforced in studies by Frederick Hilles[22] and Arthur Sherbo,[23] to mention only two. And, more recently, Shirley Van Marter has painstakingly detailed and perceptively explained the enormous number of crucial and frequently brilliant alterations Richardson made in—among others—the last edition of the novel, not only, as is sometimes suggested, for the sake of improved moral instruction, but for clearly conceived and realized aesthetic ends.[24]

When, inevitably, Krutch's critique was reinforced by the latest psychoanalytic perversion, which relates Richardson's artistic efforts less to the tragedian's art than to the sadist's fantasy, a number of fine historical scholars and critics came quietly and convincingly to Richardson's rescue. Carefully reading Richardson's novels, postscripts, and letters, John Dussinger has shown the novelist's reliance on Rapin's interpretation of Aristotle, on Philip's *The Distrest Mother*, on Rowe's *Fair Penitent*, on Otway, and on others, so that his ironic conclusion seems quite convincing: "The inescapable pornography of Richardson's style, more obviously pronounced in *Clarissa* than in *Pamela* or *Sir Charles Grandison*, may perhaps reflect the sadistic perverseness of a constitution wracked with nervous disorders; but it seems just as likely, and more relevant to the literary historian, to be an inherited characteristic from the author's early interest in drama."[25] In turn, William Farrell's stylistic studies neatly demonstrate that Lovelace's writing is in the courtly love letter tradition, and show that the heroine "resists his advances in the pathetic language of contemporary 'she-tragedy.' "[26]

Most recently, in an essay on "Aspects of Sentimentalism in Eighteenth-Century Literature," Arthur Friedman presents a convincing explanation of how sentimental expectations may inform us about eighteenth-century audiences' pleasure in a number of ostensibly very different types of literature. Among others he deals fully with Rowe and Lillo—both very important to Richardson—and as he explains the sentimental effectiveness of each play, he is able to explain quite fully what he considers the far more important and permanent aesthetic value of the Christian catastrophe of Clarissa. He quotes from the following letter by Edward Moore about the narrative of Clarissa's death:

> Whoever will take the Trouble to question his own Feelings, will learn that Joy has a much greater Share in his tears than Sorrow. The Distresses of a Lear, however undeserved or strongly painted, will affect an Audience with no other Passion than Terror; and if Clarissa, innocent as she was, had lingered in Torments and died without Hope, the Reader had been frozen and not melted. It is her noble forgiveness of Injuries, her Humanity, her Friendship, her Sweetness of Mind, and above all the Praises which are bestowed upon her that compell Tears, and not that we have lost her.[27]

Friedman concludes, "If Moore was able to shed tears of joy at the release by death of the angelic Clarissa, he must indeed have found the novel the perfection of sentimental fiction."[28]

Surely Friedman is correct and has shown us a crucial sense in which Richardson, paying his debt to a literary tradition of his own century, created one of the few great ornaments of that tradition. Yet tracing the origins of *Clarissa* back to respectable and viable literary conventions of its own day cannot do complete justice to the extent of Richardson's accomplishment: in creating a new kind of tragic action in which those literary conventions, incorporated in narrative rather than dramatic devices, became the virtues of an emotionally powerful literary "whole," Richardson initiated the tradition of the tragic novel in English.

What he had recognized far more clearly than his critics was that, if one were to do justice to the resources of narrative rather than to those of drama, one would not necessarily present a character's psychology through a sequence of inept choices that reveal his moral being as they move him towards destruction. Since narrative offers special resources of technique to avoid presenting a character as tragically deficient, reduced through unjust suffering to a crushed worm, the degree of the complicity of a tragic hero in his own doom through inadequate choices could be remarkably de-emphasized, or perhaps even ignored. The consequence of such recognition was the creation of an especially moving kind of tragic experience in which an inevitable but undefined destruction is fully assured for a sympathetic character as the consequence of a terrible but psychologically blameless blunder. In such a context, the tragic action can be developed through the protagonist's suffering in a plausible progression towards an increasingly less shadowy doom, by means of a sequence of choices that gradually reveal those that seem to promise temporary felicity as ethically inferior to those that ensure a form of destruction that must not be interpreted as being the result of a neurotic desire for death. Under such circumstances, the emotionally satisfying conclusion of the action is likely to be one in which the realized form of catastrophe stresses simultaneously the sense in which the character's fate is the inevitable destruction promised by the initial "blunder" and the sense in which the catastrophe is nevertheless the ethical victory foreshadowed by the complex but essentially "correct" ethical choices the protagonist has become capable of making as a consequence of revealed suffering during the middle parts of the action. Though even subtle variations of this pattern may equally violate the demands of "poetical justice" and of "the tragic vision," one finds magnificent concrete realizations of the humanly moving potentialities of such a tragic pattern in important novels of both the nineteenth and twentieth centuries. One need only touch upon a few of them to see the viability of the "new" tradition for the future of narrative tragedy.

Surely it is no accident that Thomas Hardy, always appreciative of the value of Richardson's sense of the architecture of tragedy, explicitly warns the reader of *Tess of the D'Urbervilles* that his "pure woman" will suffer in the opening chapters a fate usually reserved for the final catastrophe of tragedy.[29] In turn, the grotesque but powerful final night of satisfaction for Tess, still the pure woman but now a murderess as well, is a unique realization of the dual emphasis embodied in the ending of *Clarissa*, and stands in a similar relation to the intense suffering of the middle sections.

Again, it is as much to the complex demands that must be satisfied in creating a moving tragedy of this order as it is to any particular belief about the limitations of human knowledge that we owe many of Conrad's brilliant narrative experiments in *Lord Jim*. Marlowe may not enter the scene until the initial narrator has so fully revealed the internal consciousness of the callow, romantic boy that, given the conditions on the *Patna*, we are forced to regard

Jim's leap both as a psychological inevitability and as an act that ensures his still undefined but immutable doom. Only after what might have been seen as tragic choice has been transmuted into an illusion of an immutable tragic blunder can Marlowe's attempt to reconcile his disgust at Jim's fall and his perception that, despite it, Jim "is one of us" convey the significance of Jim's doom so forcefully that even the multiple ethical doubts raised about his sacrifice only increase its emotional value as a complex and richly significant tragic catastrophe.[30]

Such tragedies of the psychologically inevitable and ethically forgiven blunder are closely related to another sort, in which the blunder itself is replaced by elements of thought that convey a strong sense of a fictional universe intrinsically destructive. In such a universe the protagonists' ethically positive choices are seen as the cause of what is rich and fruitful in their lives and, simultaneously, as the complete assurance of their destruction. So, for example, many intelligent and sensitive readers not intellectually wedded to pre-conceived notions of tragic principles have been deeply moved by the tragedy of suffering realized in *A Farewell to Arms*, in which Frederick Henry survives the disastrous retreat from Caporetto, and escapes from Stresa, only to watch Catherine, remote from the chaos of war, plausibly die giving birth to their child, leaving the hero "desolate and alone in a strange land." No traditional literary probability operates here, nor does one discern any obvious victory, except for the magnificent emphasis of the immutable value of what has been lost in Catherine's death and the increased significance of that death in the hero's dignified but intense sense of loss. Nor is there any sense of culpable complicity of choice. Destruction is our common destiny, but it happens sooner to those particularly good or especially beautiful. Yet, neither Henry nor Catherine are crushed worms, for somehow Hemingway's grim vision, embodied in a variety of narrative techniques that border on lyrical modes of conveying strong feeling, has ensured the persistence of the value of their love in an otherwise meaningless universe that ensures its destruction.

Or, to end with a more recent example of an experiment in narrative tragedy, we might recall Ken Kesey's popular novel *One*

Flew Over the Cuckoo's Nest. An odd, even a grotesque, tragedy, as rich, in parts, with bitter laughter as with the more dolorous emotions. Narrated by a speechless Indian in a madhouse run by a terrifying and potentially castrating Big Nurse, the novel represents the protagonist MacMurphy making a sequence of choices that lead to the lobotomy that is his destruction. But each choice that leads him closer to that inevitable doom is precisely the choice that is deemed desirable; each choice that temporarily delays that doom is momentary weakness, understandable but nevertheless ethical cowardice. In short, Kesey absolutely reverses the requirement that in a good tragedy, characters, preferably great ones, should by their acts—that is, by the revealed choices that substantially define their characters—become sufficiently complicit in their own destruction to prevent the sheer horror implicit in the vision of a blameless human being, worm-like, crushed, defeated. Instead, Kesey relies on the reactions of the narrator, mad, silent Chief Bromden, and on the manner in which he relates the effect of MacMurphy's destruction upon the other "psychopaths." The protagonist's monstrous doom is consequently seen as a victory, and his human quality, though in all conventional ways mundane, unlovely, self-seeking, as one we must newly conceive of as great.[31]

Indeed, begin where one will, with Sophocles or Ken Kesey, with Aristotle or Murray Krieger, all trails to comprehension of the forms that tragic novels were to take lead backwards or forwards to Richardson's remarkable achievement in *Clarissa*; and *Clarissa*, I would like to argue, finally, is not merely a work with local effects so powerful and with accidental psychological revelations so moving that for their sake we forgive its formless prolixity and its occasional descents into the maudlin. On the contrary, Richardson's objections to Prevost's omissions in the French translation, and his decision to restore passages he had himself painfully deleted, were completely justified. Omit for example, as Prevost did, such a scene as Belton's despondency and death, or Anna Howe's lamentation over the corpse of her beloved friend and it is true that one does not destroy anything that eighteenth-century criticism would consciously have recognized as unity of action, or unity of anything else—one simply reduces the full effect of the tragedy to the exact degree that he reduces the significance of the heroine's doom. Even so sensitive an abridgment as that by George Sherburn alters subtle variations of consciousness both in Clarissa and Lovelace, and reduces the necessary sense of the incredible struggle that Clarissa must undergo at the end to prepare herself to leave a world whose attractions—despite her suffering —remain a threat until the very end of the seventh volume, almost before her death. (The omissions actually increase the sense of the maudlin.)[32] To understand the force of that threat and the heroism of Clarissa's victory is to see her domestic goodness raised to pathetic greatness; but the force of her final heroism requires us to feel the initial strength of her love for her implacable family, her horror of her father's curse, and a desire for reconciliation with them so strong that it becomes a major cause of Lovelace's destructive jealousy, as he recognizes quite accurately that, however attractive she finds him, she would in fact prefer reconciliation with the "implacables" to life with him. In Volume IV, for example, the cruel Tomlinson trick actually fools Clarissa into a belief that such a reconciliation is nigh; it is Lovelace who quotes the phrases of her ecstatic happiness:

> "You see me already," said she, "another creature. You know not, Mr. Lovelace, how near my heart this hoped-for reconciliation is. I am now willing to banish every disagreeable remembrance. You know not, sir, how much you have obliged me. And oh Mr. Lovelace, how happy shall I be, when my heart is lightened from the all-sinking weight of a father's curse! When my dear mamma—you don't know sir, half the excellences of my dear mamma! and what a kind heart she has when it is left to follow its own impulses—when this blessed mamma shall once more fold me to her indulgent bosom! . . . And you, Mr. Lovelace, to behold all this, and to be received into a family so dear to me, with welcome—What though a little cold at first? When they come to know you better, and to see you oftener . . . all will be warmer and warmer love on both sides, till every one will perhaps wonder how they came to set themselves against you."[33]

Of course, Captain Tomlinson is merely Lovelace's tool, Patrick M'Donald, and while Clarissa's transport is sufficient again to arouse admiration and love for her virtue in the complex Lovelace, marriage to him has already been so unpleasantly represented to the reader by a number of powerful narrative devices that even if he were to be converted, their union would be an undesirable debasement, not a reward, for Clarissa Harlowe. Lest the reader momentarily forget this, Richardson uses a device which he introduces in the first volume and continues to employ until Clarissa is actually raped: occasionally the pairing of the two is made to seem remotely possible or sufficiently desirable to destroy the tragic expectations fully established by the end of Volume II, as it does, for example, when Clarissa reveals an ability to love the antagonist, immediately after Lovelace reflects upon the Rosebud episode—the incident that had revealed in him not only latent charity and an actual reservoir of goodness, but also special conditions for the exercise of magnanimity, charity, and even continence. In circumstances like these, Richardson makes it clear that such traits are exactly those Clarissa Harlowe must frustrate by exercise of her own peculiar virtues. Accordingly, just before the innocent girl expresses her joy at the prospect of being accepted once more by her family, in the letter from which I have just quoted, Lovelace says he wishes she "would lay aside, like the friends of my uncontending Rosebud, all thoughts of defiance—would she throw herself upon my mercy. . . ." Of course the context makes it clear that she will not, should not, and cannot. But the main point I would like to focus attention upon here is the transport of happiness at the mere prospect of reconciliation with her family, reinforced by her feeling that Lovelace can become part of their world. She continues in every possible way—thus increasing Lovelace's jealousy, discomfiture, and desperation—to attempt to obtain her family's forgiveness until she is raped. After that point, all she begs for— and beg she does—is the removal of the curse and, later, a father's blessing before death. She is reluctantly granted the first and brutally denied the second. Gradually, as she becomes more certain of her death, she comes, in an extremely subtle shift of consciousness, to wish the blessing more for their own sake than for her own. But, finally, her consciousness subtly alters again, and when her kind physician offers to send for her family,

Clarissa *and the Tragic Traditions*

she paused; and at last said, "This is kind, very kind of you, sir. But I hope you do not think me so perverse, and so obstinate, as to have left until now any means unassayed which I thought likely to move my friends in my favour. But now, Doctor, said she, I should be too much disturbed at their grief, if they were any of them to come or send to me: and, perhaps, if I found they still loved me, wish to live; and so should quit unwillingly that life, which I am now really fond of quitting, and hope to quit as becomes a person who has had such a weaning-time as I have been favoured with."[34]

Richardson's tragic novel did not merely have a unified "fable" that allowed him to include moving incidents—the positive counterparts of sentimental rants—but an integral plot to which all these techniques, innumerable details, and extremely subtle shifts of consciousness were effectively subordinated, and in which they were necessary qualitative parts. In other words, I am attributing to the ostensibly rambling volumes of *Clarissa* the kind of "artistic integrity" or "synthesis" or "sense of wholeness" that we normally reserve for our critical appraisal of novelists like Henry James. Admittedly, bibliographical knowledge of the painfully shrunken, then restored, then further expanded versions of *Clarissa*—including some alterations and additions undertaken in response to friends' criticisms—make that claim seem unlikely. Yet it does seem to accord with the intuition of no less a critic than Dr. Johnson who, shortly after he received his copy of the greatly expanded and revised third edition, wrote Richardson on March 9, 1751, that he was "glad to see her improved in her appearance, but more glad to find that she was now got above all fears of prolixity, and confident enough of success to supply whatever had hitherto been suppressed." More relevant still is the complex relation of literary conventions to literary principles as new forms develop in ways admittedly somewhat mysterious, but apparently most successfully when a writer's style, stock of techniques, and characteristic interests cease to be the virtues of conventional forms at his disposal and, as a consequence, he "slowly feels his way" towards a new form that is, nevertheless, a unique realization of principles that had always been latent in the construction of—let us say—good tragedies. Not always, but occasionally, an author will in fact develop under such conditions "a new species of writing" in which his characteristic style, interests, and mode of procedure can actually become the viable virtues of the new form.

Let us imagine, for example, that when Shakespeare started to write *Macbeth* he had not become aware of the potentialities of the soliloquy—a palpable falsehood—and had, up to this point, written only tragedies in which characters are revealed through choice, statement, or action; internal states of consciousness could not be conveyed except through these. He could not, in other words, write the "tomorrow and tomorrow and tomorrow" speech; yet, a magnificent writer of lyrics, he realizes that such an innovation is a possibility. Now new effects become possible—but to be powerful they cannot result merely from lyric-like musings inserted in just any kind of play—they must become the virtues of that play. He has already had experience—let us say with *Richard III*—in the creation of a protagonist who plausibly commits deeds so villainous that his destruction grows increasingly desirable; when he is appropriately destroyed, the audience receives the aesthetic satisfaction made possible by punitive drama, whose effect, by the way, is quite opposite that of tragedy except insofar as it deals with dolorous emotions. Now Shakespeare creates just such another villain in Macbeth who, doomed by the proclamation of witches, makes choices so monstrous that Shakespeare even experiments with the bloody murder of children either on or immediately off stage—something usually considered a defect of excess in tragedy. But now, aware of a new way of conveying aspects of the illusion of "personage," Shakespeare can use his lyric gift and indeed every other linguistic, technical, and structural device at his masterly command to reveal the increasing intensity of Macbeth's terrible suffering as a consequence of stressed qualities so human—even humane—that the audience will desire his death at least as much for his own sake as for that of the world made victim to his monstrous acts. He has, in other words, suffered a significant doom. The emotional richness and complexity of the tragedy can be seen as the consequence of the humanly interesting and moving aspects of a unique literary experience made possible by Shakespeare's brilliant and profound creation of a new *form* of tragic plot which is, nevertheless, a special realization of principles on which good, bad, or indifferent tragedies have been and can be constructed.[35] Again let me stress the purely heuristic aspect of this example; historically it didn't develop quite that way.

But now turn to something closer to actual history. A printer with a comparatively limited education but a strong Christian moral sense, a hunger for praise, and considerable literary talent has had an incredible success with one epistolary novel. Indeed, he has become respected, admired, and even deferred to as a moral oracle and as an artist by some of the best-known men of his day—and even more their daughters. Can his considerable gifts for creating character and sentiment be employed in a thoroughly moral and serious way to produce a work of greater artistic significance and even greater moral import than his earlier and less conscious effort? Letter writing—actual rather than imaginary—is his avocation, his great love. There is even some evidence that correspondence is for him the most important form not only of amusement but of the exercise of friendship itself. It is natural under these circumstances that any future narrative should be written in epistolary form. The potentialities of the narrative epistle he has come to know very well indeed by this point. He has learned, for example, that the writer of a letter can create a dramatic scene just as surely as a third-person narrator can, and that, in fact, when the effect of writing to the moment is called for, he may actually have to remind the reader, subtly, "Look, reader, I'm writing a letter about what has just happened to *me*, and I'm revealing my sensations about it." He knows also, though, that he must use dialogue scenes as sparingly as, let us say, Shakespeare used the soliloquy, or else the special resources of his medium will seem extraneous, digressive, like a drama wholly the soliloquy of a single character. On the other hand, he has learned that even when a character is revealed through a letter, there are at least two resources for the revelation of internal states of consciousness and feeling. If the character is as intelligent as, say, Clarissa Harlowe, she can sometimes analyze herself and others, and give direct insight into the moral calibre of other persons, or, by contrast, into her own moral fiber. But one of the most effective devices Richardson had used previously *required* that the heroine fail fully to understand herself until the end, and fail particularly to understand her feelings for her seducer, whereas the reader was made aware of her latent attraction to him. Very well, to create the illusion of a heroine less than omniscient is a matter simple enough. First, give her the right correspondent who, though her moral inferior in many ways, possesses a set of traits—not especially admirable—that allows her to see things the heroine cannot. Second, create a correspondence between the hero-villain and others that will enable the writer to reveal things directly to the reader that the heroine cannot know; this might indeed mean giving him—the antagonist—a full personality and a complex internal life of his own. In addition, specially powerful emotional effects are possible if the occasional scene is followed by an epistolary emotional outburst, which in turn is followed by an epistolary analysis, which in turn is followed by an actual dispute between correspondents.

This of course is only a fragment of the knowledge and skills of narrative technique possessed by the writer consciously or intuitively. But still, he needs a noble, serious, and moral plan. A tragedy is almost the inevitable choice—but what kind of tragedy? Obviously one that has an improving moral fable and, at the same time, allows for that other and even greater source of tragic pleasure and profit, a number of incidents which express deep feeling and which, as the surest sign of the moral effect on the audience, lead to tears. But the audience should not weep, should not sympathize, should surely not be morally moved by such evil characters as, for example, have affected them in plays like Nicholas Rowe's *The Fair Penitent*; one's heroine must be thoroughly good if one is to weep over her fate. Still, one deviation from this norm may prove acceptable. The heroine may make a fatal blunder, a blunder that leads to an act in some sense morally culpable, but one that may be represented as primarily a consequence of the villainies of others and that may be seen to result from the heroine's virtues. All her other choices may then be noble, especially if the virtuous choice, recognition, state of mind, emotion is that which ensures the doom—though not the moral culpability—that was ineluctably present from the moment the blunder was made. But her suffer-

Clarissa *and the Tragic Traditions*

ing must then somehow be given as full and moving a sense of significance as one can contrive. A plan can be drawn like that which Richardson actually drew up and sent to Young, who thoroughly approved it. The plan itself is something like the description that Belford is to give when he contrasts the proposed tragedy of Clarissa with the inferior though much relied upon *Fair Penitent*:

> ... here is Miss Clarissa Harlowe, a virtuous, noble, wise, and pious young lady; who being ill used by her friends and unhappily ensnared by a vile libertine, whom she believes to be a man of honour, is in a manner forced to throw herself upon his protection. And he, in order to obtain her confidence, never scruples the deepest and most solemn protestations of honour.
>
> After a series of plots and contrivances, all baffled by her virtue and vigilance, he basely has recourse to the vilest of arts, and, to rob her of her honour, is forced first to rob her of her senses.
>
> Unable to bring her, notwithstanding, to his ungenerous views of cohabitation, she overawes him in the very entrance of a fresh act of premeditated guilt, in the presence of the most abandoned of women assembled to assist his devilish purpose; triumphs over them all . . . and escapes. . . . She nobly . . . refuses to see or marry the wretch; who repenting his usage of so divine a creature, would fain move her to forgive his baseness, and make him her husband: and this though persecuted by all her friends and abandoned to the most deep distress. . . .
>
> Though longing for death, and making all proper preparation for it . . . she abhors the thought of shortening her alloted period; and as much a stranger to revenge as despair, is able to forgive the author of her ruin . . . and is solicitous for nothing so much in this life, as to prevent vindictive mischief *to* and *from* the man who used her so basely.
>
> This is penitence! This is piety! And hence a distress naturally arises that must worthily affect every heart.[36]

Perhaps. Clarissa's destruction, despite the fact that she was not guiltily complicit in her own victorious doom, moves at least some readers to those feelings of pity and fear that only high tragedy is capable of. One wonders, though, about the worthy effect it might have had on the heart of John Dennis, fortunately deceased long before its publication. At least he might have been pleased by the anguish it caused Richardson to marry the skills we enumerated to the plan drawn up for the first tragic novel in English. He had to cut and restore, to add and to answer and to explain, as each letter began to take on a life of its own, as the correspondence grew till it seemed it would never end, as some admirers of *Pamela* failed to read initially with sufficient care to see that, in fact, Lovelace had converted and repented far more than Mr. B. had ever done, but that Clarissa's marriage to him, long before his most dastardly act, had been an impossibility, a nominal worldly triumph (an actual degradation) of far less consequence than the significant and tragic doom that in fact destroyed them both. In addition, Richardson had to learn to create an antagonist who could display many of the virtues of the Restoration rake, from which his being derived, in sufficiently attractive form to make plausible the heroine's attraction to him, yet to convey the sense in which those ostensible virtues could never be exercised towards a heroine with the real virtues of Clarissa. (It is no accident that in the garden from which the heroine is to be spirited by Lovelace, Richardson deftly emphasizes precisely those qualities in Lovelace that have just previously been displayed in his treatment of Rosebud; he can be generous, but only to those who stoop, who acknowledge his tyrannical power over them. In contrast, Clarissa seals her inevitable doom, and our sense of that inevitable doom, when, at the end of the beginning, she cries, "I have no patience, Sir, to be thus constrained. Must I never be at liberty to follow my own judgment? Be the consequence what it may I will not be thus constrained.")[37] And Richardson had to master the extremely complex task of conveying in the middle the sense in which Clarissa's love of life, including her own recognition of her attraction to Lovelace, is revealed only in circumstances that simultaneously indicate the undesirability of her acceding to the only conditions that might lead to apparent felicity. So, for example, Richardson brilliantly creates a scene in which Clarissa, thinking Lovelace is deathly ill, reveals her love to him and to herself, but only when the reader has been fully steeped in the disgusting details of the trick—including chewing a bloody animal bladder—by which he has deluded her. He has had, above all, to learn how to make plausible and acceptable those subtle alterations of sensibility that lead her, finally, to prefer death to any form of life open to her.

The degree to which he succeeded should, perhaps, not be measured by admired conventions of the seventeenth or the twentieth century. The last word should appropriately be given to Thomas Hardy, the greatest English tragedian of his day, who writes of the "artist spirit that [Richardson] everywhere displays in the structural part of his work" and who insists on his "consummate skill in evolving a graceful, well-balanced set of conjectures, forming altogether one of those circumstantial wholes which . . . cause the observer to pause and reflect, and say, 'what a striking history!' . . . No person who has a due perception of the constructive art shown in Greek tragic drama can be blind to the constructive art of Richardson."[38]

Poetical justice indeed.

NOTES

1. Quoted in Donald F. Bond, ed., *The Spectator* (Oxford, 1965), I, 168, n. 3.
2. *Ibid.*
3. John Dennis, "To the Spectator on his Paper on the 16th of April," *An Essay on the Genius and Writings of Shakespear: With Some Letters of Criticism to the Spectator* (London, 1712), pp. 39–42.
4. In his Introduction to *Clarissa: Preface, Hints of Prefaces, and Postscript*, Augustan Reprint Society Publication 103 (Los Angeles, 1964), p. iii. See also Ira Konigsberg, *Samuel Richardson and the Dramatic Novel* (Lexington, Ky., 1968), pp. 88–91.
5. *Selected Letters of Samuel Richardson*, ed., John Carroll (Oxford, 1964), p. 118.
6. *Ibid.*, p. 139.
7. See A. D. McKillop, *Samuel Richardson: Printer and Novelist* (Chapel Hill, 1936), pp. 159–60.
8. Elizabeth Drew, *The Novel: A Modern Guide to Fifteen English Masterpieces* (New York, 1963), p. 50. As an antidote see the important essay by Christopher Hill, "Clarissa Harlowe and Her Times," *Essays in Criticism*, V (1955), 315–40.
9. Murray Krieger, *The Tragic Vision: Variations on a Theme in Literary Interpretation* (Chicago and London, 1966), pp. 193–94. For heuristic reasons my essay stresses overmuch my disagreements with a book that contains some of the most illuminating discussions of tragic fiction yet published.

10. Elder Olson, *Tragedy and the Theory of Drama* (Detroit, 1961), pp. 207–8.
11. I have elaborated on the concept of "literary power" as a kind of intuitive knowledge in "The Psychological Implications of Generic Distinctions," *Genre*, I (1968), 106–15, and in "Golden Birds and Dying Generations," *Comparative Literature Studies*, VI (1969), 274–91.
12. Bond, I, 169–70.
13. Dennis, pp. 38–48. Admittedly my paraphrase is very free.
14. *Selected Letters*, p. 199.
15. *Ibid.*
16. *Ibid.*, p. 200.
17. *Ibid.*, pp. 203–4.
18. *Ibid.*, p. 98.
19. Joseph Wood Krutch, *Five Masters: A Study in the Mutations of the Novel* (New York, 1930), p. 158.
20. Especially his *Samuel Richardson: Printer and Novelist* (Chapel Hill, 1936).
21. *The Rise of the Novel: Studies in Defoe, Richardson and Fielding* (Berkeley, 1957).
22. "The Plan of Clarissa," *PQ*, XLV (1966), 236–48.
23. "Time and Place in Richardson's *Clarissa*," *Boston University Studies in English*, III (1957), 139–46.
24. Shirley Van Marter, "Richardson's Aesthetic Theory and Practice in Variant Editions of Clarissa" (University of Chicago thesis, 1969). But see, of course, M. Kinkead-Weekes' Seminal "Clarissa Restored?" *RES*, X (1959), 156–71. Cf. also T. C. D. Eaves and Ben Kimpel, "The Composition of *Clarissa* and Its Revision Before Publication," *PMLA*, LXXXIII (1968), 416–28.
25. John Dussinger, "Richardson's Tragic Muse," *PQ*, XLVI (1967), 33.
26. William J. Farrell, "The Style and Action in Clarissa," *SEL*, III (1963), 365.
27. Arthur Friedman, "Aspects of Sentimentalism in Eighteenth-Century Literature," in *The Augustan Milieu*: Essays presented to Louis A. Landa (Oxford, 1970), p. 261. Despite one important divergence of opinion, many of my concerns about the nature of tragic endings derive from Friedman's essay.
28. *Ibid.*
29. Thomas Hardy, *Tess of the D'Urbervilles*, "Preface to the Fifth and Later Editions." His additional brief preface, written March, 1912, in which he insists again on the appropriateness of the subtitle is equally relevant to my conception of the "tragedy of the blunder."
30. For a detailed analysis along these lines see Harry Epstein, "Conrad as a Tragic Novelist" (University of Chicago dissertation, 1972).
31. For a detailed analysis along these lines see Robert Victor Wess, "Modes of Fictional Structure in Henry Fielding and Jane Austen" (University of Chicago dissertation, 1970), Appendix i.
32. Many students of my generation were introduced to *Clarissa* by way of

John Angus Burrell's abridgement (New York, 1950), and I fear that even some serious students of the eighteenth century know the novel only in that form. Burrell explains that since the "scenes in which Tomlinson appears seem artificial and forced . . . his scenes and his machinations . . . are for the most part omitted" (p. 364). Unfortunately, the emphasis on Clarissa's love for life and her explicitly recognized hopes for meaningful marriage with Lovelace are consequently omitted as well, while such incidents as those in which Clarissa's coffin appears are given undue prominence which, in fact, they do not have in the full-length novel.

33. *The History of Clarissa Harlowe, complete in eight volumes*, in *The Novels of Samuel Richardson*, ed., William Lyon Phelps (New York, 1902), IV, 287–88, Letter LV. I shall include further references to this edition in my text.
34. *Ibid.*, VII, 297, Letter XCV.
35. This interpretation of *Macbeth* is based on that of R. S. Crane, *The Languages of Criticism and the Structure of Poetry* (Toronto, 1953), pp. 169–74; I have discussed the idea of literary history embodied here in greater detail in my introduction to Crane's *Critical and Historical Principles of Literary History* (Chicago, 1971).
36. *The History of Clarissa Harlowe*, VII, 183–84, Letter LXVII.
37. *Ibid.*, II, 320, Letter LII.
38. Thomas Hardy, "The Profitable Reading of Fiction," *Forum* (New York), 1888. Quoted here from Harold Orel, ed., *Thomas Hardy's Personal Writings* (Lawrence, Kansas, 1969), pp. 121–22.

Symposium: Irrationalism in the Eighteenth Century

Introduction

*Ralph Cohen**

WE LIVE TODAY hypnotized by the imagination of disaster, the threat of catastrophe, and visions of tragedy. This helps explain our hospitality for irrationalism and the ambiguous delight we take in the dark side of the soul. It explains too the recurrent choice of subject among many of the papers given at this conference and the subject of this symposium—irrationalism in the eighteenth century. If scholarship were immediately rather than distantly responsive to contemporary experience, scholars would long ago have made evident the distrust which many eighteenth-century thinkers had for reason and for rationality. Still, it is fortunate that we have our prejudices and our preferences, because some of these, like the preference for irrationality, help us to assess those held by our predecessors. If we have any faith at all in the hypothesis that the eighteenth century has given us legacies, then one legacy must surely be the distrust of some kinds of reasoning. For more than a century, interpretations of this distrust have been categorized as reason versus enthusiasm, orthodoxy versus unorthodoxy or paganism, peace versus revolution, general nature versus eccentricity; and each of us here can continue to add contrasts, antitheses, and paradoxes. But we can recognize that the pairing of opposites, and sometimes the resolution of contraries, belong to a post-Kantian or dialectical analysis of our ex-

---

* Professor Cohen was chairman of the section devoted to irrationalism in the eighteenth century at the Society's second annual meeting. The papers following his introduction in the present volume were delivered at that section meeting. Ed.

perience of the world. This position has been changing, and the evidence for the change imposes itself upon our consciousness wherever we turn. We find, for example, that in multiplying ourselves we subtract from the human race. We find that in reason there is madness, in peace there is war, in eccentricity there is general nature. We are prepared to reject the earlier and antithetical categories because we find that each member of the antithesis is a complex more difficult and less consistent than we imagined. This inquiry into irrationalism, therefore, beginning as I believe it does with the rejection of earlier approaches, is consistent with the assumption that for us the irrational is as accessible as, if not more accessible than, the rational.

Precisely because our experience of disaster prepares us to abandon old clichés about reason and enlightenment, we wish to avoid new clichés about irrationality and emotion. To seek ways of exploring such new interpretations is the purpose of this symposium. The participants have not been given a definition of irrationalism or of rationalism, but they have been asked to define the subject in ways they find appropriate to their argument. If it turns out that there are various definitions present, this procedure ought to be considered a necessary part of our exploration, because, indeed, this symposium ought to be seen as exploratory. Only two of the papers have been read by us. The others we shall be hearing for the first time. Thus we hope to develop a discussion of the subject with you rather than before you.

The Retreat from Reason

Bertrand H. Bronson

LEST I STUMBLE, and because the time is short, I will state at once the propositions I would try to illustrate in what follows. As generalities, they are unlikely to excite disagreement, and the interest must lie in the fluctuations of thought and feeling that differentiate those generations, chronologically viewed.

1. At the opening of the eighteenth century there is a weakening of conviction of the importance of man's personal relation to God the Father.
2. There is a depersonalizing of external nature, from the cooperative universal Mother to universal, unalterable physical laws.
3. There is a shrinkage of assurance of the potency of man's rational powers, no longer seen as "infinite in faculty," yet a keener sense of reliance on them.

As the century passes its meridian, values are gradually rescaled and redefined, roughly as follows:

4. Nature in a "state of nature" is preferred to nature domesticated.
5. Irregularity enforces a lawless appeal that surpasses rational ordering.
6. Sudden irrational conversion and conviction of salvation by faith returns to religion.
7. Emotional assurance tends to supplant the appeal to reason as expressed in logical trains of thought.

It may be laid down as an axiom, as Dr. Johnson would say, that everything had already begun before we realized. In the context of the moment, this truth if pursued would take me back straightway into the seventeenth century, where I have no wish to go, further than to acknowledge that the beginnings are there, Pyrrhonism and all.

About 1700 there was an unusually pervasive sense of the opening of a century as a true beginning: almost the birth of a "brave new world." The shadows and superstitions of the past were being dispersed by Newton's universal light, swept away like ghosts:

> 'Tis well an Old Age is out,
> And time to begin a New.[1]

As Newton had disclosed the laws of celestial mechanics, Locke had found a key to the inner world, which could open the mechanics of the mind—or a clue, a method, if not a key. The new revelations, fortunately, did not require the sacrifice of cherished beliefs. Locke and Newton were devout. God was still Creator and Lord of all, and the natural universe bore witness to His power and glory: "The works of Nature everywhere sufficiently evidence a Deity," declared Locke. "The spangled heavens proclaim their great Original," sang Addison. But now the old ideal system of orders, each hierarchically ascending, and bound together in mutual cooperative obedience to divine command, needed reformulation in less spiritual terms—the political order in Britain having already been reconstituted by the simple stroke of an ax. The new world-view still assumed a Divine Author, but shifted the focus of attention, in Tuveson's phrase, from *why* to *how* He did it.

The prevailing optimism of the age rested in the conviction that the physical universe was based on natural laws which could be discovered—gradually—by man, and understood as being fixed, regular, unalterable procedures; not beyond the capacity of human mentality to grasp as principles, though too vast to be comprehended as a whole, and too complicated to be known except piecemeal; but not supernatural, not outside or alien to intellectual process as we know it. Underlying this confidence is faith—faith in the Creator, faith in the stability of Nature, and faith in rationality as humanly conceived. The supreme expression of this confidence is paragraph IX of the first Epistle of Pope's *Essay on Man*, beginning:

> All are but parts of one stupendous whole,
> Whose body Nature is, and God the soul.

Because of its very lack of philosophical originality, Pope's statement is a paradigm of its century's characteristic attitude toward the Cosmos; it was so widely accepted as to be translated into twenty languages, and into some of them many times. Catholics, Protestants, and deists could join in adopting it, punctuating or footnoting to suit themselves.

But when God said, "Let Newton be!" a part of His meaning perhaps was, "If undisturbed, he will look after things so competently that I can afford to relax." If, in other words, the physical universe was so perfectly organized as Newton had made manifest, it needed no divine tinkering to keep it going—had needed, did, and would need none. This thought, of course, had far-reaching implications that could be chilling. How could man know that he was an object of any concern or interest to a God so impalpable and aloof? It was easy to believe in a divine original, a *causa causans*; but revelation might be *essential* to convince us any longer of our own importance. On the other hand, the deist position was a great simplifier, liberating those who embraced it from a load of worrying theological dogma. The climate of optimism, an inherited feeling-tone common to the age, and not directly subverted by the new world-view, remained emotionally operative.

If there was a slackening in man's communion with a personal God as the Age of Enlightenment began, two concomitants—and perhaps, partly, consequences—were: (1) the elevation of Nature as a surrogate for a present, immanent Deity; and (2) a closer scrutiny of the thinking process. Descartes had failed to break out of the octopus-like stranglehold of seventeenth-century Pyrrhonism to any objective truth ("I thought, then perhaps I was," in Pierre-Daniel Huet's wicked paraphrase of 1689). But Locke had begun to collect the evidence of what seems normally to be going on in our minds, and this appeared to be a hopeful method and a stimulating exercise. Perhaps God had, after all, provided us with the necessary tools for acquiring knowledge suited to existence on this "isthmus of a middle state."

Following the hopeful track, Shaftesbury, Locke's too-bright pupil, discovered that man is naturally virtuous, sociable, beauty-loving. And why not? For proof, one need only consult one's uncorrupted responses to the positives and negatives of experience, and find where one's instinctive preferences lie. For Shaftesbury, to cultivate and possess the social affections completely is, in his words, "to live according to Nature, and the Dictates and Rules of supreme Wisdom. This is Morality, Justice, Piety, and natural Religion." It is only necessary, for everyone's good, to restrain the "self-affections." Shaftesbury, Basil Willey declares, is the *typical* English moralist of the "Enlightenment"; and Hume notices that he first occasions the distinction between two theories of morals, "that which derives them from Reason, and that which derives them from 'an immediate feeling and finer internal sense.'"

Already, then, in the century's first decade, the breeze is setting toward "immediate, undefinable perception" as a more dependable criterion than reason, in moral discriminations as in questions of art. This tendency picks up strength from the academic authority and respectability of Hutcheson, who systematized Shaftesbury's elegant rhapsodizing. Sorley has neatly summarized his work in a sentence: "Hutcheson maintained the disinterestedness of benevolence; he assimilated moral and aesthetic judgments; he elaborated the doctrine of the moral sense. . . ; and he identified virtue with universal benevolence: in the tendency towards general happiness he found the standard of goodness."[2]

To make the emotions a basis of ethics is something like inverting Pope's dictum to read, "Passion the card, while Reason trims the sail." To accept it, one must have faith in natural instincts, must believe in the morality of Nature, and that human nature, as servant of that divinity, is most moral when likest to her. Shaftesbury's impassioned invocation exemplifies the faith: "O Glorious *Nature*! supremely Fair, and soveraignly Good! All-loving, and All-lovely, All-divine! . . . O mighty Nature! Wise Substitute of *Providence*! impower'd *Creatress*! . . . Thee I invoke, and Thee alone adore."[3] The date of this outburst is 1709. It could be part of the youthful Goethe's pantheistic hymn "Ganymed" ("Wie im Morgenglanze Du rings mich anglühst, Frühling, Geliebter!"), the pitch of exaltation is so close. How wholeheartedly Thomson would have endorsed this natural morality I must leave to Professor Cohen to determine. *The Seasons* is descriptive rather than prescriptive; but in general, Nature and God are not indistinguishable in Thomson, however harmonious; and I suspect that he would not have subscribed to the ethics of cultural primitivism. Nevertheless, the doctrine of the moral sense, as taught by Shaftesbury and Hutcheson, was potent, both at home and abroad. It suited an age of sensibility, and increasingly as the century wore on. Anyone who has leafed through the amazing compilation of Margaret Fitzgerald, *First Follow Nature*, and the equally surprising survey by Lois Whitney of primitivistic popular fiction must realize how inescapable the sympathetic theme of rural felicity soon became.[4]

In contrast, Johnson placed the Golden Age firmly in pre-lapsarian days. His suspicions of hypothetical subsequent golden ages in conditions of pastoral life were confirmed by sociological enquiry in the Highlands and Western Islands, of which he gave a remarkably fair-minded and dispassionate report. Apart from human hardships and deprivations, his reaction to wild Nature deserves to be recalled in this connection:

> Regions mountainous and wild, thinly inhabited, and little cultivated, make a great part of the earth, and he that has never seen them, must live unacquainted with much of the face of nature, and with one of the great scenes of human existence ... ; the imaginations excited by the view of unknown and untravelled wilderness are not such as arise in the artificial solitude of parks and gardens, a flattering notion of self-sufficiency, a placid indulgence of voluntary delusions, a secure expansion of the fancy, or a cool concentration of the mental powers. The phantoms which haunt a desert are want, and misery, and danger; the evils of dereliction rush upon the thoughts; man is made unwillingly acquainted with his own weakness, and meditation shews him only how little he can sustain, and how little he can perform.[5]

Very different was the purely aesthetic response of Gray to untouched natural grandeur. Extremely different were the sentiments and operations on Nature of the landscape gardeners of the age, whether Pope, or Shenstone, or Jago, or Capability Brown, or Repton. Pope had said,

> But treat the Goddess like a modest fair,
> Nor over-dress, nor leave her wholly bare;
> Let not each beauty ev'ry where be spy'd,
> Where half the skill is decently to hide.[6]

In fact, for such as these nature was something of a commodity to be altered at will and exploited to suit man's immediate taste and enjoyment. The point of view was not, any more than Johnson's, indicative of union with Nature. Rather, it was basically utilitarian, and exclusive of objectionable society. Only that part of external Nature was required that could serve as the club-house grounds. There were members privileged to use the grounds for health and pleasure, and others who worked on them for a livelihood, furthering thereby the aesthetic enjoyment of the members.

It is clear that the aesthetic tastes of the members were changing rapidly as the century proceeded. There was a growing appetite for more challenging, more esoteric, excitements than domesticated nature could supply. A clear preference was developing for the irregular—even the disorderly and wild.

A. R. Humphreys makes a startling generalization in his admirable little book on Shenstone: "The attack on geometry is perhaps the most significant fact of eighteenth-century aesthetics."[7] Certainly, the statement could be amply illustrated in the arts of gardening, architecture, and interior decoration. As the decades pass, we can observe everywhere a relinquishing of mathematical rule, exact equations, right lines; and everywhere a liberation of fancy. There is nothing serpentine—or even symmetrical—about a subterranean grotto: "Would not this, Dr. Johnson, make a pretty, cool place in summer?" "Madam, I think it would—for a toad." Crudely put, the movement is from reason to imagination, from rational to whimsical. Simultaneously, the temperature gradually rises, the pitch of excitement increases—more often to hot tears than to laughter.

Symposium: *The Retreat from Reason*

The signs of a will to escape from common daylight are everywhere. Into the Past, through Gothicizing (Strawberry Hill, Abbotsford, Fonthill Abbey) and bogus ruins in landscaping (Sanderson Miller, Shenstone's ruined Priory). "It is not every one that can build a ruin," declares Gilpin, "to suggest Time—Decay—Evanescence of Joy."

> LORD OGLEBY: Your Ruins, did you say, Mr. Sterling?
> STERLING: Ay, ruins, my Lord! and they are reckoned very fine ones too. You would think them ready to tumble on your head. It has just cost me a hundred and fifty pounds to put my ruins in thorough repair.[8]

Into the Distant and Strange: the craze of the 'fifties for Chinoiseries (designs for Chinese buildings; Oriental gardening; Chinese bridges, pagodas, furniture—Garrick's Chinese bed—tableware [china!], wall-paper). To the pursuit of the Primitive, of the South Seas and Savannahs—a contemporary human Past. The increasing delight in irrational forms, in nature, from the Sublime of "mountain gloom and glory" to the less ecstatic Picturesque ("artful wildness to perplex the scene"); in art, the cult of the restless and wayward Rococo. Away with straight lines and right angles—Nature abhors them! Follow the involuted curves till the eye is mazed and the mind takes flight.

Midway in the century came Hume. And, intellectually speaking, Hume is the watershed. Up to him, as Basil Willey has noted, it is possible to hold that Reason and Nature go hand in hand. Although, as Douglas White in his recent book *Pope and the Contest of Controversy*[9] takes pains to emphasize, the emotions, or Passions, in Pope's view of human nature, play a dominant, motivating role; yet Reason, in its function of comparing and judging alternative values and purposes, still serves as a brake on headlong, thoughtless impulse:

> Self-love, the spring of motion, acts the soul;
> Reason's comparing balance rules the whole.
> Man, but for that, no action could attend,
> And, but for this, were active to no end.[10]

Reason's business is "to check, delib'rate, and advise." Its restraint is essential. But now comes Hume to prove that it is utterly impossible to get outside our own perceptions to an objective reality, even so far as to verify in a single instance the relation of cause and effect. "Our reason," he says, "neither does, nor is it possible it ever shou'd, upon any supposition, give us an assurance of the continu'd and distinct existence of body. That opinion must be entirely owing to the imagination." "By the very completeness of his destructive efficacy," as Basil Willey remarks, Hume ". . . showed that man cannot live by Reason alone."[11] And if we are driven to admit the utter inadequacy of reason to cope with the most elementary phenomena of human existence, we must choose one of two alternatives: either to give up our trust in it, or to pretend that the truth is false, and go on believing in the fiction. But if any considerable number of people were actually convinced "that our perceptions are not possest of any independent existence," it is obvious that our confidence in rationality would be irreparably weakened, and that we should at the very least be thrown back upon a greater reliance upon our natural feelings and common-sense conclusions. This at any rate did occur. Although Hume's absolute philosophical skepticism is unacceptable to the normal mind, it cannot but shake our confidence that we are standing on terra firma. And I, moreover, am ready to suppose that there is some obscure connection between the simultaneous emergence of the extreme Pyrrhonism of Hume's treatise, and the revival of religious faith manifest in the tidal wave of the Wesleys' and Whitefield's Methodism. Driven to a complete dead-end, we turn back to escape. As Hume himself writes, "Nature is obstinate, and will not quit the field, however strongly attack'd by reason." If not brute instinct, we must trust the extra-rational, "believing where we cannot prove," and dismissing, like Rochester a century earlier,

> Reason, an *ignis fatuus* in the mind,
> Which, leaving light of nature, sense, behind,

leads its misguided follower on a grotesque pursuit of the dancing vapor,

Till, spent, it leaves him to eternal night.[12]

Intellectual convictions probably played a relatively small part in directing the current of thought and feeling. If we look at the poetry and fiction of the century, we can observe the same tendencies as were noticed in the physical arts: a freer and usually more irresponsible play of fancy, though not yet full-fledged Romantic Imagination; a growing refusal to be regulated by precedent; a desire to range; and a taste for higher seasoning. Instances spring to mind: fiction with an odd angle of vision—a lapdog, a guinea, a sofa; fantastical travel-books and imaginary voyages, St. Pierre's *Paul et Virginie*, Paltock's *Peter Wilkins*; Sterne's psychological capers on prostrate Locke; *The Man of Feeling*; *The Castle of Otranto*; *Vathek*; Gothic romances by the score. In the last-named, the supernatural element, an injection of irrational dread. Patricia Spacks has traced the far-reaching effects in eighteenth-century poetry of the powerful appeal of fear of the supernatural in her significant study *The Insistence of Horror*.[13] She brings out the fact that, whereas earlier in the century the treatment of the supernatural is habitually deprecatory, in the latter half it is made evident that our "secret terrours and apprehensions" of the unearthly cannot be dismissed as unimportant, they are so deeply rooted in the human psyche.

Other evidences of emotional involvement with the past and the distant are of course widespread in poetry of the age. The so-called Antiquarian Revival had important results for poetic practice and theory: Joseph Warton's manifesto that Invention and and Imagination are the chief sinews of a poet, repudiating Dryden and Pope; Thomas Warton's celebration of feudal society as the most poetically satisfying material: "We have parted," he declared, "with extravagancies that are above propriety, with incredibilities that are more acceptable than truth, and with fictions that are more valuable than reality."[14] After this, Percy's interest in the bards and in primitive and early popular poetry; melancholy Ossian; anachronistic Chatterton. Pursuit of the geographically distant was more successful in prose than in verse. But the same urge was behind it as underlay the interest in the past: the

233

perspective of distance from the present-and-immediate excited and fed the imagination. Warton's *Oriental Eclogues*, Gray's interest in Welsh and Norse poetry and poetics, Collins' in Scottish superstition show how the distances, spatial and temporal, interact.

All these manifestations were more or less timid ventures into the unknown, forays on the frontiers of the rational and familiar world. What to do with what some may think the main business of our announced subject, the out-and-out irrational (or the suprarational), I do not know. Smart, in *Jubilate Agno*, quite obviously has crossed boundaries into a country with strange laws, though not too far to be visited by familiar beings. But the light slants from a surprising angle on everything. Take a cat or a mouse as instances. They do not resemble Chaucer's cat and mouse, which obey the habits of their kind, the cat in occupying the most comfortable seat or in chasing the mouse, the mouse in running away. Smart's Jeoffrey the cat is by now too well known to need more than naming; but his mouse also deserves consideration, because his timidity has probably never before been seen in quite so favorable a light: "For," says Smart, "the mouse is a creature of great personal valor." Suddenly we find ourselves in Brobdingnag with Gulliver.... As the monkey replied to the elephant, "I can't help it if I's puny: I been sick."

William Blake is a still more dangerous case, more frightening to me because he seems to be on his way to Olympus, if not already arrived, and I cannot follow him in that rarefied atmosphere. We know, I think, that when he set out on his earthly pilgrimage, his feet were in firm contact with his place and time. We know what books he read and whom he talked to. So that we have good reason to regard him as a phenomenon of his age. But I will not undertake to explain him, nor to situate him within the context we have been considering.

> Non ragioniam dell'uom, ma guarda e passa!

At my commencement, the last proposition was: "Emotional conviction tends to supplant the appeal to Reason as expressed in logical trains of thought." But that Blake speaks with a private "symbolic logic," I do most powerfully and potently believe—on hearsay.

As for Cowper, who might have completed the triumvirate of the transcendentally enlightened, he was—I cannot think unfortunately—not often seized, in his fits of manic depression, with a *cacoethes scribendi*. He summed up his despair in words of blinding *clarity*:

> No voice divine the storm allay'd,
>   No light propitious shone;
> When, snatch'd from all effectual aid,
>   We perish'd, each alone:
> But I, beneath a rougher sea,
> And whelm'd in deeper gulphs than he.[15]

In the end, I suspect, we are driven to rest uneasily in a conviction of the irrationality of the totally rational. And with this point of view we shall find Johnson in staunch agreement. His dislike of scholastic reasoning was inveterate, as we see in his treatment of Harris ("a prig, and a bad prig"), or system-builders like Berkeley ("I refute him thus"), or dogmatists like Monboddo, or brandishers of the "terrific" or "bugbear" style like Petvin ("when speculation has done its worst, two and two still make four"). "Perhaps," as Imlac once remarked, "if we speak with rigorous exactness, no human mind is in its right state. There is no man whose imagination does not sometimes predominate over his reason, who can regulate his attention wholly by his will, and whose ideas will come and go at his command."[16] Although Johnson was impatient with nature-as-guide-ers, with those he called "feelers," and with ultra-sensibilitarians, he never forgot how small a part reason, or rationality, played in the conduct of mundane daily living, or how little likely even the wisest planning was to be justified in the sequel. Man, he insisted, is not endowed with either the faculties or the knowledge to make the wisest choices, being uncertain of the future.

In May of 1778, Boswell had a conversation with Lord Marchmont, some of which he set down:

> I know not how it came in that somebody did not act by reason. "Who does?" said Lord Marchmont. "Do you know the man who does? No man but one in Bedlam." Said I, "By what principle then *do* we act?" Said my Lord, "Why, by a variety of motives: by habits, by passion, by a liability to impressions." He said a brahmin said of human life, "The Creator meant to have a comedy." "But," said Lord Marchmont, . . . "No audience would bear such a comedy." He said our finding that we do not act by reason should teach us to be humble, to remember what we are—poor worms."[17]

Boswell was puzzled; but in the main Johnson would have agreed. Twenty years earlier, he had set down a memorable conversation between Rasselas and his sister Nekayah:

> "I cannot," protested Rasselas, "forbear to flatter myself that prudence and benevolence will make marriage happy. . . . Whenever I shall seek a wife, it shall be my first question, whether she be willing to be led by reason?" "Thus it is, said Nekayah, that philosophers are deceived. There are a thousand familiar disputes which reason never can decide; questions that elude investigation, and make logick ridiculous; cases where something must be done, and where little can be said. Consider the state of mankind, and enquire how few can be supposed to act upon any occasions, whether small or great, with all the reasons of action present to their minds. Wretched would be the pair above all names of wretchedness, who should be doomed to adjust by reason every morning all the minute detail of a domestick day."[18]

Johnson's fundamental distrust of systematic rationality may shed at least a flickering light on his unquenchable hilarity over his friend Bennet Langton's making his will. Neither Boswell nor Chambers, who had executed it, could perceive any reason for for Johnson's immoderate laughter, which Boswell unforgettably describes. Johnson creates an elaborate imaginary picture of Langton's triumphal return to his country estate, bearing his trophy and displaying it as he proceeds, with the appropriate explanatory monologue to innkeepers by the way. He carried this play of fancy to such a pitch of Falstaffian exuberance that his host was impatient to be rid of him. Even then, says Boswell,

Johnson could not stop his merriment, but continued it all the way till we got without the Temple-gate. He then burst into such a fit of laughter, that he appeared to be almost in a convulsion; and, in order to support himself, laid hold of one of the posts at the side of the foot pavement, and sent forth peals so loud, that in the silence of the night his voice seemed to resound from Temple-bar to Fleet-ditch.[19]

The scene has frightening overtones. Such cosmic mirth seems so far beyond the occasion that gave rise to it as to belong rather to a Ninth Symphony, to Olympus, to a volcanic eruption. But one jocular exclamation of Johnson's to Chambers echoes in the mind: "I trust you have had more conscience than to make him say, 'being of sound understanding;' ha, ha, ha!" Is it the laughter of Democritus?

To thee were solemn toys or empty shew:
The robes of pleasure and the veils of woe
All aid the farce, and all thy mirth maintain,
Whose joys are causeless, or whose griefs are vain.[20]

But who is to say whether tears or laughter is the more appropriate?

NOTES

1. John Dryden, *The Secular Masque*, lines 90–91.
2. William Ritchie Sorley, *A History of English Philosophy* (New York and London, 1921), p. 161.
3. "The Moralists," in *Characteristics of Men, Manners, Opinions, Times, etc.*, 2 vols., ed. J. M. Robertson (London, 1900), II, 98.
4. Fitzgerald, New York, 1947; Whitney, *Primitivism and the Idea of Progress in English Popular Literature of the Eighteenth Century* (Baltimore, 1934).
5. *A Journey to the Western Isles of Scotland*, ed. Mary Lascelles (New Haven and London, 1971), pp. 40–41.
6. Pope, "Epistle to Burlington," lines 51–54.
7. Humphreys, *William Shenstone: An Eighteenth-Century Portrait* (Cambridge, 1937), p. 48.
8. George Colman the Elder and David Garrick, *The Clandestine Marriage*, II, i.
9. White, Chicago, 1970.

10. *An Essay on Man*, II, lines 59–62.
11. *The Eighteenth Century Background* (London, 1940), p. 111.
12. "A Satyr against Reason and Mankind," lines 12–13, 24.
13. Spacks, Cambridge, Mass., 1962.
14. *The History of English Poetry*, 3 vols. (London, 1774–81), II, 463.
15. "The Cast-Away," lines 61–66.
16. *Rasselas*, chap. 44.
17. *Boswell in Extremes*, ed. C. McC. Weis and F. A. Pottle (New York, 1970), p. 335.
18. *Rasselas*, chap. 29.
19. Boswell, *Life of Johnson,* May 10, 1773.
20. Johnson, "The Vanity of Human Wishes," lines 65–68.

Irrationalism and Politics in the Eighteenth Century

George Armstrong Kelly

I

THE INTELLECTUAL object had fled before the concept was invented. *Irrationalism* is a neologism coined in the nineteenth century for its own particular uses.[1] Though the denizens of the *siècle des lumières* might flay one another's rational capacities, they found no need for this word (their word was "enthusiasm" or "superstition"). Thus our topic is focused around a linguistic anachronism. But this is a formalistic objection; let us pass on regardless.

If politics had been rational in the eighteenth century, it is unlikely that its pattern would have been broken by a massive upheaval in France with enduring fallout elsewhere. If the thinking about politics that led to the collapse of the *ancien régime* had itself been entirely rational, it is unlikely that so much intellectual provender for future antagonisms, extending even to our own times, could have been harvested.

Once these banalities are stated, we pass to more difficult matters. We may criticize either the timidity or the temerity of Enlightenment political thinkers; but we are faced with a strong common presumption that Enlightenment means the orderly application of reason to the organization and conduct of human affairs.

To be sure, it would not be hard by ordinary standards to find unreasonable people—even mild proponents of unreason—writing about or active in politics in the Age of Reason, through both premeditation and ignorance. The greatest writer of its earlier half, himself a onetime political pamphleteer, "gave the little wealth he had/To build a house for fools and mad," apparently with some conviction.² Mesmer, Cagliostro, the physiognomist Lavater, the Marquis de Sade, miscellaneous *illuminati*, the "*philosophe inconnu*," and the strange entourage of Frederick William II saw the century out. Obscure Gothicists and antiquarians like Gebelin, the boy Chatterton who wrote in excruciating and mimed fifteenth-century language, and the "magician of the North" Hamann clattered around its fringes. Whether or not they were irrational is a matter of argument. At least they were not the Comte de Lautréamont, or Franz von Baader, or Carlyle, or Nietzsche. Their real importance is conjectural. Their impacts on politics are entirely nebulous. In general, politics—and political theory—resisted the more extreme rejections of reason afforded by certain culture-clusters of the eighteenth century. Nobody yet dreamed of a "magic idealism," or of a blending of Machiavellism and metaphysics, or of a social reconstruction supported by "positivistic religion."

No doubt there was a normal cargo of misfits, fools, and fanatics—though rather fewer mystics than usual. But to inventory that cargo is not as interesting as cracking the nervous rational solidarity of the thinking man's eighteenth century with finger-exercise psychoanalyses of both practical politicians and *gens de lettres* who were perilously close to the brink. Can one not say that Diderot and Swift glimpsed the pit of the irrational? That Doctor Johnson's melancholy is not entirely wholesome? That Rousseau's logic found its deepest sources in a pathologic? Is there not general agreement that the German Enlightenment was skin-deep, masking *Sturm-und-Drang* pathos, Rosicrucian profundity, soil-and-altar localism, pantheosophic vitalism, bardic feudalism, and filigreed Masonic cultism? There can be no doubt that as we travel east we discover the century's darker features and trail off into something that is less than a kosher Age of Reason. How frail, anyway, is the crust of reason, as Freud reminds us; how close to its surface are the succubi and incubi of the steamy pudding beneath.³

That much can scarcely be in dispute. Local history of the twentieth century alone shows us that the sapience of the Encyclopedia of Diderot and d'Alembert did not belong to the mass of men or to practically anyone who lived beyond the fringes of Edinburgh, London, Paris, Bordeaux, Milan, Geneva, Berlin, and Weimar. The Enlightenment prophesied; it should not have so readily presumed to achieve.

Our main problem lies not so much in the concept of "irrationalism" (which we shall take to mean a faith in hyperintuitive or absurd evidence contrary to ordinary experience and logical inference, and a bold willingness to plan, propagandize, and act thereon) as in the various potencies assigned to its opposite "rationalism," taken in a weak sense, that of a systematic method of thought and action derived from rational precepts and guided by rational judgment.

As we know, there were at least two dozen or more isolable definitions of reason current in the eighteenth century.[4] Reason could mean a transcendental concept by which men attuned themselves universally to their rights and duties; or an instrument by which men serviced their natural passions at least cost; or a historical convergence toward which perfectible humanity was striving; or, finally, as with Kant, the medium in which the mind adequately examines itself and which protects the will from the impurities of transient desire. The ambiguous point of balance is well expressed by Burlamaqui in his *Principles of Natural Right*: "If it is true that man acts only for his own happiness, it is no less certain that reason shows the only way in which it [i.e., true happiness] can be attained."[5] However, just as happiness is a verbal snare (except possibly to the individual taste of the man seeking it), so there are more grandiose than humble, more active than complacent, more public than self-serving uses of reason. There are Christian, Stoic, hedonist, pantheist, civic, and experimental ways of rational discovery and application. Yet it is more the diversity of reason's proper goals than its emblematic integrity that makes political reason an open question in the eighteenth century. A self-stipulated "reason" becomes a field on which duels instigated by diverse parties and involving weapons of the most singular manufacture will be fought. If, on this field, it can be shown that serious strains of irrationalism insinuate themselves or that the combats are themselves irrational, and not merely capricious or dogmatic, then the slogan "Enlightenment" might cloak some irony as well as flashing some truth. However, so long as opponents persist in calling each other "unreasonable," there is presumptive hope of a common reason to arbitrate their quarrels; when they begin to use the epithets "immoral," "mad," or "degenerate," that hope has been lost.

II

Since my subject is politics, I can assume or avoid the abysmal metaphysical arguments opening out before us. Still, taking very wide liberties, I will suggest that we can make some advance on the question of irrationalism in politics by examining a dichotomy of political antagonism, followed by the construction of a typology of three "rationalisms." The dichotomy involves, of course, a clash between a political world in being (usually called the *ancien régime*) and one coming into being; but it is also connected to jarring principles of political realism and idealism that by no means correlate with any simple historical succession, as the following discussion should make clear. To complicate the matter further, this dichotomy lies athwart the three rationalisms to be discussed afterward. These latter I shall designate, for shorthand purposes, as "legitimacy-rationality," "power-rationality," and "habit-rationality." I shall deal mostly with France, because here the issues are most closely joined.

In France, the antagonism between theory and practice was real, but it was mollified by a common culture. The dichotomy is neither between "theory" and "life" nor between "ins" and "outs," but something in between. The Enlighteners were basically public men; but their ideas went beyond normal public receptiveness and debate, and into explosiveness, because of the absence or corruption of the filtering organs of representation and response. Pirate editors in Amsterdam and Geneva could not play the role of a parliament, and neither could poor M. Malesherbes or the merchants of Grub Street.

In a précis one must initially draw a heavy line between rulers and Enlighteners. Were not the practical politics of the period either statist and megalomaniac, or else, as a friend of mine writes with regard to England, "awkward, local, and corrupt?"[6] And did not, *grosso modo*, the "party of humanity" of Professor Gay turn its siege guns on both folklore and the *arbitraire*, having first managed to blast holes in the Church Visible which was protecting both through casuistry, miracles, and the confessional?

All this is broadly true: insofar as the Enlighteners conceived of themselves as a political opposition (a dawning that came late and ambiguously, and only in the wake of the anti-religious and anti-feudal battles), they came to recognize that either public opinion or ministerial cabal could be a springboard. But the Enlighteners were not so much a political opposition as they were angry petitioners for a not always unresponsive royal ear. Had not the discerning Voltaire exclaimed in 1776, when Turgot took over the Finances: "Here we are in the *siècle d'or*, up to the neck?"[7] Did not Diderot confide to Sophie that Catherine II "concealed the soul of Caesar beneath the features of Cleopatra?"[8] Had not Raynal goaded Frederick II: "Dare even more than you have; . . . bring peace to the earth"?[9] And had not Joseph II, who shared a Jesuitical education with the *gens de lettres*, declared in response: "I have made philosophy the legislator of my empire"—with the results one knows?[10]

Still, despite philosophical monarchs, despite the high statecraftsmanship of men like Pitt, Vergennes, and Kaunitz, even despite superior blends like d'Argenson, Turgot, Burke, and Goethe —political thought and action do divide. This is truistically expressed in the contrast *lumières du siècle* and *raison d'Etat*—a perennial problem that all men of thought and action face. Leo Strauss, with an intrusion of his own preference, tells us what this means: "The 'reason of state' school replaced the 'best regime' by 'efficient government.' The 'natural public law' school replaced the 'best regime' by 'legitimate government.' "[11] Let us forget Strauss' "best regime" for these purposes. I think one could argue, abstractly and contextually, that both the other notions possess their own brand of rationality. "Whate'er is best administer'd is best," if the administration contents us, is no doubt just as true as "obedience to a law which we prescribe to ourselves is liberty," so long as the collective *us* does not irresponsibly tyrannize over the individual *me*.[12] Sir Isaiah Berlin has applied these notions in a special form in his essay "Two Concepts of Liberty," where the first idea can be seen as a variant of "freedom from" (negative liberty) and the second a condition of "freedom to" (positive liberty). Perhaps they are even conciliable so long as efficiency promotes the sentiment of allegiance or legitimacy forwards a will to efficiency.

But in the eighteenth century these coexistent ideas tended to produce an irrational *mélange*, and this for two reasons. In the first place, efficiency continued to imply the prerogatives of the state in its insatiable, if limited, competition with other states,[13] and this at a time when domestic pressures were subterraneously broadening; consequently, legitimacy theory tended to deny to the state prerogatives that it had long considered second nature. Secondly, irrational consequences were promoted by a system that contained these opposites without accommodating them. Here, one must agree with Bertrand de Jouvenel that political differences cannot be solved, they can only be "settled."[14] But state power was certainly not inclined to a settlement. Thus rationality in both camps declined toward irrational goals and behavior. Despite "philosophic" inputs, the *raison d'Etat* of the eighteenth century certainly did not tend toward real efficiency. Finances were a scandal. No statesman, for example, knew or cared much about political economy, except the scholarly Turgot and the managerial "younger" Pitt. Rather, politics became a kind of frenetic and irresponsible zero-sum game, distorted by antechamber cabals. "He who gains nothing, loses," Catherine II wrote to Grimm on the eve of the final partition of Poland in 1794.[15]

Moreover, despite the ambiguous defense of Montesquieu, venality sapped the state's efficiency and reason—from the Clyde to the Tiber and from the Guadalquivir to the Don. As the Marquis d'Argenson confided to his journal on 26 February 1749: "[The King] sees and feels the wretchedness of his subjects and how bad choices have given him terrible ministers, bad *intendants*, bad generals: feudal practices, family connections, marriages, personal patronage are responsible for it all, and have distorted it all."[16]

Symposium: Irrationalism and Politics

The *lumières* had their excesses, too. These surely did not consist in the pandering to absolute power at a time when public opinion was weak and the liberal aristocracy barely stirring. Voltaire, Diderot, and others ambiguously "broke" with their monarchs of preference.[17] But there was excess in the compression of the "agenda"—the assumption that something wonderful might happen fairly soon because it had been thought of, without any real attention to social realities or the functional attributes of social habit and conditioning: here only Hume, Montesquieu, and a handful of others preached settlement instead of solution. As Judith Shklar writes of Godwin's problematic tutelage of the Romantics: "The attractions of Godwinism, one suspects, were in its excesses. There is a degree of reasonableness that borders on the irrational."[18] "*Truth* does not make any fanatics," wrote Deleyre in the Encyclopedia.[19] But he was indulging in false confidence. In the end this immoderate attitude must lead to a utopian contempt for all politics. "The whole world, my dear Aristias," Mably writes, "is one huge map of political blunders."[20]

Also, one concludes on sober reflection that, despite their gifted and responsible vulgarization of new knowledge, the Enlighteners scarcely contemplated the ways that their views would be used in a violent political struggle. Would they have sanctioned this as Condorcet did and Raynal apparently did not? Even Rousseau counselled: "Let us throw a bit of meat [i.e., culture] to these tigers, lest they devour our own children."[21] If the final pages of Taine's *Ancien Régime* were not so didactically theatrical, they might have some ring of truth. Madame de Staël, a child of Enlightenment, writes of the "mobs . . . rising from their pestilential swamps,"[22] those same sympathetic mobs or crowds described recently by George Rudé,[23] those masses of whom the Procuror-General Daguesseau wrote to Desmarets on 24 April 1709, saying: "Nothing is so terrible or dangerous as to maintain wheat at an excessive price."[24] Did the *philosophes* know what they were doing when they added a hunger of liberty to the hunger for bread? Did the Gordon Riots suit the philosophical posture of Charles James Fox? Were Mably's *Entretiens de Phocien* intended for Voltaire's servants? In a final analysis, the Enlighteners wished for political continuity. This they did not obtain, but they obtained an increment of immortality in the cultural continuity that the violent transfer of power achieved. The potential of their ideas was never truly weighed by their contemporaries. Malesherbes, the liberal censor who was later to die in the Terror for his judicial defense of Louis XVI, wrote to a noble correspondent in 1766: "A certain number of public events have more advanced the progress of the tyranny of the powerful than the philosophy of equality could pose obstacles to it in a whole century."[25]

Foreign relations and their extreme form, war, of course distinguish philosophy and statecraft very clearly, even though philosophy reduced to practise, after 1792, will merely reassert their similarity. Cardinal de Retz sensed this discrepancy when he wrote that the "rights of common men and those of kings are never better in agreement than when the subject is not brought up."[26] In war, Damilaville wrote, "the happiness of [a ruler's] people is the first victim sacrificed to his capriciousness or to the self-interest of his courtiers."[27] For Rousseau, who judged that "the human race had not been created simply for mutual slaughter,"[28] the matter was quite clear:

> I open the books of law and ethics, I listen to the learned and to the public law specialists. Filled with their provocative sayings, I deplore the wretchedness of nature; I admire the peace and justice established by civil order; I bless the wisdom of public institutions; and, seeing myself as a citizen, I am consoled at being a man. Well instructed in my duties, I close the book, leave the class, and cast my eyes around. I see disadvantaged peoples groaning beneath an iron yoke; the human race crushed by a handful of oppressors; a famished crowd burdened with pain and hunger, with the rich complacently drinking their blood and tears; and everywhere I see the strong, armed with the fearful power of the laws, against the weak.[29]

This is as strong a statement against the feudalism and *mon plaisir* of existing government as we are likely to find in serious literature before the Revolution. Yet even Rousseau, while fearing upheaval, did not wish it. He preached instead an "enclave strategy," and hurled his own structure of reason against the injustice that posed deceitfully as "order," the result of that corrupted state of nature which, hypostasized, had become international anarchy.[30] And while the Enlighteners on the whole showed no taste for modern war beyond a few Roman martial reminiscences, they were prone to accept a balance of power if it could prove an instrument of Enlightenment. Despite his unequivocal treatise *Perpetual Peace* (1795), Kant's earlier essay "Idea for a Universal History" (1784) has a passage in its *fourth principle* that could be read in this sense: "Thanks are due to nature for his quarrelsomeness, his enviously competitive vanity, and for his insatiable desire to possess and to rule, for without them all the excellent natural faculties of mankind would forever remain undeveloped."[31] We reach, then, a point of tension where, far from being abstractly removed, the Enlightener seeks a progressively self-fulfilling humanity unfolding out of a naturally competitive instinct that could be merely regarded as the methodological individuation of *raison d'Etat*. (In fact, since it can be broadly shown that the earlier generation of Enlighteners were more willing to accept *raison d'Etat* as a tool of culture than were their successors, it may be hypothesized that Richelieuvian-Colbertian-cameralist politics has a paradigmatic connection with the mathematical rationalism that had lost its leading role in France by the 1750s. The real war for and against *raison d'Etat* was fought out among the Enlighteners themselves.)

III

This analysis suggests two of the categories in which our interpretation of rationalism will be cast. First of all, there is the rationalism of legitimacy or natural right, a legacy of the previous century, which the Enlighteners, in a variety of ways, desacralized, simplified, radicalized, and even practicalized. Yet few, if any, Enlighteners accepted the full burden of this doctrine without serious historical or prudential qualifications.[32] We do not generally find in the pre-Revolution explicit espousals of what Weber was to call *Wertrationalität*, if only because the fact-value controversy was meaningless to these intellectuals, except to Hume, who having discovered it, dismissed it, and to Kant, in the later stages of his critical philosophy. Yet, in another Weberian sense, we do perceive in the greatest Enlighteners that blend of *ira et studium* which he so much prized.[33] Though the epigoni of Enlightenment had many indiscretions to answer for, their illustrious forefathers usually kept the balance between passion and diligence.

In the second place, we might identify the mode of action that Weber called *Zweckrationalität* with the principles, if not the conduct, of the ruling dynasts. It is not so much that their inherited axioms were disorderly or even in flagrant contradiction with the tactics of philosophy (as Rousseau was bold to say) as that they progressively lost the moral and intellectual capacity to carry through. The degeneration theme of Taine and the elite theorists is not a barren formula for assessing what went wrong in the eighteenth century: even Marxist writers have yielded to its power. If one understands political strategy properly, it was the confusion of *raison d'Etat*, rather than its logical pursuit, that disabled the politics of eighteenth-century monarchy.

But thirdly and finally, there is another powerful species of political thought that can no more be separated from the rationalism of legitimacy than it can be confused with any blind deference to Throne and Altar. If the word "rationalism" is taken in its strong sense, then it might be argued that what I am about to describe is a specious rationalism. On the other hand, the mainstream Enlighteners had lashed out against the "spirit of system" and willingly taken their stand on a messier and more multiple understanding of social fact, indeed a rudimentary social anthropology.[34] What I am trying to convey broadly is a rationalism of experience and *a posteriori* judgment, dependent on an associationalist psychology relieved of its abstract and puppeteering tendencies. Let us even call this conservatism, though that term, too, is an anachronism. In one sense, this frame of thought is carried out in the moderate political conclusions of Hume or developed in new interpretations of man stimulated by travel and archeological discovery. It certainly promoted historical thinking; but, as Cassirer effectively reminded us, the Enlighteners thought historically without ulterior prompting.³⁵ In another sense, it is true, this "rationalism of common sense" could also lead to deferential assumptions that the present should sit at the feet of the past, a past gracious and rich in endowment. It is also true that while this rationalism shared with the tribe of Diderot an appreciation of fossil-digging, it was lukewarm about the severe conclusions regarding legitimacy based on deductive natural right—a distinction of powerful importance. Yet I would propose that Burke's substitution of "principle" for "theory" is not fundamentally an anti-rational or anti-Enlightenment act.

Jacques Godechot, in his interesting study *La Contre-révolution*, finds the Restoration germinating in the pre-Revolutionary writings of Burke, Möser, Herder, and some other figures.³⁶ No doubt the point has some substance. But we must be careful to specify whether we mean the Restoration of Chateaubriand or of Von Haller. And we must beware of retrospective illusionism. Was there an intellectual "counter-revolutionary" who did not find reasons to hail the American Revolution? Had the French Revolution not happened, how would we then judge the "counter-revolutionaries" and trimmers on their previous records? Indeed, as one knows, the Republic of Letters greeted 1789 with almost unanimous acclaim; and the keeping and shedding of allegiances thereafter was a complex affair. If the Revolution felt compelled to decapitate men like Malesherbes and Bailly, who can say, from the intellectuals' point of view, that there was any coherent "counter-revolution?"

In brief, if we draw the curtain at 1788, we see a considerable continuum between our species of rationalism. There is no instigation of an onslaught on reason here. Michael Oakeshott has claimed of the rationalist that "his ambition is not so much to share the experience of the race as to be demonstrably a self-made man [who] believes that to form a habit is to fail."³⁷ In a similar vein, F. A. Hayek has written that "reason, with a capital R, does not exist in the singular . . . as the rationalist approach seems to assume."³⁸ I think that this kind of controversialism applies much less easily to the real Age of Reason than to our retrospective impressions of it. Moreover, it would be absurd to begin calling Oakeshott and Hayek irrationalists. Our net is cast wide enough to capture the "rationalism of common sense."

IV

Before concluding these findings, there is a less tractable problem that needs canvassing. Was not the Revolution itself basically an outburst of political irrationalism? One knows that there is a disconcerting gap between the great Enlighteners and the *déluge*, covering about a decade. What intellectual movements filled that gap? Or, at least, wasn't reason becoming hysterical? From the early 1790s on, polemicists like the picturesque Abbé Barruel argued the existence of a great underground conspiracy of mystics, Masons, *philosophes*, and radical sectarians, driven by mad systems, preparing an onslaught "more numerous and more destructive than the innundation of the Vandals."[39] The ever-sober J.-J. Mounier, no lover of Jacobins or *illuminati*, effectively put the *abbé* down.[40] But of late the historian Robert Darnton has raised the far subtler point of the influence of Mesmerism and medico-cosmological quackery upon selected figures like Lafayette, Brissot, Bergasse, and Marat.[41]

I can only record some brief reactions. Darnton's work in pinning down the nature of these irrational currents and making their political connections more explicit is important. Indeed, given the context of the immediate pre-Revolutionary period, it will be astonishing if these quaint ideas cannot be imputed to others. However, as Darnton himself recognizes and writers like Thomas Kuhn have shown, the competition of allegedly scientific paradigms and their translation into thought-systems is a very tricky business, especially when it is a question of judging rationality. In the second place, again on the basis of Darnton's findings about Brissot's career as a police spy,[42] it may not be so much the irrationalism of these men as their burning desire to thrust themselves into the limelight and out of the *Lumpen-intelligentzia* that accounts for some of their exotic commitments.

Symposium: Irrationalism and Politics

To summarize my argument, then:

The Enlightenment was both rational and irrational in political matters. The collision of its three strains of rationality, in the context of concrete political event, could not have produced a rational solution. Legitimacy-rationality, power-rationality, and habit-rationality could not be contained in a single system, though each had a claim to be called political rationality in its own right.

Why could these three gears not have been made to mesh efficiently? It might be said that *raison d'Etat*, the *lumières*, and empirical traditionalism belong, according to Aristotelian graphics, to the one, the few, and the many in the eighteenth century. However, in the ideological terms of that century, the position of the last two is switched. The *lumières*, the possession of the few, are propagated on behalf of the many; while the traditionalism of the many becomes the ideological resource of another waning few. Perhaps what we have is a paradigm of how oligarchies are exchanged; Pareto somewhere suggests this. Only in England was this contradiction papered over with some effectiveness. Only in France was it perfectly ripe to explode.

When traditionalistic reason with its cluttered venerability is joined on a single plane of action with a radical reason that takes nature as ordering and not as given, as well as with a reason which, though debased by the players, finds its consistent expression in the theory of games, the outcome cannot be a higher multiple of reason. It is not a question of anticipating nineteenth-century obscurities. It is rather that axioms which are rationally extensible in their solitude produce a higher irrationality of conjugation and come to seem irrational in themselves when reanalyzed in the light of public passions and the subsequent historical record.

NOTES

1. According to the *OED*, "irrationalism" is first identified in English in 1811 with reference to the poet Shelley; quoted in Dowden's *Life* (1887). From the mid-seventeenth century on, "irrationality" (originally from mathematics) had been an increasingly familiar word. In French, "irrationalisme" is a very recent neologism; *Robert* cites Malraux's *Les voix du silence* as a reference. However, "irrationabilité,"

meaning "état de déraison," can be located in the sixteenth century (*Littré*).
2. Jonathan Swift, "Verses on the Death of Dr. Swift," *in fine*.
3. Cf. Sigmund Freud, "Thoughts on War and Death," in Joan Riviere (ed.), *Collected Papers*, 5 vols. (London, 1949), IV, 298–99.
4. For a brief canvass of uses of "*reason*," see Gilles-Gaston Granger, *La Raison* (Paris, 1958). For the Enlightenment view of the mid-eighteenth century, see the article "Raison (logique)," in *Encyclopédie ou Dictionnaire raisonné des arts, des sciences et des métiers*, 17 vols. (Paris, 1751–65), XIII, 773a–774a.
5. Jean Jacques Burlamaqui, *Principles of Natural Law*, 2 vols. (Boston, 1792), I, chap. 5, viii, p. 31.
6. Eugene C. Black, *The Association* (Cambridge, Mass., 1963), p. 9.
7. Letter to Condorcet, 3 April 1776, in *Oeuvres complètes*, 52 vols. (Paris, 1877–82), XLIX, 574.
8. Letter, 30 March 1774, *Lettres à Sophie Volland*, 3 vols. (Paris, 1930), III, 250.
9. Guillaume Thomas François Raynal, *Histoire philosophique et politique des établissemens et du commerce des Européens dans les deux Indes*, 6 vols. (Amsterdam, 1770), II, bk. 5, 185.
10. Cited by Albert Sorel, *L'Europe et la Révolution française*, 6 vols. (Paris, 1905), I, 120.
11. Leo Strauss, "On the Spirit of Hobbes' Political Philosophy," *Revue internationale de Philosophie*, IV, 14 (1950), p. 415.
12. Cf. Diderot's typical interpretation in "Autorité politique," in *Encyclopédie*, I, 899a: "The crown, the government, and the public *authority* are possessions owned by the body of the nation, held as a usufruct by princes and as a trust by ministers."
13. Cf. Richard Pares, *King George III and the Politicians* (Oxford, 1953), p. 4: "The Government existed, in those days, not in order to legislate but in order to govern: to maintain order, to wage war and, above all, to conduct foreign affairs. These things made up, in those times, nine tenths of government...."
14. Bertrand de Jouvenel, *The Pure Theory of Politics* (Cambridge, 1963), p. 207.
15. Cited by A. Sorel, *Europe et révolution*, I, 19.
16. Armand Brette (ed.), *La France au milieu du XVIII$_e$ siècle, d'après le journal du Marquis d'Argenson* (Paris, 1898), p. 51.
17. One recent interesting attempt to "preserve" Voltaire from his princely preferences is by the Soviet writer I. I. Sivolap, "Voltaire et le rôle social de l'écrivain," in *Au siècle des lumières* (Paris, 1970), esp. pp. 270–77.
18. Judith N. Shklar, *After Utopia: The Decline of Political Faith* (Princeton, 1957), p. 31.
19. Article "Fanatisme," in *Encyclopédie*, VI, 398a.
20. Mably, *Entretiens de Phocien*, in *Oeuvres complètes*, 12 vols. (Paris, 1794), X, 135.

21. Rousseau, "Observations sur la réponse qui a été faite à son discours," in *Oeuvres complètes*, 4 vols. (Paris, 1959–), III, 56.
22. *Considérations sur la Révolution française* (Paris, 1862), I, 379.
23. George Rudé, *The Crowd in the French Revolution* (Oxford, 1959).
24. Quoted by Gérard Walter, introduction to Edgar Faure, *La disgrace de Turgot* (Paris, 1961), p. xix.
25. Malesherbes to Comte de Sarsfield, 28 November 1766, in Pierre Grosclaude (ed.), *Malesherbes et son temps: nouveaux documents inédits* (Paris, 1965), p. 47.
26. *Mémoires du Cardinal de Retz, adressés à Madame de Caumartin* (Paris, 1912), I, pt. 1, ch. iii, p. 131.
27. Article "Paix," *Encyclopédie*, XI, 768b–769a.
28. Rousseau, "État de guerre," in *Oeuvres complètes*, III, 602.
29. *Ibid.*, 608–9.
30. See Stanley Hoffmann's edifying interpretation "Rousseau on War and Peace," *American Political Science Quarterly* (June 1963), pp. 317–33.
31. "Idea for a Universal History from a Cosmopolitan Point of View," in L. W. Beck (ed.), *Kant on History* (New York, 1963), p. 16.
32. For cases in point, see Voltaire's article "Egalité," in his *Dictionnaire*, or d'Holbach's "Représentatifs," in the *Encyclopédie*.
33. Cf. Max Weber, "Politics as a Vocation," in H. H. Gerth and C. W. Mills (eds.), *From Max Weber: Essays in Sociology* (New York, 1967), p. 95.
34. See René Hubert's study, *Les sciences sociales dans l'Encyclopédie* (Paris, 1923).
35. Ernst Cassirer, *The Philosophy of the Enlightenment* (Boston, 1951), pp. 197–98.
36. Jacques Godechot, *La Contre-révolution, 1789–1804* (Paris, 1961), esp. pp. 56–70, 113–19.
37. Michael Oakeshott, *Rationalism in Politics* (London, 1961), p. 2.
38. F. A. Hayek, *Individualism and Economic Order* (Chicago, 1948), p. 15.
39. Augustin de Barruel, *Mémoires pour servir à l'histoire du jacobinisme* (London, 1797), I, iii.
40. Jean-Joseph Mounier, *De l'influence attribuée aux philosophes, aux franc-maçons et aux illuminés sur la Révolution de la France* (Paris, 1822; first ed. Tubingen, 1801).
41. Robert Darnton, *Mesmerism and the End of the Enlightenment in France* (Cambridge, Mass., 1968).
42. Darnton, "The Grub Street Style of Revolution: J.-P. Brissot, Police Spy," *Journal of Modern History*, XI, 3 (September 1968), 301–27.

Forms of Irrationality in the Eighteenth Century

George Rosen

COMPLEXITIES AND AMBIGUITIES

FOR THOSE SATISFIED by a simplistic tag, the eighteenth century continues to remain the "Age of Reason." Under closer and more penetrating scrutiny, however, the homogeneity which the designation seems to imply dissolves. Homogeneity was no more characteristic of the eighteenth century than of any other historical period. Behind the seemingly serene certitude of the smile of reason lurked complexities and ambiguities that cannot be reduced to any simple pattern or slogan. The *siècle des lumières* was as much the critic of reason as its apostle. Johann Georg Hamann (1730–88), who repudiated all rationalistic abstractions and insisted on the primacy of sense experience and imagination, was the contemporary of Richard Price (1723–91), an uncompromising rationalist for whom "reason . . . is the natural and authoritative guide of a rational being."[1] Yet to view these divisions in the consciousness of the period simply as unrelated polar antitheses is equally superficial and misleading. Both reason and feeling were recognized as springs of human behavior in the eighteenth century, and contemporaries were aware that there were complicated and intricate reciprocal relations between them. As Pope put it in the *Essay on Man*:

> Two Principles in human nature reign;
> Self-love, to urge, and Reason, to restrain, . . .
> Self-love, the spring of motion, acts the soul;

> Reason's comparing balance rules the whole . . .
> On life's vast ocean diversely we sail
> Reason the card, but Passion is the gale.[2]

But when a rupture of the relations between the head and the heart led to a fundamental rift, the ensuing gap opened a way for the emergence of the dark, the weird, and the demonic—in short, the irrational—from the depths of the eighteenth-century psyche. In this sense there is a closer connection than appears at first glance between the tears of Goethe's Werther and the stratagems of Laclos' Valmont. Both exemplify forms of irrationality arising out of a separation of emotion and reason leading to an exaggerated emphasis on the waywardness of feeling or on insensitive rationality as a basis for personality and interpersonal relations.

Illustrative of another facet of the emotional climate of the eighteenth century and its imaginative peculiarities is the cult of melancholy, which distinguishes the later decades of the period, and to which the pleasures of horror were added.[3] The latter tendency reached certain psychological extremes toward the end of the eighteenth century and during the early nineteenth century, especially in France before and during the Revolution. It was an emotional climate which expressed the moral nihilism of men who threw off the bounds and obligations of humanity and sought for extremes of experience in the morbid developments possible to the human psyche.[4]

As one examines the culture of the eighteenth century, it is evident that such instances are not unique and isolated; they are indicative of the psychological make-up and modes of behavior of individuals and groups in relation to the larger structure of social and cultural life. Historical periods are characterized by different sensibilities, that is, modes of feeling shared in varying degree by those living at a particular time. An awareness that the personal and the public interpenetrate within the framework of society must underlie any endeavor to understand these psychological characteristics. Individuals and groups cannot be divorced from the larger institutions within which they carry on their lives, since it is within this framework that their psychologies are formulated.

The way in which an individual in a given historical period perceives his world, the feeling he has about it, depends on his interests, beliefs, and values, on the intricate connections between his inner life, his life pattern, and the specific social and cultural conditions which he encounters in his environment. This characteristic mode of perceiving and feeling, which I call sensibility, is an expression of the way in which the personality integrates these diverse elements.

Such relationships are as complex for groups as they are for individuals. In any given historical period, a society or a group within it may exhibit a characteristic pattern of emotional attitudes. A prevalent psychological orientation of this kind, which by analogy with Whitehead's idea of a climate of opinion can be called an emotional climate, develops out of social and cultural conditions specific to a society or group and is related to its historical development. Numerous individual sensibilities contribute to an emotional climate, and in turn the prevalence of such a complex of feelings tends to stimulate individuals and groups to perceive their socio-cultural environment, the various aspects of society, along certain lines and to act in characteristic ways. But even when an emotional climate tends to pervade a given historical period or society, this does not preclude the presence at the same time of other, possibly opposed, complexes of feeling.[5]

A SPECTRUM OF IRRATIONALITY

The difficulty, if not impossibility, of comprehending the complexity of the eighteenth century as a whole with a few limited phrases or concepts includes as well the problem of its irrationality. In 1762, William Hogarth issued a satiric print entitled "A Medley—Credulity, Superstition and Fanaticism."[6] This attack on superstitious absurdities was called "Enthusiasm Delineated" in its first state, and it had been preceded in 1726 by an equally anti-enthusiastic engraving. In this virulent attack, Hogarth presents among other items a grotesque congregation of men and women in various stages of frenzy and emotional disorder, and a thermometer for reading the temperature of a Methodist's brain. The thermometer, resting on Joseph Glanvill's book about witchcraft and John Wesley's sermons, is provided with a scale which runs the gamut from raving madness through ecstasy and lust to despair and suicide.

Hogarth's association of unreason with extremely emotional religious behavior reflects sentiments and attitudes that were widely shared and that prevailed throughout the eighteenth century. In this vein, Addison informed readers of the *Spectator* "that since Devotion itself . . . may disorder the Mind, unless its Heats are tempered with Caution and Prudence, we should be particularly careful to keep our Reason as cool as possible, and to guard ourselves in all Parts of Life against the Influence of Passion, Imagination and Constitution." He went on to stress that "Devotion, where it does not lie under the check of Reason, is very apt to degenerate into Enthusiasm," which is "a kind of Excess in Devotion," and which has "something in it of Madness."[7]

Later in the century, the alarm aroused by the rapid growth of Methodism produced comparable reactions. Quite typical is *The Spiritual Quixote*, by Richard Graves, a gentle satire on Methodism published in 1773. Intended by its author as "an attempt to expose the ill-judged zeal of a frantic enthusiast," Graves relates how Mr. Geoffrey Wildgoose is seized by the spirit of Methodism and sets out as a saint-errant to revive true Christianity. The stimulus to this course was "a miscellaneous collection of godly discourses . . . , the productions of those self-taught preachers and self-called pastors of the Church, in the time of Cromwell's usurpation." The reading of these works, "some Presbyterian, some Independent, some Anabaptist, some Fifth-monarchy men . . . quite unsettled Mr. Geoffrey's mind; and filled his head with such a farraginous medley of opinion, as almost turned his brain."[8]

Religious movements frequently endeavor to mobilize the emotions in order to intensify the fervor of their adherents or to convert more believers. Many religions from ancient times to the present have done so to produce phenomena of group excitation, states of possession or trance accompanied by physical activity, in order to demonstrate the truth of their doctrines and claims. During the eighteenth century there appeared in several parts of Europe and

America religious groups and movements which found a characteristic expression not only in their doctrines but equally in strange bodily agitations and extravagant behavior. These include the Camisard prophets of the Cévennes in southern France; the Jansenist convulsionaries at the cemetery of St. Médard in Paris; the sect called Shakers; the Great Awakening led by Jonathan Edwards in New England; the early Methodists; the mystical, enthusiastic Russian sects, particularly the Chlysti; and the Jewish sects, specifically the Frankists and the Hasidim of the Baal-Shem Tov, that developed in the wake of the messianic movement of Sabbatai Zevi.

To discuss any of these groups in detail would exceed the limits of this presentation, nor is it necessary. All of them are characterized by a distrust of human thought-processes, of reason, and all had practices which produced an excitement of overstimulated passions, an orgy of the emotions. When adherents to Methodism underwent the "new birth," many indulged in hysterical outbursts which were regarded as manifestations of divine grace. The Journal of John Wesley contains numerous accounts such as the entry for August 11, 1740:

> Forty or fifty of those who were seeking salvation desired leave to spend the night together, at the society-room, in prayer and giving thanks. Before ten I left them and lay down. . . . Between two and three in the morning I was waked, and desired to come downstairs. I immediately heard such a confused noise, as if a number of men were all putting to the sword. It increased when I came into the room and began to pray. One whom I particularly observed to be roaring aloud for pain was J―― W――, who had been always, till then, very sure that "none cried out but hypocrites": so had Mrs S――ms also. But she too now cried to God with a loud and bitter cry. It was not long before God heard from His holy place. He spoke, and all our souls were comforted. He bruised Satan under our feet; and sorrow and sighing fled away.[9]

The Shakers represent another example of emotional religion, of the primacy of belief over doctrine. They took their origin from a religious sect brought over from France by a group known as the

French Prophets, which had developed after 1685 among the persecuted Huguenots of the Cévennes, the Camisards.[10] In 1702 these Frenchmen revolted against their oppressors, but by 1704 they had been defeated, and many, including the leaders, fled. A number of these refugees came to England, where they attracted a good deal of attention and even found some followers, among whom Sir Richard Bulkeley and John Lacy were most prominent.[11] The religious meetings of the Camisards in France had been accompanied by religious exaltations, prophetic trances, and violent transports, and this tradition was continued in England.[12] According to Benjamin Franklin, his first employer, the Philadelphia printer Keimer, "had been one of the French Prophets and could act their enthusiastic agitations."[13] Among the adherents whom the Camisards gained in England was a small group of Quakers near Manchester, led by James and Jane Wardley. They adopted the more extreme beliefs and practices of the Camisards—the ecstatic trances, the agitations of the body, the millennial prophecies, the signs of supernatural assistance in times of trouble. While they still affected some aspects of Quaker worship, participants would more often exhibit

> a mighty trembling, under which they would express the indignation of God against all sin. At other times they were affected under the power of God, with a mighty shaking; and were occasionally exercised in singing, shouting, or walking the floor, under the influence of spiritual signs, shoving each other about, — or swiftly passing and repassing each other, like clouds agitated by a mighty wind.[14]

In September, 1758, this group known as Shaking Quakers or Shakers were joined by Ann Lees, a young woman of twenty-two, who in consequence of a number of tragic occurrences following her marriage experienced a conversion leading to the conviction that her soul could be purified only if she abstained from every kind of carnal gratification. Ann Lees became a zealous member of the Wardley sect, and eventually the head of the group. Except for a few members, the Shakers at this time were poor laborers, mechanics, servants, and housewives. Their exuberant, strange mode of worship led to conflicts with the authorities, to imprisonment, and ultimately to migration to America, where Ann Lees established a permanent center near Albany, New York. The Shakers profited in part from the backwash of the Great Awakening of the 1740s, for western New York drew its population in large measure from the hill country of New England, where between 1740 and 1800 wave upon wave of religious enthusiasm rose and broke at frequent intervals. Many of those who experienced these emotional eruptions joined the Shaker settlements that were organized from 1787 to 1794.

Comparison of the religious behavior of the Shakers with that of the participants in the various religious revivals reveals many similarities. The Great Awakening associated with Jonathan Edwards produced the screaming, trembling, physical collapse, protracted stupor, speaking with tongues, and other phenomena attendant upon religious frenzy and excessive rapture.[15] As already noted, the Methodist revival produced comparable phenomena, as did the Great Revival of 1797–1805 in Kentucky and several adjoining states.[16]

These phenomena are irrational in that among those who exhibit such behavior emotion overrides reason, but this does not mean that they are inaccessible to rational analysis. How to explain these phenomena is a question to be answered on several levels, social, cultural, and psychological. The bizarre behavior exhibited by such religious groups is not accidental, in that it occurs within emotionally charged and explosive situations, under circumstances where there is intense dissatisfaction with existing conditions, and where there is a contradiction between cultural goals and the institutional means to attain them. Under the stimulus of intense desire and yearning and of the tensions that build up, there develops a need for emotional expression and action. An important factor in creating these circumstances is socio-cultural alienation which may be a consequence of repression on grounds of religion, race, ethnicity, class, or sex. Alienation develops where desires and aspirations of individuals and groups are blocked by the absence of suitable channels and means for expression and achievement, by deliberate policies of repression and segregation, and above all where fear, insecurity, and a sense of powerlessness pervade the socio-psychological atmosphere.

Thus, the feeling among the Jansenists after 1730 that "the Church had unchurched herself" was at the same time a recognition that the movement of Port-Royal had met defeat. The desire to transcend this situation betrayed these enthusiasts into fantasy, produced an apocalyptic atmosphere, and led to the ecstasies, convulsions, and other phenomena at the tomb of François de Paris in the cemetery of Saint Médard.[17] Similarly, Hasidism, the ecstatic religious movement which appeared among the Jews of eastern Poland (Podolia and Volhynia) in the eighteenth century was a product of prolonged experience of stress—religious, economic, political, and social—and an endeavor to find a way of supporting the conditions of life other than the unsatisfactory one provided by the official communal and religious authorities.[18]

But religion was not the only sphere of life in which alienation expressed itself in irrational thought and action. In an early diary of 1852, Wilhelm Dilthey attempted an analysis of *Weltschmerz* in the eighteenth and early nineteenth centuries, in which he asserted that this was a period which had inevitably produced a pathological literature. It was a period of individualism, but since the time was not ripe, the striving of individuals to realize the ideal frequently led to a painful and mortal sickness. "This is the source," he said, "from which flow the mortal pains of Werther and Hyperion."[19] Dilthey's reference to Goethe and Hölderlin points to the problem of irrationality in eighteenth-century Germany, which derived from alienation and its consequences. *The Sorrows of Young Werther* is the story, as Goethe wrote to Schönborn in 1774, of a young man "endowed with a profound, pure sensibility and genuine perceptiveness, who loses himself in ineffable dreams and undermines the foundation of his being through speculation, until finally deranged by additional unhappy passions, especially a fruitless love, he puts a bullet through his head."[20] The sentimental, pessimistic mood, the melancholy of sensibility, epitomized by the lachrymose, suffering Werther was not restricted to Germany. Indeed, its greatest devotee was Rousseau, depicted by Byron as

faction with existing institutions, opposition to authority, economic hardships, and nationalistic enthusiasms, emotional unrest, and a desire for socio-cultural change spread among the younger generation of the middle and professional classes.[24] This trend is to be found not only in Germany, but also in various European countries in the last third of the eighteenth century. France, for example, had large numbers of unemployed or underemployed young intellectuals who were ready and available to alter social circumstances. As Brinton notes, "One is struck in studying French society in the years just preceding the Revolution with a kind of jam in the stream of bright young men descending on Paris to write and talk their way to fortune. Mercier in his *Tableau de Paris* tells us how every sunny day young men might be seen on the Quays, washing and drying their only shirts, ruffled and lacy symbols of high social status."[25] Toward the end of the century this unrest found an outlet in revolutionary activism, and a number of rebellious young Germans participated prominently in the French Revolution and its later developments, for example, Georg Kerner and Georg Forster.[26]

But such a course was either not possible for the *Stürmer und Dränger*, or was not attractive to them. Thus, Merck visited Paris in 1791, where he met Jacques-Louis David, who introduced him to the Jacobin Club, which he joined four days after his arrival. Nonetheless, he did not remain in Paris but returned to Darmstadt, where later that year the hopelessness of his economic prospects drove him to suicide.[27] Most though not all the members of the *Sturm und Drang* group were impulsive and unstable in character. Merck's temperamental restlessness and lack of persistence were probably an expression of recurrent episodes of depression which plagued him and eventually contributed to his suicide. In their sharpest form, however, the perils and the consequences of the *Sturm und Drang* temperament appear in Lenz. Unable to master the conflict between inner life and external reality, his life and works are a record of a torn, tragic personality. Tortured by a sense of guilt and by hallucinations at times, Lenz attempted suicide on several occasions. Moods of enthusiasm and despair, fantasy, irony, and satire alternately overcame him, driving him to excess and cari-

The apostle of affliction, he who threw
Enchantment over passion, and from woe
Wrung overwhelming eloquence.[21]

Melancholy and *Weltschmerz* were themselves products of a kind of social situation which was not limited to Germany but which was most marked there and can be examined more specifically in the *Sturm und Drang* movement.[22] *Sturm und Drang* was a reaction against the accepted rationalism of the period, a reaction that was all the stronger because the young generation was profoundly dissatisfied with the prevailing political and social systems.[23] They protested against the rule of reason and dreamed of men who, trusting entirely to their emotions, would break down all social barriers.

The *Sturm und Drang* took shape about 1770 and came to an end around 1780. The central group of the *Stürmer und Dränger* were young men; Merck, the oldest, was 29 in 1770, Herder was 26, Goethe 21, Lenz 19, and Klinger 18. Associated with them were a number of sympathetic contemporaries who shared some of their views and attitudes. The members of the central group were all university men, trained or studying for the learned professions. With the exception of Goethe, economic reasons made a profession essential. Nor did this circumstance tend to dispel their dissatisfactions with their occupation or profession, which they felt to be confining, boring, and dull, a sentiment that also united the group.

A trait shared by almost all the members of the group and their temporary or partial associates was a temperamental instability, which they justified by their belief in the truth of intense feeling. They were motivated by a desire to live in terms of instinctive feelings, to shape their lives by intuition and revelation, not by social norms and practical reasonableness. They refused to fit themselves into accepted patterns of existence and thought, and strove to formulate new principles of personality as well as of literature. As the social, personal, and professional circumstances seemed to conspire to intensify the temperamental restlessness and unease common to the *Stürmer und Dränger*, their situation gained a wider social, cultural, and philosophical significance. Fueled by dissatis-

cature. Lenz was aware of this dissonance between his feelings and reality, yet he was convinced that life would be unbearable unless lived at a high emotional pitch.

This emphasis on the supreme value of direct experience and dynamic feelings bears all the marks of youthful turbulence endeavoring to assert itself against the restricted social life of Germany in the later eighteenth century. For the *Sturm und Drang* was a movement of young men who, with the not unexpected disregard of youth for practical obligations, also claimed that they were only expressing the needs of youth and its impatience against the domination of their elders. There is an illuminating report of a conversation between Goethe and his aunt, in which he comments resentfully on Wieland's review of *Götz*. "Wieland is wrong," insisted Goethe, "perhaps he is suitable for persons of his age, but he can't expect a young man to think as he does. It's the tone that annoyed me about him and made me so furious.... That's *just* how my father talks."[28]

But the emphasis on the subjective has even wider implications in terms of a dynamic, dialectical interaction between nature (or society) and the individual. Internal psychological processes are given priority over all external standards, all practical and moral achievement. This conflict between personal values and conventional social forms (family, religion, profession, morality) is depicted and analyzed in novels and plays in which the hero tragically asserts his values rather than renounce them and submit to standards that he considers meaningless. This conflict between personal psychological urges and social reality is presented as inevitable and tragic with but one outcome: the impassioned individual striving for freedom perishes. Their protagonists are enmeshed in a web from which they are unable to escape. They are both creatures of passion and self-pitying victims. The "revolutionary" moral significance of these individuals lies not in any attack on specific social evils, though some like Lenz were sharp social observers, but rather in the depiction of the dilemma of man as a personality in society, of the contradiction between inner urges and social constraints, in short, an exposure of the basic problem of man in society.[29]

Though activity was conceived as a means toward self-realization, and achievement as the measure of psychological intensity, these young Germans were unable to define the way in which they could most effectively direct their energies to the world about them. They attempted, though vainly, to conceive a mode of action which would do justice to the potentialities they felt within themselves, and would successfully challenge and overcome the social rigidities under which they chafed. Yet as members of a middle-class intelligentsia in eighteenth-century Germany they were powerless to do more than to challenge society and its purposes in the name of uninhibited self-expression and a creative social culture; but how their world could be altered, what form such change should take, or in what direction it ought to move they could not say.

Emphasis on individualism, spontaneity, and sensibility was a protest by middle-class intellectuals against absolute authority, whether exercised by the state, the family, or the church, and a rejection of the dominant values of the social order, especially those of the aristocracy. In this respect, *Sturm und Drang* expressed the feeling of a much larger social group. But there were few possible courses of action. One was to retreat from revolt and reach some form of accommodation with the established order, a route taken by Goethe, Klinger, and later Hegel. Another alternative was to escape from the unwanted social reality into a more acceptable world of heart's desire by taking refuge in an emphasis on emotional and spiritual independence as expressed in the ubiquitous feeling of *Weltschmerz*, the cult of sensibility, the flight to nature, and the preference for solitude.

The feeling of *Weltschmerz* arises from a psychological state which develops when there is a profound gap between an individual's expectations and the reality he confronts, a gap which because of circumstance and temperament he considers impossible to bridge. Nonetheless, the longing for the unattainable may continue and even intensify. In such a situation where society is perceived as hostile and unwilling to accept the individual on his own terms, he can seek compensation in the cultivation and evaluation of his psychological life, considering himself all the more significant as a person the more seriously and intensely he examines his emotions, feelings, and moods. Solitude provides the most propitious situation for the achievement of this goal, and it is no accident that solitude was a major theme of eighteenth-century writers, particularly during its second half. But to obtain solitude it was necessary to abandon society, and if possible flee to nature. Johann Georg Zimmermann's famous book *Uber die Einsamkeit* (1784) praises the tendency to leave society behind and to resort to nature where the soul can commune with the infinite.[30] However, nature was not essential for solitude; even those who remained in society could live alone, separated from their fellow men. An example is the translator Johann Nicolaus Meinhard, who chose to live and work in "quiet and idyllic" Erfurt, ostensibly because it was allegedly best for his health but actually because there he could carry on his work in melancholy solitude without being disturbed. Thus he spent almost two years at an inn as a stranger, without making any acquaintances.[31]

However justified it may have been, it is clear that the emotional climate of the later eighteenth century, particularly in Germany but elsewhere as well, strongly encouraged forms of narcissism. Psychological solipsism not only accepted the predominance of emotion in human behavior but regarded its varied expressions with approval. To yield to one's emotions, even if this meant emotional instability and rapid shifts of mood, was highly desirable. When Egmont's Clärchen sings "Himmelhoch jauchzend, zum Tode betrübt," she describes precisely this state. The tendency to allow the emotions free reign led inevitably to the enjoyment of emotional expression for its own sake, a development which could descend to ludicrous levels and which had its pathological side. Most pleasurable were the emotions and moods produced by sorrow and pain. An example is Klopstock's *Ode an Ebert*, where he evokes a feeling of melancholy and sorrow by imagining his live friend dead in the tomb, and alleviates his grief by crying copiously.[32] Both in literature and reality this peculiar pleasure to be derived from the experience of grief and melancholy, *die Wonne der Wehmut*, could be carried to laughable extremes. There is a letter from Claudius to Gerstenberg in which he asks for "a tragedy or some other dramatic plays so that one can have a really good cry." More extreme and more amusing is the behavior of Louise Zeigler (Darmstädter Lila), who had a crypt dug in her garden where when she felt so inclined she could lie down to experience the feelings of the dying, or even of the dead, and to cry.[33] The literary nadir of this exaltation of unhappiness and melancholy was probably achieved in Johann Martin Miller's novel *Siegwart. Eine Klostergeschichte*, published in 1776. This attitude was well expressed by Miller when he wrote of one character, "His soul was now as soft as wax; involuntary tears shone in his eyes, holding the balance between melancholy and joy."[34] Emotional release through tears is indeed the salient feature of *Siegwart*; it is so lachrymose that even the moon sheds tears. Martin Greiner counted the number of times the characters in *Siegwart* cried; he found that in the three volumes totalling 1179 pages they cried 555 times. On this basis he seems justified in referring to them as "chain weepers" (*Kettenweiner*).[35]

In a conversation with Eckermann, Goethe expressed the view that *Die Leiden des jungen Werther* was pathological and unwholesome.[36] Nor was he alone in the opinion that there was a psychopathological element associated with *Weltschmerz*, the emphasis on emotionalism, the flight to nature, and the cultivation of solitude. Reflecting on society and solitude, Christian Garve noted that solitude had certain disadvantages, even perils, in that it tended to lead to dejection, lethargy, and indolence. Moreover, it seemed to be the natural refuge of the sick, the downcast, and those who had been crushed by misfortune.[37] A poem by Lenz reveals the pathological aspect even more specifically:

> Lieben, hassen, streben, zittern,
> Hoffen, zagen bis ins Mark
> Kann das Leben zwar verbittern
> Aber ohne sie wärs Quark.

And in a letter to Lavater he wrote: "My own heart causes my greatest sorrow, but despite that I find it most unbearable not to suffer at all."[38]

Lonely and embittered Lenz, bearing his suffering as a mark of his individuality, presents in a more extreme form the imbalance between reason and emotion which encouraged the morbid developments possible to the human psyche. The masochistic element in his personality is paralleled by the hypochondriacal enjoyment of depression and misery exhibited by Karl Philipp Moritz, the neurosis of Goethe, and the hysterical characteristics of Heinrich Jung-Stilling and Adam Bernd.[39] Their counterparts in Britain, to name but a few, include Thomas Warton, William Cowper, Christopher Smart, Thomas Parnell, and William Collins.[40]

Irrationality and psychopathology, the consequences of emotional hedonism and unbalanced passions as exhibited by their contemporaries, were explored by eighteenth-century writers, especially in the novels of the period. For this was a century with a particular interest in understanding the hidden springs of behavior and therefore concerned with psychological analysis. The recesses of the human psyche are explored more or less profoundly by numerous authors, among them Prévost, Diderot, Richardson, Rousseau, Laclos, Fielding, Sterne, and Jean Paul, whose novels are filled with psychological observations. Common to all in some degree is a psychological naturalism which leads them to present their characters in human terms, with all the strengths and weaknesses, the admirable and repulsive traits to be found among men and women. This tendency is already evident in Marivaux, for example, in the *Vie de Marianne*, but it is Prévost who employs this approach to depict the madness of passion and its baneful consequences. The passion of love as portrayed through the behavior of the Chevalier des Grieux and Manon Lescaut degrades them morally and socially when permitted to reign unchecked.[41] In this situation love is a misfortune, an ignominy, a sickness; indeed, its pathological characteristics are brilliantly portrayed in the protagonist Des Grieux. Describing his inglorious love, he does not spare himself in the least, and manifests what amounts to a masochistic pleasure in confessing his lack of character and exposing his shameful, humiliating state. The dissociation of conscience from sentiment is also explored by Prévost in the *Histoire d'une Grecque moderne*, but whereas *Manon Lescaut* is a study of self-destruction due to unbridled passion, the *Grecque moderne* is a portrayal of inhibition and frustration resulting from a separation of reason and feeling, and an imbalance between them produced by an exaggeration of the former at the expense of the latter.⁴² The narrator of the *Grecque moderne*, a sophisticated man of the eighteenth century, buys a young Greek slave girl in Constantinople in order to free her, to teach her European morals and sentiments, and ultimately to enjoy her love. Unable truly to understand the ambiguities and nuances of the Occidental values and sentiments which are revealed to her, the girl Théophé accepts the concept of virtue at face value. Intoxicated with virtue, she stubbornly repulses even the slightest hint of surrender, an attitude which prevents her from accepting her benefactor's love. By carrying virtue to an extreme, Théophé turns this value into a magical and oppressive ideal which prevents her from living.

This conflict between behavior based on a social code and one's own deepest feelings, between conscience and emotion, ultimately between the conscious and the unconscious were profoundly explored by Samuel Richardson, particularly in *Clarissa* (1748), where his probing of the unconscious forms taken by the sexual impulse carried him into the realm of psychopathology. Diderot acclaimed his insights into the frightening reality of the unconscious which lies hidden beneath the most virtuous exterior. In his view Richardson illuminated the recesses of the mind and taught his contemporaries to recognize the sophistries and the dishonest motivations that are concealed behind apparent virtues. "He murmurs," wrote Diderot, "to the sublime spirit who presents himself at the entrance of the cave, and the hideous Moor appears from behind the disguise."⁴³

Samuel Johnson said that Richardson's novels taught the passions to move at the command of virtue. Though this may have been Richardson's larger purpose, his fascinated absorption in the sexual issue produced a much more complex and problematical relationship in *Clarissa*. His imagination supplied the personalities of his protagonists with psychological undertones which reveal his awareness of the morbid aspects of their behavior. The contemporary social context explains in part Lovelace's single-minded and self-conscious pursuit of his prey. For the eighteenth-century rake the male sexual role was that of a hunter who preferred to pursue a human and feminine quarry.⁴⁴ Lady Mary Wortley Montagu relates that in 1724 the Duke of Wharton was active among the Schemers, a "committee of gallantry" which met "regularly three times a week to consult on gallant schemes for the advantage and advancement of that branch of happiness."[45] In their pursuit of women the leisured sons of the upper classes, having little else to do, carried on a mode of life which had characterized their predecessors of the Restoration and which was to continue through the Regency. With political action often denied them, they expended their energies on dandyism, gaming, drinking, and wenching, with the last not necessarily the least of these pursuits.[46]

In this sense, Lovelace is a credible representative of his social class. But Richardson breaks through the genteel veneer of rakery and exposes the barbarous, exploitative, and even pathological aspects which lie beneath the surface. Lovelace is portrayed as basically cruel and callous, and his thoughts and actions reveal a personality in which sadism is a prominent element. Anna Howe sees Lovelace as a hyena, and Belford finds him as "cruel as a panther." These descriptions are substantiated by Lovelace's comparison of bird hunting with the pursuit of women. In a letter to Belford, he says, "We begin when boys, with birds, and when grown up, go on with women; and both, perhaps, in turn, experience our sportive cruelty." To which Belford replies: "Thou ever delightedst to sport with and torment the animal, whether bird or beast, that thou lovedst and hadst a power over." For Lovelace, man is a spider in whose web of deceit and trickery woman is destined to be trapped. And the more she struggles against the unfair and outrageous means which man employs to gain his ends, the more he can gloat and derive pleasure from the spectacle. In pursuit of this aim, sexual conquest, Lovelace represses all immediacy of response to goodness, and obsessively concentrates consciously on the achievement of his fell purpose. "What sensibilities," Clarissa says to him, "must thou have suppressed! What a dreadful, what a judicial harshness of heart must thine be; who canst be capable of such emotions as sometimes thou hast shown; and of such sentiments as sometimes have flown from thy lips; yet canst have so far overcome them all, as to be able to act as thou hast acted and that from settled purpose and premeditation."

If man is a conqueror, woman must be a victim, and this is how Richardson presents the sexual relationship in *Clarissa*. But his heroine is not just a victim who has been sexually violated; she is a victim who expresses her suffering in terms strongly tinged with masochistic sensuality, and who represses her normal erotic impulses and narcissistically enjoys the preparations for her approaching *Liebestod*. For example, just before eloping with Lovelace, Clarissa dreamt that he stabbed her in the heart, and then "tumbled me into a deep grave ready dug, among two or three half-dissolved carcasses; throwing in the dirt and earth upon me with his hands, and trampling it down with his feet." Then when she is dying, the pleasure which Clarissa takes in the preparations for her funeral, her preoccupation with her "wedding garments . . . , the easiest, the *happiest* suit, that ever bridal maiden wore," with her own coffin, is not only in the tradition of an *ars moriendi* but expresses as well morbid tendencies in her social and cultural environment.

Richardson's exploration of the consequences of unbridled sexual hedonism, of the pursuit of sexual conquest divorced from any deeper feeling, reveal aspects of the irrational and psychopathological which were intended to point a moral lesson. But Richardson's insights could be used without his moral values, as was done with elegance and considerable psychological penetration by Laclos in *Les Liaisons dangereuses* (1782). Indeed, La Harpe pointed specifically to Lovelace as one of the sources of Valmont. André Malraux has described *Les Liaisons dangereuses* as the story of an intrigue based on the premise that people can be manipulated by appealing to their passions, that is, where they are most vulnerable.[47] The intrigue is a game in which the players pursue their aims by manipulating vanity and sexual desire. In the *Liaisons dangereuses*, Laclos presents the reader with a precise sequence of manoeuvres and their consequences. Moreover, he emphasizes the intelligence and rationality of his protagonists, but does not endow them with any moral sentiments. By divorcing reason from feeling, by turning seduction and debauchery into a game to be enjoyed without any consideration of the victims, Laclos creates another form of irrationality. Valmont is a very Machiavelli of seduction. The scientific rigor with which he plans his conquests reminds one of the behavior of academic war strategists. After all, Laclos was a soldier. Had he lived today he might have had Valmont work out his moves using game theory. Indeed, so obsessed is he with his game that his scheming continues even as he makes love. On one occasion he writes a letter to Mme. de Tourvel, using as a desk a girl with whom he has gone to bed, as he says, "a letter written in bed, practically while in a woman's arms, and even interrupted so as to render the infidelity complete."[48] By repressing all emotion except his desire for sexual conquest and the need to support his vanity, by distancing himself totally as a person from others, Valmont acts according to a kind of surrealistic rationality—a rationality that is under no restraint so that when carried to its logical culmination it becomes a form of irrationality.

Valmont's obsessive rationality has novelistic as well as artistic and political counterparts. The protagonist of Wilhelm Heinse's novel *Ardinghello* (1787) is a ruthless, amoral hedonist who relentlessly endeavors to express his egoistic sensualism in his behavior. For him, too, women are objects to be used for pleasure. Eventually, he flees to the Aegean where he forms a utopian community based on piracy, whose members are completely free to follow their own desires, and in which all property, including the women, is shared. Ultimately, however, the plan fails due to the incompatibility of its basic principles, amoral individualism and abstract communism, and the irrationality of endeavoring to combine them.[49]

Similarly, appeals for a rational architecture, for an architecture cleansed of the artificialities and bizarre fancies of the Rococo, led to visionary structures dominated by formal purity and intended to create an environment which would influence the citizens' soul in a moral sense. Underlying this development is a belief in the educative mission of the artist, no matter whether he uses the pen, the brush, or the chisel. In this sense, an expressive architecture, an *architecture parlante*, based upon irreducible geometric forms, spherical, cubical, pyramidal, could provide a vocabulary to communicate universally valid truths uncovered by the pure light of reason. This aim, to activate the subconscious implications of architecture and thus to foster the moral sensibility, was pushed to its farthest extreme by the French architects, E.-L. Boullée (1728–99) and J.-J. Lequeu (1757–1825).[50] The latter designed visionary structures of which the various elements corresponded to certain dominant passions or states of the soul. Examples are Lequeu's "Temple of Divination" and "Island of Love."[51] Boullée's fantastic and megalomaniac designs exemplify Wordsworth's "reason in her most exalted mood." In explanation of his project for a monument to Newton, Boullée wrote: 'O Newton! since you by the extent of your knowledge and the sublimity of your genius have determined the shape of the earth, I conceived the idea of enclosing you in your own discovery. . . . For how can one find anything worthy of you apart from you. For this reason I wanted to characterize your tomb by the shape of the earth."[52] By designing a monument where the cenotaph would be placed within a hollow sphere, Boullée not only paid homage to Newton, but also symbolized the union of science and art in the spirit expressed by André Chenier.

> Tous les arts sout unis: les sciences humaines
> N'ont pu de leur empire étendre les domaines
> Sans agrandir aussi la carrière des vers.[53]

Other projects conceived by Boullée were even more extreme. A vast library which he designed was intended more as a monument to learning than to be a repository for books. Also in his plan for a cemetery entrance, Boullée produced a severely triangular mass, a geometric form, reminiscent of modern abstractionism. Clearly, the architecture of reason was carried in these instances to a point where reason was transformed into exaltation, where visionary structures exemplified purification of thought and form, but from the point of view of the builder and user were impractical and irrational.

The eighteenth century produced analogous examples in the political arena. Ideas were pushed with inexorable logic to extremes where, as if by the operation of a Hegelian dialectic, they emerged as their very opposites. This process is most evident in the evolution of the principles which Robespierre and Saint-Just set forth in their speeches and writings, though it is not limited to them, and which were inspired by a desire to create a republic that would inaugurate a reign of virtue under which free men and women would live in harmony and peace. As Saint-Just expressed it, "Our aim is to create an order of things which would establish a universal tendency toward the good . . . to establish a sincere government so that the people would be happy, and wisdom and eternal Providence only would preside over the creation of the Republic. . . ."[54] But to ensure the achievement of this goal there could be no compromise with any opponents who were wicked and criminal by definition. Even rational argument was suspect in this context. Robespierre might have been echoing Pope when he said in 1794 that reason in any man "misled by his passions is frequently only a sophist pleading their cause." It is essential "to create in him an instinct for moral things which will enable him to act rapidly to do good and avoid evil without the slow assistance of reasoning."[55] The achievement of these aims required the creation of a proper environment in which the formative influence of republican institutions could be effective. "I imagined," said Saint-Just in 1793, "that if man was given laws in accord with his nature and his heart he would cease to be unhappy and corrupt." The correct organization of the social order would lead to control of human motivation and behavior. "The legislator commands the future; to be weak will avail him nothing. It is for him to will the good and to perpetuate it, to make men what he wishes them to be." "Institutions have as their object the establishment in fact of all social and individual guarantees so as to avoid dissension and violence; they substitute the power of morals for the power of men."[56] Proceeding logically and rationally from the premise that self-interest and indifference to the welfare of the community were the source of all evil, the institutions to be established were to inculcate love of the nation, ascetic living and spartan self-control, and sacrifice of self-interest for the public good, and to eliminate pride, cupidity, factionalism, and social passivity. By directing the emotional energies and loyalties of the citizens toward the state and applying the same rigorous standards to all, a social organization would be produced in which virtue could express itself and in which harmony would reign. The Republic would be the source of all moral values, and loyalty to it would supersede all other loyalties. But as Malraux says, for Saint-Just and those who listened to him, "the Republic was not simply a system of government, but primarily an apocalypse and the hope of an unknown world."[57] It was a utopian vision based on faith, a vision of a Republic "less concerned with making people happy than with preventing them from being unhappy," indeed primarily concerned with an absolute moral order comparable to that of a militant religion. Because Saint-Just was capable of dealing realistically with immediate problems, some have considered him a rationalist, which he was not. He was a visionary, a believer in a Republic which was guillotined with him, a man imbued with a burning faith which carried him for good and ill far beyond the bounds of reason.

THE IRRATIONALITY OF CREDULITY

Commenting on the susceptibility of his contemporaries for marvels, Louis-Sebastien Mercier noted in 1782 that "Love of the marvellous always ensnares us, because sensing confusedly how ignorant we are of the forces of nature, anything which leads us to discover something about them is welcomed enthusiastically."[58] Mercier's perceptive remark calls attention to still another aspect of irrationality in the eighteenth century. Not only was the eighteenth century a period of enlightenment; it was also a period of pseudo-science, charlatanism, and quackery, of which some practitioners are still remembered, e.g., Casanova and Cagliostro. The progressive separation of science and theology in this period helped to create some of the conditions favorable to charlatanism. Scientific investigation left many unanswered questions and gaps that could be answered and filled by imagination and fiction. To draw the line between science and pseudo-science was difficult even for scientists; how much more so was it for uncritical laymen. Under such conditions the transition from what is strange to what is marvelous is easy and imperceptible. Without realizing that the real world has been left far behind, one is soon surrounded by the fantastic. As long as it is not possible to verify assertions or products of thinking by well-established methods linking them to empirical phenomena, analogies and similarities are exploited, honestly and dishonestly, without regard for any empirical verification.[59] Among the semi-educated, the phenomena of electricity, magnetism, and gases seemed to endow nature with forces which were not far from the older occult doctrines of astrology, alchemy, divination, theurgy, and the like.[60] To a considerable extent the latter were a part of the popular culture of the eighteenth century; it was enough to accept new marvels without any real understanding and to assume that it would be possible to achieve the impossible for anyone who knew the secrets involved.[61] Furthermore, one of the vicissitudes to which human beings are subject is disease, and the uncertainty associated with its occurrence and outcome often arouses emotional distress. This is true at present, particularly in the case of disorders not readily amenable to treatment, and was certainly the case in the eighteenth century, when the obscurity of the causal relationships was even greater. Such a situation opens the door to all kinds of irrational and often fraudulent forms of therapy, particularly those that can make use of the placebo effect to a considerable degree. Finally, one cannot overlook the fact that science, or what people thought of as science, became fashionable—it was *à la mode*.

The situation was well characterized in October 1789 by the German physician C. W. Hufeland in Bertuchs *Journal des Luxus und der Moden*. In an article entitled "Über die neuesten Modearzneyen und Charlatanerien," he dealt with the science fad of his day and with fashionable diseases and cures. "We live in a time of popularity," he wrote, "and even the most serious sciences must now lay aside their pedantic mien and learn to clothe themselves in a pleasingly fashionable dress so that they will no longer be denied entrance to any female society." Quacks, he continued, "have made themselves truly indispensable. Indeed, where can one now find a group marked by good taste where one does not hear talk of elemental fire, magnetism, electricity, the primal causes of things, even about the most abstract topics of metaphysics, and all with an ease and interest that astound one? Medicine was one of the first to have the honor of embarking on this course."[62] In medicine, this trend was most prominent with respect to fashionable ailments and their treatment. Hufeland diagnosed this tendency as a consequence of

> semi-enlightenment in medical matters. The world wants to be deceived, a proverb which was never truer than it is today. People insist on having something new and wonderful. Ordinary medicine is boring, puts one in an ill humor, and is not in tune with the frivolous life of our time. And so this army of ignoramuses, swindlers and cunning rogues trumpet forth ever new, ever more promising things, and mistreat our health and our pocket books in the most wretched way.[63]

Under these circumstances, there were enough individuals to clutch credulously at the appeals and promises of a variety of adventurers, nature healers, layers-on of hands, and other charlatans. Some were local celebrities, such as the Swiss "mountain doctor," Michael Schüppach (1701-81), who employed uroscopy, electrotherapy, plant remedies, a theatrical atmosphere, and an ability to size up his customers, so as to attract a clientele of touring aristocrats and celebrities, as well as numerous peasants and others of lower social position.[64] Another was the Scottish quack James Graham (1745-94) of Edinburgh, who exploited electricity and magnetism in his Temple of Health, opened in London in 1780.[65] The Temple was sumptuously furnished in an Oriental manner. In the Great Apollo apartment, patients and visitors could participate in mysterious rituals in an atmosphere of soft music and attractive perfumes, hailing the magic of magnetism and viewing the rosy Goddess of Health (a part played by Emma Hart, later Lady Hamilton). The chamber where patients were received was equipped with a very large air pump and an enormous metallic conductor, intended presumably to impress them with Graham's scientific background. By 1782, Graham had exhausted the potentialities of his Temple and he turned to advocacy of mud baths.

These are only two of the eighteenth-century charlatans. There were many others, among whom may be mentioned Elisha Perkins of Connecticut, who in 1798 patented metallic tractors, of which the active principle was supposed to be like that of galvanism or animal magnetism; and the self-styled Chevalier John Taylor

(1708–72) who actually took a medical degree at Basel and was the most notorious quack oculist of his time.[66] Taylor travelled about Europe extolling his merits, attracting patients, and accumulating wealth; he left behind him many victims blinded by his hand.

Another of these medical deviants, but one who was a better doctor, was Gottfried Christoph Beireis (1730–1809), professor of physics and medicine at the small University of Helmstedt, a singular individual in whom self-deceit, vanity, and a desire to shock and to mystify combined strangely to produce a form of charlatanism which attracted numerous visitors and patients to him. Achim von Arnim visited Beireis in 1806 at the suggestion of Goethe and based a chapter in his novel *Gräfin Dolores* on this experience. The atmosphere surrounding the singular doctor and the effect created by his person are well portrayed at the very outset, when the protagonist arrives in Helmstedt. "Only now the Count recalled that without noticing it he had come into the atmosphere of a wonder worker who for almost fifty years had given everyone much to guess at even though this half-century had completely rejected all riddles and miracles." At the doctor's house, "the servant knocked three times on the door; a man in fine black clothes, wearing an oddly stiff, white wig of spun glass, with a broad forehead and deep gray, friendly eyes, his fingers covered with magnificent rings, inquired what we wished." After his visitor had entered, the doctor excused himself, as he had to visit a patient, "the town crier, whom he had to cure of a pulmonary disorder in eight days."[67]

In this instance as in so many others, the charlatan endeavors to build up a *persona* which will appeal to the wishes and desires of a certain kind of audience, of individuals who want to believe that they can be helped, that they can be relieved of insecurity, pain, doubt, alienation, or whatever else troubles them. Quick and simple remedies have been desired by men since time immemorial, and those who promise to provide them tend to secure a following, if only for a time. This was certainly true in the eighteenth century, and contemporaries were aware of the irrational aspects of quackery. As Southey put it, "The operations of sickness and healing are alike mysterious, and hence arises the predilection of many enthusiasts for quackery, and the ostentation which all quacks make of religion, or of some extraordinary power in themselves."[68]

IRRATIONALITY AND ECCENTRICITY

The eccentric and the bizarre may be linked with the irrational, and the eighteenth century had its examples. Although eccentricity in the age cannot be explored in any detail here, a few samples of its occurrence may be offered. As Mercier reports, there were to be found in Paris, on the street or in cafes, individuals whose peculiarities of dress or behavior did not attract undue notice, though people commented on them. Encountering a crack-brained maker of projects in a coffeehouse, Mercier remarked that there were others like him who had the public weal at heart "but who unfortunately were addlepated."[69] Diderot's brilliant portrayal of Rameau's nephew presents another social deviant who is a strange mixture of good sense and folly. Delineated with great acuteness and intelligence, he was according to Diderot, "One of the most bizarre fellows in a country where God has seen to it that there is no lack of them."[70]

Mercier includes as irrational the mania of collectors, those who buy pictures, drawings, china, or jewels, and he ends by dubbing the extravagant collector a maniac.[71] Self-indulgence and indolence are also regarded as irrational, because individuals exhibiting such characteristics were often considered socially disruptive.[72] Similarly, because of the frivolity of his behavior, the fop, the macaroni, the *incroyable*, the dandy, was viewed as high in the scale of folly. Those "who decide upon the length of a neckhandkerchief, and who regulate the number of buttons at the knees of their breeches" and thus prescribe fashions, exist in a social world organized according to strict but capricious conventions.[73] The epitome of the type is George Brummell (1778–1840), who satisfied his need to be an aristocrat without hereditary privileges by acting as the arbiter of fashion in a social universe of extremely limited dimensions, so limited that in the last analysis the dandy was his own best audience.[74] The dandy as his own creation expresses a desire for social recognition of imagination in a form which is essentially peripheral if not opposed to the prevalent major values of society. The consequence is that the socially irrelevant and eccentric position of the dandy can lead to an ever increasing narcissism and a loss of relation to reality in matters of money and social rank. Whereas Beau Nash in the earlier eighteenth century had as Master of Ceremonies served a social function in developing at Bath an agreeable summer retreat for people of fashion and for those who aspired to that designation, Beau Brummell developed the doctrine that the essence of elegance was not to attract attention by dressing gaudily, but rather to express oneself through the tailoring of one's clothes, a subject to which he devoted the greatest care, as he did also to the dressing of his hair and the making of his gloves.[75] As the eighteenth century changed into the nineteenth, the role of the "Beau," the beautiful person, was narrowed down more and more, until Baudelaire summed it up in the sentence "A dandy does nothing," and to paraphrase him, his glory is to be unique and alone.[76] And so through the eighteenth century, the folly of dandyism moved from social frivolity through individualistic eccentricity to eventual irrelevance, to become a spectacle for astonished stares or indifference.

MADNESS IN THE 18TH CENTURY

There is little point in emphasizing the occurrence of mental and emotional disorders among people of the eighteenth century. As in any other period of human history there were enough unfortunates who suffered from such conditions, nor were they limited to any social class.[77] For an estimate of this aspect of irrationality one must draw upon the non-medical as well as the medical literature; not only Pinel but also Diderot must be consulted. For example, in *La Religieuse* Diderot describes lesbianism, depression, and acute mania. He also follows step by step the development of a mental disorder in the mother superior of the convent. In the *Bijoux indiscrets* Diderot depicts an astrologer so obsessed by his observations that he finally goes mad. Naturally such materials must be used with caution, especially in assigning current diagnostic categories to delineations of eighteenth-century behavior.[78] The same caution is equally if not more applicable to ideas concerning normal and disordered states of mind. For example, the view was held in the eighteenth century that the normal and the abnormal were closely related. This may appear similar to a view held today that there is a fluid continuum between normality and abnormality, between health and sickness. It does not follow, however, that the explanations for the view held in the eighteenth century have much in common with our ideas. When Imlac, in Johnson's *Rasselas*, says that "if we speak with vigorous exactness, no human mind is in its right state," he is referring to the balance between imagination and reason, categories which do not have the same meanings and connotations today.[79]

REASON AND UNREASON: THE UNSTABLE BALANCE

Irrationality was an integral element in the fabric of eighteenth-century life, appearing in various forms ranging from run-of-the-mill crotchets and phobias to serious mental and emotional disorders. Religion, literature, politics, fashion—all show reason in differing combinations with emotion, imagination, and various morbid psychological states. The relationship between these elements varied in terms of personality, changing fashions in expression, alterations in the social position and function of individuals and groups, institutional pressures, and the like.[80] The uneasy balance of these elements in the social context is evident from Hölderlin's advice:

Hast du Verstand und ein Herz, so zeige nur eines von beiden!
Beides verdammen sie dir, zeigest du beides zugleich.

And it is this shifting and unstable balance between mind and heart in a changing social order which provides the wide-ranging gamut of irrationality in the eighteenth century.

NOTES

1. Richard Price, *A Review of the Principal Questions of Morals* (3rd ed., 1787), ed. D. Daiches Raphael (Oxford: Clarendon Press, 1948), p. 109.
2. John Butt, ed., *The Poems of Alexander Pope* (New Haven: Yale University Press, 1963), pp. 517–19.
3. L. J. Bredvold, *The Natural History of Sensibility* (Detroit: Wayne State University Press, 1962), pp. 53–62, 77–97.
4. A. Camus: *Essais*, Bibliothèque de la Pléiade (Paris: Gallimard, 1965), pp. 447–57; "Sade," *Yale French Studies*, No. 35 (New Haven, 1965); P. Trahard, *La Sensibilité révolutionnaire (1789–1794)* (Paris: Boivin et Cie., 1936).
5. For a development of these concepts and their application as analytic tools see George Rosen, "Emotion and Sensibility in Ages of Anxiety: A Comparative Historical Review," *American Journal of Psychiatry*, 124: 771–84 (1967).
6. Frederick Antal, *Hogarth and His Place in European Art* (New York: Basic Books, 1962), pp. 166–67; for enthusiasm as used in the seventeenth and eighteenth centuries see George Rosen, " 'Enthusiasm: a dark lanthorn of the spirit,' " *Bull. Hist. Med.*, 42:393–421 (1968).
7. *The Spectator*, edited with an introduction and notes by Donald F. Bond, 5 vols. (Oxford: Clarendon Press, 1965), II, 289.
8. Richard Graves, *The Spiritual Quixote, or the Summer's Ramble of Mr. Geoffrey Wildgoose*, edited with an introduction by Clarence Tracy (London: Oxford University Press, 1967), pp. 3, 19–20.
9. *The Journal of John Wesley*, abridged by Nehemiah Curnock (New York: Capricorn Books, 1963), pp. 100–101; see also Sydney G. Diamond, *The Psychology of the Methodist Revival* (London: Oxford University Press, 1926), pp. 125–39.
10. Charles Allmeras, *La Révolte des camisards* (Arthaud, 1960); R. A. Knox, *Enthusiasm. A Chapter in the History of Religion with special reference to the XVII and XVIII centuries* (New York: Oxford University Press, 1950), pp. 356–71.
11. James Sutherland, *Background For Queen Anne* (London: Methuen and Co., 1939), pp. 36–74.
12. George B. Cutten, *Speaking with Tongues Historically and Psychologically Considered* (New Haven: Yale University Press, 1927), pp. 48–66.
13. Benjamin Franklin, *The Complete Works of Benjamin Franklin*, 10 vols., ed. J. Bigelow (New York-London: G. P. Putnam, 1887–88), I, 66.
14. Edward D. Andrews, *The People Called Shakers. A Search for the Perfect Society* (New York: Oxford University Press, 1953), p. 6.
15. Perry Miller, *Jonathan Edwards* (New York: Meridian Books, 1959), pp. 133–63, 170–77; idem, *Errand into the Wilderness* (Cambridge,

Mass.: Belknap Press, 1956), pp. 153–66; Jonathan Edwards, *A Treatise concerning Religious Affections*, ed. John E. Smith (New Haven: Yale University Press, 1959), pp. 285–89; Whitney R. Cross, *The Burned-Over District. The Social and Intellectual History of Enthusiastic Religion in Western New York, 1800–1850* (Ithaca, N.Y.: Cornell University Press, 1950), pp. 6–9.

16. Catharine C. Cleveland, *The Great Revival in the West, 1797–1805* (Chicago: University of Chicago Press, 1916), pp. 128–58; Richard M'Nemar, *The Kentucky Revival; or A Short History of the Late Extraordinary Out-Pouring of the Spirit of God in the Western States of America* (New York: Edward O. Jenkins, 1846); W. L. Sutton, "Reports on the medical topography and the epidemic diseases of Kentucky," *Trans. A.M.A.* 11(1858):77–123, esp. pp. 110–23.

17. Carré de Montgeron, *La Verité des Miracles operés par l'intercession de M. de Paris, demontrée contre M. l'Archevêque de Sens*, 2 vols. (Utrecht and Paris(?), 1737–42); C. A. Saint-Beuve, *Port-Royal*, Bibliothèque de la Pléiade, 3 vols. (Paris: Gallimard, 1952–55), III, 526, 531; Ph. Hecquet, *Le naturalisme des convulsions dans les maladies de l'épidémie convulsionnaire*, 2 vols. (Soleure, 1733); Knox, *op. cit.*, pp. 374–85.

18. Gershom-Gerhard Scholem, "Le mouvement sabbataïste en Pologne," *Revue de l'histoire des religions* 143:30–90, 209–32, 42–77 (1953–54); *idem*, "The Holiness of Sin," *Commentary* 51:41–70 (1971); Jacob Katz, *Tradition and Crisis. Jewish Society at the End of the Middle Ages* (New York: Free Press, 1961), pp. 213–44; Torsten Ysander, *Studien zum B'eštschen Hasidismus in seiner religionsgeschichtlichen Sonderart*, Uppsala Universitets Årsskraft, Bd. I, Teologi 2 (Uppsala, 1933), pp. 17–61.

19. Wilhelm Dilthey, *Der junge Dilthey. Ein Lebensbild in Briefen und Tagebüchern 1852–1870*, zusammengestellt von Clara Misch geb. Dilthey (Leipzig and Berlin: B. G. Teubner, 1933), pp. 2–3.

20. J. W. Goethe, *Die Leiden des jungen Werthers. Frühe Prosa*, mit einem Nachwort von Peter Boerner (Munich: Deutscher Taschenbuch Verlag, 1962), p. 263.

21. Byron, *Childe Harold's Pilgrimage*, III, 77.

22. William Rose, "Die Anfänge des Weltschmerzes in der deutschen Literatur," *Germanisch-Romanische Monatsschrift* 12:140–55 (1924); Max Wieser, *Der sentimentale Mensch. Gesehen aus der Welt holländischer und deutscher Mystiker im 18. Jahrhundert* (Stuttgart, 1924), pp. 7–9.

23. For a wider discussion of the *Sturm und Drang*, see H. A. Korff, *Geist der Goethezeit. Sturm und Drang* (New York, 1953); Hans Gerth, *Die sozialgeschichtliche Lage der bürgerlichen Intelligenz um die Wende des 18. Jahrhunderts* (Berlin, 1935).

24. F. Valjavec, *Die Entstehung der politischen Strömungen in Deutschland 1770–1815* (Munich: Oldenbourg, 1951), pp. 185–86, 214–24, 235–37; H. Brunschwig, *La Crise de l'état prussien à la fin du XVIII_e*

siècle et la genèse de la mentalité romantique (Paris: Presses Universitaires de France, 1947), pp. 176–96.
25. Crane Brinton, *The Anatomy of Revolution* (New York: Vintage Books, 1957), p. 66.
26. Justinus Kerner, *Das Leben des Justinus Kerner, Erzählt von ihm und seiner Tochter Marie*, herausgegeben von Karl Pörnbacher (Munich, Kösel Verlag, 1967), pp. 36–72, 166–68, 175–80; Georg Forster, *Das Abenteuer seines Lebens unter Wiedergabe vieler Briefe und Tagebucheintragungen*, erzählt von Wilhelm Langewiesche (Ebenhausen im Isartal and Leipzig: Verlag von Wilhelm Langewiesche-Brandt, 1923), pp. 158–272.
27. J. H. Merck, *Briefe*, herausgegeben von Herbert Kraft (Frankfurt a. M., 1968), p. 632; *idem*, *Werke*, ausgewählt und herausgegeben von Arthur Henkel (Frankfurt a. M.: Insel Verlag, 1968), pp. 16–17.
28. *Goethe's Gespräche*. . . . auf Grund der Ausgabe und des Nachlasses von Flodoard Freiherrn von Biedermann, ergänzt und herausgegeben von Wolfgang Herwig (Zürich and Stuttgart: Artemis Verlag, 1965), 1, 90–93.
29. See for example the plays by Lenz, *Der Hofmeister* and *Die Soldaten*.
30. J. G. Zimmermann, *Über die Einsamkeit*, 4 vols. (Leipzig, 1784); Ernst Bloch, *Das Prinzip Hoffnung*, 2 vols. (Frankfurt a. M.: Suhrkamp, 1959), II, 1125–28.
31. Helmut Rehder, *Johann Nicolaus Meinhard und seine Übersetzungen*, Illinois Studies in Language and Literature, Vol. 37, No. 2 (1953), pp. 1–5.
32. Friedrich Gottlieb Klopstock, *Ausgewählte Werke* (Munich: Carl Hanser Verlag, 1962), pp. 27–29.
33. Leo Balet and E. Gerbard, *Die Verbürgerlichung der deutschen Kunst, Literatur und Musik* (Strassburg, Leipzig, Zürich, 1936), pp. 307, 316–19.
34. Rose, *op. cit.*, p. 147.
35. Martin Greiner, *Die Entstehung der modernen Unterhaltungsliteratur. Studien zum Trivialroman des 18. Jahrhunderts* (Reinbek bei Hamburg, 1964), pp. 48 ff. Anyone wishing to sample *Siegwart* may turn to Horst Kunze, *Lieblingsbücher von dazumal. Eine Blütenlese aus den erfolgreichsten Büchern von 1750–1860* . . . (Munich: Ernst Heimeran, 1938), pp. 87–96.
36. J. P. Eckermann, *Gespräche mit Goethe in den letzten Jahren seines Lebens*, neue Ausgabe herausgegeben von Fritz Bergemann (Wiesbaden: Insel Verlag, 1955), pp. 489–91.
37. Christian Garve, *Über Gesellschaft und Einsamkeit, Versuche über verschiedene Gegenstände aus der Moral, der Literatur und dem gesellschaftlichen Leben* (Breslau, 1801), 3. Theil, pp. 66, 296, 368; cited in Wolf Lepenies, *Melancholie und Gesellschaft* (Frankfurt a.M.: Suhrkamp Verlag, 1969), p. 92.
38. Rose, *op. cit.*, p. 147; J. M. R. Lenz, *Gedichte*. . . . herausgegeben von Karl Weinhold (Berlin: Wilhelm Hertz, 1891), p. 112.

39. Karl Philipp Moritz (1756–93) author of the autobiographical novel *Anton Reiser* (1785); Heinrich Jung-Stilling (1740–1817), medical man and author of mystical verse, whose best-known work is his autobiography *Heinrich Stillings Jugend* (1777); Adam Bernd, *Eigene Lebens Beschreibung* . . . (Leipzig, 1738).
40. See, for example, G. A. Aitken, *The Poetical Works of Thomas Parnell*, 1894, p. iiii.
41. Abbé Prévost, *Histoire du Chevalier des Grieux et de Manon Lescaut* (1731), in *Romanciers du XVIII$_e$ Siecle*, textes établis, présentés et annotés par Etiemble, Bibliothèque de la Pléiade, 2 vols. (Paris: Gallimard, 1960), I, 1219–1371. See for example pp. 1225–26, 1259–84.
42. Abbé Prévost, *Histoire d'une Grecque moderne* (1740), introduction par Robert Mauzi (Paris: Bibliothèque 10–18, 1965).
43. Diderot, *Oeuvres*, Texte établi et annoté par Andre Billy. Bibliothèque de la Pléiade (Paris: Gallimard, 1951), p. 1091.
44. H. T. Hopkinson, "Robert Lovelace, the Romantic Cad," *Horizon* 10:80–104 (1944).
45. Mary Wortley Montagu, *Letters and Works*, ed. Lord Wharncliffe; 3rd ed, rev. by W. Moy Thomas, 2 vols. (London, 1861), I, 476–77.
46. Barbey D'Aurevilly, *Oeuvres Romanesques Complétes*, Textes présentés, établis et annotés par Jacques Petit, Bibliothèque de la Pléiade, 2 vols. (Paris: Gallimard, 1966), II, 667–733.
47. André Malraux, *Le triangle noir, Laclos, Goya, Saint-Just* (Paris: Gallimard, 1970), pp. 23–51.
48. Choderlos de Laclos, *Oeuvres Complètes*, Texte établi et annoté par Maurice Allem, Bibliothèque de la Pléiade (Paris: Gallimard, 1957), p. 125.
49. A. Jolivet, *Wilhelm Heinse* (Paris, 1922), pp. 266–69; Rose, *op. cit.*, pp. 149–50; Walter Brecht, *Heinse und der ästhetische Immoralismus* (Berlin, 1911), p. x.
50. Etienne-Louis Boullée, *Architecture. Essai sur l'art*, Textes réunis et présentés par J.-M. P. de Montclos (Paris: Hermann, 1968); Emil Kaufmann, "Etienne-Louis Boulée," *Art Bulletin* 21:213–27 (1939); idem, *Three Revolutionary Architects, Boullée, Ledoux and Lequeu*, Transactions of the American Philosophical Society, Vol. 62, part 3, (October, 1952), pp. 436–73; Helen Rosenau, *Boullée's Treatise on Architecture* (London, 1953); Emil Kaufmann, *Architecture in the Age of Reason* (Cambridge, Mass., 1955); Helen Rosenau, "Architecture and the French Revolution: Jean Jacque Lequeu," *Architectural Review* 106:111–16 (1949).
51. André Chastel, "The Moralizing Architecture of Jean-Jacques Lequeu," in *The Grand Eccentrics*, ed. Thomas B. Hess and John Ashbery (New York: Collier Books, 1966), pp. 57–66.
52. Boullée, *op. cit.*, pp. 137–38.
53. André Chenier, *Oeuvres complètes*, Texte . . . établis par Gérard Walter, Bibliothèque de la Pléiade (Paris: Gallimard, 1950), p. 125.
54. Saint-Just, *Oeuvres* (Paris: Prévot, 1834), p. 208.

55. Robespierre, *Textes Choisis*, ed. Jean Poperen, 3 vols. (Paris: Editions Sociales, 1956), III, 168.
56. Saint-Just, *op. cit.*, pp. 71, 74, 365.
57. André Malraux, "Préface" to Albert Ollivier, *Saint-Just et la force des choses* (Paris: Gallimard, 1954), p. 23.
58. L.-S. Mercier, *Tableau de Paris*, Nouvelle édition corrigée et augmentée (Amsterdam, 1782), II, 300.
59. For a discussion of the various factors which lead people to accept the imaginary, the marvelous, and the fantastic and to hold fast to such beliefs see Gustav Jahoda, *The Psychology of Superstition* (Harmondsworth, Middlesex: Penguin Books, 1969).
60. Robert Darnton, *Mesmerism and the End of the Enlightenment in France* (Cambridge, Mass.: Harvard University Press, 1968), pp. 12–36; Mercier, *op. cit.*, pp. 299–300; Auguste Viatte, *Les Sources occultes du romantisme, illuminisme-théosophie, 1770–1820*, 2 vols. (Paris, 1928); "Aspects de L'Illuminisme au XVIIIe Siècle," *Les Cahiers de la Tour Saint-Jacques*, II, III, IV (Paris: H. Roudil, 1960).
61. Robert Mandrou, *De la culture populaire aux 17e et 18e siècles, La Bibliothèque bleue de Troyes* (Paris: Stock, 1964), pp. 55–75 and *passim*.
62. Grete de Francesco, "Scharlatane aus drei Jahrhunderten," *Ciba Zeitschrift* 4:1259–76 (1936); see p. 1267.
63. Grete de Francesco, *The Power of the Charlatan* (New Haven: Yale University Press, 1939), p. 166.
64. *Ibid.*, pp. 188–92.
65. C. J. S. Thompson, *The Quacks of Old London* (London, 1928), p. 333; F. H. Garrison, *An Introduction to the History of Medicine*, 4th ed. (Philadelphia: W. B. Saunders Co., 1929), p. 387; Robert Southey, *Letters from England* (1807), edited with an introduction by Jack Simmons (London: Cresset Press, 1951), pp. 297–98.
66. Eberhard Buchner, *Ärzte und Kurpfuscher. Kulturhistorisch interessante Dokumente aus alten deutschen Zeitungen (17. und 18. Jahrhundert)* (Munich: Albert Langen, 1922), pp. 73–88.
67. Achim von Arnim, *Sämtliche Romane und Erzählungen*, 3 vols. (Munich: Carl Hanser Verlag, 1962–63), I, 271–72. The whole of Chapter 9 deals with the marvelous doctor.
68. Southey, *op. cit.*, p. 295.
69. Sebastien Mercier, *Tableau de Paris* (Hamburg and Neuchatel, 1781), pp. 103–4.
70. Diderot, *Oeuvres*, Texte établi et annoté par Andre Billy, Bibliothèque de la Pléiade (Paris: Gallimard, 1951), p. 425.
71. Mercier, *op. cit.* (1782), IV, 54–56.
72. For a fuller examination of this point see George Rosen, "Social Attitudes to Irrationality and Madness in 17th and 18th Century Europe," *Journal of the History of Medicine* 18:220–40 (1963).
73. Southey, *op. cit.*, pp. 447–49.
74. Otto Mann, *Der Dandy. Ein Kulturproblem der Moderne* (Heidel-

berg, 1962), pp. 48, 57; Simone François, *Le dandyisme et Marcel Proust. De Brummell au Baron de Charlus* (Brussels, 1956), p. 17; Barbey d'Aurevilly, *Oeuvres romanesques complètes*, Bibliothèque de la Pléiade, 2 vols. (Paris: Gallimard, 1966), II, 670–718.

75. Oliver Goldsmith, *The Bee and other Essays, together with the Life of Nash* (London: Oxford University Press, 1914), pp. 279–409; Edith Sitwell, *Bath* (London: Faber & Faber, 1932), pp. 41–57 and *passim*; Egon Friedell, *Kulturgeschichte der Neuzeit*, Vollständige ungekürzte Ausgabe, Drei Teile in einem Band (London and Oxford: Phaidon Press, 1947), Dritter Teil, p. 68.

76. Baudelaire, *Oeuvres complètes*, Bibliothèque de la Pléiade (Paris: Gallimard, 1961), pp. 1278–94.

77. See for example C. H. Spiess, *Biographien der Wahnsinnigen* (1795–96) (Neuwied-Berlin: Luchterhand Verlag, 1966); also, Rosen, *op. cit.*, Note 72.

78. For a discussion of this problem see George Rosen, "Mental Disorder, Social Deviance and Culture Pattern: Some Methodological Issues in the Historical Study of Mental Illness," in *Psychiatry and Its History*, ed. G. Mora and J. L. Brand (Springfield, Ill.: Charles C Thomas, 1970), pp. 172–94.

79. Samuel Johnson, *Prose and Poetry*, selected by Mona Wilson (Cambridge, Mass.: Harvard University Press, 1957), pp. 468–69.

80. For example see Dieter Claessens, *Angst, Furcht und gesellschaftlicher Druck und andere Aufsätze* (Dortmund: Fr. Wilh. Ruhfus, 1966), pp. 61–69, 88–101.

Un Aspect de l'irrationnel au XVIIIème siècle:

La Démonologie et son exploitation littéraire

P. Vernière

IL N'EST PAS DE PROBLÈME plus irritant, pour l'historien des idées, que cette schématisation pédagogique qui impose à chaque siècle une caractéristique dominante. Le véritable responsable de cette vision contrastée, Hegel, a voulu coûte que coûte construire une dialectique de l'esprit occidental qui non seulement symboliserait, mais aurait plus ou moins inspiré, l'histoire de l'Occident. "L'histoire de l'Esprit" serait ainsi l'histoire des hommes. La réalité des faits détruit cette grandiose ordonnance. Nous savons maintenant opposer un XVIème siècle rationaliste à un XVIème siècle mystique: la Renaissance selon Henri Busson n'est pas celle d'Albert-Marie Schmidt ou de Marguerite Yourcenar. Le siècle classique est aussi le siècle du baroque; les libertins érudits de M. Pintard sont les contemporains des possédés de Loudun, des têtes rondes de Cromwell, des prédicateurs fous des Cévennes. Ces diversités sociales expliquent sans doute les contradictions psychologiques des plus grands esprits: Descartes, inventeur de la géométrie analytique, eut comme Pascal son illumination mystique dans son poêle d'Allemagne. Leibniz auprès de Knorr von Rosenroth recherchait la pierre philosophale.

Il en est de même au XVIIIème siècle. Ce n'est que par schématisation, ou ce qui est plus dangereux, par goût et par choix, que nous en faisons le siècle de la "raison," "the age of reason." Notre but aujourd'hui serait d'aller dans le sens même de votre colloque et d'insister sur un aspect de l'irrationnel au siècle des lumières. Au lieu d'insister sur la fin du siècle où les résurgences mystiques et religieuses se font plus nombreuses, avec certaines sectes d'illuminés et d'occultistes parmi lesquels dominent les noms de Swedenborg, Martinez de Pasqually, Saint-Martin "le philosophe inconnu," où les imposteurs comme Cagliostro et Mesmer sont légion, nous voudrions marquer la continuité à travers les siècles classiques des rêveries irrationnelles. M. Milner a fait débuter avec Cazotte son étude littéraire du diable, alors que le diable n'a cessé de sévir depuis son antique invention. MM. Viatte et Cellier n'étudient les sources du romantisme que dans un tardif XVIIIème siècle. Je crois au contraire, en vous proposant *la démonologie et son exploitation littéraire*, montrer la persistance dans l'âme occidentale d'exigences tantôt poétiques, tantôt religieuses, qui vont d'ailleurs de la fantaisie amusée à la connivence, de la curiosité à la crédulité.

I. LA DÉMONOLOGIE ÉLÉMENTAIRE

Me permettrez-vous d'évoquer sans rire ces vieilles spéculations qui firent tant délirer les philosophes d'autrefois? J'entends par "démonologie" la doctrine des "esprits élémentaires," telle qu'elle prévalut dès la Renaissance et telle qu'on la retrouve dans le romantisme allemand et dans une certaine mythologie wagnérienne. La distinction des quatre éléments *air*, *feu*, *eau*, *terre* remonte aux présocratiques et fonde la cosmologie des philosophes ioniens. Mais l'idée de lier aux éléments quatre groupes, quatre peuples de génies, est relativement récente. Très différente de la théorie des "démons" selon Platon ou Pythagore, elle se développe chez les néo-platoniciens de l'antiquité décadente, Porphyre, Jamblique, et Proclus; les exégètes de la Renaissance la remanient avec Marsile Ficin, Cardan, Pic de la Mirandole. Ronsard en est informé; les premiers occultistes s'en emparent; Paracelse sera leur grand-maître.

Si nous exceptons *L'Hymne sur les démons* de Ronsard, l'exploitation littéraire de cette doctrine est sous la Renaissance d'une rare prudence. Volontairement, le potentiel poétique en est négligé, ce qui prouve qu'elle est matière de créance et de crainte. Pour

Symposium: Un Aspect de l'irrationnel

l'Eglise, elle est hérésie et domaine diabolique. Lorsqu'en 1580 l'illustre jurisconsulte Jean Bodin publie sa *Démonomanie*, toute l'érudition humaniste est mobilisée pour prouver qu'elle correspond aux témoignages quotidiens des tribunaux. La sorcellerie existe; les sorcières établissent des associations charnelles avec les esprits démoniaques. L'Eglise et les instances judiciaires doivent sévir. Bodin propose le supplice du feu et l'étranglement pour ceux qui se repentent. Quant à ceux qui, par scepticisme, réclament l'indulgence et des peines mineures, ce sont les complices de Satan. Huit ans plus tard, en 1588, dans son chapitre des *Boiteux*, Montaigne courageusement réfutera Bodin, verra dans les sorciers des fous et des malades, refusera d'utiliser d'aussi douteuses conjectures pour "faire cuire, selon ses termes, un homme tout vif" (Essais, III, II).

II. LE COMTE DE GABALIS

C'est en 1670, l'année même où paraissait les *Pensées* de Pascal, que le livre essentiel, j'entends le livre de vulgarisation, répandra la doctrine: nous avons peine à croire à l'importance du *Comte de Gabalis*, qui fut pourtant le relais majeur de la pensée irrationnelle entre la Renaissance et le Romantisme. L'ouvrage est charmant, humoristique, écrit dans le français lumineux de Mme. de La Fayette ou de Perrault. Anatole France s'en inspirera encore dans sa *Rôtisserie de la reine Pédauque*. L'auteur, mort jeune, l'abbé de Montfaucon de Villars, est très évidemment rationaliste et tient à ridiculiser cabalistes et occultistes; mais le merveilleux a son charme, et quoi qu'en ait l'auteur, la poésie du sujet l'emportera dans l'esprit des lecteurs sur le rationalisme de la thèse. Même aventure arrivera pour un autre rationaliste: Charles Perrault écrira des *Contes de fées*.

L'histoire est simple et pratiquement sans intrigue: un amateur d'occultisme, sceptique et curieux, reçoit à Paris un grand maître rose-croix, le comte de Gabalis, venu des confins de l'Allemagne et de la Pologne. Gabalis en cinq entretiens lui confie ses secrets, dans les allées mystérieuses du château de Rueil, près de Paris. Si nous excluons deux entretiens sur la cabale et sur les oracles, les trois autres traitent de la nature et des moeurs des esprits élémentaires. Les *sylphes* sont liés à l'air, les *ondins* à l'eau, les *salamandres* au feu, les *gnomes* à la terre. Pour accéder à la maîtrise des génies, il faut renoncer aux femmes. Les hommes sont immortels, mais les génies ne le sont pas. En s'unissant à un génie, on lui confère l'immortalité et il devient votre serviteur pour maîtriser la nature. L'abbé de Villars dépense des trésors d'érudition pour prouver que, dans une perspective chrétienne, tous les dieux du paganisme sont des génies, inoffensifs d'ailleurs et sans lien avec le diable. Quant aux héros de la mythologie, ce sont des enfants nés d'hommes et de génies: Hercule, Alexandre, Apollonios de Tyane, ou Merlin l'Enchanteur qui épousa la nymphe Mélusine. Mais l'auteur ne se borne pas à ces perspectives fabuleuses de l'histoire, où tous les grands hommes de Carlyle prennent une dimension divine. Interviennent alors des exemples contemporains: deux nous intéressent par leur élaboration déjà littéraire. Le premier est celui d'un sylphe amoureux d'une *Demoiselle de Séville* dont l'amant rebuté était parti aux Indes; le sylphe prend le visage de l'amant, séduit la fille, et lui donne deux enfants: on imagine la surprise de l'amant terrestre à son retour de voyage. Non moins curieuse l'histoire du *Seigneur de Bavière*, qu'une sylphe console de sa femme morte en prenant ses traits et en prétendant qu'elle est sa femme ressuscitée.

C'est cet aspect littéraire, poétique plus que dogmatique, qui fera le succès durable du *Comte de Gabalis*. Oeuvre rationaliste d'un libertin érudit? Peut-être. Mais il suffit de comparer cette oeuvre charmante avec le lourd traité rationaliste de Balthazar Bekker, *Le Monde enchanté*, paru à Amsterdam en 1694, pour saisir la différence de portée. Bekker, comme Spinoza, veut démystifier le monde, réduire rationnellement le miracle. Par la critique des témoignages humains et la connaissance des lois de la nature physique, tout merveilleux devient imposture. Bekker est un pasteur protestant sévère, épris de vérité et de christianisme épuré; pour ce cartésien, la doctrine des deux substances exclut la croyance aux esprits; dans son tome IV, la formule est nette: "La droite raison interdit d'admettre le commerce des esprits et des hommes" (t. IV, p. 9). Tous ces phantasmes sont un abus du christianisme, favorisé par l'Eglise de Rome.

Symposium: Un Aspect de l'irrationnel

Les libertins français sont heureusement moins raides et l'exploitation littéraire du *Comte de Gabalis* commence assez tôt. C'est Thomas Corneille qui en 1681 donne le divertissement de la *Pierre philosophale*. Son neveu Fontenelle en 1689 en tire une comédie en un acte, malheureusement perdue: le lien littéraire et même stylistique est évident entre l'abbé de Villars et l'auteur des *Oracles*. En 1714, Beauchamp adapte en deux actes le *Comte de Gabalis* pour divertir la Duchesse du Maine. Faut-il rappeler à nos amis anglicistes que Pope en 1717, dans *The Rape of the Lock*, utilise Gabalis pour exposer la doctrine des Rose-Croix? Mais je voudrais faire un sort à *L'Histoire de M. Oufle* de l'abbé Bordelon, étrange petit roman paru en 1710. Un brave bourgeois, M. Oufle, a perdu la tête à force de lire Bodin, l'abbé de Villars et Bekker; dans un cadre moliéresque qui fait penser au *Malade imaginaire*, il persécute sa famille, femme et enfants, par ses folies. Tour à tour loup-garou, sorcier ou génie, assiégé de fantômes, il cherche à séduire les bourgeoises du crû ou à vérifier par des maléfices la fidélité de son épouse. Chacune de ses aventures se termine par des coups de bâton et des retours ridicules à la maison. *M. Oufle* n'est pas un chef-d'oeuvre; l'abbé Bordelon encombre de notes érudites et de citations curieuses cette histoire indigeste, dont Marivaux ou même Dancourt aurait pu faire une pièce charmante. Mais il n'était pas inutile de montrer la précocité de cette double postérité littéraire du *Comte de Gabalis*: l'une est poétique, l'autre philosophique et morale. Nous retrouverons ce double courant au XVIIIème siècle.

III. L'IRRATIONNEL AU DÉBUT DU XVIIIÈME SIÈCLE

Il existe une très mauvaise petite thèse de 1925 de Constantin Bila, dont le sujet mériterait d'être entièrement repris. Le titre en est *La Croyance à la magie au XVIIIème siècle* (Paris, Gambier, 1925). Mais elle a le mérite d'insister sur la persistance des pulsions irrationnelles dans les esprits et dans les goûts d'un siècle qu'on dit "éclairé." L'incroyable vogue des contes de fées aurait dû éclairer la critique. Le *Cabinet des fées* de Charles Mayer, compilé entre 1785 and 1789, comporte 41 volumes et plus de 80 auteurs. A-t-on mesuré ce qu'exige le conte de fées, cette âme d'enfant, cette créance sans mélange à l'égard du merveilleux ? Je ne veux pas ignorer le XVIIIème siècle des traités politiques et des campagnes philosophiques et humanitaires. Encore faut-il concevoir les besoins psychologiques d'un monde raffiné, sceptique, blasé sur les plaisirs du sexe et de la table. A côté d'un édifice demeuré classique, celui des tragédies de Voltaire, les petits genres, voyages imaginaires, opéras, contes de fées, manifestent la persistance du goût baroque, dans sa quête de l'irrationnel, dans son indulgence pour la poésie, dans son besoin d'évasion.

Nous concevons dès lors le succès persistant du *Comte de Gabalis*, réédité d'ailleurs en 1700, 1742, 1788. Rappelons-nous ce parisien moqué par Montesquieu dans la 58ème *lettre persane*: "Un autre vous promet de vous faire coucher avec des esprits aériens, pourvu que vous soyiez seulement trente ans sans avoir de femmes." C'est une allusion certaine à l'abbé de Villars. Le cardinal de Bernis, favori de la Pompadour, rappelle ses jeux d'enfant dans ses *Mémoires*: au fond du parc paternel, il célébrait des messes noires, le *Comte de Gabalis* à la main. C'est encore Gabalis qu'évoque Casanova, dans son premier voyage en France, vers 1750; c'est ainsi qu'il dupera le comte de La Tour d'Auvergne et sa vieille folle de tante, la marquise d'Urfé. D'après Casanova et les *Souvenirs* de Gleichen, Versailles même n'était pas à l'abri des magiciens et des imposteurs: un nouveau Gabalis, le Comte de Saint-Germain, fut accueilli dans les petits appartements par Louis XV et la Pompadour. Les bibliothèques ésotériques pullulent. On réédite en 1703 le *Grand Albert* et en 1722 le *Petit Albert*. Pierre Cayet en 1712 adapte en français l'histoire de Faust (Cologne, 1712). Dom Calmet écrit en 1751 une *Dissertation sur les revenants et les vampires*. Henri Decremps donne en 1785 *La Magie blanche dévoilée*. Mais le répertoire le plus extraordinaire des sciences occultes se trouve dans le catalogue de la bibliothèque de l'abbé Sépher, mort en 1786.

A telle enseigne que cette vogue, plus ou moins innocente, de la magie, inquiète les philosophes au même titre que l'Eglise officielle. La plupart ont pris position; d'Argens dans ses *Lettres juives* de 1736 et dans ses *Lettres cabalistiques* de 1741; l'*Encyclopédie* dans l'article "Magie"; Voltaire dans le *Dictionnaire philoso-*

phique; Rousseau dans sa *Lettre à Christophe de Beaumont*, archevêque de Paris; le médecin Tissot dans son traité *De l'Imagination*.

L'abbé Coyer dans ses *Bagatelles morales* constate l'universalité de la magie dans la littérature: son porte-parole, un rabbin, déclare que la scène française en est encombrée, cite quelques titres: *le Combat magique, Coraline la magicienne*. Nous trouverions quelques autres pièces, plus proches de la démonologie de l'abbé de Villars; le répertoire du théâtre italien vers 1740 comporte une *Sylphide* que nous avons perdue. Laffichard, en 1744, donne une allégorie comique intitulée *La Salamandre*. Mais nous voudrions insister longuement, dans le genre si révélateur du "conte," sur un thème dont la signification psychanalytique est assez évidente pour les modernes, au point de constituer, à notre sens, dans l'étude de la femme au XVIIIème siècle, un contre-poids nécessaire aux insolences libertines de Crébillon fils, de Duclos, et de Laclos.

IV. TROIS VARIATIONS SUR LE SYLPHE AMOUREUX

Trois variations sur le même thème, le *Sylphe* de Crébillon fils, le *Sylphe amoureux* d'auteur anonyme, le *Mari-Sylphe* de Marmontel. Les éléments communs de ces trois contes sont évidents et prouvent une nécessaire filiation. Même origine: les amours éthérées des esprits de l'air et des humains. Même point de départ: une femme prude, une "précieuse" comme l'on aurait dit au siècle précédent, refuse les hommages charnels qu'elle juge vulgaires et dégradants.

1) *Le Sylphe* de Crébillon fils, oeuvre de jeunesse, date de 1730 et contraste moins qu'on ne croirait avec les contes ultérieurs. Une jeune femme rêve une nuit d'été d'un sylphe qui la viendrait entretenir. Il vient: c'est un esprit invisible qui la rassure en lui disant qu'il ne saurait lui faire violence et qu'il ne peut l'aimer qu'avec son accord. D'ailleurs il sait toutes ses pensées. Il sait notamment qu'il n'y a pas de femme vertueuse. Mais les sylphes exigent la fidélité sous peine de mort. La dame se récrie: "Point de commerce, Monsieur le Démon. Il fallait me cacher la perversité de votre caractère et les risques des engagements qu'on prend avec vous." Sommé de montrer son visage, le sylphe se révèle enfin; il est d'une

admirable beauté. Mais une femme de chambre survient et le fait s'enfuir, au grand regret de la rêveuse. Allégorie psychanalytique d'une étonnante modernité, le *Sylphe* de Crébillon échappe trop vite à ses sources occultistes. Il n'en est pas de même de ses successeurs.

2) *Le Sylphe amoureux*, d'après les éditeurs de 1788, daterait des années 30. J'en ai recherché vainement l'auteur et l'édition originale. L'intrigue se dégage de la pureté psychologique de Crébillon et revêt tous les oripeaux des contes de fées. Jugez-en. La belle marquise d'Autricourt refuse les hommages des hommes. Mais une nuit, à la suite de la lecture propice du *Comte de Gabalis*, des évènements extraordinaires surviennent dans sa chambre: des bracelets de diamants, accompagnés de petits vers, révèlent la présence d'un sylphe amoureux. Des clefs descendent mystérieusement du plafond, ouvrent des cassettes pleines d'élixirs précieux. Tous les désirs qu'elle exprime sont exaucés. Souhaite-t-elle que le sylphe prenne la figure de papillon? Et le soir même, d'un tiroir de sa commode, cent papillons s'envolent. Pour échapper aux sortilèges, la marquise s'enfuit à sa campagne de Suresnes. Le sylphe l'a devancée et continue ses enchantements. L'affaire s'éclairera: ce sont les machinations galantes du comte de Ponteuil, un ami de la marquise, qui a acheté les complaisances des serviteurs. La belle marquise s'incline devant tant de grâce. C'est Ponteuil qui a déclenché les rêveries galantes en lui faisant prêter le *Comte de Gabalis*. Riche de vingt mille livres de rente, il fera un excellent époux.

3) Troisième variation, *Le Mari sylphe* de Marmontel vient trente ans plus tard en 1761. La filiation est évidente avec l'anonyme, sauf que l'amant dans la ligne toute édifiante des *Contes moraux* devient le mari. Elise, sortie du couvent pour épouser le marquis de Volanges, déteste les hommes et croit à la guerre des sexes: "La fable des sylphes était à la mode, dit Marmontel. Il lui était tombé dans les mains quelques-uns de ces romans où l'on a peint le commerce délicieux de ces esprits avec les mortels." Chimère dont elle rêve et dont elle espère le bonheur. Volanges, averti par la suivante Justine de la folie de Madame, monte un scénario avec sa complicité. Il deviendra le sylphe amoureux.

Le sylphe s'annonce en répandant de l'essence de rose; la nuit, il parle à voix basse au chevet du lit et dit des choses exquises.

Elise charmée engage le dialogue: elle ne saurait se faire à la matérialité des époux et souhaite la communion des purs esprits. Le sylphe aussitôt se présente sous le nom de Valoë qui veut dire "tout âme." Tous les désirs d'Elise sont exaucés: une robe souhaitée est aussitôt fournie. Une harpe désirée est apportée par un maître de musique qui récite des vers en son honneur. A la campagne, une tonnelle de lilas est aménagée en une nuit; au bain un portrait d'elle est encastré dans un miroir. Le sylphe sollicité promet de se montrer, mais sous les traits du mari. Au rendez-vous dans un bosquet du parc le sylphe, au grand émoi d'Elise, lui apprend qu'il est devenu un être de désir. Mais Elise la prude préfère sa vertu à son amour et repousse l'audacieux. Volanges tout joyeux, et qui aurait été fâché de se tromper lui-même, avoue qu'il est le mari terrestre, que tout est illusion et badinage galant. Le témoignage de Justine détrompe Elise, qui se félicite que Valoé le sylphe soit son mari Volanges.

Saisissons les différences entre les trois sylphes: celui de Crébillon est illusion nocturne; les deux autres sont de galants imposteurs. Mais il n'y a pas croyance aux esprits dans ces trois contes, rien qui traduise l'irrationnel, dira-t-on? La conclusion est retour au réel, démystification. Nous ne pensons pas qu'une telle interprétation soit la bonne. Rien ne traduit mieux, sinon le conte de *La Belle et la Bête*, contemporain d'ailleurs, les exigences poétiques d'un monde qu'on a cru fermé à toute poésie. Le *Comte de Gabalis*, loin d'apparaître, comme l'ont cru certains historiens des idées, comme un manifeste rationaliste, ouvre un champ poétique nouveau, au même titre que les contes de *Ma mère l'Oie* ou les *Mille et une Nuits*. Villars, Perrault, Galland sont les vrais magiciens du dix-huitième siècle, les maîtres du rêve comme Bayle et Fontenelle sont les maîtres du réel. Nous ne saurions pour notre compte mutiler indûment le siècle de Voltaire; la critique moderne devrait, à propos des sylphes, revenir sur ses préventions et ses oublis, et réhabiliter ces jeux subtils de miroirs que n'aurait pas désavoués Jean Cocteau.

V. LE DIABLE AMOUREUX DE CAZOTTE

Parmi les sylphes, n'oublions pas l'*Amant-Salamandre*, oeuvre unique d'un auteur obscur appelé Cointreau. L'oeuvre est de 1756 et ramasse des données connues: Julie refuse elle aussi les hommages masculins; sa gouvernante tout enfant lui a promis l'amour d'un esprit du feu, une *salamandre*. Cette folie fait le malheur de ses parents qui meurent, pendant que la gouvernante disparaît. Riche, la jeune inhumaine vit retirée dans une maison solitaire près du Luxembourg. Voici que la gouvernante revient, se fait reconnaître et promet la venue de la salamandre. Une nuit, un splendide jeune homme apparaît dans le parc, au milieu de pièces d'artifice et de boules de feu. Chaque nuit, pendant un an, l'amant-salamandre revient. Mais un soir l'amant est blessé à mort devant le porche de l'hôtel. Il avoue la supercherie: c'est sa mère, la gouvernante, qui a fait jouer ce rôle à son fils pour capter la richesse de Julie. Mais Julie pardonne.

Plus grossier dans ses données comme dans sa conclusion mélodramatique, l'*Amant-Salamandre* tourne au roman noir. Mais jugez des éclairages et des prestiges poétiques mis en oeuvre! C'est l'apparition du génie du feu:

> Le jour de ma fête étant arrivé, ma gouvernante me proposa de faire tirer un petit feu d'artifice dans le jardin. Il fut exécuté dans la dernière perfection; on avait mis des lampions autour des murs et sur les fenêtres. Après le feu, nous voulûmes profiter de la plus belle nuit du monde. Nous marchions à pas comptés, lorsque je vis venir au devant de nous un globe de feu qui se soutenait de lui-même. . . . Je frémis à cette vue et je voulus retourner sur mes pas, lorsque ma bonne me força de continuer la promenade. . . . Le globe était toujours au-devant de nous. . . . Nous aperçumes contre le mur un homme d'une riche taille. . . .

Sans vouloir écraser l'obscur Cointreau en rappelant Shakespeare et *Le Songe d'une nuit d'été*, nous solliciterons en sa faveur votre indulgence.

Cazotte, lui, n'a besoin d'indulgence. De Nerval à Jean Cocteau, par le mystère de sa vie et le drame de sa mort sur l'échafaud, il a séduit les meilleurs esprits. Par le *Diable amoureux* aussi, son oeuvre essentielle. Grand initié pour Nerval et le Sar Péladan, il est avant tout pour nous l'initiateur du conte fantastique. Depuis le *Comte de Gabalis*, ce fut au XVIIIème siècle le relais essentiel de

Symposium: Un Aspect de l'irrationnel

la littérature irrationnelle, relais européen, comme nous le verrons bientôt.

Nous ne voudrions pas résumer une oeuvre trop célèbre. Rappelez-vous seulement les aventures du jeune officier espagnol Alvare, capitaine aux gardes du roi de Naples. Par bravade, il évoque le diable dans les ruines de Portici. Belzébuth apparaît sous forme d'une tête de chameau et se met à son service, improvisant fêtes et festins; devenu Biondetta, étrange serviteur au sexe ambigu, il espère séduire son maître qui, catholique résolu, se méfie de la beauté du diable. C'est à Venise que la tentation se précise: Biondetta, poignardée par une courtisane, fait oublier à Alvare son origine diabolique et exige un amour absolu. Mais des signes miraculeux l'avertissent du danger: Alvare fuit en Espagne, propose un mariage chrétien. Au cours d'une fête dans un mystérieux château, Biondetta réussit enfin à faire céder le pieux Espagnol. Le diable triomphe; la tête de chameau apparaît au milieu de monstres phosphorescents. Triomphe sans lendemain, car il n'a pas su entamer la réelle vertu d'Alvare.

Mais un tel résumé détruit le charme, l'intense poésie, le symbolisme subtil de l'oeuvre de Cazotte. L'humour n'est pas absent, mais le ton est neuf. Nous sommes loin des impostures galantes de Marmontel et des jeux nocturnes de Crébillon. Biondetta est le diable en personne. Car c'est cette présence du diable et de Dieu, par cet irrationnel qui dépasse la fantaisie poétique, qui confère au *Diable amoureux* une dimension nouvelle. L'idée du pacte faustien fait de Cazotte un frère de Marlowe ou de Goethe, plus qu'un contemporain de Diderot ou d'Helvétius. Pour goûter le *Diable amoureux*, il faut une certaine adhésion au sujet, une certaine connivence; il faut ressentir soi-même l'effroi d'Alvare. Un exégète de Cazotte, Lucien Maury, parle d'un "reflet de flamme souterraine." Cazotte en 1772 n'est pas encore le grand initié, le maçon mystique, le fanatique qui mourra en martyr du royalisme. Mais son christianisme intact lui fait réfuter la démonologie rassurante du *Comte de Gabalis*: les esprits élémentaires existent, mais ce ne sont plus les émanations inoffensives de la nature; ce sont les "incubes" et les "succubes" démoniaques de l'orthodoxie théologique.

Est-ce à dire que dans cette dialectique nouvelle le contact est rompu avec le *Comte de Gabalis*? Nullement. Biondetta pour séduire Alvare se dira "fille de l'air." Ecoutons sa profession de foi:

> Je suis *sylphide d'origine* et une des plus considérables d'entre elles. . . . Je reçus vos ordres et nous nous empressâmes tous à l'envi de les accomplir. Je me soumis avec joie, et goûtai de tels charmes dans mon obéissance que je résolus de vous la vouer pour toujours. . . . Décidons, me disais-je, mon état et mon bonheur. Abandonnée dans le vague de l'air à une incertitude nécessaire, sans sensations, sans jouissances, balancerai-je davantage sur le choix des moyens par lesquels je puis ennoblir mon essence? Il m'est permis de prendre un corps pour m'associer à un sage: le voilà. Si je me réduis à un simple état de femme, si je jerds, par ce changement volontaire, le droit naturel des sylphides et l'assistance de mes compagnes, je jouirai du bonheur d'aimer et d'être aimée. Je servirai mon vainqueur, je l'instruirai de la sublimité de son être: il nous soumettra, avec les éléments dont j'aurai abandonné l'empire, les esprits de toutes les sphères. Il est fait pour être le roi du monde, et j'en serai la reine et la reine adorée de lui.

Même si le poète faustien transparaît, avec le thème déjà romantique de "la puissance et de la gloire," Biondetta suit de très près le quatrième entretien du *Comte de Gabalis* dont je rappelle le titre: "Sur les mariages des enfants des hommes avec les peuples élémentaires." La sylphide exige un philosophe, un sage, pour confirmer sa propre incarnation. La fidélité absolue est de rigueur: "Il ne me suffit pas de promettre d'être à moi, dit Biondetta. Il faut que vous vous donniez, et sans réserve, et pour toujours." Mais Cazotte apporte à la démonologie une dimension métaphysique. Le *Comte de Gabalis*, dans ses rêveries rosicruciennes, développait avec humour un espoir d'eugénisme, celui d'une race humaine améliorée par le contact des génies. Cazotte, par les tentations de son diable femelle qui sait pleurer et émouvoir, prendre l'homme au piège de sa sensibilité et tirer le pire de ce qu'il pense être tre le meilleur de lui-même, construit au delà d'une fable un mythe qui exprime à merveille la condition de l'homme moderne, pris entre le désir de jouissance, la volonté de puissance et les exigences infantiles d'une bonne conscience.

CONCLUSION

Nous ne saurions pousser au delà de Cazotte l'étude de cette "démonologie littéraire." Mais dans la mesure où Cazotte cite encore, dans la conclusion du *Diable amoureux*, la *Démonomanie* de Bodin et le *Monde enchanté* de Bekker, nous espérons avoir prouvé la continuité historique de ce thème depuis le XVIème siècle. A la vision hégélienne des pulsions dialectiques contradictoires, puis réconciliées, nous préférons constater, dans leurs lignées parallèles, l'extraordinaire survie des exigences fondamentales de l'esprit. La démonologie est un aspect de l'exigence de l'irrationnel, aussi respectable, aussi irrépressible que celle de la raison. Nous espérons avoir montré la survie au XVIIIème siècle, dans la littérature comme dans les goûts du public "éclairé," des valeurs irrationnelles qu'on déguise sous les mots de "fantaisie," de "rêve," de "poésie."

Mais la persistance de ce thème démonologique, outre qu'il nous impose de reconnaître définitivement le double visage du XVIIIème siècle, nous permettra de lier les siècles d'autrefois avec notre propre monde mental, façonné par cent cinquante ans de romantisme. Quelques jalons suffiront: Mathieu Lewis dans son roman noir *Le Moine (The Monk)* fait séduire Ambrosio par une nécromancienne qui, introduite dans le cloître, le livre à Satan. Nouvelle incarnation de la Biondetta de Cazotte, le *Visionnaire* de Schiller (*Der Geisterseher*): nous voyons vivre près de Venise, sur les rives de la Brenta, un prince entiché de magie avec un serviteur suspect, Biondello. Hoffmann enfin, dans son *Elementargeist (L'Esprit élémentaire)* avoue sa dette envers Cazotte et le "Teufel Amor": son héros, Victor, est l'amant d'une salamandre.

Faut-il évoquer, dans le domaine des lettres germaniques, les ondines de La Motte-Fouqué, la petite sirène d'Andersen, les gnômes wagnériens gardiens des trésors de la terre et des eaux? Dans le domaine français, les sylphides romantiques éviteront de s'incarner pour nourrir les rêveries de Chateaubriand. Nerval écrira les *Filles du feu*. Baudelaire dans "Le Possédé" (*Fleurs du mal*, XXXIV) et Théophile Gautier dans *Albertus* se souviendront des diablesses de Cazotte et de l'aveu d'Alvare: "Mon cher Belzébuth, je t'adore!" Plus tard enfin, Giraudoux fera revivre l'*Ondine* de La Motte-Fouqué.

Je ne sais si, en notre siècle de fer, il n'est pas dérisoire d'évoquer, même dans leur exploitation littéraire, les esprits élémentaires qui firent rêver nos ancêtres—qui d'ailleurs, au même titre que nous, se croyaient "éclairés." Nous avons, avec Freud, intériorisé le mythe, tout simplement. Et lorsque Gaston Bachelard, au delà d'une dimension psychanalytique, nous révèle esthétiquement grâce aux rêveries de l'eau, de la terre et du feu, fait-il autre chose que de rajeunir l'antique démonologie et de découvrir, en ceux d'entre nous qui sont poètes, autant d'ondines, de sylphes, et de salamandres?

The Irrational and the Problem of Historical Knowledge in the Enlightenment

Hayden White

IT IS CONVENTIONAL nowadays in any discussion of eighteenth-century historical thought to make at least a small gesture in the direction of rebalancing the nineteenth-century charge that the Enlightenment was deficient in historical sensibility. And it would seem obligatory to make such a gesture in a discussion of the concept of the irrational in eighteenth-century historical thinking, for the nineteenth century's indictment of the historical sensibility of the age turns in large part on allegations regarding the Enlightener's incapacity to entertain sympathetically any manifestation of the irrational in past ages or cultures whose devotion to reason did not equal its own. But it seems to me that any analysis of eighteenth-century historical thinking which begins with the assumption that the nineteenth century was justified in making the *kind* of criticism it did of the eighteenth century grants too much to the nineteenth-century historians' conception of what a proper historical sensibility *ought to be*. It was Nietzsche who reminded his age that there are different kinds of historical sensibility, and that sympathy and tolerance are not necessarily the most desirable attributes for all historians in all situations. There are times, he said, in the lives of cultures no less than in the lives of individuals, when the "proper" historical sensibility is marked by a selective forgetfulness rather than by an indiscriminant remembering. And part of his respect for the Enlightenment derived from his appreciation of its willingness to practice "critical" history rather than the "monumental" and "antiquarian" varieties which constituted the historiographical orthodoxy of his own time.

If we were to use Nietzsche's terminology, we would be permitted to say that the Enlightenment attitude towards the past was less ahistorical or unhistorical than "superhistorical," willing to bring the past to the bar of judgment, to break it up and, when necessary, condemn it in the interests of present *needs* and the *hope* of a better life. To be sure, as even Nietzsche admitted, this willingness to "annihilate" the past is as dangerous in its way as that indiscriminate sympathy for old things just because they are old which is the sign of a culture grown stale. For once one begins the work of annihilation, it is difficult to set a limit on it and to retrieve that reverence for roots and respect for the conservative virtues without which the human organism cannot survive. Still, *for its time,* the Enlightenment's "superhistorical" attitude was as necessary as it was desirable, and its consistent hostility to unreason was not unproductive of significant historical insights. Without their uniquely "critical" approach to history, the Enlighteners would not have been able to carry out their work of dismantling tired institutions and discrediting the authority of a tradition long since degenerated into mechanical routine. A critical approach to the historical record as given by tradition was a necessary precondition of the Enlighteners' program for planting a second nature in place of the first, which had been willed to them by their predecessors as *the sole possible* form that any specifically *human* life might take.

The principal charge against the Enlighteners is that their militant rationalism short-circuited any impulse to entertain sympathetically and to judge tolerantly the many manifestations of the irrational that they found in the historical record, and especially in the records of the Middle Ages and remote antiquity. The charge is accurate enough as a *description* of the approach of the best historical thinkers of the age in the main line of rationalism —Bayle, Montesquieu, Voltaire, Robertson, Hume, and Gibbon— though it hardly does justice to representatives of the variant convention—Leibniz, Vico, Möser, and Herder. But as a *judgment* suggesting a crucial limitation on the rationalists' historical sense, it implicitly begs the question of the uses to which knowledge in general, and historical knowledge in particular, ought to be put. This question is *meta*historiographical—having to do with the *value* that one assigns to the *disinterested* study of the past—and cannot therefore be adjudicated from within historical thinking itself. The way one approaches the past, the posture one assumes before the data of history, the voice with which one reports one's findings about the past, the ratio between one's capacities for tolerance and one's interest in interpreting and criticizing—all these are functions of a *meta*historiographical, and specifically ethical, decision regarding the uses to which one's knowledge ought to be put. It is true that eighteenth-century historical thinkers tended to *overvalue* the irrational as a causal factor in the historical process and to *undervalue* it as a possible source of creative social force. But if they were intolerant of what *we* no longer regard as unreason but value rather as faith, they were guilty only of a misjudgment; their instinct was sound enough. The important point is not whether they failed to distinguish between unreason and faith but what critical insights into the nature of historical existence their failure to draw that distinction adequately may have provided them with.

It is not as if the eighteenth century was unacquainted with the *forma mentis* which, in the nineteenth century, would triumph as historicism and which would, in the event, establish tolerance and sympathy for everything in the past, rational as well as irrational, as an unquestioned canon of orthodoxy in historical thought. In Leibniz' philosophy, for example, we encounter attitudes which do not so much endow the irrational with a specific value as simply dissolve the distinction between reason and unreason as a criterion of evaluation. In the *Monadology* (1714), the very concept of the irrational is ruled out as a category of significant historical being, since the notion of *intrinsic* irrationality would have suggested some inadequacy in the Creation and hence, by implication, in the Creator. Leibniz' doctrine of continuity, with its cognate ideas of analogical reasoning in epistemology and of evolution in ontology, generates the conception of *transition by degrees* from one spatial location to another and from one temporal instant to another, which effectively denies the adequacy of any characterization of the world in terms of *oppositions*. So too, in his conception of human nature, Leibniz sees no discontinuity between the physical and spiritual attributes of men, between different kinds of men, or between different spiritual states within men. Just as the very notion of a "monstrous" man was an anomaly, reflecting more a failure of knowledge or imagination in the knower than an inadequacy in the thing known, so too the notion of an inherently "irrational" man reflected either a want of knowledge or an inadequate conception of human nature. Contiguous in space, continuous in time: such were the presuppositions of the notion of the historical process which Leibniz brought to his attempts at historical writing. The "annalistic" form of historical representation which he promoted was thus more than a device for mechanically organizing the historical field: it reflected the order of being in time, *evolution by degrees*, that *continuity* in the historical process of which the cosmos itself was a spatial equivalent.

The implications of this conception of history were fully worked out only during the last two decades of the eighteenth century, particularly by Herder, whose *Ideen zur Philosophie der Geschichte des Menschheits* appeared between 1784 and 1791. Between 1714, the year of Leibniz' *Monadology*, and the 1780's the doctrine of continuity, the concept of evolution, and the principle of analogical reasoning had fallen on evil days, not only in natural philosophy, from which they had been expelled by Newton and Locke, but from historiography as well. Their return to historiography with Herder, however, does not so much signal the rebirth of a *genuine* historical sensibility as mark an important transition from one *form* of historical thought to another, a transition from the "critical" historiography of the Enlightenment to the historical "pietism" of the nineteenth century. Such a transition can be regarded as an absolute *progressus* only to those who fail to credit the Nietzschean distinction between different ways of approaching the historical field.

Even Cassirer, who was among the first to oppose the view that the Enlightenment was deficient in historical sensibility, has stressed the *revolutionary nature* of Herder's attack upon "analytical thinking and the principle of identity" that—in Cassirer's view —had hampered the development of a fully tolerant historiography throughout most of the preceding century. Herder, Cassirer says, "dispells the illusion of identity"; nothing for him is really identical with anything else, nothing ever recurs in the same form. For Herder:

> History brings forth new creatures in uninterrupted succession, and on each she bestows as its birthright a unique shape and an independent mode of existence. Every abstract generalization is, therefore, powerless with respect to history, and neither a generic nor any universal norm can comprehend its wealth.

But, revolutionary as this application of the doctrine of continuity may have been, it does not follow, as Cassirer believed, that the historical sensibility of the next age was absolutely superior to that of the rationalists of the eighteenth century. For Herder's type of thinking not only dissolved the distinction between the "exotic" and the "familiar," it also dissolved the distinction between the rational and the irrational, without which "critical" historiography cannot be practical at all.

To Herder, everything in history is equally exotic or equally familiar, that is to say, equally worthy of being entertained as simply one more manifestation of man's marvelous capacity for survival, adjustment, accommodation, growth, or adaptation. For Herder, existence itself is a value. He delights in the fact that "what can anywhere occur, does occur; what can operate, operates." And on the basis of this fact, he is permitted to warn his readers against any "concern" about history of either a "provident or retrospective" sort. "All that can be, is," he says, again and again; "all that can come to be, will be, if not today, then tomorrow.... Everything has come to bloom upon the earth which could do so, each in its own time and in its own milieu; it has faded away, and it will bloom again, when its time comes."

Herder does not presume to place himself above, or to judge, anything in the historical record. He has neither more nor less respect for the Romans than he has for the slovenly natives of Southern California, news of which has reached him from missionaries to those exotic shores. These Californians, who change their habitation "perhaps a hundred times a year," who sleep wherever and whenever the urge seizes them "without paying the least regard to the filthiness of the soil or endeavouring to secure themselves from noxious vermin," and who feed on seeds which, "when pressed by want, they pick with their toes out of their own excrement"—these humble Californians are neither more nor less than the noblest of Romans. Both were, as he says of the Romans specifically, "precisely what they were capable of becoming: everything perishable belonging to them perished, and what was susceptible of permanence remained." It is in history as it is in nature, Herder concludes, "all, or nothing, is fortuitous; all, or nothing, is arbitrary.... This is the only philosophical method of contemplating history, and it has been even unconsciously practiced by all thinking minds."

Of course, needless to say, for Herder nothing is fortuitous, nothing arbitrary; and nothing—not even the most irrational act—is without its reasons for being precisely what it was in the time and place in which it occurred.

This "pietistic" posture before the particular historical event—before the irrational as well as the rational in human nature—differs radically from that *ironic* attitude which prevails in the main line of historical thought in the eighteenth century from Bayle to Gibbon. Which is not to say that the rationalists were utterly lacking in sympathy for irrational humanity or totally incapable of tolerance for the irrationality of man displayed all too amply in the historical record. In general, the scepticism of the Enlighteners guarded them well enough against the tendency to set the folly of past men over against the presumed wisdom of their contemporaries. That kind of simple-minded Manichaeism which saw reason and folly as opposite and mutually exclusive states of mind is to be found among doctrinaire rationalists such as Turgot and Condorcet; but among the best historians in the rationalist tradition —Voltaire, Hume, Gibbon—such Manichaeism functions more as a rhetorical device than as a notion about the relation of reason to unreason in mankind everywhere and in all times and places.

As historians, the Enlighteners tend in general to ground their apprehension of—and consequently their judgments on—folly in the *situation* in which it is manifested. In his *History of Charles XII*, for example, Voltaire distinguishes quite rigorously and consistently between the kind of *miscalculation* which led Charles to undertake the conquest of Russia and the deeper *folly* reflected in his attempts to win glory through conquest. Unlike the *Philosophy of History*, which *is* marked by a tendency to conceive the conflict between reason and unreason (or charlatanry and stupidity) in Manichaean terms, the *History of Charles XII* subtly distinguishes between a number of different *kinds* of irrationality in Charles' career. Voltaire is not above taking delight in the exposure of stupidity in the past as well as in the present, but this mock-epic (as Lionel Gossman has called it in his brilliant analysis of it as a work of art) is shot through with a sympathy for a ruler whose reason was insufficient to guide him to use his talents for pacific rather than martial ends. The passages in which Voltaire describes the death of Charles in the trenches before Frederikshall and goes on to draw the moral of a life misspent in pursuit of martial glory are worthy of comparison with anything produced by the historians of the next century. The didactic aim is manifest, but the judgments as specifically *historical* judgments are unexceptionable. And they are rendered more convincing by the presence of a melancholy recognition that neither talent itself nor even reason of a certain kind is sufficient warrant against the power of folly. Voltaire, like Bayle, took a perverse delight in cataloguing the wide range of forms that folly might take; but this very apprehension of the various forms that irrationality might take drives him in the end to the recognition that folly might prevail in human nature in the long run. And his knowledge of folly's power over men of even the most exceptional talents guarded Voltaire against the naive optimism which a doctrinaire rationalist faith in the power of reason fostered in thinkers like Turgot. And much the same can be said of both Hume and Gibbon.

In my view, the causes of the Enlighteners' failures as well as their successes as historians are not to be found in any inability of theirs to understand, or even to sympathize with and to tolerate, the irrational in history. They lie rather in their incapacity to conceive historical knowledge in general as a *problem*. When they write on the question of historical knowledge or the writing of history, both Bayle and Voltaire tend to draw the line too rigidly between *history* on the one side and *fable* on the other. Although recognizing that "history, generally speaking, is the most difficult composition that an author can undertake," Bayle seems to think that the principal requirement for the writing of good history is a *desire* to tell the truth. Thus in the article on "Historical Talent" in his *Dictionnaire historique*, Bayle remarks: "I observe that truth being the soul of history, it is an essential thing for a historical composition to be free from lies; so that though it should have all other perfections, it will not be a history, but a mere fable or romance, if it want truth." But the will to truth is an insufficient methodological principle for the production of an adequate history. The great antiquarians of the age, men like Muratori and Curne de la Sainte-Palaye, appear to have recognized this truth when they stressed the necessity of philological, epigraphical, and numismatic evidence for the proper assessment of the documentary record. But even they did not appreciate the difficulty of choosing among several different *possible* accounts of the past, and they appeared to have no notion at all of the problem of translating an apprehension of the past into a plausible picture of it in a narrative account.

The historical Pyrrhonism which flourished at the beginning of the eighteenth century, and which could be used to justify the writing of *histoire galante* or *romanesque* on the one side and what Bayle and Voltaire called satirical history on the other, was effectively demolished by the antiquarians' achievements in actually reconstructing a true *chronicle* of remote ages. But the translation of a chronicle into a history required more than erudition, and it required more than learning augmented by common sense. Learning alone could yield what Nietzsche called "antiquarian" historiography, necessary for the promotion of the human capacities for reverence and respect for the roots of human culture and society, and common sense could promote that "monumental" historiography which inspired heroic actions in the interest of a better future. But something more was required if historical knowledge was to contribute to that effort to "distance" the past, an act necessary for the proper assessment of present possibilities. Voltaire was on the right track when, in the *Philosophy of History*, he insisted on reason's right to submit the historical record to criticism in the light of current science, on the right of critical intelligence to treat past pieties with the scorn which present exigency required. Yet not even he was able to appreciate the ambiguity of the messages which the past transmitted to the present in the form of historical documents and records.

The failure of the age to appreciate the problematics of historical knowledge is shown clearly in the work of the Abbé de Mably. In his *De la manière de l'écrire l'histoire* (1782), a work which is sensibly critical of the "ironical" element in the histories of Voltaire, Hume, and Robertson, Mably suggests that "character" is the ultimate basis of good historiography. Historians are born, he says, not made. According to Mably, the historian's principal *problem*, once his investigation of the historical record was done, was to choose between the plot-structures of Comedy and Tragedy for depicting those events in the past worthy of having a history written about them. And in his discussion of this problem, Mably assumes, as most of his contemporaries appear to have done, that the rules of *classical* rhetoric and poetics are sufficient for its resolution. All historical manifestations of heroism and villainy, of good and evil, or of reason and folly could be drawn together and woven into a story of general human interest and edification by the application of the principles of narration contained in tested classical models. Wisdom was necessary for the selection of the model to be used in a specific instance, but in Mably's view one was either born wise or not. Tact was the important thing, to know how to "emplot" the events appropriately.

Mably's counsels on how to write history reveal an important hidden assumption in Enlightenment historiography, a contradiction which hindered the efforts of its best historians to deal with the main problems of historical representation, whether of the irrational or of anything else. This contradiction is caused by Enlightenment historians' dependence upon the rules of classical rhetoric and poetics as the methodology of historical representation and a simultaneous suspicion of the figurative language and analogical reasoning required for their proper application. Voltaire still views historiography in classical terms; it is philosophy teaching by example, imagistically as it were rather than by discursive logic. At the same time, however, he explicitly rules out figurative language as an appropriate instrument for conveying the meaning of an historical account. Thus he writes in his *Philosophical Dictionary*, "Ardent imagination, passion, desire—frequently deceived—produce the figurative style. We do not admit it into history, for too many metaphors are hurtful, not only to perspecuity, but also to truth, by saying more or less than the thing itself." And in his discussion of poetic tropes, he criticizes the Fathers for their excessive use of them, which in his view leads to *fabulation* rather than a *representation of the truth*. Figurative language can be appropriately used only in poetry, he says; and he cites Ovid as a poet who uses figures and tropes in such a way as to "deceive" no one.

What Voltaire and most of the Enlighteners failed to see was that figurative language is just as often a way of expressing a truth incompletely grasped as it is of concealing an error or falsehood incompletely recognized. The rigid distinction between figurative language for poetic effects on the one side and discursive prose representation for reporting the truth of things on the other prevented the Enlighteners from taking seriously the fables, legends, and myths which came to them as the truths by which men in past ages had lived. The Enlighteners did not regard the passions or the imagination as expungeable elements of human nature, to be set over against the reason as its enemies; on the contrary, what they sought was a judicious balancing of the reason and the emotions in the construction of a just humanity. But they did tend to compartmentalize the psyche in such a way as to lead them to draw rigid distinctions between the imagination's area of legitimate expression on the one side and reason's proper domain on the other. And this compartmentalization of the psyche blocked their understanding of the ways in which reason and the imagination might work in tandem as both guides to practical activity and as instruments of understanding. And therefore, in their contemplation of the evidence of the remote past, they failed to see how truth might be contained in fable, and fable in truth, in civilizations whose commitments to reason were not as fully developed as their own.

Peter Gay has recently argued that, whatever the limitations of the Enlighteners' historical sensibility, in the distinction which they drew between mythical thought on the one side and scientific thought on the other they anticipated the modern scientific histories of culture produced by our own age. But that distinction was not unique to Enlightenment thought; it was as old as Greek philosophy and was a mainstay even of Christian theology during the Patristic period. In any event, modern scientific theories of culture are as much dependent on the conception of the functional *similarities* between mythic and scientific thinking as upon the recognizable formal differences between them. Where the Enlighteners failed was in their inability, once they had drawn the distinction between mythical thinking and scientific thinking, to see how these might be bound up with one another as *phases* in the history of a single culture, society, or individual consciousness. As long as they identified the "fabulous" with the "unreal," and failed to see that fabulation itself could serve as a means to the apprehension of the truth about reality and was not simply an alternative to or an adornment of such apprehension, they could never gain access to those cultures and states of mind in which the distinction between the true and the false had not been as clearly drawn as they hoped to draw it.

To put the matter another way, to conceive the "fabulous" as the opposite of the "true" was legitimate enough as a principle by which to characterize the differences between an aesthetic apprehension of reality on the one side and a scientific, or philosophical, comprehension of it on the other. But when treated as a principle of psychology, or of epistemology, such an opposition dissolved any effort to search for the ground on which mediations between them might be achieved. Truth and fable are no more *opposed* than science and poetry, and to make of the "true" and the "fabulous" the categories of a historical method is as dangerous as the *opposition* of reason to imagination in a psychological theory or a theory of knowledge. And it was the mark of Vico's genius to perceive the fallacies contained in such oppositions and to attempt, in the *New Science* (first edition, 1725, definitive edition, 1744), to provide a historical method in which the principle of *distinction* would supplant the reductionist tendencies in both the Leibnizian and Lockean approaches to the study of human consciousness.

In the *New Science* Vico criticizes Bayle for advancing the belief that nations might grow and prosper without *any* belief in God; but it is the *kind* of scepticism about the beliefs of primitive peoples in general which Bayle's rationalism fosters that is a principal target of his book. The historical consciousness of his own age, Vico believed, was informed by misconceptions about primitive peoples that engendered two conceits, that of the "scholars," who tended to assume that earlier peoples must have possessed the same learning as that possessed by the scholars themselves, and that of the "nations," which assumed that primitive peoples must have conducted their affairs in the ways that fully civilized peoples do. These two conceits permitted the philosophers to solve the historical problem, which is to explain how humanity might have lived on the basis of principles *different* from those honored in the present, by simply denying that the problem existed: by simply asserting that primitive man must have solved his problems in the same way, and by the same means, that modern men do. This in turn promoted the conviction that all of the original evidence—oral, written, and monumental—about the style of life of ancient peoples, evidence which was uniformly "fabulous" in nature, was a product either of error or duplicity.

Yet, Vico argued, such an assumption offended against reason itself, which taught that humanity in general and society in particular could not survive if founded on nothing but error and deceit. There must have been some adequacy of mythical belief to reality, or pagan humanity could not have raised itself from the condition of savagery to that of civilization. And this suggested the possibility of a third kind of knowledge between the literally true and the fabulous, on the basis of which the relationship between primitive consciousness and the world could be mediated and the adequacy of the one to the other be *progressively* realized.

This third order of knowledge, which is a combination of truth and error, or is rather half-truth treated as "certain" truth for practical purposes, is a species of what we would call the *fictive* in a precise sense. What Vico does is transform the notion of the "fabulous" into a generic concept, generally descriptive of consciousness, of which the literally true and the poetic are species. If we admit the use of the notion of the "fictive" as a way of designating the general nature of human consciousness, we can then regard the "true" and the "fabulous" as simply *different* ways of signifying the relationship of the human consciousness to the world it confronts in different *degrees* of certitude and comprehension. Vico conceives the "fictive" as unconscious hypothesis-making of the sort consigned by Aristotle to the poets; for him, "poetry" figures reality. And his conceptualization of the notion of the "poetic wisdom" of primitive man as a form of proto-science permits him to break down the distinction between the true and the fabulous which blocked the rationalists' understanding of those ages not endowed with a commitment to rationality commensurate with their own.

Instead of setting the imagination over against the reason as an *opposed* way of apprehending reality, and poetry over against prose as an *opposed* way of representing it, Vico argues for a *continuity* between them. This conceptualization of consciousness gives him a way of reconceiving the relationship between the irrational and the rational in the life of culture. Moreover, it allows him to view philosophy not as an *alternative* to, but as merely a *different way* of speaking about, truths originally apprehended in poetic forms. By reversing the relationship between the imagination and the reason, and seeing the former as the necessary basis of the latter, Vico succeeds in clearing the way to an understanding of those myths and fables in which earlier cultures expressed their lived experiences of the worlds they occupied.

Unlike Leibniz, then, who was inclined to place everything on the same ontological plane and thus dissolve the distinction between the rational and the irrational in life, Vico provides a means of at once distinguishing between the irrational and the rational manifestations of consciousness and then linking them in time as stages of a single evolutionary process. The mechanism which directed this evolutionary process was in his view neither rational nor irrational *per se*, but a pre-rational factor, unique to man, which served as a mediating agency between mind and body on the one side and between human consciousness and its milieux on the other. This mediating agency was speech, which, in the dialectical relationship between its capacities for poetic articulation and prosaic representation, provides the model for comprehending human evolution in general.

The most significant difference between the first edition of the *New Science* (1725) and the last edition (1744) was the expansion of the discussion of the *creative* aspects of language. In the first edition, Vico does little more than assert that language is the clue to the understanding of primitive man's construction of a world in which he can feel at home. But in the later editions he goes on to explain how poetic language might have served as the basis of primitive man's closure with a natural world that must have appeared alien and threatening to him in all its aspects. It was by *metaphorical projection* of his own nature onto that world, Vico theorizes, that primitive man was able progressively to *humanize* it. By identifying the forces of nature as man-like spirits, primitive man invented religion. By the progressive tropological reductions of those forces—by metonymy and synecdoche especially—primitive men gradually came to the realization of their own godlike natures. Then, by the trope of irony, they came to an awareness of the possibility of distinguishing between truth and error in the conceptualization of both the natural world and society. Thus, science and philosophy themselves were rendered possible by an insight into the nature of the relationship between consciousness and reality provided by poetry; they were not to be viewed as creations of reason, but rather as products of poetic, and specifically tropological, consciousness. And thus, the relation between the imagination and reason can be conceived as *both* a temporal *and* an ontological relationship, the one being contained in the other rather than being opposed to it.

These insights into language and consciousness permitted Vico to break down the opposition of truth to fable and to conceive the fictive as a third ground between them, but they also permitted him to conceive of the *theory of language* as the *methodology* for comprehending the function of myth and fable in primitive and archaic cultures. This was the basis of his attack upon the philological method of the antiquarian historiography of his time, which assumed that it was enough to know the history of words and their etymologies without inquiring into the more basic problem of the function of language in the process of civilization.

The Enlighteners' indifference to the kinds of questions that Vico raised helps illuminate some significant presuppositions of their thought. One way of characterizing the thought of an age is to identify the questions which its representative thinkers consistently beg. One question begged by the Enlightenment was that of the nature of historical knowledge—not the question of *what happened* in history or the *meaning* of the historical process, but of *how historical knowledge is possible*. This is what I meant when I said that history as such was not a problem for the Enlighteners. By the same token, neither was language a problem for them. This is not to say that they did not study languages or recognize the importance of language in the evolution of culture, but rather that they did not take language itself, with its powers to illuminate as well as to obscure, as a problem. And this crucially limited their capacities for understanding the modes of expression of cultures radically different from their own.

As long as it was considered sufficient for the historian simply to learn the language in which documents from the past had been written, rather than to penetrate the *modes of thought* reflected in different linguistic conventions, the minds of past ages had to remain closed to anything approximating full understanding of their operations. The Enlighteners' bias in favor of recent, as against remote, history therefore reflected a commendable tact. As long as they were dealing with cultures not too dissimilar from their own, they produced historiography such as the History of Charles XII, The Age of Louis XIV, or the Decline and Fall of *the Roman Empire* that was as good as anything produced by later historians. When they tried to deal with radically different ages and cultures, they tended to overvalue or undervalue their originality and uniquenesses, as Gibbon did with Byzantium, Winckelmann with Greece, Robertson with America, and Hume with the Middle Ages. When they found things to admire in these remote ages and cultures, they were inclined to temper their admiration with benign irony. When they found things they despised, they were inclined simply to berate them rather than to try to comprehend their functions in worlds different from their own. Their failure lay in their unwillingness to credit fully their own prodigious capacities for poetic identification with the different and strange. They did not trust their own oneiric powers. But given the task they had set themselves, which was to discredit any institution or idea that hampered the construction of a just society in their own time, this was a legitimate decision. For as Nietzsche said, it is not always a creative decision to seek understanding when the situation calls for criticism, or to show tolerance when what is needed is an assertion of the rights of the present over the claims of the past.

Vico remained unappreciated throughout the eighteenth century, not merely because his thought was especially complex, but because the most progressive thinkers of the age could not, given their purpose, afford the luxury of conceiving historical knowledge in general as a problem. The historical thinkers in the main line of rationalism—Bayle, Montesquieu, Voltaire, Hume, and Gibbon—were engaged in a ground-clearing operation on behalf of an ideal which necessarily required that the crucial cultural relationships be conceived in terms of oppositions rather than continuities or subtle gradations. Their most creative work was critical rather than constructive, directed against irrationalism in whatever form it appeared, whether as superstition, ignorance, or tyranny, or as emotion, myth, or passion. It was in their interest to view the past (and especially the remote past) as *the opposite* of that which they valued in their own present, not as *the basis* of it. Vico appeared to make reason dependent upon unreason, to make of it a refined form of unreason, the products of which were essentially the same as those produced by unreason. But if the *philosophes* had seriously entertained the notion of the identity of reason with unreason in human consciousness, at whatever level, their critical work would have been undermined from the beginning.

The essentially conservative implications of Vico's system conflicted with the conscious interests of the rationalist philosophers of history and their counterparts in historiography. Vico had to be ignored or set aside for the same reasons that Leibniz had to be rejected and satirized. His system might be recognized as doing more justice to the facts of history, but it was not justice so much as truth that the Enlighteners demanded. Justice was what was demanded for living men, and justice for living men could be provided in part by bringing those residues of the past still living in the present to the bar of judgment, exposing their irrational bases and the unreason involved in continued loyalty to them, and consigning them to a past that was genuinely dead, a fit object of antiquarian interest but nothing more.

Yet, the radical scepticism of the age, a scepticism which existed alongside of a conscious devotion to reason, was ultimately destructive of the faith in reason which it had originally promoted in its purely critical function vis-à-vis tradition and custom. Reason itself, reason hypostatized, could not long remain exempted from the second thoughts about the irrationality of its own hypostatization which scepticism inevitably inspired. We can see, in the best historical thought of the age and in Hume especially, a growing recognition of the limitations of a historical vision dedicated to the unmasking of past folly as its principal aim. Hume's ironical approach to history breeds *ennui*, turns upon and dissolves the conviction originally inspiring it that men in the present age had progressed absolutely beyond the irrationality characteristic of their remote ancestors.

Actually, Hume is forced to conclude that the ratio of folly to reason in his own age had not significantly changed from what it had been in different ages in the past, that the only change had been in the *forms* which reason and unreason assumed over time. Gibbon was still able to maintain the fiction that his own age was superior to the Dark Ages, but this was largely an aesthetic preference, the result of a decision to treat his own time with more sympathy than he might lavish on the Middle Ages, not a conclusion derived by a reasoned argument. And Kant himself, in a late essay, "An Old Question Raised Again: Is the Human Race Constantly Progressing?" was forced to concede that the best grounds for believing in progress were moral, not scientific.

Historical evidence alone, Kant noted, permitted belief in any of three views of history: eudaemonistic, terroristic, and abderitic, reflecting belief in historical progress, decline, or stasis respectively. It was one's moral duty to believe in the progressivist view, because the other two views promoted attitudes unworthy of a morally responsible man. One's view of the meaning of history depended, Kant insisted, on the kind of man one was, the kind of man one wanted to be, and the kind of humanity that one desired to see take shape in the future. If one *chose* to believe that humanity was either declining or remaining essentially the same, one would live one's life in such a way as to bring to pass the condition of degeneration or stasis perceived to be reflected in the record of the past. The way one looked at the past of the race conditioned and in the long run actually determined the shape that the future must have. Kant continued to believe to the end of his life that past history taught nothing about human nature that could not be learned from the study of humanity in its present incarnations. But he insisted that we are not permitted to believe that there has been no progress in the passage from past to present lest we prohibit ourselves from believing that the future will be better than the present, and cut the nerve of human effort to bring such a better future to pass in the process.

This growing desire to believe in progress in the face of scepticism's teaching that we have no rational grounds for believing in it, accounts for the enthusiastic reception of Herder's philosophy of history at the end of the eighteenth century. Here the problem of the relationship between reason and unreason is placed on another ground, though in such a way as to dissolve the distinction as a criterion for assessing the nature of the relationship between past, present, and future. Everything exists in a timeless present for Herder; history is a totality of individualities, each of which is equally valuable *as an individual* and all of which manifest the same mixture of reason and unreason in their specificity. Herder's insistence that reflection on history be informed by no "concern" either of a "provident or a retrospective" sort removes from the historian the burden of *judging* the past. But at the same time, it removes from him the burden of having to judge the present and, moreover, all responsibility for having to speak about the course that human society in the future ought to take. The naive faith which Herder has in the power of history to take care of itself, to produce what is required for the whole of humanity in the time and place that it is required, is the perfect antithesis of that scepticism, with its debilitating irony, which Hume had brought to perfection as a system of thought.

Yet, what Herder experienced as a rebirth of man's capacity of faith in the essential adequacy of individuated existence, Kant recognized as the dogmatism which it truly was. The Herderian belief in the adequacy of the whole, and in the adequacy of the individual parts of the whole to the totality, denied the problematics of historical existence quite as effectively as Hume's scepticism did. The principal difference between Hume's scepticism and Herder's dogmatism lay in the fact that, whereas the former led to despair in the face of history's meaninglessness, the latter promoted a groundless optimism which neither reason nor morality sanctioned. It put historical reflection back on the ground of aesthetic sensibility, made of it nothing more than the endless entertainment of things in their *formal* coherency, the richness and variety of their forms, and the ceaseless coming to be and passing away of things each in its own season. The tone was different but the resultant picture of the whole was the same.

THE AMERICAN SOCIETY FOR
EIGHTEENTH-CENTURY STUDIES

PROGRAM
OF THE SECOND ANNUAL MEETING

April 22–24, 1971
College Park, Maryland

Thursday, April 22

Morning Session

Presiding: Lester G. Crocker, president of the Society

"The Sublime or the Grotesque: From Fantasy to Monsters in Eighteenth Century Art"
  Charles Fleischauer (department of French, Carleton University)

"Battles of Style and the Beginnings of Romanticism"
  Frederick J. Cummings (The Detroit Institute of Arts)

Afternoon Session

Presiding: William MacBain (department of French, University of Maryland)

"Concepts of Progress in the European and American Enlightenment"
  Henry Steele Commager (department of history, Amherst College)

"*Opéra Comique* and Revolution: An Eighteenth-Century Paradox"
  Paul Henry Lang (department of music, Columbia University)

"Un aspect de l'irrationnel au dix-huitième siècle: La démonologie et son exploitation littéraire"

Paul Vernière (faculté des lettres et des sciences humaines, Université de Paris)

Evening

A Concert of Eighteenth-Century Music: The Juillard Quartet and George Malcolm

Friday, April 23

Morning Session

Presiding: Stephen G. Brush (department of history, University of Maryland)

"Tragic Novels and the Tragic Tradition"

Sheldon Sacks (department of English, The University of Chicago)

"Leonhard Euler, Supreme Geometer (1707–1783)"

Clifford A. Truesdell (department of mechanics, The Johns Hopkins University)

Afternoon Session

Presiding: Morris Freedman (department of English, University of Maryland)

Symposium: Irrationalism in the Eighteenth Century

Moderator: Ralph Cohen (department of English, The University of Virginia)

George Rosen (department of the history of science and medicine, Yale University)

Ronald Paulson (department of English, The Johns Hopkins University)

Bertrand H. Bronson (department of English, The University of California at Berkeley)

Hayden V. White (department of history, The University of California at Los Angeles; Society for the Humanities, Cornell University)

Program of the 1971 Meeting

George A. Kelly (department of politics, Brandeis University)

Evening Banquet

Master of Ceremonies: Arthur M. Wilson (department of history, Dartmouth College)

Remarks: Lester G. Crocker, president of the Society

"Three Generations: A Plausible Interpretation of the French *Philosophes?*"
Louis Gottschalk, first vice-president of the Society

Saturday, April 24

Morning Session

Section Meetings

Section A: English and American Literatures
Chairman: Howard Anderson (department of English, Michigan State University)

"Structuralism and Eighteenth-Century Literature"
  Peter Hughes (department of English, Victoria College, University of Toronto)

Section B: Other Modern Languages and Literatures
Chairman: Jean A. Perkins (department of modern languages and literatures, Swarthmore College)

"Iriarte and the Neo-Classical Theater: A Reappraisal"
  R. Merritt Cox (department of Spanish, Duke University)

"The Problem of Scientific Versus Alphabetical Order in the *Encyclopédie*"
  Hugh M. Davidson (department of French, Ohio State University)

"The Sick Rose as an Aesthetic Idea: Kant, Blake, and the Symbol in Literature"

John Neubauer (department of German, Case Western Reserve University)

Section C: Classics, Comparative Literature, Linguistics, Speech, and Drama

Chairman: A. Owen Aldridge (department of comparative literature, University of Illinois)

"The First English Translation of Marivaux's *Le Jeu de l'amour et du hasard*"

Robert Halsband (department of English, Columbia University)

"Ludwig Tieck: French and English Sources of His *William Lovell* (1795/96)"

François Jost (department of comparative literature, University of Illinois)

"The Correspondence of Metastasio as an Expression of Eighteenth Century Culture"

Elio Gianturco (departments of Italian and comparative literature, Hunter College)

Section E: Philosophy, History of Ideas, Religion

Chairman: Richard H. Popkin (department of philosophy, The University of California at San Diego)

Papers and panel discussion: "Emerging Problems in Eighteenth Century History of Ideas"

Other section programs to be announced at the meeting.

Saturday, April 24

Afternoon Session

Business Meeting

Presiding: Lester G. Crocker, president of the Society

"*La Philosophie dans le boudoir*: or, A Young Lady's Entrance into the World"

R. F. Brissenden (department of English, Australian National University; president, Australasian Society for Eighteenth-Century Studies)

Officers and Executive Board Members to June 30, 1972

ORGANIZING COMMITTEE
DECEMBER 1968 TO JULY 1969

James L. Clifford, *Columbia University*
Lester G. Crocker, *Case Western Reserve University* (chairman)
Peter Gay, *Columbia University*
Donald Greene, *University of Southern California* (secretary)

PROVISIONAL EXECUTIVE BOARD
JULY 1969 TO JUNE 30, 1970

President: Lester G. Crocker, *Case Western Reserve University*
Secretary: Donald Greene, *University of Southern California*
Treasurer: Peter J. Stanlis, *Rockford College*
    A. Owen Aldridge, *University of Illinois, Urbana*
    James L. Clifford, *Columbia University*
    Louis Gottschalk, *University of Illinois, Chicago Circle*
    Warren Kirkendale, *Duke University*
    Richard H. Popkin, *University of California, San Diego*
    Charles R. Ritcheson, *Southern Methodist University*
    Robert R. Wark, *Henry E. Huntington Library and Art Gallery*
    Roy M. Wiles, *McMaster University*

EXECUTIVE BOARD
JULY 1, 1970 TO JUNE 30, 1971

President: Lester G. Crocker, *Case Western Reserve University*
First Vice-President: Louis Gottschalk, *University of Illinois, Chicago Circle*
Second Vice-President: Robert R. Wark, *Henry E. Huntington Library and Art Gallery*

Secretary: Donald Greene, *University of Southern California*
Treasurer: Peter J. Stanlis, *Rockford College*
    A. Owen Aldridge, *University of Illinois, Urbana*
    James L. Clifford, *Columbia University*
    Warren Kirkendale, *Duke University*
    Hilda Neatby, *Queen's University*
    Richard H. Popkin, *University of California, San Diego*
    Charles R. Ritcheson, *Southern Methodist University*

EXECUTIVE BOARD
JULY 1, 1971 TO JUNE 30, 1972

President: Louis Gottschalk, *University of Illinois, Chicago Circle*
Past President: Lester G. Crocker, *University of Virginia*
First Vice-President: Robert R. Wark, *Henry E. Huntington Library and Art Gallery*
Second Vice-President: James L. Clifford, *Columbia University*
Secretary: Donald Greene, *University of Southern California*
Treasurer: Peter J. Stanlis, *Rockford College*
    A. Owen Aldridge, *University of Illinois, Urbana*
    William J. Cameron, *University of Western Ontario*
    Adrienne D. Hytier, *Vassar College*
    Warren Kirkendale, *Duke University*
    Richard H. Popkin, *Lehman College, City University of New York*
    Charles R. Ritcheson, *University of Southern California*

American Society for Eighteenth-Century Studies List of Members

INSTITUTIONAL MEMBERS

Alfred University
Bryn Mawr College
Butler University
University of California, Berkeley
University of California, Davis
University of California, Irvine
University of California, Los Angeles
University of California, Riverside
Case Western Reserve University
University of Cincinnati
City College of New York
Claremont Graduate School
Cleveland State University
University of Colorado, Denver
University of Connecticut
Detroit Institute of Arts, Founders' Society
Fordham University
Georgia State University
University of Illinois, Chicago Circle
University of Illinois, Urbana
University of Iowa
Kent State University
Lehigh University
Lehman College of the City University of New York
The Lewis Walpole Library
University of Maryland
University of Massachusetts, Boston
The Paul Mellon Center for British Art and British Studies
Michigan State University
Middle Tennessee State University
University of Minnesota
State University of New York, Fredonia
State University of New York, Oswego
University of North Carolina, Chapel Hill
Northwestern University
Ohio State University
University of Pennsylvania
University of Pittsburgh
Portland State University
Princeton University
Rice University
Rockford College
University of Southern California
Stanford University
Swarthmore College
Sweet Briar College
Temple University
Tulane University
University of Virginia
Washington and Lee University
University of Western Ontario
The Henry Francis du Pont Winterthur Museum
Yale University

INDIVIDUAL MEMBERS

C— Charter member (joined before April 17, 1970)

Sp—Sponsoring member

S— Student member

Members not so indicated are regular members

ABDELLA, Christina
Comparative and foreign literature
 (assistant professor)
Rutgers University
314 Glenn Avenue
Trenton, N. J. 08638

ACOMB, Frances D.   C
History (associate professor)
Duke University
Box 6777 College Station
Durham, N. C. 27708
Political and social ideas, esp. Mallet du Pan

ADAMS, Betty S.   C
English (associate professor)
Ohio State University
138 Arden Road
Columbus, Ohio 43214

ADAMS, Geoffrey   C
History (associate professor)
Loyola College
7141 Sherbrooke St. W.
Montreal 262, Quebec
Relation between French protestants and philosophes

ADAMS, Leonard   C
French (lecturer)
University of Guelph
Guelph, Ontario
Eighteenth century in France

ADAMS, Margaret E.   Sp
Modern languages (associate professor)
State College at Boston
Woods End Road
Lincoln, Mass. 01773
Development of liberal thought; early encyclopedists

ADAMS, Percy G.
English (professor)
University of Tennessee
Knoxville, Tenn. 37916
Travel literature; novel; Franco-British relations

ADAMS, Thomas M.
History
University of Kansas
Lawrence, Kansas 66044
The "dépots de mendicité," 1764-1789

ADLER, Jacob H.   C
English (professor)
Purdue University
Lafayette, Indiana 47907
Pope; literary criticism

AGNIERAY, Gérard   C
Romance languages (lecturer)
University of Arizona
Tucson, Arizona 85721
Pierre Bayle

ALDRIDGE, A. Owen   C
Comparative literature (professor)
University of Illinois
Urbana, Illinois 61801
Ibero-American enlightenment

ALKON, Paul K.   C
English (associate professor)
University of Minnesota
Minneapolis, Minn. 55455
English literature, esp. Samuel Johnson

ALLAIN, Mathé   C
Foreign languages (instructor)
University of Southwestern Louisiana
Box 1542
Lafayette, Louisiana 70501
Voltaire; colonial Louisiana

ALLEGO, Donna M.   C
English (instructor)
Western Illinois University
Macomb, Illinois 61455
Burke; Swift; Johnson; American political writing

ALLEN, Robert R.
English (assistant professor)
University of Southern California
Los Angeles, California 90007
Bibliography; printing; Samuel Johnson

ALLENTUCK, Marcia   C
English (associate professor)
City College, CUNY
5 West 86th St. Apt. 12B
New York, N. Y. 10024
Aesthetics and criticism; British and American literature

ALLISON, Daniel Brian   S
English (teaching assistant)
University of Southern California

List of Members

2077 Chestnut Ave.
Long Beach, California 90806
English literature

ALVERSON, J. Stewart   S
History
Case Western Reserve University
315 Wyandot Place
Huron, Ohio 44839
French revolution; intellectual history

AMETER, Brenda   S
English
Indiana University
1303 North Allen Street
Robinson, Illinois 62454
Fiction: Richardson, Gothic

AMMERLAHN, Hellmut
Germanic languages and literature
  (assistant professor)
University of Washington
Seattle, Washington 98105
Goethe; philosophy; music

ANDERSON, David L.   C
French (assistant professor)
Pennsylvania State University
S-408 Burrowes
University Park, Pa. 16802
French literature

ANDERSON, George L.   C
English (professor)
University of Hawaii
Honolulu, Hawaii 96822
*Queen Anne period; criticism; literature
  and politics*

ANDERSON, Howard   C
English (professor)
Michigan State University
East Lansing, Michigan 48823
Novel, esp. gothic novel; Laurence Sterne

ANDERSON, Rodney E.   S
History
Southern Illinois University
Rural Route No. 1
Eldorado, Illinois 62930
French and German history

ANDERSON, William L.   C
History (assistant professor)
Western Carolina University

Box 888
Cullowhee, North Carolina 28723
European history (1700-1815)

ANDREWS, Norwood, Jr.
Classical and Romance languages
  (professor)
Texas Tech University
Lubbock, Texas 79409

ARNASON, H. Harvard   C
Art history
1075 Park Ave., Apt. 14D
New York, N. Y. 10028
French sculpture; Jean-Antoine Houdon

ASKEW, Pamela
Art (professor)
Vassar College
Poughkeepsie, New York 12601
Art history

ASTMAN, Joseph G.
Foreign languages (professor)
Dean, College of Liberal Arts and
  Sciences
Hofstra University
2 Border Lane
Levittown, New York 11756
*German literature; influence of Greek
  tragedians on dramas of Kleist*

ATKINS, G. Douglas   C
English (assistant professor)
University of Kansas
Lawrence, Kansas 66044
*Restoration and eighteenth-century
  English literature*

ATTERIDGE, Thomas
English (lecturer)
Syracuse University
203 Hall of Languages
Syracuse, New York 13210
Swift

AUBERY, Pierre
French (professor)
State University of New York at Buffalo
Buffalo, New York 14214

BACKSCHEIDER, Paula   S
English
Purdue University
1515 Marilyn Avenue
W. Lafayette, Indiana 47906
Defoe, Swift, Wycherley

BADIR, Magdy Gabriel
Romance Languages (lecturer)
University of Alberta
Edmonton, Alberta
Voltaire and Islam

BADURA-SKODA, Eva   C
Music (professor)
University of Wisconsin
1D University Houses
Madison, Wisconsin 53705
History of music in Vienna

BAER, Joel H.   C
English (instructor)
Macalester College
St. Paul, Minn. 55101
Swift; Defoe; Johnson; Scottish folksong

BAHR, Ehrhard
Germanic languages (associate
   professor)
University of California
Los Angeles, California 90024
Goethe; Lessing; irony

BAIRD, John D.   C
English (assistant professor)
Victoria College, University of Toronto
Toronto 5, Ontario
*William Cowper; later eighteenth-
   century literature*

BAIRD, Thomas R.
History (assistant professor)
St. Francis College
159 West 12th Street
New York, New York 10011
*Social origins of notables born after
   1750*

BAKER, Van R.   C
English (associate professor)
York College
York, Pennsylvania 17403
English literature; Pennsylvania history

BALKAN, Katherine S.
Art history (graduate student)
University of California, Los Angeles
10554 Lauriston Avenue
Los Angeles, California 90064
Art history (England)

BALL, David   C
French (lecturer)
Smith College
Northampton, Mass. 01060
Swift, Voltaire

BAMFORD, Paul W.
History (professor)
University of Minnesota
Minneapolis, Minnesota 55455
*France, social history,
   maritime history (Old Regime)*

BANERJEE, Chinmoy
English (assistant professor)
Simon Fraser University
Burnaby 2, British Columbia
Novel in English

BANNON, Peter   C
English (professor)
Memphis State University
340 South Prescott St.
Memphis, Tennessee 38111
*Eighteenth-century poetry: Pope and
   Blake*

BARKER, David E.
Modern foreign languages (instructor)
Saginaw Valley College
2250 Pierce Road
University Center, Michigan 48710
*Voltaire et "l'infâme";
   histoire des idées*

BARKER, Gerard A.   C
English (assistant professor)
Queens College, CUNY
Flushing, New York 11367
Novel; history of ideas

BARKER, Rosalind   C
English (lecturer)
Victoria College
University of Toronto
Toronto 5, Ontario
Drama; literary criticism

BARLOW, Walter L.   S
French (graduate student)
Rice University
Houston, Texas 77001
Rousseau

List of Members

BARNES, Clifford R.   C
Music (associate professor)
Brigham Young University
HFAC E454
Provo, Utah 84601
Opéra-Comique

BARNES, Donald Grove   C
History (professor emeritus)
Case Western Reserve University
2300 Overlook Road
Cleveland, Ohio 44106
British history

BARR, Mary-Margaret H.   C
French
P.O. Box 716
Portland, Indiana 47371
Voltaire; Franco-American relations

BARTON, H. Arnold   C
History
Southern Illinois University
Carbondale, Illinois 62901

BASNEY, Lionel
English (assistant professor)
Houghton College
Box 25
Houghton, New York 14744
Johnson; development of aesthetics

BATTEN, Charles L., Jr.   C
English (assistant professor)
University of California
Los Angeles, California 90024
Non-fiction travel literature

BATTERSBY, James L.
English (associate professor)
Ohio State University
Denney Hall
164 West 17th Avenue
Columbus, Ohio 43210
Samuel Johnson; critical theory

BATTESTIN, Martin C.   C
English (professor)
University of Virginia
Charlottesville, Virginia 22901
Fielding and the novel; the period 1660-1750

BAUKE, Joseph   C
German (professor)
Columbia University
423 W. 120th Street
New York, N. Y. 10027
Enlightenment and classicism in Germany

BAXTER, Charles Langtry, Jr.   C
English (associate professor)
Northern Michigan University
Marquette, Michigan 49855
Richardson; Swift; history of ideas

BEALE, Georgia Robison   C
History (professor)
University of Kentucky
Lexington, Kentucky 40506
Directory; L.-A.-G. Bosc

BEATTIE, J. M.   C
History (associate professor)
University of Toronto
Toronto 5, Ontario
Social history; crime and the administration of justice

BEAUMONT, Charles
English (professor)
University of Georgia
Athens, Georgia 30601
British literature; satire in general

BECK, Lewis White
Philosophy (professor)
University of Rochester
Rochester, New York 14627
Philosophy; history of ideas

BEDFORD, Emmett G.   C
English (assistant professor)
University of Wisconsin-Parkside
Kenosha, Wisconsin 53140
Alexander Pope; religious symbolism

BEIK, Paul H.   C
History (professor)
Swarthmore College
Swarthmore, Pa. 19081
French revolution

BEIT-ISHOO, Benedict   C
French and Italian (instructor)
University of Southern California
Los Angeles, California 90007
Pre-Romanticism; French and Middle Eastern studies

BELCHER, William F.   C
English (professor)
North Texas State University
Denton, Texas 76203
Pope; Swift; the novel

BENHAMOU, Paul
Modern languages (assistant professor)
Purdue University
Lafayette, Indiana 47907
French periodicals—l'Encyclopédie, les antiphilosophes

BENNETT, Fordyce
English (professor)
Pasadena College
Howard at Bresee
Pasadena, California 91104
Johnson; Prior; Cowper

BENNETT, Pamela J.   S
English (graduate student)
Indiana University
Bloomington, Indiana 47401

BENTON, Rita
Music (associate professor)
University of Iowa
School of Music Library
Iowa City, Iowa 52240
France

BERGMANN, Frederick L.   C
English (professor)
DePauw University
Greencastle, Indiana 46135
Drama; David Garrick

BERKVAM, Michael L.
French and Italian (lecturer)
Indiana University
Bloomington, Indiana 47401
Society and Literature in 18th-Century France; Pierre-Michel Hennin

BETTS, Marilyn J.   S
University of Florida
3722 S.W. 19th Street
Gainesville, Florida 32601

BEVILACQUA, Vincent M.   C
Speech (associate professor)
University of Massachusetts
367 Bartlett Hall
Amherst, Mass. 01002
Rhetorical literature; aesthetics and art theory

BEYER, Charles J.   C
French (professor)
State University of New York
Buffalo, New York 14214
Montesquieu

BILL, Shirley A.
History (professor)
University of Illinois at Chicago Circle
1907 University Hall
Chicago, Illinois 60680
U.S. constitutional and early national history; U.S. Revolution

BILLINGS, Elizabeth
Modern languages (instructor)
Dickinson College
Route 944, R.D. 2
Carlisle, Pa. 17013
French and German literature; music

BINGHAM, Alfred J.   C
French (professor)
University of Maryland
College Park, Maryland 20742
Voltaire; philosophical controversies

BIRN, Raymond   C
History (associate professor)
University of Oregon
Eugene, Oregon 97403
France; the press and the book trade

BJORNSTAD, William B.   C
English (professor)
Drake University
Des Moines, Iowa 50311
Swift, Pope, French-English intercultural relations

BLAYDES, Sophia B.
English (associate professor)
West Virginia University
Morgantown, West Virginia 26505
Christopher Smart

BLEWETT, D. L.   C
English (lecturer)
McMaster University
Hamilton, Ontario
Fiction

BLYTHE, Harold R., Jr.
English (assistant professor)
Adrian College
Adrian, Michigan 49221
Eighteenth-century novel; Smollett

List of Members

BOERNER, Peter C
Comparative literature (professor)
Indiana University
1213 East First Street
Bloomington, Indiana 47401
Prose fiction; autobiography; Goethe

BOGORAD, Samuel N. C
English (professor)
University of Vermont
Burlington, Vermont 05401
Drama; satire; Swift

BOHNE, Frederick J. C
English (professor)
Edinboro State College
R.D. 3
Edinboro, Pa. 16412
Literature; esp. Swift, Pope

BOND, Richmond P. C
English (professor)
University of North Carolina
101 Pine Lane
Chapel Hill, N. C. 27514
Periodicals

BONGIE, Laurence L. C
French (professor)
University of British Columbia
Vancouver 8, British Columbia
David Hume; French history of ideas

BONNEVILLE, Douglas A.
Romance languages (associate professor)
University of Florida
Box 415 GSIS
Gainesville, Florida 32601
Voltaire's romans; Diderot's early works; Eighteenth-century French novel

BORDEN, Gavin
English
Garland Press, Inc.
24 West 45th Street
New York, New York 10036
Novel and criticism

BOSSE, Malcolm J. C
English (lecturer)
City College, CUNY
91 Charles Street
New York, N. Y. 10014
Late eighteenth-century fiction

BOULBY, Mark C
German (professor)
University of British Columbia
Vancouver 8, British Columbia
Pietism and mysticism in German literature

BOULLE, Pierre H. C
History (assistant professor)
McGill University
Montreal 110, Quebec
History of France; colonies

BOWEN, Vincent
French (associate professor)
University of Illinois
Urbana, Illinois 61801
French fiction, esp. Diderot

BOWERS, Bro. Francis R., FSC C
English (associate professor)
Manhattan College
Bronx, New York 10471
George Crabbe; drama

BOYCE, Benjamin C
English (professor emeritus)
Duke University
1200 Dwire Place
Durham, North Carolina 27706
English and French prose fiction

BOYER, Bruce H. C
Theater arts
University of California
Los Angeles, California 90024
1015 Michigan Avenue
Evanston, Illinois 60202
Plays and play publication (printing history) 1700-1750

BOYER, G. Bruce
English (instructor)
Allentown College
Center Valley, Pennsylvania 18034

BOYER, Mildred
Spanish and Portuguese (professor)
University of Texas
902 Lund Street
Austin, Texas 78704
Spanish literature; drama

BRACK, O. M., Jr. C
English (associate professor)

University of Iowa
Iowa City, Iowa 52240
History of printing; prose fiction

BRACKEN, Harry M.
Philosophy (professor)
McGill University
Montreal 110, Quebec
Bayle; Berkeley; Scottish philosophy

BRADBURY, Miles L.
History (assistant professor)
University of Maryland
College Park, Md. 20740
Political theory; education; religion

BRADHAM, Jo Allen
English (assistant professor)
Agnes Scott College
Box 923
Decatur, Georgia 30030
Pope, Swift

BRADY, Patrick
Modern languages (professor)
Florida State University
Tallahassee, Florida 32306
Rococo style; the novel form

BRANAM, George C.   C
English (professor; vice chancellor)
Office of Academic Affairs
Louisiana State University
New Orleans, Louisiana 70122
Theater and literary criticism

BRAUDY, Leo   C
English (assistant professor)
Columbia University
416 Hamilton Hall
New York, N. Y. 10027
Novel; history; satire

BRAUER, George C., Jr.   C
English (professor)
University of South Carolina
17-G Cornell Arms Apartments
Columbia, South Carolina 29201
*Classical influences; Swift; Pope;
   Johnson; novel*

BRAUN, Theodore E. D.   C
Languages and literature (professor)
University of Delaware
Newark, Delaware 19711
*French literature; poetry; theater;
   Voltaire*

BRENNER, Rosamond Drooker   C
Music history
726 North Park Boulevard
Glen Ellyn, Illinois 60137
*German baroque opera (Reinhard
   Keiser)*

BREWER, Gwen W.
English (associate professor)
San Fernando Valley State College
Northridge, California 91324
Restoration drama; novel; folklore

BRICKE, John J.   C
Philosophy (assistant professor)
University of Kansas
Lawrence, Kansas 66044
*British empiricist philosophers, esp.
   David Hume*

BRIDGMAN, Richard
English (associate professor)
University of California
Berkeley, California 94720

BROFSKY, Howard   C
Music (professor)
Queens College, CUNY
Flushing, New York 11367
*Musicology: Italian and French
   instrumental music*

BRONSON, B. H.   C
English (professor emeritus)
University of California, Berkeley
927 Oxford St.
Berkeley, California 94707
*Arts and literature (esp. music and
   poetry)*

BROOK, Barry S.   C
Musicology (professor)
City University of New York
505 West End Ave.
New York, N. Y. 10024

BROOKS, Douglas
English (lecturer)
University of Manchester
11 Agnes Road
Blundellsands
Liverpool L23 6ST, England
Literature; music; art/architecture

List of Members

BROOKS, Richard A.   C
Humanities (professor)
Richmond College, CUNY
Staten Island, N. Y. 10301
Voltaire; French Enlightenment; bibliography

BROWN, Jack R.   C
English (professor)
Marshall University
Huntington, West Virginia 25701
Fielding; drama

BROWN, Lorraine A.
English (assistant professor)
George Mason College of the University of Virginia
4400 University Drive
Fairfax, Virginia 22030

BROWN, Richard G.   C
English (assistant professor)
Ball State University
Muncie, Indiana 47306

BROWNE, Dennis J. M.   S
English
Queens College, CUNY
5719 65th Street
Flushing, New York 11378
Pope and his circle; Addison

BROWNELL, Morris R.
English (assistant professor)
Cornell University
Ithaca, New York 14850

BROYLES, Michael E.   C
Music history (assistant professor)
University of Maryland, Baltimore County
5401 Wilkens Avenue
Baltimore, Maryland 21228

BRÜCKMANN, Patricia
English (associate professor)
Trinity College, University of Toronto
Toronto 5, Ontario
Pope; Scriblerus Club

BRYAN, Paul R.   C
Music (associate professor)
Duke University
Box 6695 College Station
Durham, N. C. 27708
Music: Mozart and Haydn milieu

BUCHANAN, Michelle
French and Italian (assistant professor)
University of Southern California
Los Angeles, California 90007
Novel; memoirs; theater

BUCSELA, John   C
Russian (associate professor)
Emory University
Atlanta, Georgia 30322
Russian language and literature

BUFORD, Lenore V.   C
Foreign languages (head)
Cuyahoga Community College
13800 Terrace Road, Apt. 717
East Cleveland, Ohio 44112
Voltaire, Diderot, theater

BURLINGAME, Leslie J.
History (assistant professor)
Mount Holyoke College
South Hadley, Mass. 01075
French biological ideas, esp. evolutionary speculations (Lamarck)

BURNETTE, Rand   C
History (assistant professor)
MacMurray College
Jacksonville, Illinois 62650
American colonial history and English history

BUSCH, Gudrun   C
Music (assistant professor)
D 4050 Mönchengladbach
Roermonder Str. 58
Germany
History of eighteenth-century German Lied

BYRNES, Joseph A.   C
English (assistant professor)
New York University
P.O. Box 283
Elizabeth, New Jersey 07207
Dramatic literature; theater history

CALDWELL, Gilbert L., Jr.   C
English (teaching fellow)
Bowling Green State University
Bowling Green, Ohio 43403
Drama

CALLAHAN, Anne M. C
French (assistant professor)
Chestnut Hill College
2100 Walnut Street
Philadelphia, Pa. 19103
French literature of Enlightenment

CAMERON, William J.
Library and information science (dean)
University of Western Ontario
London 72, Ontario

CANAVAN, Francis, S.J. C
Political science (associate professor)
Fordham University
Loyola Hall
Bronx, New York 10458
Edmund Burke; political philosophy

CANE, Edric S
Romance languages
University of Michigan
2307 Fernwood
Ann Arbor, Michigan 48104
Influence of John Locke

CANEPA, Andrew M. S
History
University of California
Los Angeles, California 90024
Italian and French intellectual history; travel accounts

CANFIELD, J. Douglas C
English (assistant professor)
University of California
Los Angeles, California 90024
Restoration drama

CAPRIO, Anthony Salvatore
French (instructor)
Lehman College, CUNY
P.O. Box 765
Poughquag, N. Y. 12570

CARELS, Peter Edgerton C
German and Russian (instructor)
Miami University
5730 County Line Road
Oxford, Ohio 45056
Satire, decorative arts

CARNIE, Robert Hay
English (professor)
University of Calgary
Calgary 44, Alberta
Bibliography; Scottish literature; Johnson group

CARNOCHAN, W. B. Sp
English (associate professor)
Stanford University
Stanford, California 94305
Swift; satire; the "Augustans"

CARRITHERS, David W.
History (assistant professor)
University of Tennessee at Chattanooga
304 Hemphill Avenue
Chattanooga, Tennessee 37411
French Enlightenment; Montesquieu

CARTWRIGHT, Michael T. C
French (assistant professor)
Peterson Hall
McGill University
Montreal, Quebec
Diderot; aesthetics and art criticism

CASH, Arthur H. C
English (professor)
State University of New York
New Paltz, New York 12568
Novel, esp. Laurence Sterne

CASSIDY, Hélène Monod-
French (associate professor)
Van Hise Hall
University of Wisconsin
Madison, Wisconsin 53711
Novel; theater; history of science

CASTELLANI, Joseph C
English (instructor)
Ball State University
14 Duane Road
Muncie, Indiana 47304

CAVANAUGH, Gerald J. C
History (assistant professor)
University of California
Berkeley, California 94720
Old regime France; European Enlightenment

CAVE, Michael
Romance and classical languages (lecturer)
19 Little Bay Lane

List of Members

Short Beach, Connecticut 06405
Spanish literature; baroque; the Commedia

CHAPDU, Robert E. C
English (instructor)
University of Illinois
330 David Kinley Hall
Urbana, Illinois 61801
Johnson; Boswell; printing house practice

CHAPIN, Chester F. C
English (professor)
University of Michigan
College of Engineering
Ann Arbor, Michigan 48104
Johnson; history of ideas

CHERPACK, Clifton C
Romance languages (professor)
University of Pennsylvania
Philadelphia, Pennsylvania 19104
French fiction

CHRISTIAN, William
Economics and political science (assistant professor)
Mount Allison University
P.O. Box 1233
Sackville, New Brunswick

CHRISTIANSON, Eric Howard S
History (graduate student)
University of Southern California
Los Angeles, Calif. 90007
Science; cultural, social, and intellectual history

CHUBB, Charles Stuart S
English (graduate student)
Queen's University
King Pitt Road
Kingston, Ontario
Augustan journalism; personal literature

CHURGIN, Bathia C
Music (professor)
Bar-Ilan University
Ramat Gan, Israel
Music (eighteenth-century symphony)

CLARK, Anthony Morris Sp
Art history
Director, The Minneapolis Institute of Arts

201 East 24th Street
Minneapolis, Minn. 55404
18th-c. Roman painting, other arts, social history

CLARK, E. Roger C
French (assistant professor)
Memorial University of Newfoundland
St. John's, Newfoundland
Utopian novel in French

CLARK, Evalyn A. C
History (professor emeritus)
Vassar College
Poughkeepsie, New York 12601
French Enlightenment and French Revolution

CLARK, John R. C
English (associate professor)
New York University
30 Woodcliff Drive
Madison, New Jersey 07940
Swift; Pope; English literature; satire

CLEMENTS, Frances M. C
English (assistant professor)
University of Wisconsin
Green Bay, Wisconsin 54305
Novel and social history

CLEVER, Glenn
English (assistant professor)
University of Ottawa
Ottawa 2, Ontario
Novel; narrative poetry; diaries

CLIFFORD, James L. C
English (professor emeritus)
Columbia University
25 Claremont Avenue
New York, N. Y. 10027
English literature; Samuel Johnson and his circle

COBURN, William Leon
English (assistant professor)
University of Nevada
Las Vegas, Nevada 89109
The novel; Henry Fielding; criticism

COGEN, Jill R. C
Music (librarian)
University of California, Los Angeles
5072 Gaviota Ave.

339

Encino, California 91316
*Cultural history of French Revolution;
English political history, 1750-1800*

COHEN, Murray   C
English (assistant professor)
University of California
Berkeley, California 94720
Novel; intellectual history

COHEN, Ralph   C
English (professor)
University of Virginia
Wilson Hall
Charlottesville, Va. 22901

COHEN, Richard   C
English (professor)
Illinois Benedictine Hall
Lisle, Illinois 60532
The novel

COLE, Malcolm S.   C
Music (assistant professor)
University of California
Schoenberg Hall
Los Angeles, California 90024
Haydn; Mozart; Beethoven; instrumental rondo

COLEMAN, Philip C.
English
Charles Scribner's Sons
597 Fifth Avenue
New York, N. Y. 10017
English belles lettres

COLTON, Judith
Visual Arts
Bennington College
240 East 82nd Street
New York, New York 10028
Eighteenth-Century French and British art: social and intellectual background

COLUMBUS, Thomas M.   C
English (instructor)
University of Dayton
Dayton, Ohio 45409
English literature; Augustan age

COMER, David B., III   C
English (professor)
Georgia Institute of Technology
Atlanta, Georgia 30332

COMMAGER, Henry Steele   Sp
History (professor)
Amherst College
405 S. Pleasant St.
Amherst, Mass. 01002
European relations; American Enlightenment

COMPEAN, Richard   S
English (graduate student)
University of California
Davis, Calif. 95616
Religion; wit; humor; satire; Swift

CONLON, Pierre M.   C
French (professor)
McMaster University
Hamilton, Ontario
Voltaire

CONNORS, Joseph B.   C
English (professor)
College of St. Thomas
St. Paul, Minnesota 55101
Johnson circle; 18th-century London

COOK, Cynthia M.   S
French (graduate student)
University of Texas
208 Lee Hall
Austin, Texas 78712
French literature; Voltaire

COOK, Marlinda Bruno   S
French
University of Pittsburgh
1617 C. L.
Pittsburgh, Pennsylvania 15213
Les Mémoires secrets de Bachaumont

COPELAND, Thomas W.
English (professor)
University of Massachusetts
251 Sunset Avenue
Amherst, Mass. 01002
Edmund Burke

CORMICK, Jean A.   S
Literature (graduate student)
University of California, San Diego
La Jolla, California 92037
Literature; satire

List of Members

COSENTINI, John W. C
French (professor)
St John's University
Jamaica, New York 11432
The Dialogue

COUGHLIN, Donald J.
English (assistant professor)
Loyola University
6525 N. Sheridan
Chicago, Illinois 60626
Samuel Johnson; Jonathan Swift; genre

COUGHLIN, Edward
Romance languages (assistant professor)
University of Cincinnati
Cincinnati, Ohio 45221
Spanish literature

COUMONT, Eileen S
English
Rice University
Houston, Texas 77001
English and classical literature; imitations of Greek and Latin poetry; epic

COURTNEY, Alice K. C
Romance languages (instructor)
Ohio Wesleyan University
Delaware, Ohio 43015
French literature, esp. the novel

COWLER, Rosemary E. C
English (professor)
Lake Forest College
Lake Forest, Ill. 60045
Pope; Richardson

COX, R. Merritt
Romance languages (assistant professor)
Duke University
Durham, North Carolina 27706
Spain: critical theory, poetry

CRAGG, Olga B.
French (assistant professor)
University of British Columbia
Vancouver 8, B. C.
Novel; Mme Riccoboni

CRANDALL, Joan S
Interdisciplinary (graduate student)
Michigan State University
863 N. Kentview Drive, NE
Grand Rapids, Michigan 49505
History; Art; Literature

CRAWFORD, Frederic M., Jr. C
History (assistant professor)
Middle Tennessee State University
Box 142
Murfreesboro, Tenn. 37130
Communication of ideas; intellectual history

CREIGHTON, Douglas G.
French (associate professor)
University of Western Ontario
London 72, Ontario
French literature and thought; Diderot

CROCKER, Lester G. C
French (professor)
University of Virginia
Charlottesville, Virginia 22903
French literature; European thought

CRONIN, Grover, Jr. C
English (professor)
Fordham University
Bronx, N. Y. 10458
Eighteenth-century England

CROUT, Robert Rhodes S
History Department
University of Georgia
Athens, Georgia 30601
French imperialism

CUMMINGS, Frederick J. C
Art history
Assistant director, Detroit Institute of Arts
5200 Woodward Ave.
Detroit, Michigan 48202

CUNNINGHAM, William F., Jr. C
English (associate professor)
Le Moyne College
Syracuse, New York 13214

CURLEY, Thomas M.
English (assistant professor)
Fordham University
294 Bronxville Road, Apt. 4-A
Bronxville, New York 10708
English literature; Samuel Johnson; prose fiction

DAGHLIAN, Philip B.   C
English (professor)
Indiana University
Bloomington, Indiana 47401
Johnson; Boswell; Horace Walpole

DALSANT, John B.
English (assistant professor)
Humboldt State College
Arcata, California 95521
Pope; Hogarth and graphic art; novel

DARNTON, Robert
History (associate professor)
Dickinson Hall
Princeton University
Princeton, New Jersey 08540
Grub Street literature in France, publishing, and J. P. Brissot

DASH, Irene   S
English (graduate student)
Columbia University
161 West 16th Street
New York, N. Y. 10011
Shakespeare's plays in eighteenth century

DAUTERMAN, Carl C.   C
Art history (curator)
The Metropolitan Museum of Art
New York, N. Y. 10028
Western European arts

DAUTERMAN, (Mrs.) Carl C.
1326 Madison Avenue
New York, N. Y. 10028

DAVIDSON, Hugh M.   C
Romance languages (professor)
Ohio State University
3838 Chiselhurst Place
Columbus, Ohio 43220
Rhetoric and "philosophie"; Montesquieu; Rousseau

DAVIE, Donald   C
English (professor)
Stanford University
989 Cottrell Way
Stanford, California 94305
Poetry; scientific vocabulary; Jefferson and John Adams

DAVIES, Richard A.
English (assistant professor)
Box 168
Acadia University
Wolfville, Nova Scotia
Laurence Sterne

DAVIS, Bertram H.
English (general secretary AAUP)
3009 Daniel Lane N. W.
Washington, D. C. 20015
Sir John Hawkins; Samuel Johnson; music

DAVIS, Charles George
English
Boise State College
Boise, Idaho 83704
Novel; satire; Henry Fielding

DAVIS, James Herbert, Jr.   C
Romance languages (associate professor)
University of Georgia
Athens, Georgia 30601
Eighteenth-century French theater

DAVY, Francis X.
English (professor)
Box 1031
Eastern Kentucky University
Richmond, Kentucky 40475
Jonathan Swift; the rise of the novel

DAY, Robert Adams   C
English (professor)
Queens College, CUNY
Flushing, New York 11367
English fiction, poetry, bibliography

DESAUTELS, Alfred R., S.J.   C
Modern languages (professor)
Holy Cross College
Worcester, Mass. 01610
Intellectual history of the philosophes

DESCHÊNES, Martin O.   C
French (assistant professor)
Tennessee State University
411 North Wilson Blvd.
Nashville, Tenn. 37205
Voltaire

DESOLE, Gloria M.   C
English (assistant professor)

List of Members

Skidmore College
Saratoga Springs, N. Y. 12203
The Scriblerians

DESROCHES, Richard H.   C
Romance languages (associate professor)
University of Oregon
Eugene, Oregon 97403
French literature, esp. novel

DEWEES, Charles W., Jr.   C
English (associate professor)
Philadelphia College of Textiles and Science
Schoolhouse Lane & Henry Ave.
Philadelphia, Pa. 19144
Fiction

DICKEY, William   C
English (associate professor)
San Francisco State College
San Francisco, Calif. 94132
Augustan poetry; Swift; eighteenth-century novel

DIRCKS, P. T.   C
English (assistant professor)
C. W. Post College of Long Island University
72 Halstead Ave.
Yonkers, N. Y. 10704
Eighteenth-century drama

DIRCKS, Richard J.   C
English (professor)
St. John's University
72 Halstead Ave.
Yonkers, New York 10704
Henry Fielding; eighteenth-century drama and novel

DOBSON, Paul   C
History (assistant professor)
University of Houston
Cullen Boulevard
Houston, Texas 77004
Historiography; dissemination of ideas of philosophes

DOCK, Terry Smiley   S
French (graduate student)
Vanderbilt University
Box 1651, Station B
Nashville, Tennessee 37203

DOLMETSCH, Carl R.
English (professor)
College of William and Mary
Williamsburg, Virginia 23185
American literature

DOLMETSCH, Joan
Art history
Department of Collections
Colonial Williamsburg
Williamsburg, Virginia 23185

DONNELLY, Jerome
English (assistant professor)
Florida Technological University
Box 25000
Orlando, Florida 32816

DONOVAN, Arthur
History (assistant professor)
University of Illinois, Chicago Circle
Chicago, Illinois 60680
History of science and technology; Scottish Enlightenment

DORRIS, George   C
English (assistant professor)
York College, CUNY
Bayside, New York 11363
Augustan poetry, tragedy, opera

DOWLING, John
Spanish and Portuguese (professor)
Indiana University
Bloomington, Indiana 47401
Drama

DOWNEY, James   C
English (associate professor)
Carleton University
Ottawa 1, Ontario
Church history, esp. homiletics; Laurence Sterne

DOYLE, Charles Clay   C
English (assistant professor)
University of Southern California
Los Angeles, Calif. 90007
Interregnum and Restoration verse

DRUESEDOW, John E., Jr.   C
Music (instructor)
Miami University
Oxford, Ohio 45056
Music in Spain and Latin America

DUBRO, James R.
English (teaching fellow)
Victoria College, University of Toronto
51 Grosvenor St., Apt. 206A
Toronto 5, Ontario
Johnson; Lord Hervey; Lady Mary Wortley Montagu

DUCHOVNAY, Gerald C.   C
English
JU Box 27
Jacksonville University Station
Jacksonville, Florida 32211
Prose fiction; literature and the arts

DUIKER, Yvonne V.   S
French (graduate student)
Pennsylvania State University
430 Sylvan Drive
State College, Pa. 16801
Eighteenth-century French novel

DU PONT, Bernard L.   S
Romance languages (teaching assistant)
University of Washington
Seattle, Washington 98105
Eighteenth-century novel; Anglo-French relations

DURER, Christopher S.
English (assistant professor)
University of Wyoming
Box 3353, University Station
Laramie, Wyoming 82070

DUSSINGER, John A.   C
English (associate professor)
University of Illinois
1612 Chevy Chase Drive
Champaign, Illinois 61820
Fiction; history of ideas; Johnson and his circle

EBERWEIN, Robert   C
English (assistant professor)
Oakland University
379 West Frank
Birmingham, Michigan 48009
Criticism

EDINGER, William Carter
English (assistant professor)
University of California
405 Hilgard Avenue
Los Angeles, California 90024
Literary criticism, esp. Johnson's

EHRENPREIS, Irvin
English (professor)
University of Virginia
1830 Fendall Avenue
Charlottesville, Virginia 22903
Jonathan Swift

EINBOND, Bernard L.   C
English (assistant professor)
Lehman College, CUNY
Bronx, New York 10468
Samuel Johnson; poetry and poetics

EISEN, Donald G.   C
English (associate professor)
Indiana University of Pennsylvania
Indiana, Pennsylvania 15701

EISENSTEIN, Elizabeth L.   C
History (adjunct professor)
American University
82 Kalorama Circle, N. W.
Washington, D. C. 20008
Enlightenment and French Revolution

ELDER, A. T.   C
English (professor)
University of Alberta
Edmonton 7, Alberta
Johnson; periodicals

ELIOSEFF, Lee Andrew   C
English (associate professor)
University of Kentucky
Lexington, Ky. 40506
Literature: intellectual history

ELLIOTT, Robert C.   C
Literature (professor)
University of California, San Diego
La Jolla, Calif. 92037
Literary satire; Swift

ELLIS, William D., Jr.   C
English (professor)
St. Peter's College
Jersey City, N. J. 07306
Theory of genres

EMERSON, Roger   C
History (associate professor)
University of Western Ontario
London, Ontario

List of Members

ENGLAND, R. Dickinson S
English (graduate student)
University of Wisconsin
308 North Bassett
Madison, Wisconsin 53703
Smollett; Vanbrugh

ENGLISH, John C. C
History (professor)
Baker University
P.O. Box 537
Baldwin, Kansas 66006
*Empiricism, Platonism, and
   Augustinianism; John Wesley*

EPSTEIN, William H.
English (instructor)
Purdue University
Heavilon Hall
Lafayette, Indiana 47907
British literature; English novel

ESSICK, Robert N.
English (assistant professor)
San Fernando Valley State College
100 South Chester Avenue, Apt. 9
Pasadena, California 91106
*William Blake and the relationship
   between the pictorial and literary arts
   in the 18th century*

EVANS, David L. C
English
University of British Columbia
Vancouver 8, B. C.

EVANS, Howard V. C
History (associate professor)
Central Michigan University
30 Cedar Drive
Hiawatha Hills
Mt. Pleasant, Michigan 48858
*European Enlightenment; French
   Revolution*

EVANS, James E.
English (assistant professor)
University of North Carolina
   at Greensboro
Greensboro, North Carolina 27412
English novel; Swift

EVANS, John Maurice C
English (associate professor)
Washington and Lee University
Lexington, Virginia 24450
Augustan satirists

EVERSOLE, Richard C
English (assistant professor)
University of Kansas
Lawrence, Kansas 66044
Eighteenth-century poetry

FALK, Joyce Duncan C
History
1231 Harvard, Apt. O
Santa Monica, Calif. 90404
*French political and social thought;
   European history*

FALLE, George C
English (professor)
Trinity College, University of Toronto
Toronto 5, Ontario
Dryden; Restoration drama; Swift

FARBER, Paul C
History of science
Indiana University
1658 N.W. Harrison Blvd.
Corvallis, Oregon 97330
History of science; Buffon

FAULKNER, Thomas C.
English (assistant professor)
Washington State University
Pullman, Washington 99163
*Political literature; late
   18th-century poetry*

FEDER, Lillian C
English (professor)
Queens College, CUNY
80 Central Park West
New York, N. Y. 10023
Classical backgrounds; satire

FEILER, Seymour C
Modern languages (professor)
University of Oklahoma
Norman, Oklahoma 73069
French literature

FELD, Patricia L. (Mrs.) S
Drama (graduate student)
Tufts University
46 Coolidge Hill Road

Watertown, Massachusetts 02172
*Drama on the English and
American stages*

FENNER, A. F.
English (professor)
University of Detroit
Detroit, Michigan 48221
Pope; satire; music

FERGUSON, Oliver W.   C
English (professor)
Duke University
Durham, North Carolina 27706
Swift; Goldsmith

FERLING, John E.
History (assistant professor)
West Georgia College
Carrollton, Georgia 30117
*The American Revolution; loyalism in
American Revolution; political theory*

FIFER, Charles N.   C
English (professor)
Stanford University
Stanford, California 94305
*Johnson and Boswell; biography
and autobiography*

FINK, Beatrice C.   C
French and Italian (assistant professor)
University of Maryland
6111 Madawaska Rd.
Washington, D. C. 20016
*Eighteenth-century French literature,
esp. Diderot, Rousseau, Sade*

FINNELL, Robert
English (assistant instructor)
University of Texas
Austin, Texas 78712
Pope; architecture

FITZGERALD, Robert P.   C
English (associate professor)
Pennsylvania State University
33 South Burrows Building
University Park, Pa. 16802
Swift; pre-Romantic poetry

FITZSIMONS, James M., Jr.   C
English (assistant professor)
University of Detroit
4001 W. McNichols Rd.
Detroit, Michigan 48077
*Swift; Fielding; parodic shapes and
strategies*

FLAGG, James   C
Romance languages (lecturer)
Boston College
148 Oak Crest Drive
Framingham, Mass. 01701
Early 18th-century French literature

FLAHERTY, M. G.   C
German (assistant professor)
Bryn Mawr College
Bryn Mawr, Pa. 19010
Literary criticism; aesthetics; opera

FLEISCHAUER, Charles   C
French (associate professor)
Carleton University
Ottawa 1, Ontario
*Voltaire; Diderot; French art;
rationalism*

FOLKENFLIK, Robert   C
English (assistant professor)
University of Rochester
Rochester, New York 14627
*Biography, criticism, novel, Johnson,
Fielding*

FONTAINE, Ligeia Z.   S
English (graduate student)
University of Pennsylvania
4605 Cedar Avenue
Philadelphia, Pa. 19143

FORD, Alvin E.   C
Foreign languages (lecturer)
San Fernando Valley State College
Northridge, Calif. 91324

FOREMAN, Kenneth J., Jr.
Executive Director, Historical Foundation of the Presbyterian and
Reformed Churches
Box 847
Montreat, North Carolina 28757
*Presbyterian and Reformed Church
history*

FORTUNA, James Louis, Jr.   S
English (graduate student)
University of Florida
1009 SW 6th Avenue
Gainesville, Florida 32601
Richardson; Fielding; Smollett

List of Members

FOWLER, W. Robert C
History (teaching assistant)
American University
17 Webster St.
Lynn, Mass. 01904
British intellectual and social history

FRANK, Charles E.
English (professor)
Illinois College
Jacksonville, Illinois 62650
Poetry; novel; Edward Young

FRAUTSCHI, Richard L. C
Romance languages (professor)
Pennsylvania State University
602C Parkway Plaza
State College, Pennsylvania 16801
Prose fiction; quantitative stylistics

FREASE, Cynthia R.
English (associate professor)
University of Northern Colorado
1901 21st Ave. Court
Greeley, Colorado 80631
Biography, letters, drama

FREEMAN, Robert N. S
Music
University of California, Los Angeles
505 Hillgreen Drive
Beverly Hills, Calif. 90212
History of musicology

FRENCH, David P. C
English (professor)
University of Oklahoma
Norman, Oklahoma 73069
English literature

FRICKE, Donna G.
English (assistant professor)
Bowling Green State University
Bowling Green, Ohio 43403
Swift; novel

FRIEDLAND, Bea S
Music (graduate student)
City University of New York
155 W. 20th Street
New York, N. Y. 10011
Haydn; Sturm und Drang in music

FRIEDMAN, Glenn S. S
French (graduate student)
Pennsylvania State University
413 South Burrowes
University Park, Pa. 16802

FRIGUGLIETTI, James C
History (assistant professor)
Case Western Reserve University
Cleveland, Ohio 44106
Reign of Louis XVI, origins of Revolution

FRITZ, Paul S.
History
McMaster University
Hamilton, Ontario

FRUSHELL, Richard C. C
English (assistant professor)
Indiana State University
Terre Haute, Indiana 47809
Drama

FUCHS, Jacob S
English and comparative literature
University of California, Irvine
335 Lakeview Ave.
Long Beach, Calif. 90803

FULLER, David R. C
Music (associate professor)
State University of New York
Buffalo, New York 14214
French keyboard music

GAGLIARDO, John G. C
History (associate professor)
Boston University
Boston, Mass. 02215
German history; history of absolute monarchy

GALLANAR, Joseph M. C
History (associate professor)
Claremont Graduate School
Claremont, California 91711
Intellectual history, 1760-1800; historiography

GALLIANI, Renato C
French (assistant professor)
Carleton University
Ottawa 1, Ontario
Mably and history

GANNON, Susan R. C
English (instructor)
Pace College, Westchester
861 Bedford Road
Pleasantville, N. Y. 10570
English literature

GARBER, Frederick
Comparative literature
 (associate professor)
SUNY, Binghamton
Binghamton, New York 13901
*Comparative literature; literature
of sensibility; fiction: sentimental
and Gothic*

GARDNER, Paula R.
French
Boston University
5 Purchase Street
Salem, Massachusetts 01970
*Montesquieu; crisis between 17th and
18th centuries*

GAROSI, Frank J. C
History (associate professor)
Sacramento State College
Sacramento, California 95819
History of Italy, France, Central Europe

GARRARD, John G. C
Slavic languages and literatures
 (associate professor)
University of Virginia
Charlottesville, Va. 22903
*Cultural relations between Russia and
Western Europe*

GARSON, Helen S.
English (professor)
George Mason College of the University
 of Virginia
4400 University Drive
Fairfax, Virginia 22030
English novel

GAYLORD, Susan Delaronde S
English (teaching assistant)
Michigan State University
1572K Spartan Village
East Lansing, Michigan 48823
English novel; Samuel Richardson

GEIRINGER, Karl C
Music (professor)

University of California, Santa Barbara
1823 Mira Vista Avenue
Santa Barbara, California 93103
Music

GENDZIER, Stephen J. C
Romance languages and comparative
 literature (associate professor)
Brandeis University
36 Hayes Avenue
Lexington, Mass. 02173
French and English novel; Encyclopédie

GERSHOY, Leo C
History (professor emeritus)
New York University
29 Washington Square
New York, N. Y. 10011

GERSON, Frederick C
French (assistant professor)
New College, University of Toronto
Toronto 5, Ontario
Les philosophes

GIANTURCO, Elio C
Italian and comparative literature
 (professor)
Hunter College
2025 Huidekoper Place, N.W.
Washington, D. C. 20007
Anglo-Italian literary relations; Vico

GIBBS, Thomas, Jr. C
Music (graduate student)
University of Texas
1217 Greensboro Road
Birmingham, Alabama 35208
Musical classicism; Haydn; Mozart

GILBERT, Bennett Bruce S
History and philosophy (student)
Yale College
1042 Yale Station
New Haven, Connecticut 06520

GILBERT, Vedder M. C
English (professor)
University of Montana
Missoula, Montana 59801
*Thomas Edwards; dramatists and
novelists*

GILLIARD, Fred, Jr. C
English (teaching assistant)

348

List of Members

University of Utah
411 K Street
Salt Lake City, Utah 84103
Drama

GINSBERG, Elaine K.
English (instructor)
West Virginia University
Morgantown, W. Va. 26506
American literature

GINSBERG, Robert   C
Philosophy (assistant professor)
Pennsylvania State University
Delaware County Campus
25 Yearsley Mill Road
Media, Pennsylvania 19063
Theories of war, peace, and revolution; aesthetics

GLENN, Jerry
German (associate professor)
University of Cincinnati
Cincinnati, Ohio 45221
Influence of Latin literature on German; G. E. Lessing

GLOCK, Waldo S.
English (assistant professor)
New Mexico State University
Las Cruces, New Mexico 88001
Fielding; the novel

GOARD, Robert R.   C
Romance languages (instructor)
Ohio Wesleyan University
Delaware, Ohio 43105
French novel, esp. 1750-89

GOETZ, Walter L.   S
English (associate)
University of California, Irvine
Irvine, California 92664
Literary and aesthetic theory from 1660-1798

GOLDEN, Herbert H.   C
Romance languages and literatures (professor)
Boston University
Boston, Mass. 02215
French literature; history of ideas

GOLDEN, Morris   C
English (professor)
University of Massachusetts
Amherst, Mass. 01002
English literature

GOLDSTEIN, Harvey D.   C
English (associate professor)
University of Southern California
Los Angeles, Calif. 90007
Criticism; aesthetics

GOLDSTEIN, Morton Ellis   C
History (assistant professor)
Callison College, University of the Pacific
Stockton, California 95204
Spain, France

GOOD, Stephen H.   C
English (assistant professor)
Mount Saint Mary's College
Emmitsburg, Maryland 21727

GOODREAU, David A.   S
Art history (graduate student)
University of California
16704 Ardita Drive
Whittier, California 90603
Eighteenth-century English art

GOSSMAN, Lionel   C
French (professor)
Johns Hopkins University
Baltimore, Maryland 21218

GOTTSCHALK, Louis   C
History (professor)
University of Illinois, Chicago Circle
5551 University Avenue
Chicago, Illinois 60637

GOTWALS, Vernon   C
Music (professor)
Smith College
Sage Hall
Northampton, Mass. 01060
Bach; Handel; Haydn; Mozart

GOUREVITCH, Victor
Philosophy (professor)
Wesleyan University
Wesleyan Station
Middletown, Conn. 06457
Rousseau

GRANNIS, Harvey Newell, Jr.
R. R. 2
Ewing, Ky. 41039
History of 18th-century France

GRAY, James   C
English (professor)
Bishop's University
Lennoxville, Quebec
Johnson circle; religion, theater, biography in later 18th century

GREASON, A. LeRoy, Jr.
English (professor)
Bowdoin College
256 Maine Street
Brunswick, Maine 04011
English literature

GREEN, Mary Elizabeth   C
English (assistant professor)
Arizona State University
Tempe, Arizona 85281
Augustan satires on learning

GREENBAUM, Louis S.   C
History (professor)
University of Massachusetts
Herter Hall 636
Amherst, Mass. 01002
French church and social history; Lavoisier

GREENBERG, Bernard L.
English (professor)
Director of Admissions
Gallaudet College
Washington, D. C. 20002
Sterne; novel; history of ideas

GREENBERG, Irwin L.
Romance languages (assistant professor)
University of Cincinnati
Cincinnati, Ohio 45221
Diderot; French novel

GREENE, Donald J.   C
English (professor)
University of Southern California
Los Angeles, California 90007
Johnson; English intellectual and cultural history

GREENE, Mildred S.   C
English (assistant professor)
Arizona State University
Tempe, Arizona 85281
17th-, 18th-century English and French novel

GREENWAY, John L.   C
English (assistant professor)
University of Kentucky
Lexington, Kentucky 40506
Scandinavian literature; German literature; mythology

GREENWOOD, David C.
English (assistant professor)
University of Maryland
College Park, Maryland 20742
Neo-Latin; history of England

GRIFFIN, William D.   C
History (assistant professor)
St. John's University
Grand Central & Utopia Parkways
Jamaica, New York 11432
Ireland in era of Grattan's Parliament (1782-1800)

GRIFFITH, Philip Mahone   C
English (professor)
University of Tulsa
600 South College
Tulsa, Oklahoma 74104
Novel; Samuel Johnson and his circle; periodical

GRIMALDI, Alfonsina Albini   C
French and Italian (teacher)
Hoboken High School
204 5th Street
Hoboken, New Jersey 07030
Giambattista Vico

GRINDELL, Robert M.   C
English (assistant professor)
State University College
Geneseo, New York 14454
English novel

GROLLMAN, Marilynn   C
Romance languages
Douglass College
New Brunswick, N. J. 08901
The Jew in 18th-century French literature

350

List of Members

GROSS, Doris Koren   S
French
Boston University
45 Verndale Street
Brookline, Mass. 02146
French literature

GROSS, Jeffrey T.
English (assistant professor)
St Andrews Presbyterian College
Laurinburg, North Carolina 28352
*Pope, Johnson, music in the
early 18th-century*

GRUDER, Vivian R.   C
History (assistant professor)
Queens College, CUNY
890 West End Avenue
New York, N. Y. 10025
France; Ancien Régime and revolution

GRUSHOW, Ira
English (associate professor)
Franklin and Marshall College
Lancaster, Pennsylvania 17604
English literature; bookbinding

GUÉDON, Jean-Claude
Natural Science (lecturer)
York University
Glendon College
2275 Bayview Avenue
Toronto 317, Ontario, Canada
*History of chemistry and related sciences
in the 18th century*

GUILHAMET, Leon M.   C
English (assistant professor)
City College, CUNY
New York, N. Y. 10031
English literature

GUY, Basil   C
French (professor)
University of California
4125 Dwinelle
Berkeley, Calif. 94720
Voltaire; novel; cosmopolitanism

HAAC, Oscar A.   C
Romance languages (professor)
SUNY, Stony Brook
Stony Brook, N. Y. 11790
Marivaux; Voltaire

HAFTER, Monroe Z.
Romance languages (professor)
University of Michigan
Ann Arbor, Michigan 48104
Spanish literature

HAGSTRUM, Jean H.   C
English (professor)
Northwestern University
819 Michigan Avenue
Evanston, Illinois 60202
Visual arts; Johnson; Blake

HAHN, H. G.
English (assistant professor)
Towson State College
Linthicum Hall
Baltimore, Maryland 21204
English novel; literary biography

HAHN, Roger   C
History (associate professor)
University of California
Berkeley, California 94720
*Science and technology; institutional
history; history of ideas*

HAIG, Robert   C
English (professor)
University of North Carolina
Chapel Hill, N. C. 27514

HALL, Inez Jean   C
English (instructor)
Ball State University
North Annex 217
Muncie, Indiana 47306
Major English writers, esp. Swift

HALL, Thadd E.   C
History (assistant professor)
State University of New York
Binghamton, New York 13901
Eighteenth-century France

HALSBAND, Robert   C
English (professor)
University of California
Riverside, California 92502
Literary and social history, 1700-1750

HAMBRIDGE, Roger A.   S
English (student)
University of California, Los Angeles

1520 S. Purdue Ave. No. 4
West Los Angeles, Calif. 90025
Alexander Pope

HAMILTON, James F.
Romance languages (assistant professor)
University of Cincinnati
Cincinnati, Ohio 45221
Rousseau

HAMMOND, Antony
English (assistant professor)
McMaster University
Hamilton, Ontario
Theater; drama; biography (Langbaine, Oldys)

HANDLER, Pearl P.
English (lecturer)
University of California, Los Angeles
2931 Club Drive
Los Angeles, California 90064
Mandeville; Johnson; science and medicine

HANKINS, Richard   C
English (assistant professor)
Baldwin-Wallace College
559 Prospect Rd.
Berea, Ohio 44017
Biography as a genre

HANKINS, Thomas L.
History (associate professor)
University of Washington
315 Smith Hall
Seattle, Washington 98105
History of science; Jean d'Alembert

HANNA, Blake T.   C
French, modern languages (professor)
Université de Montréal
C.P. 6128
Montreal 101, Quebec
Denis Diderot

HANSELL, Sven H.   C
Music (assistant professor)
University of California
Davis, California 95616

HANSEN, David A.   C
English (assistant professor)
University of California
Riverside, Calif. 92502
Theories of prose style

HANSON, Blair   C
Modern languages (professor)
Allegheny College
Meadville, Pennsylvania 16335
French eighteenth century

HARBERT, Earl H.
English (associate professor)
Tulane University
New Orleans, Louisiana 70118
American literature; autobiography; biography

HARDESTY, Kay
Modern languages (instructor)
Tougaloo College
Tougaloo, Mississippi 39174
Encyclopédie and its supplement; American-French relations

HARDIE, Graham   S
Music (graduate student)
University of Michigan
Ann Arbor, Michigan 48105
Early eighteenth-century Italian opera

HARE, Robert R.
English (associate professor)
Youngstown State University
3805 Sampson Road
Youngstown, Ohio 44505
The later period 1750-1800, English, French, American; St. John de Crèvecoeur

HARRIS, Svetlana Kluge   C
History (graduate student)
Columbia University
55 Park Avenue
New York, N. Y. 10016
France; Russia; international relations

HARROLD, Frances   C
History (associate professor)
Georgia State University
33 Gilmer St. S.E.
Atlanta, Georgia 30303
18th-century constitutional and legal ideas, esp. Jefferson

List of Members

HART, Edward L.   C
English (professor)
Brigham Young University
Provo, Utah 84601
English literature (age of Johnson)

HARTH, Phillip   C
English (professor)
University of Wisconsin
352 Bascom Hall
Madison, Wisconsin 53706
Dryden; Swift; intellectual history

HARVEY, A. Mosby
Romance languages and literatures
  (assistant professor)
Dartmouth College
RFD 331
Norwich, Vermont 05055
French law; French literature

HASSLER, Donald M.   C
English (associate professor)
Kent State University
Kent, Ohio 44242
Late 18th-century poetry; science; Erasmus Darwin

HATZFELD, Helmut A.   C
Romance languages (professor
  emeritus)
Catholic University of America
2401 Calvert St. N.W.
Washington, D. C. 20008
Rococo

HAVENS, George R.   C
Romance languages (professor
  emeritus)
Ohio State University
415 Glen Echo Circle
Columbus, Ohio 43202
France, esp. Voltaire, Rousseau

HAWES, Lloyd E., M.D.   C
Art history
Harvard Medical School
690 Beacon Street
Boston, Mass. 02215
Ceramics

HEARTZ, Daniel   C
Music (professor)
University of California
Berkeley, California 94720
Italian opera; French theater; Mozart

HECHLER, Sandra S.   C
French (assistant professor)
Cleveland State University
922 Dresden Road
East Cleveland, Ohio 44112
Diderot; women in 18th century

HEHR, Milton G.   C
Music (associate professor)
University of Missouri, Kansas City
4420 Warwick Blvd.
Kansas City, Missouri 64111
Music

HEIN, Rebecca F.   C
Romance languages
University of Michigan
2890 Pebble Creek Road
Ann Arbor, Michigan 48104
French-American intellectual relations

HEITNER, Robert R.   C
German (professor)
University of Illinois at Chicago Circle
Chicago, Illinois 60680
Drama (German): Lessing, Schiller, Goethe

HELSING, Lyse D.   S
Romance languages (graduate student)
Johns Hopkins University
2730 Wisconsin Avenue N.W.
Washington, D. C. 20007

HENRY, Rolanne   C
English (instructor)
Rutgers University
10 Pine Tree Terrace
Madison, New Jersey 07940
Thomas Birch; biographical dictionaries

HERBY, Valdo
French (instructor)
Sacramento State College
Sacramento, Calif. 95819

HERRING, Maben D.   S
English (graduate student)
University of Notre Dame
1139 Helman Drive
South Bend, Indiana 46615
English literature; Afro-American literature

HERRMANN, Rolf-Dieter
Philosophy (associate professor)
University of Tennessee
Knoxville, Tennessee 37916
Philosophy (Baumgarten, Kant, Rousseau)

HESSE, Alfred W.   C
English
U. S. Department of Defense
86 Eldrid Drive
Silver Spring, Maryland 20904
Nicholas Rowe; early 18th-century English drama

HESTER, Robert F.   C
Interior design (professor)
Virginia Commonwealth University
901 West Franklin Street
Richmond, Virginia 23220
Art and architecture

HEUSTON, Edward F.   C
English (associate professor)
Plattsburgh State Univ. College, SUNY
Plattsburgh, N. Y. 12901
Augustan satire

HICKS, Thomas William   C
English (assistant professor)
Georgia State University
33 Gilmer Street, S.E.
Atlanta, Georgia 30033
Restoration drama; influence of science on English literature

HILL, John   C
Music (graduate student)
Harvard University
24 West Delaware Avenue
Newark, Delaware 19711
Eighteenth-century music

HILLES, Frederick W.   C
English (professor emeritus)
Yale University
P.O. Box 553
Old Lyme, Connecticut 06371
Johnson's Lives of the Poets; Boswell's letters

HINNANT, Charles H.   C
English (assistant professor)
University of Michigan

2615 Haven Hall
Ann Arbor, Michigan 48104
Dryden; Swift

HNATKO, Eugene
English (professor)
State University of New York
Cortland, New York 13045
Laurence Sterne; drama; prose style

HODGSON, Judith F.   S
English (graduate student)
University of Pennsylvania
4513 Pine Street
Philadelphia, Pennsylvania 19143

HOFFMAN, Arthur W.   C
English (professor)
Syracuse University
203 Hall of Languages
Syracuse, New York 13210
Dryden; Congreve; Pope; Fielding

HOLLY, Grant Innes
English (instructor)
Hobart and William Smith Colleges
Geneva, New York 14456
Novel

HONICK, Lois
6736 Wilmont Drive
Baltimore, Maryland 21207
Biography; history of ideas

HOPKINS, Robert H.   C
English (associate professor)
University of California
Davis, California 95616
The Johnson circle; Swift; Pope

HOTCH, Douglas R.   C
English (assistant professor)
University of Illinois
100 English Building
Urbana, Illinois 61801
Swift; Sterne

HUANG, Roderick   C
English (professor)
University of Windsor
Windsor, Ontario
Pope; late Augustan poets

HUEBNER, Wayne V.   C
English (associate professor)

List of Members

California State College at Fullerton
930 Barbara Avenue
Placentia, Calif. 92670
Augustan satire

HUGHES, Peter M.   C
English (associate professor)
Victoria College, University of Toronto
17 Elm Avenue, Rosedale
Toronto 5, Ontario
English literature; comparative literature (English and French); intellectual history

HUME, Robert D.   C
English (assistant professor)
Cornell University
Ithaca, New York 14850
Literary aesthetics and criticism; English drama

HUNT, Russell A.   C
English (assistant professor)
Saint Thomas University
Fredericton, New Brunswick
Politics in literature; development of drama

HUNTER, J. Paul   C
English (professor)
Emory University
Atlanta, Georgia 30322
Satire and the novel

HUNTER, Kathryn Montgomery   C
English (assistant professor)
Morehouse College
Atlanta, Georgia 30314
Satire; Dryden; the Restoration

HUTCHENS, Eleanor N.   C
English (professor)
University of Alabama
300 Williams Ave., S.E.
Huntsville, Alabama 35801
Fielding

HYDE, Mrs. Donald F.   C
English
Four Oaks Farm, RFD #3
Somerville, New Jersey 08876
Johnson; Boswell; Mrs. Thrale

HYTIER, Adrienne D.   C
French (professor)
Vassar College
Poughkeepsie, N. Y. 12601
Philosophes and enlightened despotism; Jacobites

ILIE, Paul
Romance languages (professor)
University of Michigan
Ann Arbor, Michigan 48104
Spanish intellectual history, 1701-1759; aesthetics

ISHERWOOD, Robert M.   C
History (assistant professor)
Vanderbilt University
Box 1667
Nashville, Tenn. 37203
Musical ideas and influence of the philosophes

IVKER, Barry   C
English (assistant professor)
Dillard University
New Orleans, La. 70122
Libertinism; fiction; history of ideas

JACOBSON, David Y.   S
History (graduate student)
Brown University
387 Angell St.
Providence, R. I. 02906
French history

JAMIESON, Suzanne
French and Italian (instructor)
University of Texas
Austin, Texas 78712
French eighteenth century

JANES, Regina Mary   C
English (teaching fellow)
Harvard University
Eliot House N-43d
Cambridge, Mass. 02138
English literature

JARRETT, H. Marshall   C
History (associate professor)
Washington & Lee University
Lexington, Virginia 24450
D'Alembert; Encyclopédie; social, political theory

JEFFREY, David K.   C
English

Haley Center
Auburn University
Auburn, Alabama 36830
Smollett

JEFFRIES, Theodore
History of science (associate professor)
Lorain County Community College
North Abbe Road
Elyria, Ohio 44035
Science and technology

JENKINS, Annibel   C
English (associate professor)
Georgia Institute of Technology
Atlanta, Georgia 30332
Early 18th-century drama; periodicals; N. Rowe

JENKINS, Clauston
English (assistant professor)
North Carolina State University
201 Holladay Hall
Raleigh, North Carolina 27607
Textual criticism; Swift

JENNINGS, Edward M.   C
English (assistant professor)
State University of New York
Albany, New York 12203
Narrative (English); "time"

JENSEN, H. James   C
English (assistant professor)
Indiana University
Ballantine Hall
Bloomington, Indiana 47401
Dryden; 18th-century criticism and aesthetics

JOHNSON, Lathrop P.   C
German (instructor)
University of Illinois
Urbana, Illinois 61801
German lyric

JOHNSON, Maurice
English (professor)
University of Pennsylvania
Philadelphia, Pennsylvania 19104
English literature; satire

JOHNSON, Neal R.
Languages (assistant professor)
University of Guelph
Guelph, Ontario
Public opinion in 18th-century France

JOHNSTON, Shirley W.   C
English (assistant professor)
University of Colorado, Denver Center
2311 S. High St.
Denver, Colorado 80210
Samuel Johnson

JOLY, Raymond   C
French (associate professor)
Faculté des Lettres
Université Laval
Quebec 10, Quebec
Eighteenth-century French literature

JONES, B. W.   C
English (associate professor)
Carleton University
Ottawa, Ontario
Collins; symbolic theory; Blake

JONES, William Powell   C
English (professor emeritus)
Case Western Reserve University
Berkshire Rd.
Gates Mills, Ohio 44040
Gray; relations of science and literature

JORDAN, Daniel P.
History
Virginia Commonwealth University
9405 University Boulevard
Richmond, Virginia 23229

JOSEPHS, Herbert   C
Romance languages (associate professor)
Michigan State University
East Lansing, Michigan 48823
Diderot; 18th-century novel

JOSEPHSON, David   C
Music (lecturer)
Columbia University
629 West 115th St.
New York, N. Y. 10025
Music (Canadian history)

JOST, François
French and comparative literature (professor)
University of Illinois
244 Lincoln Hall
Urbana, Illinois 61801
Novel; history of ideas (French, German, English)

List of Members

JOVICEVICH, Alexander
French (professor)
126 Oakview Ave.
Maplewood, N. J. 07040
French literature: Voltaire, La Harpe, and general

JOY, Neill R.   C
English (assistant professor)
Colgate University
Hamilton, New York 13346
Burke; Gibbon; satire; Richardson

JULIARD, Pierre   C
History (assistant professor)
Lehigh University
Bethlehem, Pa. 18015
French social and intellectual history

KAFKER, Frank A.   C
History (associate professor)
University of Cincinnati
McMicken Hall
Cincinnati, Ohio 45242
Encyclopedists; French Revolution

KAILIN, Susan A.   S
French (graduate student)
University of Chicago
4900 Marine Drive
Chicago, Illinois 60640
Eighteenth-century French novel and philosophes

KALLICH, Martin
English (professor)
Northern Illinois University
DeKalb, Illinois 60115

KALMAN, Harold D.   C
Art history (assistant professor)
University of British Columbia
Vancouver 8, B. C.
Eighteenth-century British architecture; art history generally

KALMEY, Robert P.
English (associate professor)
Shippensburg State College
Star Route 2
Shippensburg, Pa. 17257

KANTOR, Marvin   C
Slavic languages (assistant professor)
Northwestern University
Evanston, Illinois 60201
Russian language and literature of 18th century

KAPLAN, Steven Laurence
History (assistant professor)
Cornell University
West Sibley Hall
Ithaca, New York 14850
Comparative history and literature; social and economic history; material culture (emphasis France)

KARAFIOL, Emile
History (assistant professor)
University of Chicago
5811 South Ellis Avenue
Chicago, Illinois 60637
Administration, political theory, esp. German-speaking Central Europe

KARLE, Joan   S
History (graduate student)
Columbia University
60 Cooper Street
New York, N. Y. 10034
German intellectual history

KASINEC, Edward   S
History (graduate student)
Columbia University
438 East 75 Street
New York, N. Y. 10021
Russian history; bibliography

KATZ, Eve   C
French (assistant professor)
New York University
4 Washington Square Village 5P
New York, N. Y. 10012

KATZ, Wallace B.
History (lecturer)
Wesleyan University
Laurel Grove Road
Middletown, Connecticut 06457
Intellectual history; "Democracy in Theory and Practice: the Uses of Rousseau 1755-1794"

KAUFMAN, Paul   C
Library science (consultant in bibliography)
University of Washington Library

Seattle, Washington 98105
Popular libraries as social forces

KEEN, Sandra H. S
History (student)
New York University
24 Prescott Street
Cambridge, Mass. 02138
French Enlightenment; Diderot; poor relief; utopias

KEENAN, Joseph J., Jr. C
English (assistant professor)
Duquesne University
Pittsburgh, Pa. 15219
Late 18th-century drama, esp. comedy

KEIG, Judith C
English (assistant professor)
University of Pennsylvania
One Sherman Square, Apt. 5L
New York, N. Y. 10023
Ideas of cultural history; biography

KELLER, Theodore D. C
English (associate professor)
East Stroudsburg State College
37 Lackawanna Ave.
East Stroudsburg, Pa. 18301
Swift; satire

KENNEDY, Joyce H. Deveau C
English (assistant professor)
University of Alberta
Edmonton, Alberta
Daniel Defoe

KENNY, Shirley Strum
English (associate professor)
University of Maryland
College Park, Maryland 20742
Drama; bibliography; satire

KERN, Jean B. C
English (associate professor)
Coe College
1639 Ridge Road
Iowa City, Iowa 52240
Drama; satire; novel

KIDD, Ronald R. C
Music (assistant professor)
Purdue University
Stanley Coulter Hall

Lafayette, Indiana 47907
English instrumental music; sociology of music

KIM, Hwal S
English
Soodo Women's Teachers College
Sungdong-Ku
Seoul, Korea
English literature

KING; James
English
McMaster University
Hamilton, Ontario, Canada
Alexander Pope; The Sister Arts; William Blake; William Cowper

KING, Lester S., M. D.
American Medical Association
535 N. Dearborn Street
Chicago, Illinois 60610
History of medicine; history of ideas

KINSLEY, William C
English (assistant professor)
Université de Montréal
Montreal 101, Quebec
Pope, esp. "Dunciad"; satire; media study

KINZER, Ilona Ricardo
French (lecturer)
Massachusetts Institute of Technology
168 Winthrop Road
Brookline, Massachusetts 02146
French novel

KIRBY, John P. C
English (professor)
Randolph-Macon Women's College
Lynchburg, Virginia 24504
Boswell; Horace Walpole; novel

KIRK, Gerald A. C
English (associate professor)
North Texas State University
Denton, Texas 76203
Novel; drama

KIRKENDALE, Warren C
Musicology (associate professor)
Duke University
2422 Tryon Road
Durham, North Carolina 27705
Austrian chamber music; Austrian mass

List of Members

KLEIN, Milton M.   C
History (professor)
University of Tennessee
Knoxville, Tenn. 37916

KLEIN, Suzanne M. L.   C
French (assistant professor)
Pitzer College
18644 Galatina Street
Rowland Heights, California 91745
Novel, esp. Robert Charles to Marquis de Sade

KLINE, Richard B.   C
English (associate professor)
SUNY, Fredonia
Fredonia, New York 14063
Prior; satire, Queen Anne period

KLINGER, Uwe Roland
German (teaching intern)
Wesleyan University
Fisk Hall
Middletown, Conn. 06457
German literature

KNAPP, Mary E.   C
English (professor)
Albertus Magnus College
120 Dwight Street
New Haven, Connecticut 06511
Garrick

KNAPP, Richard Gilbert   C
Languages (assistant professor)
102 Furman Ave., No. 7
Asheville, N. C. 28801
French and English literature

KNODEL, Arthur J.   C
French (professor)
University of Southern California
Los Angeles, California 90007

KOCH, Philip
French and Italian (professor)
University of Pittsburgh
620 LIS
Pittsburgh, Pennsylvania 15213
Galiani; Diderot; Marivaux; Italo-French literary relations

KOLB, Gwin J.   C
English (professor)
University of Chicago
1050 E. 59th St.
Chicago, Illinois 60637
Johnson and his circle

KOLODNY, Annette
English (assistant professor)
University of British Columbia
Vancouver 8, British Columbia
Development of an "American" national consciousness

KOON, Helene
English (assistant professor)
California State College
5500 State College Parkway
San Bernardino, California 92407
Drama 1700-1735

KORS, Alan Charles
History (assistant professor)
University of Pennsylvania
Philadelphia, Pa. 19104
French Enlightenment

KORSHIN, Paul J.   C
English (associate professor)
University of Pennsylvania
Philadelphia, Pa. 19104
Poetics; religion and literature

KRA, Pauline   C
French (assistant professor)
Yeshiva University
109-14 Ascan Avenue
Forest Hills, New York 11375
French literature

KRANTZ, Charles K.
Humanities (associate professor)
Newark College of Engineering
Newark, New Jersey 07102
History of free-thought

KRITZER, Hildreth   C
English (associate professor)
Long Island University
Brooklyn, New York 11201
Critical theory; novel

KRIZSAN, Emery I.
French (assistant professor)
Davis and Elkins College
Elkins, W. Va.
French language and literature

359

KROITOR, Harry P. C
English (professor)
Texas A. & M. University
College Station, Texas 77843
Johnson; Pope

KROPF, Carl R. C
English (assistant professor)
Georgia State University
33 Gilmer Street, S.E.
Atlanta, Georgia 30303
Religious backgrounds of British literature

KUPERSMITH, William C
English (assistant professor)
University of Iowa
Iowa City, Iowa 52240
English satire

LABORDE, Alice M. C
French (assistant professor)
University of California
Irvine, Calif. 92664
Aesthetics; novel

LACOMBE, Anne
Romance languages (assistant professor)
University of North Carolina
313 Northampton Plaza
Chapel Hill, North Carolina 27514
French novel; theater

LACY, Margriet B.
French (graduate student)
University of Kansas
West 8th and Canterbury
Lawrence, Kansas 66044
French novel (Marivaux)

LAFARGE, Catherine
French (assistant professor)
Bryn Mawr College
Bryn Mawr, Pennsylvania 19010
Robert Challe; the myth of Paris in eighteenth-century literature

LAGARDE, Marie L. C
French (professor)
Louisiana State University
New Orleans, Louisiana 70122
French literature

LANDA, Louis A. C
English (professor emeritus)
Princeton University
Princeton, New Jersey 08540
Queen Anne period; intellectual and social background

LANE, James Martin S
History (student)
St. Francis College
28-35 34th Street
Astoria, New York 11103
Colonial and European history; Burke

LANG, Louise S. S
French (graduate student)
9211 S.W. 36th Ave.
Portland, Oregon 97219
French literature

LAPREVOTTE, Guy C
French (assistant professor)
University of Illinois
Foreign Language Building
Urbana, Ill. 61801
French and English science and poetry

LAROCH, Philippe C
Romance languages (instructor)
Banff School of Fine Arts
Banff, Alberta
Libertine novels, Crébillon fils to Laclos; Stanislas de Boufflers

LATTINVILLE, Ronald E. S
English (graduate student)
University of Southern California
1219 West 27th St.
Los Angeles, Calif. 90007
Drama

LAUDON, Robert T. C
Music (associate professor)
University of Minnesota
Minneapolis, Minn. 55455
French opera and aesthetics

LAWRY, Jon S. C
English (professor)
Laurentian University
Sudbury, Ontario
Swift; Prior

List of Members

LAWTON, Joseph   S
English (teaching fellow)
University of Oregon
Eugene, Oregon 97401

LEBRUN, Richard   C
History (associate professor)
University of Manitoba
Winnipeg 19, Manitoba
French political thought (de Maistre)

LECLERC, Paul O.
Modern languages (associate professor)
Union College
Schenectady, N. Y. 12308
Voltaire; Morellet

LEDER, Lawrence H.   C
History (professor)
Lehigh University
Bethlehem, Pennsylvania 18015
American-English politics and political thought

LEE, Douglas A.
Music (associate professor)
Wichita State University
Wichita, Kansas 67208
Instrumental music—German; pamphletizing

LEE, Jae Num   C
English (assistant professor)
Portland State University
Portland, Oregon 97207
Swift; Pope

LEE, Joseph Patrick   C
Romance languages (assistant professor)
University of Georgia
Athens, Georgia 30601
Voltaire's philosophical sermons; Matthew Maty

LEE, Vera G.   C
Romance languages (associate professor)
Boston College
Chestnut Hill, Mass. 02167

LEED, Jacob   C
English (associate professor)
Kent State University
Kent, Ohio 44240
Samuel Johnson

LEITH, James A.   C
History (professor)
Queen's University
Kingston, Ontario
Educational thought; aesthetics and the visual arts

LEMAY, J. A. Leo   C
English (assistant professor)
University of California
Los Angeles, California 90024
American literature; Benjamin Franklin

LENFEST, David S.   C
English (assistant professor)
University of Illinois at Chicago Circle
Box 4348
Chicago, Ill. 60680
Swift; Pope; eighteenth-century poetry and painting

LENNEBERG, Hans H.   C
Musicology (associate professor)
Library/Department of Music
University of Chicago
7458 S. Constance
Chicago, Ill. 60649
Eighteenth-century theory, music printing

LePAGE, Peter V.
English (associate professor)
University of Cincinnati
3535 Mooney Avenue
Cincinnati, Ohio 45208
The novel; satire; music and poetic texts

LETZRING, Monica
English (assistant professor)
Temple University
Philadelphia, Pa. 19122

LEVENTHAL, Herbert   C
History (graduate student)
Graduate Center, CUNY
New York, N. Y. 10036
Colonial American history

LEVIN, Colette G.   S
French and Italian (student)
University of Pittsburgh
820 Evergreen Drive
Washington, Pennsylvania 15301

LEVINE, George R.   C
English (associate professor)
SUNY, Buffalo
Annex B
Buffalo, New York 14214
Interdisciplinary studies; novel

LEVINE, J. A.   C
English (professor)
University of Illinois at Chicago Circle
Chicago, Ill. 60680
English literature

LEVINE, Philip
English (assistant professor)
Tulane University
New Orleans, Louisiana 70118
Johnson, Boswell

LEVY, Darline Gay
History (assistant professor)
Rutgers University, Newark
100 Bleecker St. Apt. 18D
New York, N. Y. 10012
France, social history of ideas

LEVY, Robert H.
English (assistant professor)
Brown University
Providence, R. I. 02912
English literature; Enlightenment philosophy

LEWIS, Wilmarth S.
English
The Lewis Walpole Library (Yale University)
Main Street
Farmington, Connecticut 06032
Horace Walpole and his times

LIEBEL, Helen   C
History (associate professor)
University of Alberta
Edmonton, Alberta
German-Austrian political and economic thought

LIND, Kermit   C
History (instructor)
Cleveland State University
4300 Euclid Avenue
Cleveland, Ohio 44115
Intellectual history

LINDBERG, John D.
Foreign languages (professor)
University of Nevada, Las Vegas
4505 Maryland Parkway
Las Vegas, Nevada 89109
German literature of the 18th century

LINDSTROM, David H.
English (assistant professor)
Colorado State University
Fort Collins, Colorado 80521
Swift, periodical literature, Henry Hills, satire

LINKER, Anita K.   S
Art history (graduate student)
Pennsylvania State University
636 Sunset Road
State College, Pa. 16801
British social history; 18th century art, esp. painting

LINKER, Ronald W.   C
History (associate professor)
Pennsylvania State University
University Park, Pa. 16802
English landed families, particularly Roman Catholics

LOCKE, Miriam   C
English (professor)
University of Alabama
Box 1484
University, Alabama 35486
Fielding; Swift

LODGE, Martin E.
History (assistant professor)
State University College
New Paltz, New York 12561
British colonies

LOKKEN, Roy N.   C
History (associate professor)
East Carolina University
P.O. Box 2744
Greenville, North Carolina 27834
Colonial and revolutionary American history

LONGYEAR, R. M.
Music (professor)
University of Kentucky
Lexington, Ky. 40506
Music; German literature (Empfindsamkeit, Sturm und Drang)

List of Members

LOY, J. Robert   C
Modern languages (professor)
City University of New York, Brooklyn
312 Hicks Street
Brooklyn, New York 11201
French literature and thought

LUDLOW, Gregory   C
French (instructor)
New York University
3 Washington Square Village Apt. 2E
New York, N. Y. 10012
*Comparative study of English and
French 18th-century novel*

LUNN, Alice Coyle   C
English (assistant professor)
University of Michigan
2607 Haven Hall
Ann Arbor, Michigan 48104
English literature; Alexander Pope

LUSTIG, Irma S.   C
English (lecturer)
Bryn Mawr College
2023 Boxwood Drive
Broomall, Pa. 19008
Boswell; Johnson; biography

LYLES, Albert M.
English (professor)
Virginia Commonwealth University
Richmond, Virginia 23220
*Congreve, Richardson, Boswell, and
Johnson*

McALLISTER, Harold Stanwood
English
509 Oak
Grand Forks, North Dakota 58201
Samuel Richardson; gothic novelists

MACANDREW, Elizabeth
English (assistant professor)
Cleveland State University
2804 East 130th Street
Cleveland, Ohio 44120

McCALL, Raymond G.   C
English (professor)
The College of Wooster
Wooster, Ohio 44691

McCARTHY, John A.
German (assistant professor)
Oakland University
3164 Bookham Circle
Pontiac, Michigan 48057
Ch. M. Wieland; Lessing; Goethe

McCORMICK, Thomas J.   C
Art (professor)
Wheaton College
Box 426
Norton, Mass. 02766
Architecture, esp. Neoclassicism

McCOY, Kathleen   C
English (assistant professor)
Seton Hall University
South Orange, N. J. 07079
Novel; aesthetics

McCRACKEN, David
English (assistant professor)
University of Washington
439 - 36th Avenue
Seattle, Washington 98122
Later 18th-century English literature

MACCUBBIN, Robert P.
English (assistant professor)
College of William and Mary
Williamsburg, Virginia 23185
Satire; music

McCUE, Daniel L., Jr.
English (assistant professor)
Boston College
458 Carney Center
Chestnut Hill, Massachusetts 02167
*Interaction of literature and science;
newspapers and periodicals;
England and French Revolution*

McDERMOTT, John Francis
Adjunct Research Professor
Southern Illinois University at
Edwardsville
6345 Westminster Place
St. Louis, Missouri 63130
The French in the Mississippi Valley

McDONALD, Robert H.
History (lecturer)
California State College
Hayward, California 94542
*Intellectual and cultural history, esp.
Voltaire*

MacDONALD, Russell C. C
English (associate professor)
West Virginia University
Morgantown, W. Va. 26506
Novel

McDONALD, W. Wesley S
Political science (graduate research assistant)
State University of New York
352 State Street, Apt. 3
Albany, New York 12210
Edmund Burke; political thought

McDOUGAL, Stuart Y.
4720 Huron Hill Drive
Okemos, Michigan 48864

McGHEE, Dorothy M. C
Modern languages (professor emeritus)
Hamline University
St. Paul, Minnesota 55101
The philosophic tale and moral tale; narrative devices and plans

McGILL, William J. C
History (associate professor)
Alma College
Alma, Michigan 48801
Hapsburgs, diplomatic and social history

McGUINNESS, Arthur E. C
English (associate professor)
University of California
Davis, California 95616
Eighteenth-century English literature and criticism

McHENRY, Lawrence C., Jr., M.D. C
Stroke Research Center
Philadelphia General Hospital
34th and Civic Center Blvd.
Philadelphia, Pa. 19104
Samuel Johnson; eighteenth-century medicine

McHENRY, Robert
English (assistant professor)
University of Hawaii
1733 Donaghho Road
Honolulu, Hawaii 96822
History of ideas; Pope

MacINTOSH, Fred H. C
English (professor)
University of North Carolina
Chapel Hill, N. C. 27515
Pope; Swift; literary criticism

McINTOSH, R. Carey C
English (assistant professor)
University of Rochester
Rochester, New York 14627
Johnson; Augustan genres

MacINTYRE, Jean
English (associate professor)
University of Alberta
Edmonton 7, Alberta
English literature, mostly Pope and Johnson

MacKEITH, Ronald, M.D. C
Guy's Hospital
35 Bloomfield Terrace
London, SW1, England
Samuel Johnson

McKENTY, David E. C
English (professor)
West Chester State College
West Chester, Pa. 19380
Restoration drama, history

McKENZIE, Alan T. C
English (assistant professor)
Purdue University
Lafayette, Indiana 47907
English literature; Johnson, Baretti, Pope, Swift

McKILLOP, David E. S
History (graduate student)
Case Western Reserve University
1875 Forest Hills Blvd. Apt. B-2
East Cleveland, Ohio 44112
Russo-European diplomatic history

McLEOD, W. Reynolds C
History (assistant professor)
West Virginia University
Morgantown, W. Va. 26506
Great Britain; nobility in reign of George I

McMILLAN, Cynthia Anne C
History (graduate student)
University of Virginia
1048 Ohio Avenue S.W.

List of Members

Huron, South Dakota 57350
History of science; intellectual history (European)

McTIGUE, Joan E.   S
English (assistant instructor)
Indiana University
213 North Grant Street
Bloomington, Indiana 47401

MACEY, Samuel L.
English (assistant professor)
University of Victoria
Victoria, British Columbia
Satire; German literature; influence of science and technology

MACK, Maynard   C
English (professor)
Yale University
1314 Yale Station
New Haven, Connecticut 06520

MAHAFFEY, Kathleen   C
English (professor)
University of Puerto Rico at Mayagüez
Mayagüez, Puerto Rico 00708
Writers of the Augustan period, esp. Pope

MALCOLMSON, Robert W.   C
History (lecturer)
Queen's University
Kingston, Ontario
English social history

MALEK, James S.
English (associate professor)
University of Idaho
Moscow, Idaho 83843
British aesthetics; British drama

MALUEG, Sara Ellen
Modern languages (associate professor)
Oregon State University
Corvallis, Oregon 97331
Diderot; Encyclopédie; Franco-American relations

MANCUSO, Joseph Charles
English (instructor)
University of North Carolina
Chapel Hill, N. C. 27514
Poetry of Christopher Smart

MANDLE, Earl Roger
Art history (assistant director)
Minneapolis Institute of Arts
201 East 24th Street
Minneapolis, Minn. 55404
Eighteenth-century Dutch painting

MANN, David D.
English (assistant professor)
Miami University
Oxford, Ohio 45056
Congreve; Gay; drama

MANTOVANI, Juanita Marie   S
English (teaching assistant)
University of Southern California
Los Angeles, Calif. 90007

MARKIEWICZ, Susanna   C
French and Italian (instructor)
Miami University
22 North College
Oxford, Ohio 45056
Denis Diderot

MARKS, Paul F.   C
Music (graduate student)
University of Washington
330 Marlatt St.
St. Laurent 378, Quebec
Musical Sturm und Drang; Viennese classic style

MARSAK, Leonard M.   C
History (professor)
University of California
Santa Barbara, Calif. 93106
Social history of science

MARSHALL, Donald G.   C
English (assistant professor)
University of California
Los Angeles, California 90024

MARSHALL, Geoffrey   C
English (assistant professor)
University of Oklahoma
760 Van Vleet Oval
Norman, Oklahoma 73069
Restoration, eighteenth-century drama; Dryden

MARSHALL, Robert L.   C
Music (assistant professor)

Princeton University
Princeton, N. J. 08540
Music of J. S. Bach

MARTIN, Jean-Claude   C
French (assistant professor)
City University of New York
420 East 72nd St.
New York, N. Y. 10021
French literature and art

MARTIN, Peter E.   C
English (assistant professor)
Florida Atlantic University
Boca Raton, Florida 33432
*Pope; eighteenth-century gardening;
  John Gay*

MARTINS, Heitor   C
Spanish and Portuguese (professor)
Indiana University
Bloomington, Indiana 47401
*Portuguese and Brazilian literature and
  history*

MAST, Daniel D.   C
English (instructor)
Eastern New Mexico University
Portales, New Mexico 88130
Samuel Johnson

MATHIEU, Elizabeth   S
French (student)
Vassar College
255 Waterman Street
Providence, R. I. 02906

MAY, Georges
French (professor)
Yale University
New Haven, Connecticut 06520
French literature; the novel

MAY, Gita   C
French (professor)
Columbia University
404 West 116th Street
New York, N. Y. 10027
*French Enlightenment and Revolution;
  preromanticism; aesthetics*

MAYFIELD, P. M.   C
History (professor)
Ball State University
Muncie, Indiana 47306
British naval and administrative history

MAYO, Robert D.
English (professor)
Northwestern University
Evanston, Illinois 60201
English fiction, periodicals

MAZZEO, Guido E.
Romance languages (professor)
George Washington University
6902 Highland Street
Springfield, Virginia 22150
Spanish Jesuits in exile

MEIER, Peter P.   S
Romance languages (graduate student)
175 East 151 Street
Bronx, N. Y. 10451

MELL, Donald C., Jr.   C
English (assistant professor)
University of Delaware
Newark, Delaware 19711
*Early eighteenth century; age of
  Johnson; elegy*

MENGEL, Elias F., Jr.   C
English (associate professor)
Georgetown University
1340 29th St., N. W.
Washington, D. C. 20007

MESSENGER, Ann P.   C
English (assistant professor)
Simon Fraser University
Burnaby 2, British Columbia
Drama; Restoration period

METGER, Helen Kendall
French (teacher)
Warrensburg Central School
220 Ash Street
Corinth, New York 12822
French literature

MEYER, Eve R.   C
Music (associate professor)
Temple University
Philadelphia, Pa. 19122
Music

MEYER, Paul H.   C
Romance languages (professor)
University of Connecticut
Storrs, Conn. 06268
*French philosophes; comparative
  literature*

List of Members

MICHAELS, Brian   S
English (teaching assistant)
University of Florida
P.O. Box 1336
Gainesville, Florida 32601
Swift

MIDDENDORF, John H.   C
English (professor)
Columbia University
610 Philosophy Hall
New York, N. Y. 10027
Samuel Johnson; economics and literature

MILIC, Louis T.   C
English (professor)
Cleveland State University
Euclid Ave. at 22nd St.
Cleveland, Ohio 44115
Swift and prose style

MILLER, Arnold   C
French and Italian (associate professor)
University of Wisconsin
Madison, Wisconsin 53706
French Enlightenment and its influence in 19th-century Russia; Diderot

MILLER, B. J.   C
English (assistant professor)
Bloomsburg State College
44 West Third Street
Bloomsburg, Pa. 17815
British literature

MILLER, Henry Knight   C
English (professor)
Princeton University
22 McCosh Hall
Princeton, N. J. 08540
Henry Fielding and the Augustan age

MILLNER, Stuart A.
English (assistant professor)
Suffolk University
390 Weld Street
West Roxbury, Massachusetts 02132
Thomas Gray

MILNE, Victor J.   S
English
49H McGee Ave.
Kitchener, Ontario
Aesthetics; Samuel Johnson

MINDAK, M.
French (teaching associate)
University of Texas
2301 West 11th
Austin, Texas 78703
French literature

MINER, Earl   C
English (professor)
Princeton University
Princeton, N. J. 08540
Dryden; Restoration poetry and criticism

MISENHEIMER, James B., Jr.   C
English (professor)
North Texas State University
N.T. Station, Box 13826
Denton, Texas 76203
Age of Johnson; novel; satire

MITCHELL, Daniel T.   C
English (associate professor)
Loyola University of Los Angeles
4133 Locust Avenue
Long Beach, California 90807
Oliver Goldsmith

MITTMAN, Barbara G.
French (assistant professor)
University of Illinois, Chicago Circle
640 Judson
Evanston, Illinois 60202
Diderot's theatre

MOGGIO, Anna-Maria   C
History (instructor)
College of the Holy Cross
Worcester, Mass. 01610
French Revolution

MONAHAN, Patrick J., Jr.
Modern languages (instructor)
Gonzaga University
Box 56
Spokane, Washington 99202
Diderot, Voltaire

MONTGOMERY, Lyna Lee
English (assistant professor)
University of Arkansas
Fayetteville, Arkansas 72701
Drama

MONTY, Jeanne R.   C
French (associate professor)
Tulane University
New Orleans, La. 70118
French literature

MOORE, Elizabeth L.   C
French (professor emeritus)
Western College for Women
1325 Market Street
Parkersburg, W. Va. 26101
Ethnology and French literature of the eighteenth century

MOORE, James W.
Political science (assistant professor)
Loyola College
7141 Sherbrooke Street West
Montreal 262, Quebec
Eighteenth-century political thought

MOORE, Josephine K.
English (instructor)
Foreign languages and literature
National Taiwan University
Taipei, Taiwan, China
English literature, esp. Swift

MOORE, Judith K.   S
English (graduate student)
Cornell University
1008 N. Cayuga
Ithaca, New York 14850
Relation of literature to economic, social, political thought

MOORE, Nancy   C
English (professor)
Butler University
Indianapolis, Indiana 46208
Johnson; Swift

MOORE, Robert E.
English (professor)
University of Minnesota
Minneapolis, Minnesota 55455
English literature; music and the visual arts

MOORE, William M.   S
French and Romance philology
  (graduate student)
Columbia University
1572 Massachusetts Avenue, Apt. 6
Cambridge, Massachusetts 02138
Diderot; Eighteenth-century novel

MORBY, John E.
History (assistant professor)
California State College
Hayward, California 94542
History; French musical institutions, esp. at court of Versailles

MORIN, H. S
French (associate professor)
Secretariat of State
400 Stewart Street
Apt. 1605
Ottawa 2, Ontario
Sensibility (Marmontel, Rousseau)

MORRISROE, Michael, Jr.   C
English (assistant professor)
University of Illinois at Chicago Circle
Box 4348
Chicago, Illinois 60680
David Hume and the Enlightenment

MORRISSEY, L. J.
English (associate professor)
University of Saskatchewan
Saskatoon, Saskatchewan
Drama

MORSE, Donald E.
English (associate professor)
Oakland University
Rochester, Michigan 48063
Satire

MOSS, Harold Gene   C
English (assistant professor)
University of Florida
Gainesville, Fla. 32601
Drama

MOSS, Jean D.   C
English and history (instructor)
West Virginia University
Morgantown, W. Va. 26506
*Tudor England
Drama*

MOTSCH, Markus F.
Germanic languages and literatures
University of Cincinnati

List of Members

Cincinnati, Ohio 45221
Eighteenth-century German literary criticism

MOUNT, Elizabeth F.   S
French (graduate student)
Tulane University
2224 Carondelet St., Apt. A
New Orleans, La. 70130
Diderot

MURPHY, Orville T.
History (professor)
State University of New York
Buffalo, New York 14214
Old régime France; diplomacy; education

MURPHY, Patricia   C
Modern languages (assistant professor)
University of New Mexico
Albuquerque, New Mexico 87106
French literature (novel)

MYERS, Mitzi   C
English (assistant professor)
University of California
Santa Barbara, Calif. 93106
Eighteenth-century fiction

MYERS, Robert Manson   C
English (professor)
University of Maryland
2101 Connecticut Avenue, N.W.
Washington, D. C. 20008
Handel; music criticism; music and literature in eighteenth century

MYERS, Sylvia H.   C
English
1575 La Vereda Rd.
Berkeley, Calif. 94708
Novel; life and letters of Mrs. Piozzi; women writers

NABARRA, Alain Marie
French
Lakehead University
Thunder Bay "P", Ontario
French literature (novel; literature and society)

NAUEN, Franz
History
University of California at San Diego
4437 30th St.
San Diego, California 92116

NAUGLE, Helen H.   C
English (assistant professor)
Georgia Institute of Technology
Atlanta, Georgia 30332
Periodical literature

NEATBY, Hilda   C
History (professor)
Queen's University
Kingston, Ontario
Canadian history

NEBEL, Henry M., Jr.   C
Russian (associate professor)
Northwestern University
Evanston, Illinois 60201
Russian literature of eighteenth century

NEBEL, Sylvia Sue   C
German (assistant professor)
Loyola University of Chicago
6525 N. Sheridan
Chicago, Illinois 60626
German literature of eighteenth century

NECHELES, Ruth F.   C
History (associate professor)
Long Island University
Brooklyn Center
Brooklyn, New York 11201
French Revolution (history)

NEEDHAM, Gwendolyn B.   C
English (professor)
University of California
Davis, California 95616
Novel; social milieu; arts and crafts

NELSON, Jeffrey M.   S
History (graduate student)
Harvard University
77 Trowbridge Street No. 43
Cambridge, Mass. 02138
English political thought; Hume, Burke, American Revolution

NELSON, John Walter   C
English
Eastern Kentucky University
Richmond, Kentucky 40475
William Blake

NELSON, Malcolm A.   C
English (associate professor)
State University College
Fredonia, New York 14063
Catches and glees; popular culture

NELSON, Nicholas H.
English (assistant professor)
Indiana University at Kokomo
2300 South Washington Street
Kokomo, Indiana 46901
English literature, esp. satire

NELSON, Ronald R.   C
History (professor)
Western Carolina University
Cullowhee, N. C. 28723
Eighteenth-century British

NELSON, Russell S., Jr.
History (associate professor)
Wisconsin State University
901 Illinois Avenue
Stevens Point, Wisconsin 54481
Colonial back-country

NESBITT, John D.   S
English (student)
University of California, Davis
313 K Street, No. 79
Davis, California 95616
English literature

NEUBAUER, John   C
German (associate professor)
Case Western Reserve University
Cleveland, Ohio 44106
Aesthetics; science; Romantic poetry

NEUFELD, Evelyn   C
Foreign languages (assistant professor)
State University of New York
McAllister Road, R.D. 1
Fredonia, New York 14063
Novel (Spain, France, Germany, England)

NEW, Melvyn   C
English (assistant professor)
University of Florida
Gainesville, Florida 32601
Laurence Sterne; novel; satire

NEWELL, Julia   C
French (professor)
Dawson College
4996 Victoria Ave.
Montreal 247, Quebec
French literature

NEWMAN, Edgar Leon
History (assistant professor)
New Mexico State University
Box 3-H
Las Cruces, New Mexico 88001
Bourbon Restoration 1814-30; French Louisiana

NEWMAN, Robert   C
English (assistant professor)
SUNY, Buffalo
Annex B
Buffalo, New York 14214
Criticism, drama

NICHOLLS, James C.   C
Romance languages (associate professor)
Colgate University
Hamilton, New York 13346
Anglo-French literary relations

NIEMAN, Lawrence J.   C
English (assistant professor)
Canisius College
2001 Main Street
Buffalo, N. Y. 14208
Eighteenth-century English literature

NIERENBERG, Edwin   C
English (associate professor)
San Francisco State University
1600 Holloway Avenue
San Francisco, Calif. 94132
Pope; Swift; Scriblerus group; satire

NOETHER, Emiliana P.   C
History (professor)
University of Connecticut
Storrs, Connecticut 06268
Italian intellectual history

NOLTE, Edgar V.
Moravian Music Foundation, Inc.
Drawer Z
Winston-Salem, N. C. 27108

List of Members

NORMAN, Sister Marion, IBVM C
English (associate professor)
University of Alberta
Edmonton 7, Alberta
Thomas Sprat; influence of science on literature

NORTON, David Fate
Philosophy (associate professor)
University of California at San Diego
Box 109 La Jolla, California 92037
Philosophy; Scottish Enlightenment

NOVAK, Maximillian E. C
English (professor)
University of California
405 Hilgard Avenue
Los Angeles, California 90024
Defoe; Dryden; Congreve; novel; drama

NOWINSKI, Judith C
French (assistant professor)
Hostos Community College, CUNY
90 La Salle Street
New York, New York 10027
French Enlightenment

O'BRIEN, Charles H.
History (assistant professor)
Wittenberg University
Springfield, Ohio 45501
Enlightened absolutism; religious toleration; Austria: history and culture

ODEN, Richard L.
English (assistant professor)
Texas Tech University
Lubbock, Texas 79409
Dryden; Fielding

O'DONNELL, Rev. Terrence F. X. C
Church history
Church of St. Barnabas
409 E. 241st Street
Bronx, New York 10470
Roman Catholic, esp. Papal history

O'GORMAN, Donal C
French (professor)
St. Michael's College
University of Toronto
Toronto 5, Ontario
Diderot; Rousseau; satire

O'LEARY, Kenneth C
English (assistant professor)
Seton Hall University
South Orange, New Jersey 07079
English literature

OLIVIER, Louis A. C
Romance languages (senior instructor)
University of Oregon
Eugene, Oregon 97403

OLSEN, Donald J. C
History (associate professor)
Vassar College
Poughkeepsie, N. Y. 12601
English history; urban development and estate management

OLSEN, Leslie A. C
English (assistant professor)
University of Michigan
College of Engineering
Ann Arbor, Michigan 48104
Poetry; stylistics; computer techniques

OLSHIN, Toby A. C
English (assistant professor)
Temple University
Philadelphia, Pa. 19122
Novelists; Laurence Sterne

OPPER, Jacob
Music (assistant professor)
Frostburg State College
Frostburg, Maryland 21532
Musical classicism; cosmology; science

OSBORN, James M. C
English (research associate)
Yale University
1603 A. Yale Station
New Haven, Conn. 06520

OWEN, John B.
History (professor)
University of Calgary
Calgary 45, Alberta
English history

PAGLIARO, Harold E. C
English (professor)
Swarthmore College
Swarthmore, Pa. 19081
Structural and rhetorical patterns in poetry and prose

PALMER, Joe L.
Romance languages (assistant professor)
University of Georgia
Athens, Georgia 30601
Spanish 18th Century

PALMER, R. R.   C
History (professor)
Yale University
46 Cliff Street
New Haven, Conn. 06511

PANAGOPOULOS, Beata
Tutorials (assistant professor)
San Jose State College
San Jose, California 95114
Art history

PANAGOPOULOS, Epaminondas P.   C
History (professor)
San Jose State College
San Jose, Calif. 95114
American constitutional and intellectual history

PANNELL, Anne G.   C
History (professor)
President, Sweet Briar College
Sweet Briar, Virginia 24595
Anti-slavery agitation; the Society of Friends

PAOLINI, Gilberto   C
Spanish and Portuguese (associate professor)
Tulane University
New Orleans, La. 70118
Spanish and Italian literature

PAPPAS, John N.   C
Romance languages (professor)
Fordham University
Bronx, New York 10458
D'Alembert's role in the French Enlightenment

PARK, William   C
English
Sarah Lawrence College
Bronxville, New York 10708
English novel

PARKER, James   C
Art history (curator)
Metropolitan Museum of Art
Fifth Ave. at 82nd Street
New York, N. Y. 10028
European decorative arts

PARKIN, Rebecca P.   C
English (professor)
Sacramento State College
Sacramento, Calif. 95819
Eighteenth-century verse

PASSLER, Susan M.
English (assistant professor)
Georgia State University
1481 E. Rock Spring Road, Apt. 4
Atlanta, Georgia 30306
Novel (Fielding); Johnson

PATTERSON, Emily H.
English (assistant professor)
San Diego State College
San Diego, California 92115
Swift, Pope

PATTERSON, Frank M.   C
English (associate professor)
Central Missouri State College
Warrensburg, Mo. 64093
Drama

PEACOCK, Valerie S.   S
Literature (graduate student)
University of California, San Diego
354 N. Sierra
Solana Beach, California 92075
Jonathan Swift; history of science and technology; status of women; the dance

PELLI, Moshe
Modern Hebrew literature (senior lecturer)
Negev University
P.O.B. 2053
Beersheva, Israel
Hebrew Haskalah (enlightenment); deism; Jewish intellectual history

PERKINS, Jean A.   C
French (associate professor)
Swarthmore College
Swarthmore, Pennsylvania 19081
French 18th-century literature and philosophy

List of Members

PERRY, Thomas W.   C
History (associate professor)
Boston College
Chestnut Hill, Mass. 02167
British history

PETERSON, R. G.   C
English (associate professor)
St. Olaf College
Northfield, Minnesota 55057
Dryden and Restoration; Pope; early 18th-century Neoclassicism

PETERSON, Spiro   C
English (professor)
Miami University of Ohio
115 N. University Ave.
Oxford, Ohio 45056
Defoe; novel; satire

PETIT, Bernard
French (instructor)
SUNY, Brockport
8223 Ridge Road
Brockport, N. Y. 14420
Prose fiction; journals

PETTIT, Henry   C
English (professor)
University of Colorado
Boulder, Colorado 80302
Mid-eighteenth-century poetry

PHILLIPS, Steven R.
English (assistant professor)
Alfred University
Alfred, New York 14802

PHILLIPSON, John S.   C
English (associate professor)
University of Akron
Akron, Ohio 44304
Novel

PICKEN, Robert A.   C
Romance languages
Queens College, CUNY
Flushing, New York 11367
French literature of the 18th century

PIERSON, Harry H.
3026 Harcross Road
Redwood City, California 94062
Johnson and Boswell and their circle

PIPER, William Bowman   C
English (professor)
Rice University
Houston, Texas 77001
The literature of conversation and common sense

PISANO, Brother Anthony, F.S.C.   S
Brownson Hall
University of Notre Dame
Notre Dame, Indiana 46556

PITOU, Spire   C
Language and literature (professor)
University of Delaware
Newark, Delaware 19711
Comedy; tragedy; repertory

POCOCK, J. G. A.   C
History (professor)
Washington University
St. Louis, Mo. 63130
Political and historical thought

POLT, John H. R.
Spanish and Portuguese (professor)
University of California
Berkeley, California 94720
Spanish literature

POPKIN, Richard H.   C
Philosophy (professor)
Lehman College, CUNY
Bronx, N. Y. 10468
History of philosophy; history of Judaism

PORTER, Charles A.   C
French (associate professor)
Yale University
321 W. L. Harkness Hall
New Haven, Connecticut 06520
Restif de la Bretonne; L'Encyclopédie

POSNER, Donald
Art history (professor)
Institute of Fine Arts
New York University
1 East 78th Street
New York, N. Y. 10021
French and Italian art

POWER, Mina Waterman
French
Finch College

169 East 78th Street
New York, N. Y. 10021
Voltaire, Pascal, Diderot, ethics, aesthetics

PRESTON, Thomas R.   C
English (associate professor)
University of Tennessee
Chattanooga, Tenn. 37403

PRIMER, Irwin   C
English (associate professor)
Rutgers University
Newark, New Jersey 07102
Mandeville

PROSSER, Jeanne   C
History (lecturer)
Dartmouth College
Hanover, N. H. 03755
Ancien Régime; French Revolution

PROWN, Jules D.   C
Art history (director)
The Paul Mellon Center for British Art and British Studies
Box 2120 Yale Station
New Haven, Connecticut 06520
Eighteenth-century American and English art

QUAINTANCE, Richard E., Jr.   C
English (associate professor)
Douglass College
New Brunswick, N. J. 08903
Satire and erotic poetry; novel

QUINTANA, Ricardo   C
English (professor emeritus)
University of Wisconsin
2100 Commonwealth Ave.
Madison, Wis. 53705
Swift; Oliver Goldsmith

RACEVSKIS, Karlis
Foreign Languages (assistant professor)
Antioch College
604 Phillips Street
Yellow Springs, Ohio 45387
The French Academy and the philosophes

RADFORD, James Elliot   S
English
1452 East Rock Springs Road, N.E.
Apt. 4
Atlanta, Georgia 30306
Literature and the visual arts

RADNER, John B.   C
English (assistant professor)
Harvard University
Warren House 9
Cambridge, Mass. 02138
Criticism; satire; moral philosophy

RAGUSA, Olga
Italian (professor)
Columbia University
601 Casa Italiana
New York, N. Y. 10027
Franco-Italian relations

RAINBOLT, John C.
History (associate professor)
University of Missouri
153 Arts and Science
Columbia, Missouri 65201
American colonial and Revolutionary history

RAITIERE, Anna   C
Humanities (assistant professor)
York College, CUNY
401 West 118th Street
New York, N. Y. 10027
Theater and novel in French literature

RAMSEY, Clifford Earl   C
English (assistant professor)
Bryn Mawr College
Bryn Mawr, Pa. 19010
Pope; Restoration drama; pastoral and landscape literature

RANUM, Orest
History (professor)
Johns Hopkins University
208 Ridgewood Road
Baltimore, Maryland 21210
French history, history of ideas

RAPPAPORT, Rhoda   C
History (assistant professor)
Vassar College
Poughkeepsie, N. Y. 12601
History of science (France)

List of Members

RASMUSSEN, Kirk G.   S
English (teaching assistant)
Salem College
Salem, W. Va. 26426
Studies in the novel

RASSIAS, John A.
Romance languages (professor)
Dartmouth College
Hanover, New Hampshire 03755
Diderot; theater (in general)

RAWSON, C. J.   C
English (professor)
University of Warwick
Coventry, Warwickshire
England
Fielding; Swift; Thomas Parnell; satire

RAYNAUD, Jean-Michel
French (professor)
University of Ottawa
130 Somerset West
Ottawa 4, Ontario
Voltaire

REARDON, Ruth C.   C
French (assistant professor)
New York University
New York, N. Y. 10003
French literature of the 18th century; philosophes

REEDY, Rev. Gerard, S.J.
English (student)
University of Pennsylvania
2101 Chestnut St., Apt. 1426
Philadelphia, Pa. 19103

REGAN, John   S
English (graduate student)
University of California, Davis
13-C Solano Park
Davis, California 95616
Poetry of Alexander Pope

REISH, Joseph G.   S
French (teaching assistant)
University of Wisconsin
2019 University Avenue
Madison, Wisconsin 53705
French literature; linguistics

REITAN, Earl A.   C
History (professor)
Illinois State University
Normal, Illinois 61761
British constitutional and political history, 1689-1832

RENZ, Joan K.
English (instructor)
Northern Michigan University
1420 W. Center Street
Marquette, Michigan 49855

RETZLEFF, Garry V.   S
English (graduate student)
University of Toronto
Toronto 5, Ontario
Aesthetic theory; landscape literature; the picturesque

REUTINGER, Martin   S
English (graduate student)
University of California, Berkeley
P.O. Box 126
Stinson Beach, Calif. 94970
English literature; Swift

REVITT, Paul J.   C
Music (professor)
University of Missouri at Kansas City
4420 Warwick Blvd.
Kansas City, Missouri 64111
Music

REYNOLDS, Richard
English (assistant professor)
University of Connecticut
Hillyndale Road
Storrs, Conn. 06268
Johnson; Pope

REZLER, Marta   C
Romance languages (assistant professor)
Hunter College, CUNY
695 Park Avenue
New York, New York 10021
History of ideas; D'Alembert; Voltaire

RICCIARDELLI, M.   C
Italian (professor)
State University of New York
221 Crosby Hall
Buffalo, New York 14214
Italian history, art, literature

RICE, Scott B.
English (assistant professor)
San Jose State College
125 South 7th Street
San Jose, California 95114
Travel literature; Smollett

RICHARDSON, Robert D., Jr. C
English (associate professor)
University of Denver
Denver, Colorado 80210
Mythology and mythography; American romanticism

RICHARDSON, Sharon B. S
Comparative literature (graduate student)
University of North Carolina
13708 Superior Road
Cleveland, Ohio 44112
Letters

RICHESON, Edward, Jr.
English (associate professor)
University of Texas at El Paso
Box 128, UTEP
El Paso, Texas 79902
Pope and the Augustan Age

RIDGWAY, R. S. C
French and Spanish (professor)
University of Saskatchewan
Saskatoon, Saskatchewan
Voltaire; theater; sensibility

RIELY, John C. C
English (teaching fellow)
University of Pennsylvania
2104 Walnut St.
Philadelphia, Pa. 19103
Johnson, Boswell, and their circle

RIPPEY, Arthur G.
English
2525 E. Exposition Avenue
Denver, Colorado 80223
Johnson; Boswell (early editions; collector)

RIPPY, Frances M. C
English (professor)
Ball State University
4417 W. Jackson
Muncie, Indiana 47304
Restoration and eighteenth-century British poetry

RITCHESON, Charles R.
History (professor)
University of Southern California
Los Angeles, California 90007
Late eighteenth- and early nineteenth-century British and American

ROBBINS, Caroline
History (professor)
Bryn Mawr College
815 The Chetwynd
Rosemont, Pennsylvania 19010
History of ideas

ROBERTS, David D. C
English (assistant professor)
University of Wyoming
Laramie, Wyoming 82070
English literature

ROBERTS, Edgar V., Jr. C
English (associate professor)
Herbert H. Lehman College, CUNY
Bronx, N. Y. 10468
Plays of Henry Fielding

ROBINSON, Lucius S.
German (associate professor)
California Western Campus
United States International University
3928 Milan Street
San Diego, Calif. 92106
German and French literature; U. S. cultural history

ROCHE, John F. C
History (associate professor)
Fordham University
New York, N. Y. 10023
History of American revolution; American architecture

RODES, David Stuart C
English (assistant professor)
University of California
405 Hilgard Avenue
Los Angeles, Calif. 90024
Theater; French-English relations; Dutch influences

RODEWALD, Albert F.
Music (assistant professor)
University of Virginia
113 Old Cabell Hall
Charlottesville, Virginia 22903
Opera; theatre

List of Members

RODGERS, Gary B.   S
French (graduate student)
University of Texas
Austin, Texas 78712
Diderot; 18th-century French press

ROGAL, Samuel J.   C
English (associate professor)
State University College
Oswego, N. Y. 13126
Hymnody; emphasis on Isaac Watts and the Wesleys

ROGERS, Adrienne
French (associate professor)
Russell Sage College
Troy, New York 12180
Censorship in France; Voltaire; Rousseau

ROGERS, William B.
Literature (assistant professor)
Rensselaer Polytechnic Institute
Troy, New York 12181
The novel

ROSBOTTOM, Ronald C.   C
Romance languages (assistant professor)
University of Pennsylvania
Box 4 Logan Hall
Philadelphia, Pennsylvania 19104
French literature, art, history

ROSCH, Hopewell Selby   S
English (graduate student)
Stanford University
5625 S.E. 38th Street
Portland, Oregon 97202
Swift; Restoration drama

ROSEN, George
History of science and medicine (professor)
Yale University
1480 Ridge Road
North Haven, Connecticut 06473
Medicine, science, literature, culture

ROSEN, Richard L.
History of science (assistant professor)
Drexel University
Philadelphia, Pennsylvania 19104
History of science, esp. Italy

ROSENBERG, Aubrey   C
French (lecturer)
Victoria College
University of Toronto
Toronto 5, Ontario
Voyages imaginaires and utopias

ROSENFIELD, Leonora Cohen
French and Italian (professor)
University of Maryland
3749 Chesapeake Street, N.W.
Washington, D. C. 20016
History of ideas (France); French Enlightenment and its relations with other countries

ROSENHEIM, E. W., Jr.
English (professor)
University of Chicago
Chicago, Illinois 60637
Satire

ROSOWSKI, Susan   S
English (graduate student)
University of Arizona
1810 So. 25th
Lincoln, Nebraska 68502
Laurence Sterne

ROSS, Ian   C
English (associate professor)
University of British Columbia
3845 W. 37th Avenue
Vancouver 13, British Columbia
Hume circle; Scottish vernacular poetry

ROTHMAN, Irving N.
English
University of Houston
Houston, Texas 77004

ROTHSCHILD, Harriet Dorothy
French (associate professor)
University of Rhode Island
Kingston, Rhode Island 02881
Benoit de Maillet

ROTHSTEIN, Eric
English (professor)
University of Wisconsin
7195 White Hall
Madison, Wisconsin 53706
Drama; fiction; Anglo-French literary relationships

ROUSSEAU, George S.   C
English (associate professor)
University of California
Los Angeles, California 90024
*Literature and science; medicine
1660-1800; Pope*

ROWE, Constance
French (associate professor)
Southeast Missouri State College
318 North Sprigg Street
Cape Girardeau, Missouri 63701
Voltaire

ROWSOME, Beverly   C
History
100 West Street
Geneva, New York 14456
Colonial American legal tradition

RUDOLPH, Valerie C.   C
English (instructor)
Purdue University
Lafayette, Indiana 47907
Drama; satire; Fielding

RUFF, Lawrence Albert   C
English (associate professor)
University of Dayton
Dayton, Ohio 45409
Novel

RUGGLES, Rebecca D.   C
English
Brooklyn College, CUNY
606 West 116th St. Apt. 23
New York, N.Y. 10027

RUHE, E. L.   C
English (professor)
University of Kansas
Lawrence, Kansas 66044
Johnson; Milton tradition; Edmund Curll

RULE, John C.   C
History (professor)
Ohio State University
216 N. Oval Drive
Columbus, Ohio 43210
*European history; age of Louis XIV,
French diplomacy*

RUNTE, Roseann   S
French and Italian (graduate student)
University of Kansas
Box 76
Shrub Oak, New York 10588
*La Fontaine's reputation and influence
in 18th-century France*

RUPPRECHT, Oliver C.
English and fine arts (professor)
Concordia College
1108 Kavanaugh Place
Milwaukee, Wisconsin 53213
Literature, music, art

RYLEY, Robert M.   C
English (assistant professor)
York College, CUNY
Jamaica, N. Y. 11432
Criticism

RYNES, Theodore J.
English (assistant professor)
University of Santa Clara
Faculty Residence
Santa Clara, Calif. 95053
English literature; visual arts; religion

SACKS, Sheldon   C
English (professor)
University of Chicago
Chicago, Illinois 60637
Prose fiction; Henry Fielding

SAETA, Maurice   C
English
3435 Wilshire Blvd., Suite 2510
Los Angeles, Calif. 90010
Boswell; Johnson

SAINE, Thomas P.
Germanic languages and literature
   (assistant professor)
Yale University
307 W. L. Harkness Hall
New Haven, Conn. 06520
*German literature; intellectual history;
aesthetics*

SAISSELIN, Rémy B.   C
Comparative literature (professor)
University of Rochester
Rochester, New York 14627
Aesthetic theory; art; pre-romanticism

SAKOWSKI, Wanda   S
French and Italian (teaching assistant)
Tulane University

List of Members

1327 Broadway, No. A
New Orleans, La. 70118
Diderot

SALM, Peter   C
Comparative literature (professor)
Case Western Reserve University
Yost Hall
Cleveland, Ohio 44106
Literature and philosophy; relationship between science and literature

SAMPSON, H. Grant   C
Drama (director)
Department of English
Queen's University
Kingston, Ontario
Drama

SAREIL, Jean   C
French (professor)
Columbia University
New York, N. Y. 10027
Literature; history

SARICK, Hyman
English (lecturer)
Queen's University
Kingston, Ontario
Swift; Johnson

SARICKS, Ambrose   C
History (professor)
Wichita State University
Dean, Graduate School
Wichita, Kansas 67207
Economic and religious thought; French Revolution

SASLOW, Edward L.
English (assistant professor)
University of California, Riverside
1805-I Loma Vista
Riverside, California 92507
Dryden

SAVELLE, Max   C
History (professor)
University of Illinois, Chicago Circle
Chicago, Illinois 60680
Anglo-American intellectual history; the Enlightenment and America

SCHABERT, Tilo
Hoover Institution (research fellow)
Stanford University
Stanford, California 94305
Political thought, theory of knowledge; anthropology

SCHAKEL, Peter J.   C
English
Hope College
Holland, Michigan 49423
Jonathan Swift

SCHLEGEL, Dorothy B.   C
English (professor)
Norfolk State College
476 Linkhorn Drive
Virginia Beach, Virginia 23351
Rosicrucian and Masonic symbolism; Shaftesbury (3rd Earl)

SCHLERETH, Thomas J.
History (assistant professor)
Grinnell College
Grinnell, Iowa 50112
Scottish and American Enlightenments

SCHNITZER, Shirley   C
English (graduate student)
City University of New York
430 East 86th Street
New York, N. Y. 10028
Pope; Swift

SCHNORRENBERG, Barbara B. C
History (lecturer)
University of North Carolina
Chapel Hill, N. C. 27514
English and German history, especially diplomatic

SCHOFIELD, Robert E.   C
History of science (professor)
Case Western Reserve University
Crawford Hall
Cleveland, Ohio 44106
Natural philosophy, esp. British; Joseph Priestley

SCHRADER, William C., III   C
History (assistant professor)
Tennessee Technological University
Cookeville, Tenn. 38501
Habsburgs; cultural parallels

SCHUTZ, John A.   C
History (professor)
University of Southern California
Los Angeles, Calif. 90007
Massachusetts politics; American Tories

SCHWANDT, Pamela Poynter
English
811 Greenvale
Northfield, Minnesota 55057
Pope; translation; Homeric criticism

SCHWARTZ, Judith L.   C
Music (instructor)
University of California
Riverside, Calif. 92502
Classical music and musical theory

SCHWARTZ, Leon   C
Foreign languages (professor)
California State College at Los Angeles
1032 So. El Molino
Alhambra, Calif. 91801
French literature

SCHWARTZ, Richard B.   C
English (associate professor)
University of Wisconsin
Madison, Wisconsin 53706
Literature and science; Samuel Johnson

SCHWARTZ, Robert G., Jr.   C
English (assistant professor)
Central Missouri State College
Warrensburg, Missouri 64093
English literature

SCHWARZ, Herbert J., Jr.   C
History
435 East 57th Street
New York, N. Y. 10022
History (evolution of the souvenir industry)

SCHWARZBACH, Bertram E.
French (assistant professor)
Elmira College
1304 Brooklyn Avenue
Brooklyn, New York 11203
Voltaire, Bible criticism, history of science

SCOTT, Alison   C
Germanic languages (professor)
University of Alberta
Edmonton 7, Alberta
German literature, especially Lessing; Anglo-German and Franco-German

SCOUTEN, Arthur H.
English (professor)
University of Pennsylvania
Philadelphia, Pennsylvania 19104
Restoration drama; Swift

SCRUGGS, Charles   C
English (assistant professor)
University of Arizona
Tucson, Arizona 85721
Swift

SEBBA, Gregor
Liberal arts (professor)
Graduate Institute of Liberal Arts
Emory University
Atlanta, Georgia 30322
Rousseau, Goethe, history of ideas

SEBOLD, Russell P.
Spanish (professor)
University of Pennsylvania
Philadelphia, Pa. 19104
Spanish literature; novel, pre-romanticism (European literatures); aesthetics

SEGAL, Lester A.   C
History (assistant professor)
University of Massachusetts
Boston, Mass. 02116
French intellectual history; religious skepticism

SEGEL, Harold B.   C
Slavic languages (professor)
Columbia University
213 Lewisohn Hall
New York, N. Y. 10027
Russian and Polish 18th-century literature

SELLS, Larry F.   C
English (instructor)
Westminster College
4 Beechwood Drive
New Wilmington, Pa. 16142
English novel, esp. Fielding

SELSS, Steven L.   C
History (student)

List of Members

Queens College, CUNY
192-24B 64th Circle
Flushing, New York 11365
Military, Jewish, music, N. Y. city history

SENA, John F.
English (assistant professor)
Ohio State University
Columbus, Ohio 43210
Samuel Garth; literature and medicine

SHAW, Edward P.
Romance languages (professor)
State University of New York, Albany
1400 Washington Avenue
Albany, New York 12203
French literature

SHEA, John S.   C
English (assistant professor)
Loyola University of Chicago
6525 N. Sheridan Road
Chicago, Ill. 60626
Dryden; Gay; the fable

SHEPS, Arthur   C
History (lecturer)
University of Toronto
Toronto 5, Ontario
Political philosophy; Anglo-American intellectual history; American Revolution

SHERBO, Arthur   C
English (professor)
Michigan State University
East Lansing, Michigan 48823
English literature in all its aspects

SHERMAN, Carol
Romance languages (instructor)
University of North Carolina
Chapel Hill, N. C. 27514
Diderot and the philosophic dialogue

SHERWOOD, Irma Z.
English (assistant professor)
University of Oregon
Eugene, Oregon 97403
Samuel Johnson

SHERWOOD, John C.
English (professor)
University of Oregon
Eugene, Oregon 97403
Dryden

SHIMIZU, Kazuyoshi
English (assistant professor)
Aichi University
116-68, Ippongi, Ueda-cho
Toyohashi 440, Japan
Authors, publishers and readers of 18th-century England

SHIPLEY, John B.   C
English (professor)
University of Illinois at Chicago Circle
Box 4348
Chicago, Illinois 60680
Novel; Johnson circle; aesthetics; the newspapers

SHOWALTER, English, Jr.   C
Romance languages (assistant professor)
Princeton University
Princeton, New Jersey 08540
French literature, esp. fiction

SHULIM, Joseph I.   C
History (professor)
City University of New York
2601 Glenwood Road
Brooklyn, New York 11210
Old Régime (France); French Revolution; Napoleon

SIEBERT, Donald T., Jr.   S
English (graduate student)
University of Virginia
Charlottesville, Va. 22901
English literature

SIEGEL, June Sigler   C
French, English
6 Carol Lane
New Rochelle, N. Y. 10804
French-English, esp. novel

SIEVERT, William   C
English (assistant professor)
Pace College
41 Park Row
New York, N. Y. 10038
Satire

SIGWORTH, Oliver F.   C
English (professor)
University of Arizona
Tucson, Arizona 85721
Poetry, criticism

SILBAJORIS, Frank R.   C
Slavic studies (professor)
Ohio State University
1841 Millikin Road
Columbus, Ohio 43210
Russian 18th-century poetics, drama, and prose

SILBER, C. Anderson   C
English (lecturer)
Victoria College, University of Toronto
43 Hambly Avenue
Toronto 260, Ontario
English literature, esp. poetry

SILBER, Gordon R.   C
French (professor)
SUNY, Buffalo
124 Brookedge Drive
Williamsville, N. Y. 14221
French literature; Franco-American cultural relations

SILBER, Mrs. Gordon R.
124 Brookedge Drive
Williamsville, New York 14221

SILVERBLATT, Bette G.   C
French
Case Western Reserve University
3638 Strathavon Road
Shaker Hts., Ohio 44120
Charles Pinot Duclos; French literature and thought

SIMMONS, Sarah
Romance languages (assistant professor)
Colorado College
Colorado Springs, Colorado 80903
Eighteenth-century French novel

SIMONEAU, Joseph R.   S
French (student)
Pennsylvania State University
519 West College Ave.
State College, Pa. 16801
Diderot and L'Encyclopédie

SJOGREN, Christine
Modern languages (professor)
Oregon State University
Corvallis, Oregon 97331
Enlightenment

SKINNER, Mary-Lynn   C
English (assistant professor)
Virginia Commonwealth University
Richmond, Virginia 23220
Novel; Restoration and eighteenth-century drama

SKUBLY, Jacqueline de L.
Foreign languages (assistant professor)
Housatonic Community College
555 Clinton Avenue
Bridgeport, Conn. 06605
Marivaux

SLATTERY, William C.
English (professor)
Southern Illinois University
Edwardsville, Illinois 62025
Richardson, the Dutch novel

SLAVIN, Morris   C
History (associate professor)
Youngstown State University
262 Outlook Ave.
Youngstown, Ohio 44504
French Revolution

SLOAN, Sheldon   S
English (graduate assistant)
University of Maryland
2117 Guilfor Road No. 203
Hyattsville, Maryland 20783

SMITH, D. I. B.   C
English (associate professor)
University College, University of Toronto
Toronto, Ontario
Editing; history of ideas; poetry

SMITH, D. W.   C
French (associate professor)
Victoria College, University of Toronto
Toronto 5, Ontario
Helvétius

SMITH, David E.   C
American studies (professor)
Hampshire College

List of Members

Merrill House
Amherst, Mass. 01002
American 18th-century studies

SMITH, Frederik N. C
English (assistant professor)
Case Western Reserve University
Cleveland, Ohio 44106
Swift; 17th-18th-century prose style

SMITH, Joan Van Rensselaer
Art (associate professor)
Michigan State University
East Lansing, Michigan 48823
Art and architecture

SMITH, Lyle E.
English (assistant professor)
California State College
1000 East Victoria Street
Dominguez Hills, California 90747
English literature

SMITH, Peter L. S
French and Italian (teaching assistant)
University of Wisconsin
618 Van Hise Hall
Madison, Wisconsin 53706
Correspondence of Pierre-Michel Hennin

SPACKS, Patricia Meyer C
English (professor)
Wellesley College
16 Abbott Street
Wellesley, Mass. 02181
Pope; poetry

SPEAKMAN, James S.
English (associate [in Subject A])
University of California, Davis
2821 17th St.
Sacramento, California 95818
Comic theory; theory and practice of the novel

SPEAR, Frederick A. C
French (professor)
Skidmore College
Saratoga Springs, New York 12866
Voltaire bibliography; Diderot bibliography

SPEAR, Richard E. C
Art history (associate professor)
Oberlin College
Oberlin, Ohio 44074
The rococo

SPECTOR, Robert D. C
English (professor)
Long Island University
Brooklyn, New York 11201
Novel; periodicals

SPENCER, David G. C
English (professor)
California State College
Bakersfield, Calif. 93309
Restoration and 18th-century theater; political satire

SPENCER, Jeffry B. (Mrs. David G.) C
English (adjunct associate professor)
California State College
Bakersfield, California 93309
Literature and the visual arts; poetry

SPIKER, Sina K. C
English (associate professor—retired)
Southern Illinois University
209 Brook Lane
Carbondale, Illinois 62901
Restoration literature

SPURLIN, Paul M.
French (professor emeritus)
University of Michigan
505 N. Seventh Street
Ann Arbor, Michigan 48103

STANLIS, Peter J. C
English (professor)
Rockford College
Rockford, Illinois 61101
Burke and his times

STARKEY, Margaret M. C
English (associate professor)
Brooklyn College, CUNY
1011 North Avenue
New Rochelle, N. Y. 10804
Age of Pope, dominant ideas in the poetry of the age

STARNES, Thomas C. C
German (assistant professor)
Tulane University
New Orleans, La. 70118
C. M. Wieland

383

STAVAN, Henry Anthony C
French (associate professor)
University of Colorado
Boulder, Colorado 80302
Late 18th-century French literature

STEDMOND, John C
English (professor)
Queen's University
Kingston, Ontario
Prose fiction; Laurence Sterne

STEELE, Elizabeth C
English (assistant professor)
University of Toledo
3219 Cheltenham Rd.
Toledo, Ohio 43606
Horace Walpole

STEENSMA, Robert C. C
English (associate professor)
University of Utah
Salt Lake City, Utah 84112
Jonathan Swift; Sir William Temple; naval history

STEESE, Peter C
English (associate professor)
State University of New York
Fredonia, N. Y. 14063
Biography; verse paraphrases of the Bible

STEFANSON, Donald H. S
English (doctoral candidate)
University of Iowa
2718 South Coral
Sioux City, Iowa 51106
History of printing; prose fiction

STEPP, Nancy T. C
411 South Church Street
Bowling Green, Ohio 43402
Dryden; novel; satire; satirical allegory

STERN, Monique S
Graduate student
University of Maryland
12 Furber Lane
Newton Centre, Mass. 02159

STEWART, Keith C
English (associate professor)
University of Cincinnati

Cincinnati, Ohio 45221
Literary theory—mid- and later eighteenth-century

STEWART, Maaja A. C
English (assistant professor)
Newcomb College
New Orleans, La. 70118
Fiction; novel and history, biography, journal

STEWART, Mary Margaret C
English (professor)
Gettysburg College
Gettysburg, Pennsylvania 17325
William Collins; Henry Fielding; James Boswell

STEWART, Philip C
French (assistant professor)
Harvard University
201 Boylston Hall
Cambridge, Mass. 02138
French literature, especially novel

STOCKTON, Constant Noble
History and philosophy (associate professor)
Wisconsin State University
River Falls, Wisconsin 54022
Intellectual history, philosophy, historiography, law

STOCKWELL, Joseph E.
English (assistant professor)
Mississippi State University
Box 5242
State College, Miss. 39762
Samuel Johnson's criticism

STOEFFLER, F. Ernest
Religion (professor)
Temple University
Philadelphia, Pennsylvania 19122
German criticism and German Enlightenment

STOLLERY, C. William C
R.R. 2
Aurora, Ontario
Johnsonian letters

STRAKA, Gerald M.
History (associate professor)

List of Members

University of Delaware
Newark, Delaware 19711
Political theory

STRAULMAN, Ann T.
English (assistant professor)
University of Western Ontario
London 72, Ontario
English novel and drama

STRAUSS, Albrecht B.   C
English (associate professor)
University of North Carolina
2 Dogwood Acres Drive
Chapel Hill, N. C. 27514
English novel; prose style; Johnson

STRICKLEN, Charles G., Jr.   C
History (assistant professor)
University of North Carolina
Chapel Hill, N. C. 27514
*Social and political thought
(1770-1789)*

STURGILL, Claude C.   C
History (associate professor)
University of Florida
630 N.E. 10th Ave.
Gainesville, Florida 32601
French military history

STURM, Norbert A.   C
English (associate professor)
University of Dayton
3849 Germantown Street
Dayton, Ohio 45418

SULLIVAN, Maureen   C
English
University of Pennsylvania
119 Bennett Hall
Philadelphia, Pa. 19104
Restoration, 18th-century drama; novel

SUNGOLOWSKY, Joseph
Romance languages (associate
   professor)
Queens College, CUNY
Flushing, New York 11367
*Romanticism and 18th century in
   France; theater; Beaumarchais*

SWEDENBERG, H. T.   C
English (professor)
University of California
Los Angeles, Calif. 90024
Dryden; poetry

SWITZER, Richard   C
French (professor)
California State College
San Bernardino, Calif. 92407
Theater; pre-romanticism

TARAS, A. F.
Foreign languages (professor)
Ithaca College
1137 Warren Road
Ithaca, New York 14850
Lesage; Voltaire; Rousseau

TARBET, David W.   C
English (assistant professor)
State University of New York
Buffalo, New York 14214
Johnson; philosophy

TASCH, Peter A.   C
English (instructor)
Temple University
5430 Wayne Avenue
Philadelphia, Pa. 19144
Drama; Scriblerus Club

TATE, Robert S., Jr.   C
French and Italian (assistant professor)
University of Iowa
141 Grand Avenue Court
Iowa City, Iowa 52240
French literature; Bachaumont; Lesage

TAYLOR, Charlene M.   C
English (assistant professor)
University of Arizona
8120 Calle Potrero
Tucson, Arizona 85715
Restoration and 18th-century drama

TEMMER, Mark J.   C
French and Italian (professor)
University of California
Santa Barbara, Calif. 93106
J. J. Rousseau

TEMPERLEY, Nicholas   C
Musicology (associate professor)
University of Illinois
805 W. Indiana
Urbana, Illinois 61801
Music in eighteenth-century England

THACKRAY, Arnold
History of science (associate professor)
University of Pennsylvania
117 E. F. Smith Chemistry Laboratory
Philadelphia, Pa. 19104
Science, technology, the Industrial Revolution

THELANDER, Dorothy R.   C
French (associate professor)
University of Illinois at Chicago Circle
Box 4348
Chicago, Ill. 60680
Epistolary fiction; satire

THERRIEN, Madeleine B.   C
French (associate professor)
Emory University
Atlanta, Georgia 30322
French novel; Laclos

THEILEMANN, Leland J.   C
French and Italian (professor)
University of Texas
206 Robert E. Lee Hall
Austin, Texas 78712

THIHER, Roberta Joyce
Modern languages
Saint Michael's College
Winooski, Vermont 05404
French literature

THOMASSON, Brenda Faith
French (graduate student)
University of Kentucky
Cooperstown F-312
Lexington, Kentucky 40506
Diderot; materialists

THOMPSON, Nancy M.   C
French and Spanish (assistant professor)
University of Saskatchewan
Saskatoon, Saskatchewan
Voltaire

THOMPSON, Paul V.   C
English (professor)
University of Colorado
325 16th Street
Boulder, Colorado 80302
Swift

THORNE, Charles Greenwood, Jr.   C
Cultural history
Box 427
Ephrata, Pa. 17522
Cultural and intellectual history; silver; architecture

THORSON, James L.   C
English (assistant professor)
University of New Mexico
Albuquerque, New Mexico 87106
Satire; Jonathan Swift; Hogarth

THRO, Michael   S
English (graduate student)
University of Southern California
Los Angeles, California 90007
The novel—Defoe, Sterne

TOBORG, Alfred   C
History (associate professor)
Lyndon State College
Lyndonville, Vermont 15851
Prussian history, esp. Frederick the Great

TODD, Dennis   C
English
Wayne State University
Detroit, Michigan 48202
Pope; Gay

TONELLI, Giorgio
Philosophy (professor)
State University of New York
Binghamton, N. Y. 13901
18th-century German, French, English philosophy

TOPAZIO, Virgil W.   C
French (professor)
Rice University
236 Rayzor Hall
Houston, Texas 77001
Voltaire; Rousseau; D'Holbach

TORIGIAN, Janine
French and Italian (assistant instructor)
University of Texas
11 Matador Circle
Austin, Texas 78746
Political theory of the dispersion

TOTTEN, Charles F.   S
English (graduate assistant)

List of Members

Wayne State University
Detroit, Michigan 48202
English drama, criticism

TOTTEN, Darla R.   S
Art history (graduate student)
Wayne State University
Detroit, Michigan 48202

TRACY, Clarence   C
English (professor)
Acadia University
Wolfville, Nova Scotia
Johnson

TRAPNELL, William H.   C
French (assistant professor)
Indiana University
Ballantine Hall
Bloomington, Indiana 47401
Marivaux, Voltaire

TROTT, David A.   C
French (lecturer)
Erindale College, University of Toronto
Toronto, Ontario
French drama; Marivaux

TROUT, Paul A.   S
English (graduate student)
University of British Columbia
5662 Dalhousie, No. 3
Vancouver 8, British Columbia
Swift, satire

TROWBRIDGE, Hoyt
English (professor)
University of New Mexico
Albuquerque, New Mexico 87106
Dryden, Swift, Pope, Johnson, literary criticism

TUMINS, Valerie A.   C
Russian (associate professor)
University of California
Davis, Calif. 95616
Russian literature and culture

TYNE, Rev. James L., S.J.   C
English (associate professor)
Fordham University
Bronx, New York 10458
Jonathan Swift

TYSON, Gerald P.
English (assistant professor)
University of Maryland
College Park, Md. 20740
Scottish writers and Scots' nationalism

UPHAUS, Robert W.   C
English (assistant professor)
School of English
University of Leeds
Leeds 2, England
Poetry and aesthetics

VALES, Robert L.   C
English (assistant professor)
Gannon College
Erie, Pa. 16501
Late eighteenth-century studies

VALLIER, Robert   C
English
University of Tennessee
Chattanooga, Tennessee 37403
Swift's rhetorical satire

VAN DUSEN, R.   C
German (associate professor)
McMaster University
Hamilton, Ontario
German: popular philosophie, comparative literature

VAN EERDE, John A.   C
Romance languages (professor)
Lehigh University
Bethlehem, Pa. 18015
Theater

VAN MARTER, Shirley   C
English and comparative literature (assistant professor)
University of California
Irvine, California 92664
Literature

VAN TREESE, Glenn J.   C
Modern languages (assistant professor)
Sweet Briar College
P.O. Box 18
Sweet Briar, Virginia 24595
D'Alembert; Frederick the Great

VARNELL, O. Paul   C
English (instructor)
North Illinois University

835 Edgebrook, Apt. 3
De Kalb, Illinois 60115
Swift; political and social philosophy

VARTANIAN, Aram   C
Romance languages (professor)
New York University
19 University Place
New York, N. Y. 10003

VÁZQUEZ-RAMPA, Washington   C
Spanish and Portuguese (assistant professor)
Miami University
Oxford, Ohio 45056
Spanish and Portuguese literature; esp. satire and fable

VERDURMEN, J. Peter
English (assistant professor)
University of Cincinnati
727 Red Bud Avenue
Cincinnati, Ohio 45229
Restoration drama; later 18th-century drama

VIETH, David M.   C
English (professor)
Southern Illinois University
Carbondale, Illinois 62901
John Wilmot; Restoration literature; Swift and Pope

VINCENT, Howard   C
English (professor)
Kent State University
Kent, Ohio 44240

VINCENT, Thomas B.   C
English (lecturer)
Royal Military College of Canada
Kingston, Ontario
English novel; aesthetic theory and literary criticism

VOIGT, Milton
English (professor)
University of Utah
Salt Lake City, Utah 84112
Swift

VOITLE, Robert   C
English (professor)
University of North Carolina
Chapel Hill, N. C. 27514
Johnson; 3rd Earl of Shaftesbury; deism

VOS, Marie Ann Heiberg   C
Music (assistant professor)
McHenry County College
207 North Main St., Apt. 203
Crystal Lake, Ill. 60014
J. C. Bach; 18th-century Italian church music

WACHS, Morris   C
French (professor)
Vanderbilt University
Nashville, Tenn. 37235
D'Alembert; Diderot; Voltaire

WADAS, Walter E.
3738 Miller St.
Baden, Pa. 15005
Art history

WAINGROW, Marshall   C
English (professor)
Claremont Graduate School
Claremont, Calif. 91711
Johnson and Boswell; eighteenth-century novel

WALDINGER, Renée   C
French (professor)
City College, CUNY
Convent Avenue at 138th Street
New York, N. Y. 10031
French literature

WALKER, Rev. John M., Jr.
Church history
First Presbyterian Church
16 East 5th St.
Roanoke Rapids, N. C. 27870
Theology; church history; art; Johnson

WALKER, Robert Gary   S
English (graduate student)
University of Florida
P.O. Box 13189, University Station
Gainesville, Florida 32601
Johnson; English poetry

WALLACE, J. O.
Library science (librarian)
San Antonio College
1001 Howard Street
San Antonio, Texas 78284

List of Members

WALLS, Aileen S.
English (associate professor)
George Mason College
Fairfax, Virginia 22030
Charles Brockden Brown; Phillip Freneau; William Byrd II

WANLASS, Dorothy C.   C
English (professor)
San Diego State College
4646 Norma Drive
San Diego, Calif. 92115
Architecture; painting; Neoclassicism

WARK, Robert R.   C
Art history (curator)
The Henry E. Huntington Library and Art Gallery
San Marino, Calif. 91108

WARREN, Joseph A., III
American studies (chairman)
Lansing Community College
419 N. Capitol Avenue
Lansing, Michigan 48914

WASSERMAN, George R.
English
Russell Sage College
Box 572
Newtonville, New York 12128

WATSON, Richard A.
Philosophy (associate professor)
Washington University
Philosophy 1073
St. Louis, Missouri 63130
Metaphysics; epistemology

WATT, Ian   C
English (professor)
Stanford University
Stanford, Calif. 94305
Novel; Augustan poetry; social background

WATZLAWICK, Helmut
22, chemin de l'esplanade
CH-1214 VERNIER (Geneva)
Switzerland
Anonyma and pseudonym literature; literary production of adventure writers: Casanova, Goudar, Zannowich, d'Afflisio

WEBSTER, T. S.   C
History (professor)
Queen's University
Kingston, Ontario
France-North America, 1763-1815

WEGMAN, Nola J.   C
English (associate professor)
Valparaiso University
Valparaiso, Indiana 46383
Swift; Pope; satire; theological-literary relations

WEIGAND, Ann K.
Modern languages (instructor)
Rosemont College
118 West Rittenhouse St.
Philadelphia, Pa. 19144
Novel

WEINBROT, Howard D.   C
English (associate professor)
University of Wisconsin
Madison, Wisconsin 53706
Pope; Johnson; imitation; satire

WEINSTEIN, Minna F.   C
History (associate professor)
LaSalle College
Philadelphia, Pa. 19141
English Enlightenment

WEISBERGER, R. William
Social science (instructor)
Butler County Community College
Apt. 3D, Green Acres
204 Litman Road
Butler, Pennsylvania 16001
Intellectual history

WEITZMAN, Arthur J.   C
English (associate professor)
Northeastern University
Boston, Mass. 02115
Oriental tale; satire

WENNER, Evelyn W.   C
English (professor)
Western Maryland College
158 Pennsylvania Avenue
Westminster, Maryland 21157
Life and works of George Steevens

WERNER, Stephen C
French (assistant professor)
University of California
Los Angeles, Calif. 90024
Diderot; Rousseau

WEST, Elsie L. C
English (associate professor)
Johnson State College
Box 164
Johnson, Vermont 05656
American and English literature

WEYANT, Robert G.
Psychology (professor)
University of Calgary
Calgary, Alberta, Canada
Psychological, and related philosophical and social thought; history of ideas

WEYGANT, Peter S. C
English (graduate student)
University of Pennsylvania
324 Chester Avenue
Moorestown, N. J. 08057
Restoration poetry

WHEELOCK, James T. S. C
Italian (instructor)
University of Colorado
1607-6th Street
Boulder, Colorado 80302
Anglo-Italian literary relations in eighteenth century

WHITE, Douglas H. C
English (assistant professor)
Loyola University, Chicago
6525 Sheridan Rd.
Chicago, Ill. 60611
Pope; Swift; intellectual history

WHITE, Fred H.
English (assistant professor)
Westhampton College
University of Richmond
Box 32
Richmond, Virginia 23173
Pope and his circle

WHITE, John Charles C
History (assistant professor)
University of Alabama

Huntsville, Alabama 35807
Humanitarian reform; French naval administration

WHITE, Maurice L. C
Music (honors choir director)
Detroit Schools
36408 Rayburn
Livonia, Michigan 48154
Musicology; composers (1775-1825); Cherubini

WHITE, Richard S. C
Russian (instructor)
Dept. of Slavic Languages and Literatures
Northwestern University
Evanston, Illinois 60201
Russian fiction in 18th century

WHITE, Robert B., Jr. C
English (associate professor)
North Carolina State University
Raleigh, N. C. 27607
Periodicals; early satire

WHITWORTH, Kernan B., Jr. C
French (professor)
University of Missouri
27 A and S
Columbia, Missouri 65201
French novel; Voltaire; Diderot

WICHE, Glen Norman S
History (student)
Allegheny College
655 Thornwood Drive
Napierville, Illinois 60540
Cultural life of Virginia (dramatic, musical, bibliographical aspects)

WIDMAYER, Jayne A.
English (instructor)
The College of Idaho
Caldwell, Idaho 83605
The picturesque; late 18th-century poetry

WIESENFARTH, Joseph C
English (associate professor)
241 Langdon St.
Madison, Wisconsin 53703
Novel, esp. Fielding and Sterne

List of Members

WILES, R. M.   C
English (professor emeritus)
McMaster University
Hamilton, Ontario
Johnson; provincial press

WILKINS, Kay S.   C
Romance languages (assistant professor)
SUNY, Stony Brook
Stony Brook, New York 11790
Jesuit influence in France; occult in literature

WILLCOX, William B.   C
History (professor)
Yale University
1603 A. Yale Station
New Haven, Conn. 06520
Franklin; War of American Independence

WILLEY, Edward P.
English (assistant professor)
Clemson University
Clemson, S. C. 29631
Periodicals

WILLIAMS, David   C
Romance languages (associate professor)
McMaster University
Hamilton, Ontario
Voltaire, aesthetics

WILLIAMS, Kathleen   C
English (professor)
University of California
Riverside, Calif. 92502
Swift; Pope

WILSON, Arthur M.   C
Biography and government (professor emeritus)
Dartmouth College
1 Brookside
Norwich, Vermont 05055
Encyclopédie; Diderot; the Enlightenment

WILSON, Diana G.
Art history (graduate student)
University of California, Los Angeles
20907 Via Verde
Covina, California 91724

WILSON, James R.   C
English (professor)
University of Alaska
401 Atlantis Avenue
Anchorage, Alaska 99502
Swift; drama; Pope

WILSON, JoAnn H.   S
English (graduate student)
University of Oregon
2683 Hilyard
Eugene, Oregon 97405

WILSON, Lester N.   C
History (associate professor)
Long Island University
Zeckendorf Campus
Brooklyn, N. Y. 11201
Diplomacy

WIMSATT, W. K.   C
English (professor)
Yale University
1882 Yale Station
New Haven, Conn. 06511
Pope, Johnson

WINESANKER, Michael   C
Musicology (professor)
Texas Christian University
Fort Worth, Texas 76129
English musical drama (comic opera) of the eighteenth century

WINSLOW, Donald J.   C
English (professor)
Boston University
236 Bay State Road
Boston, Mass. 02215
Biography

WINTON, Calhoun   C
English (professor)
University of South Carolina
Columbia, S. C. 29208
English and American non-fictional prose

WOLFF, C. Griffin   C
English (assistant professor)
Manhattanville College
415 West 115th St. Apt. 51
New York, N. Y. 10025
Novel

WOLFF, Christoph
Music (associate professor)
Columbia University
New York, New York 10027
Music

WOLPER, Roy S.   C
English (associate professor)
Temple University
Philadelphia, Pa. 19122
Satire of Restoration; drama; Pope, Swift, and group

WOOLLEY, James David   S
English (graduate student)
Marquette University
Milwaukee, Wisconsin 53233
Satiric verse; Swift; literature and society

WORDEN, John L., Jr.   C
English (assistant professor)
Chico State College
Chico, Calif. 95926
Johnson

WORTHINGTON, Anne   S
Graduate student
University of Maryland
12309 Stonehaven Lane
Bowie, Maryland 20715

WRAGE, William   C
Modern languages (associate professor)
Ohio University
Athens, Ohio 45701
French literature

WRIGHT, Andrew   C
English (professor)
University of California, San Diego
P.O. Box 109
La Jolla, Calif. 92037

WRIGHT, H. Bunker   C
English (professor)
Miami University
Oxford, Ohio 45056
English literature and history; Matthew Prior

WRIGHT, John W.
English (associate professor)
University of Michigan
Ann Arbor, Michigan 48104
British and German philosophy; Johnson; Blake

WRIGHT, William E.   C
History (associate professor)
Associate dean, international programs
University of Minnesota
Minneapolis, Minn. 55455
History; Austria, central Europe, Enlightenment

WUNDER, Richard P.
Art history (senior research fellow)
Smithsonian Institution
National Collection of Fine Arts
Brookside, Orwell
Vermont 05760

YASHINSKY, Jack   C
French (lecturer)
Erindale College
University of Toronto
Toronto 5, Ontario
Voltaire's theater

YOUNG, Donald L.   C
English (professor)
Dean of the College
Eastern Nazarene College
Wollaston Park
Quincy, Mass. 02170

ZANTS, Emily   C
French and Italian (assistant professor)
University of California, Davis
708 N Street
Davis, California 95616
French novel

ZIMANSKY, Curt A.   C
English (professor)
University of Iowa
Iowa City, Iowa 52240

ZIRKER, Malvin R., Jr.   C
English (associate professor)
Indiana University
Bloomington, Indiana 47401
Novel

ZOLTOWSKA, Maria Evelina   C
French (assistant professor)
Université de Moneton
Moncton, New Brunswick
The novel; Jean Potocki

List of Members

ZUCKERMAN, Arnold
History (professor)
Northeast Missouri State College
Social Science Division
P.O. Box 11
Kirksville, Missouri 63501
History of medicine

ZYLAWY, Roman
Foreign languages (instructor)
University of Montana
Missoula, Montana 59801
Marivaux, Prévost, and the feminist problem